IMPULSE CONTROL DISORDERS

FIRST EDITION

EDITED BY GEORGE KOOB

University of California, San Diego

cognella™

San Diego, CA

Bassim Hamadeh, CEO and Publisher
Christopher Foster, General Vice President
Michael Simpson, Vice President of Acquisitions
Jessica Knott, Managing Editor
Kevin Fahey, Cognella Marketing Manager
Jess Busch, Senior Graphic Designer
Seidy Cruz, Acquisitions Editor
Sarah Wheeler, Project Editor
Stephanie Sandler, Licensing Associate

First published in the United States of America in 2013 by Cognella, Inc.

Trademark Notice: Product or corporate names may be trademarks or registered trademarks, and are used only for identification and explanation without intent to infringe.

Printed in the United States of America

ISBN: 978-1-62131-212-3

www.cognella.com 800.200.3908

Contents

Introduction

One could argue that impulse control disorders form the basis for the major social and psychiatric pathology of civilization. *Impulse Control Disorders* is a compendium derived from a course I developed at the University of California, San Diego, in the Department of Psychology curriculum termed *Impulse Control Disorders*. The chapters of this book follow the course outline. The focus of the course is on self-regulation failure within the study of impulse control disorders. The curricula move through three models: social psychology domain, addiction domain, and psychiatric domain. Self-regulation failures in every day life, addiction-like disorders, and psychiatric disorders all involve elements of impulsivity and impulse control disorders.

What are impulse control disorders? They can represent disorders that have an increasing sense of tension or arousal before performing an act, pleasure, gratification, or relief during the act, and regret, self-reproach, or guilt after performing the act. Such is the definition in the *Diagnostic and Statistical Manual of Mental Disorders* of the American Psychiatric Association applied to kleptomania, pyromania, and trichotillomania, in which the disorder was listed as an impulse control disorder not otherwise specified (American Psychiatric Association, 2000). Impulsivity, as a construct, also can be defined as "actions which are poorly conceived, prematurely expressed, unduly risky, or inappropriate to the situation and that often result in undesirable consequences" (Durana and Barnes, 1993). The focus of this book *Impulse Control Disorders* is to explore the elements of impulsivity and impulse control disorders in pathology with an attempt to understand how such pathology evolves and forms elements of some of the most severe disorders of our time, including addiction, compulsive disorders, and antisocial disorder/psychopathy.

In the social psychology domain (Chapters 1 and 2), many of the principles of self-regulation failure in the social arena are explored by drawing on the seminal work of Roy Baumeister and his colleagues in *Losing Control: How and Why People Fail at Self-regulation* (Baumeister et al., 1994). The principles of self-regulation failure that involve underregulation and misregulation are explored by focusing on key elements of standards, strength, monitoring, and exerting control that fail to work (misregulation). These principles form the basis of self-regulation failure within each of the disorders discussed in the course and in the subsequent chapters that focus on the pathologies that form impulse control disorders.

In the addiction domain (Chapter 3, 4, and 5), the principles of addiction are outlined with an emphasis on how the elements of impulsivity combine with elements of compulsivity to form the predominant aspects of the addiction cycle: binge/intoxication, withdrawal/negative affect, and preoccupation/anticipation ("craving"). These stages are also pervasive and common elements in the subsequent chapters that focus on the pathologies that form impulse control disorders or nondrug addictions, termed by others, including the American Society of Addiction Medicine, as "process addictions"

The impulse control disorders elaborated in Chapters 6-15 are explored within the contexts of self-regulation failure and addiction. Common elements of self-regulation failure from a social psychology perspective and common elements related to addiction can be identified by the astute reader and related back to Chapters 1-5.

A third common element explored in Chapters 16-18 is the transition from impulse control disorders to compulsive disorders and well-documented psychiatric disorders. With elements of impulsivity, self-regulation failure merges to form some of the most pervasive disorders, including attention-deficit/hyperactivity disorder (Chapter 17), and most devastating disorders, including obsessive compulsive disorder (Chapter 18) and antisocial personality disorder/psychopathy (Chapter 16). Woven into this fabric is the transition from impulse control disorders to compulsive disorders in Chapter 18.

Finally, the brain mechanisms that drive self-regulation failure are explored throughout the chapters, but a specific focus on self-regulation failure and stress is provided in Chapter 20, in which a seminal article by Robert Sapolsky (2003) forms a unifying theme about how the body responds to stressors and how chronic stress can engage many pathologies, including the impulse control disorders outlined in this compendium.

Altogether, this book provides background reading material for a course on Impulse Control Disorders. It also forms a body of heuristic work for not only students enrolled in similar courses but also professionals who wish to compare and evaluate disorders linked by important elements of self-regulation failure and elements related to addiction. As the medical/scientific community begins to consider nondrug addiction-like disorders as serious psychiatric disorders worthy of treatment because of the misery they cause and their economic and social costs, this book will provide a heuristic framework by which to evolve key concepts.

References

American Psychiatric Association. *Diagnostic and Statistical Manual of Mental Disorders*, 4th edition, text revision. American Psychiatric Press, Washington DC, 2000.

Baumeister RF, Heatherton TF, Tice DM (eds) *Losing Control: How and Why People Fail at Self-Regulation*. Academic Press, San Diego, 1994.

Durana, J. H., and Barnes, P. A. (1993). A neurodevelopmental view of impulsivity and its relationship to the superfactors of personality. In *The Impulsive Client: Theory, Research, and Treatment* (W. G. McCown, J. Johnson, and M. B. Shure, eds.), pp. 23-37. American Psychological Association, Washington DC.

Sapolsky R. Taming stress: an emerging understanding of the brain's stress pathways points toward treatments for anxiety and depression beyond Valium and Prozac. *Scientific American*, 2003, September: 87-95.

Introduction

Self-Regulation Failure in Social and Theoretical Context

By Roy F. Baumeister, Todd F. Heatherton, and Dianne M. Tice

Self-regulation failure is the major social pathology of the present time. As America lurches toward the end of the twentieth century, it finds itself beset by all manner of social problems and discontents. Some of these reflect problems of social structure and have economic and sociological roots, but others are based in the difficulties that individual citizens have in managing their lives. Many of these individual difficulties revolve around the inability to control oneself. All over the country, people are miserable because they cannot control their money, their weight, their emotions, their drinking, their hostility, their craving for drugs, their spending, their own behavior vis-à-vis their family members, their sexual impulses, and more. America is regarded by some observers as a society addicted to addiction: Therapies and support groups proliferate, not just for alcoholics and heroin addicts, but for people who cannot control a craving for Coca-Cola, an impulse to beat their children, an urge to masturbate or sleep with multiple strangers, a debt balance on credit cards, or the daily consumption of coffee or chocolate. Some of these problems are large, while others seem small to all but those who suffer from them; but they share an acutely vexed awareness of failure at self-regulation.

The consequences of these problems go beyond individuals. Self-regulation failure is central to many of the problems that are widely discussed and bemoaned as allegedly hastening the decline and doom of America. Teen pregnancy and single parenthood, which supposedly perpetuate a cycle of poverty and which threaten the cherished images of family life, are often the result of a failure to regulate one's sexual actions—either by abstaining from intercourse or, at least, by taking contraceptive precautions. Heedless, uncontrolled, unsafe sex has also brought epidemics of several major venereal diseases, from AIDS to gonorrhea. Drug abuse, alcoholism, and binge eating all consist of an inability to stop oneself from indulging one's appetites to excess.

Economists note with chagrin that the American economy suffers because our citizens save and invest much less of their money than citizens of other industrialized countries, and one reason for this is an inability to discipline one's private finances. Indeed, the lack of fiscal discipline goes much further than an inability to save; many people find themselves chronically in debt. Many middleclass citizens struggle with huge credit card balances and ballooning mortgage payments and other debts, while some working-class citizens live in constant fear of having their telephone service or electricity shut off or their furniture repossessed because of unpaid bills, and others find themselves still making monthly payments on cars that have already gone to the junkyard.

Americans continue to pledge lifelong fidelity at their weddings, but in fact they are getting divorces in record numbers, and it took a series of major scares about incurable and deadly venereal diseases to slow the rise in extramarital sex. Instead of working out marital problems, Americans head for divorce court, and many people repeat the cycle with a series of stormy marriages and costly divorces, A new willingness to talk about family problems has revealed epidemic levels of domestic violence: One out of eight or nine American husbands admits to physically attacking his wife in the past year, and wives are equally or perhaps even more likely to attack their husbands (although the husbands

are less likely to suffer serious injury). Marital rape, once considered to be a contradiction in terms, has now become recognized as a widespread problem. Children are beaten uncontrollably and are sexually abused as well. Elderly parents are beaten by their grown offspring.

Impulsive crimes have risen steadily. Statistics on rape, muggings, murder, robbery, assault, and similar offenses show alarming increases. The increase is not primarily due to any rise of organized crime or planned criminal activity, but rather it mostly indicates a tendency for people to give in to violent impulses. One sign of this is that our prisons are overflowing, not with Mafiosi, but with school dropouts and the offspring of neglecting, absent, alcoholic or addicted, criminal, or abusive parents, who tend to fail worst at instilling self-control in their children.

Meanwhile, even the most law-abiding citizens suffer from problems arising from lack of self-control. Health experts routinely say that many, perhaps even most, causes of American deaths are preventable if only people would regulate their behaviors better: quit smoking, eat right, exercise regularly.

The school achievement of American pupils lags behind the rest of the industrialized world. There are multiple reasons for the problems of our schools, but the lack of self-discipline of our students is among them. Students cut class, fail to complete homework assignments, disrupt classrooms with misbehavior, and drop out altogether. Instead of learning, many students spend their time in school distracted with issues of violence, weapons, drugs, and sex. Even the most talented students often seem to think that the route to success is less a matter of hard work, good study habits, and meeting deadlines, than of doing extra-credit projects, being creative, and circumventing authoritarian rules with clever excuses and well-phrased requests for special treatment.

Currently there seems to be a widespread hope, which is probably no more than an absurd and idle fantasy, that raising self-esteem will solve these problems. If only we loved ourselves more, the assumption is, all our problems would vanish. From the perspective of self-regulation theory, the fascination with self-esteem is a pathetic and self-indulgent wish. People mess up their lives with various forms of irresponsible behavior, such as abusing alcohol or drugs, spending more money than they have, or abusing marital trust. When the destructive consequences of self-regulation failure catch up with them and they contemplate the sorry state of their lives, they feel a loss of self-esteem. As a result, they come to associate the problem with the loss of self-esteem—but conclude, wrongly, that the low self-esteem is the cause rather than the result of their reckless or self-destructive behavior. Solving their problems would in fact require hard work and self-discipline to change their patterns of behavior and deny themselves the instant gratification of their impulses. Instead of accepting that sober reality, however, people wish that they could effect a magical transformation by merely deciding not to feel guilty any more. They wish to forgive themselves (and be forgiven by others) for their misdeeds and to start a new chapter of their lives with a clean slate and a generous dose of self admiration. Unfortunately, this prescription does not change the core problems of poor self-regulation; in fact, it merely offers the individual a way to avoid learning from his or her mistakes. It seems likely to lead merely to another round of indulgent, irresponsible behavior and another set of problems.

The three authors of this book have spent many years doing research on self-esteem (e.g., Baumeister, 1982, 1993a; Baumeister, Heatherton, & Tice, 1993; Baumeister, Tice, & Hutton, 1989; Heatherton & Polivy, 1992; Tice, 1991, 1993). Normally, researchers like to see the variables they study become a focus of national interest, because it increases the recognition of one's own work. We cannot, however, go along with the national preoccupation with self-esteem. In our view, America is not suffering from low self-esteem. It suffers from a spreading epidemic of self-regulation failure.

The importance of self-regulation failure has not escaped the attention of social scientists. Psychological research on issues of self-control has expanded dramatically since the middle of the 1980s. Unfortunately, there is not much coordination of this research. Researchers in multiple fields have examined many phenomena in isolation from each other.

The purpose of this book is to pull together much of this work on self-regulation failure. The goal is understanding rather than intervention or social critique. We hope to assemble the information about self-regulation failure, now scattered among dozens of journals and seemingly unrelated fields of inquiry, in order to identify some general patterns and principles and to offer a resource

for others who may wish to know about self-regulation failure for other purposes, including possibly clinical work, social work, policy analysis, and basic research and theorizing. Regarding the last of these, which is closest to our own work, we note that self-regulation failure is of interest in several ways. First, it is an intriguing problem in its own right. Second, it is part of a broader theoretical question of self-regulation per se. (That is, to understand how people control themselves successfully, it is useful to have a body of knowledge about *failures* of self-regulation, so that one can understand the limits and pitfalls of efforts to regulate the self.)

Third, self-regulation is important for the compelling project of understanding the nature of human selfhood. In our view, a very significant and central part of the self is its activity as a self-regulator. No cognitive, motivational, emotional, or behavioral theory about the self can pretend to be complete without addressing the issue of self-regulation.

WHAT IS SELF-REGULATION?

If life is indeed a miracle, then it is a many-sided one, and one of the most miraculous of these sides is the ability of living things to control themselves. Among most species, the ability to alter oneself is confined to certain limited and innately prepared mechanisms, such as homeostasis, but among human beings the ability to exert control over one's own inner states, processes, and responses is extensive.

Most living things have some set of inner mechanisms that regulate the system. Homeostasis, after all, is not a neutral state or passive outcome but a dynamic state that is the product of frequent adjustments in response to constantly changing circumstances. Food is ingested and digested. Body temperature is adjusted. Cuts, bruises, and other tissue damages are repaired. Opponent processes spring into action to offset unusual states and conditions (see Solomon & Corbit, 1974). Thus, living systems are all self-regulating.

Among human beings, however, the capacity for self-regulation far exceeds what most other living things can do. Part of the reason for this is the involvement of the conscious human mind in the process. Human beings develop a broad variety of techniques for regulating their actions and inner states. They do so with reference to far more than a steady-state outcome; indeed, people regulate themselves with reference to ideals, long-range goals, others' expectations, and other standards that may not correspond to anything they have yet experienced. Some people have elevated control over bodily processes to an extraordinary level, such as the yogis who allow themselves to be buried alive for a week or who melt large blocks of ice with their naked bodies.

Human culture has long recognized people's capacity for regulating themselves. Words such as *self-control* and *self-discipline* embody popular conceptions of self-regulation. We shall favor the term *self-regulation,* but from our perspective *self-control* has a very similar meaning and *self-discipline* is only slightly narrower, and we shall use the latter two terms to connect our discussion with the way people talk about these issues and problems in everyday life.

We use the term *self-regulation* broadly, to refer to any effort by a human being to alter its own responses. These responses may include actions, thoughts, feelings, desires, and performances. In the absence of regulation, the person would respond to the particular situation in a certain way, whether because of learning, habit, inclination, or even innate tendencies. Self-regulation prevents this normal or natural response from occurring and substitutes another response (or lack of response) in its place.

Thus, the essential nature of self-regulation is that of *overriding.* In an important sense, self-regulation theory requires that the person (or other organism) have multiple processes or levels of action. One process interrupts or overrides another, for example, a person may wish to complete a certain project at work. While she works, she may feel a growing thirst, as her body uses up its moisture. Normally the increase in thirst would prompt her to get a drink; the urgency of the work, however, may prompt her to override this typical response and stay at her desk until the project is completed. She has regulated her behavior in a way to make it depart from normal or habitual ways of acting.

The concept of overriding encompasses starting, stopping, or changing a process, as well as substituting one outcome or response for another. The most basic form of override, however, is simply to bring a response sequence to a stop. The original and rudimentary form of self-regulation is therefore what we call *self-stopping:* Intervening in one action or response pattern in order to bring it to a halt. Successful self-regulation may involve stopping oneself from drinking another beer, from eating another helping, from thinking about what might have been, from yelling out one's anger, and the like.

Indeed, most forms of self-regulation can in theory be analyzed as instances of self-stopping, although there are some exceptions (such as getting oneself out of bed in the morning, which requires one to start an action rather than to stop one; although in a sense one stops oneself from indulging in the lazy desire to lie in bed). It is an instructive exercise to try to reduce all self-regulation to self-stopping. Although we do not subscribe to such extremely reductionistic views, one can analyze the vast majority of instances of self-regulation in that way. Addicts stop themselves from indulging their cravings; dieters stop themselves from eating; infantry soldiers stop themselves from running away; decision makers stop themselves from being swayed by improper sources or unwelcome evidence; persevering workers stop themselves from giving in to the pain or fatigue that sends an impulse to quit; angry or distressed people stop themselves from dwelling on what upset them; and so forth.

BASIC INGREDIENTS OF SELF-REGULATION

Although this book is focused on self-regulation failure, some initial comments about self-regulation per se need to be made. In other words, it is useful to have some grasp of what the main processes are, in order to understand how they may fail.

It is necessary to begin with the assumption that there is more than one thing going on inside a human being at any given time. Multiple processes operate in parallel in a complex creature such as a human being. At any moment, the body may be regulating temperature, breathing, and digesting food, the mind may be pondering some problem while also replaying some remembered piece of music, and the emotional system may be reacting to thoughts with various feelings. Self-regulation begins with competition among such multiple processes. Self-regulation is a matter of one process overriding another, and that result emerges from competition among these parallel processes.

To understand self-regulation, it is also necessary to have some concept of a hierarchy among these multiple processes. The competing processes are not equal. Indeed, the hierarchy concept was central to one of the most important works on self-regulation, namely the model advanced by Carver and Scheier (1981, 1982). Higher processes involve longer time spans, more extensive networks of meaningful associations and interpretations, and more distal or abstract goals (see also Baumeister, 1991a, 1991b; Vallacher & Wegner, 1985, 1987). Self-regulation involves higher processes overriding lower processes; when the reverse happens, it is *failure* of self-regulation. The person may be torn between the desire for a cigarette and the resolution to quit, and the latter is higher on the hierarchy. If the person manages to avoid smoking in that situation, then that was an instance of successful self-regulation, because the self's resolve over-rode the (lower) desire to smoke. It is not self-regulation, however, if the desire to smoke overrides the resolution to abstain. Rather, if the person gives in and has a cigarette, that is a case of self-regulation failure.

Much of the research and theorizing about self-regulation has emphasized the concept of the feedback loops, borrowed from systems theory (Miller, Galanter, & Pribram, 1960; Powers, 1973; Carver & Scheier, 1981, 1982). Feedback-loop theory was advanced in the 1940s in connection with the development of sophisticated weapons such as ballistic missiles, but the most familiar example from everyday life is the room thermostat, which turns on the furnace or air conditioner whenever the room temperature departs from a preset range. Feedback loops are also commonly called TOTE loops; TOTE is an acronym for test-operate-test-exit, reflecting the sequence of steps in such a loop. The initial *test* phase refers to a comparison of current circumstances (e.g., the room temperature, or a person's current dress) to a standard (the desired temperature, or the desired level of dress). If there is a discrepancy, such that current circumstances fall short of the standard, then there is a phase of *operation:* The thermostat turns on the furnace, or the person changes clothes. Then comes another *test,* to see whether the circumstances have reached the goal or not. If not, the system continues to operate to produce change (more heat; further changes in clothes). Finally, when the circumstances measure up to the standard, the system *exits* the loop, and the cycle ends.

The feedback loop model presupposes three things that are important ingredients for self-regulation. First, there must be *standards;* to pursue the example, the thermostat cannot operate without being set to a particular target temperature. When people seek to exert control over themselves, they invoke various standards, which are abstract concepts of how things should be. These may be social norms, personal goals, the expectations of others, and the like. When standards are unclear, ambiguous, lacking, or conflicting, self-regulation will be less effective.

Second, a feedback loop requires some way of *monitoring* the current circumstances (in the test phase). People can only regulate themselves successfully if they pay attention to what they are doing, or if they have some other way of gaining the knowledge of their responses. People who use their charge cards indiscriminately, without keeping track of how much they are spending, will have a much harder time regulating their finances than people who continue to monitor their expenditures.

Third, people must have some means of operating on themselves in order to bring about the desired changes or responses. As we have said, self-regulation involves overriding responses that might normally, naturally, or habitually occur. If people cannot override these, self-regulation will be unsuccessful.

Understanding self-regulation as an override process portrays the problem as one of competition between responses, and indeed in many instances of self-regulatory challenge people feel as if there is an inner conflict going on, in which they are pulled in opposite directions. The decision to keep to a strict diet conflicts with the urge to gobble down that doughnut that someone has placed on the table in front of you. In some sense, therefore, the stronger response wins. Successful self-regulation therefore requires that the responses high in the hierarchy carry enough strength to override the lower tendencies.

This concept of strength resembles the colloquial concept of *willpower.* In the familiar example, a person uses willpower to resist temptation. Strong people will be able to resist; weak people will not. Although this common-sense model may have some shortcomings (for example, we should not assume that strength is a constant quantity that reflects some good or bad property

of the person's character), it is valid in some important ways. We shall return to issues of strength repeatedly throughout this book. In particular, factors that deplete or decrease self-regulatory strength may increase the likelihood of self-regulation failure. By the same token, if the lower impulse becomes stronger and stronger—such as if the temptation becomes more appealing, or the person's deprivation becomes more acute—then it may be able to thwart the person's efforts to override it.

IMPORTANCE OF SELF-REGULATION

The central importance of self-regulation to human life has already been suggested by our opening remarks that linked self-regulation failure to many of the major social problems of our contemporary society. Indeed, the notion that self-regulation is important is far from new. Although ancient philosophers and wise men may have neglected to use the term, they nonetheless recognized its importance. Indeed, the Aristotelian exhortation to pursue moderation in all things can be understood as a recommendation that people regulate their desires and their actions so as to prevent destructive, undesirable extremes.

Traditional conceptions of virtue and vice have often referred to self-regulation patterns. Medieval Christians were frequently warned about the "seven deadly sins," for example. Five of the seven—greed (avarice), lust, gluttony, sloth (laziness), and anger (wrath)—referred to issues of self-regulation failure, ones that we shall cover in the pages of this book. Thus, the majority of major sins referred to selfish impulses and actions, and sinners were defined as people who failed to overcome these impulses. Meanwhile, virtues such as fidelity, temperance, loyalty, chastity, prudence, courage, humility, and steadfastness celebrated people who did manage to keep their own behavior up to high standards by resisting temptations and maintaining consistency.

Likewise, the traditional male and female sex roles embodied idealized conceptions of self-regulation, although these often tended to be expressed in somewhat different spheres. Male ideals often invoked heroic feats of self-control, such as conquering one's fear in battle so as to be able to perform effectively and aggressively despite great personal danger. Self-discipline has also been admired in male work, where great accomplishments often require laboring for long grueling hours at strenuous tasks, such as in farming. Female ideals, meanwhile, have placed even greater emphasis on self-control, usually requiring consistent exercise over long periods of time rather than more isolated, heroic feats. The culture has treated self-denial, chastity, fidelity, self-sacrifice, emotional control, and dutiful submission to the sometimes arbitrary and capricious commands of others as feminine virtues, and self-regulation is central to all of those. Indeed, it is possible to say that self-control has been the quintessential feminine virtue in Western culture. Although resisting temptation has been regarded as an important task in the achievement of virtue by either sex, there has generally been greater tolerance of occasional lapses by males (whose periodic indulgence in intoxication, sexual shenanigans, or aggressive misbehavior has been regarded as inevitable and perhaps appropriate), which implies that females have generally been held to higher standards than males for the capacity to overcome desires and impulses (for a discussion, see Bullough & Brundage, 1982).

Recent research has continued to verify the value and importance of self-regulation in various ways, as several examples will readily show. One significant problem in our society is the high divorce rate. Kelly and Conley (1987) examined a broad host of personality and attitudinal factors in order to see which ones predicted marital breakup. Three variables stood out as especially powerful predictors. Two of these were the neuroticism of the husband and the neuroticism of the wife, indicating that (not surprisingly) grumpy, unhappy, irritable people are more prone to marital dissatisfaction and divorce. The only other variable that ranked with those two obvious factors was the husband's impulse control. Thus, marriages break up in large part when husbands are deficient at self-regulation.

In a possibly related finding, Strube, Turner, Cerro, Stevens, and Hinchey (1984) linked lack of control to hostile aggression and family violence. These authors noted that many researchers had suggested that the Type A, coronary-prone personality tended to be accompanied by higher levels of aggression than other personality types, but the nature of this aggressiveness had not been spelled out. Their own research ruled out the notion that Type A aggression is instrumental; instead, it appears that Type

A people's aggression often emerges as a hostile response to frustration and an inability to prevent oneself from violent action when one has been angered.

In one of the most provocative studies to examine long-term effects of self-regulatory capabilities, Mischel, Shoda, and Peake (1988) showed beneficial effects lasting for over a decade. More precisely, children who showed a high capacity to resist immediate temptations and choose delayed gratifications while still preschoolers later became more successful and well-adjusted adolescents. In this study, researchers assessed the children's ability to delay gratification when the children were 4 and 5 years old. About 10 years later, the researchers contacted the parents for reports on how the children were doing. The adolescents who had been the most self-controlled children were superior in school performance, social competence, and coping abilities (i.e., being able to deal with frustration and stress effectively). Another follow-up study found that the children who had been most able to delay gratification at age 4 had higher SAT scores when they applied to college! (Shoda, Mischel, & Peake, 1990).

These findings suggest that self-regulatory capacity is a central, powerful, stable, and beneficial aspect of personality. Research by Funder, Block, and Block (1983) has confirmed its importance in personality. High capacity to delay gratification is linked to being attentive, reasonable, intelligent, resourceful, competent, and cooperative (all of these as perceived by teachers and psychologists). Children who have low ability to delay gratification tend to be aggressive, restless, unable to deal with stress, prone to feelings of victimization, and likely to be regarded as sulky and whiny.

Turning from beneficial to destructive patterns, self-regulation again emerges as a central factor. In an important work synthesizing a great deal of research on many types and patterns of crime, Gottfredson and Hirschi (1990) concluded that the most important generalization about crime and criminality is that they arise from lack of self-control. Most crimes are impulsive actions, and most criminals exhibit broad and multifaceted patterns of lacking self-control. We shall return to this in some detail as we examine specific processes of self-control failure; for now, the important point is that self-regulation failure has been implicated as possibly the single greatest cause of destructive, illegal, and antisocial behavior.

To put things in a broader context, it appears that self-regulation is a vital aspect of human adaptation to life. A classic paper by Rothbaum, Weisz, and Snyder (1982) argued that human adaptation involves two processes, which they termed primary and secondary control. Primary control referred to direct efforts at changing the environment in order to suit the self. Secondary control, in contrast, involved changing the self to fit in to the environment. As a way of operating on the self, secondary control can be understood as a concept that is closely related to self-regulation. Thus, self-regulation accounts for roughly half of the adaptive activities of human beings.

And, in fact, self-regulation may be the more important half. When Rothbaum et al. (1982) wrote their article, they argued that people generally began by trying to exert primary control (hence the term) and only resorted to secondary control if primary control failed, but research has failed to support that sequence. In fact, subsequent work by these authors consistently found that measures of secondary control were the ones most closely related to successful adjustment (F. Rothbaum, 1988, personal communication). In their work, as in the work by Mischel et al. (1988), self-regulation emerged as the most powerful and decisive key to becoming a successful, well-adjusted person.

Thus, self-regulation has been widely and justly recognized as an important aspect of personality and of human behavior. Society benefits when its members have high self-control, because social relations remain more orderly, predictable, and constructive. Individuals benefit from self-control, because over the long run they have a better chance of meeting their goals, fulfilling their plans, and adapting to their environment.

PLAN OF BOOK

In this book we plan to survey the research literature in several major domains where self-regulation failure has been studied. In reading these literatures, our goal has been to understand each phenomenon on its own terms and then to look for common patterns and principles that hold up across different domains. These patterns and principles constitute a general understanding of self-regulation failure, which can then be reapplied to the individual spheres and domains, It would be unrealistic to expect all self-regulation failures to follow a single causal process or to conform to a uniform pattern. Still, there do exist broad similarities across multiple spheres, and these deserve careful attention and emphasis.

Chapter 2 will discuss the general patterns and principles that we found in diverse forms of self-regulation failure. We shall present these in the form of a general theoretical discussion of self-regulation failure, derived largely from an understanding of how successful self-regulation functions.

The subsequent chapters will present the evidence about specific spheres of self-regulation failure. Our goal has been to cover the main findings and conclusions about each type of self-regulation failure, regardless of whether it fits our theoretical scheme or not. We shall of course refer back to the general theoretical discussion from Chapter 2 wherever appropriate, but we have sought to avoid a Procrustean policy of forcing all research findings to conform to our ideas.

The main body of the book, therefore, is organized by phenomenon rather than by conceptual process. Thus, for example, rather than covering all instances of underregulation together and then proceeding to all instances of misregulation, we cover both underregulation and misregulation in each chapter. The chapters cover the major areas of self-regulation failure so as to be accessible to readers who have a specific interest in one sphere. The four chapters of Part II involve self-regulation failure in several of the main spheres studied by social and personality psychologists: task performance, self-management, mental processes, and emotions. Part III covers self-regulation failures with regard to impulses and appetites, including eating, drinking alcohol, gambling, smoking, shopping, and aggressive misbehavior.

Our final chapter, then, will summarize the mass of evidence in relation to the general ideas and patterns explained in Chapter 2. We shall also seek to outline areas where knowledge remains most fragmentary and incomplete, in the hope that researchers will redouble their efforts in these areas.

General Patterns and Mechanisms of Self-Regulation Failure

By Roy F. Baumeister, Todd F. Heatherton, Dianne M. Tice

The purpose of this chapter is to outline some broad ideas and theories about how self-regulation fails. These can then be examined, tested, and refined in further chapters, in which we examine what is known about specific spheres of self-regulation failure.

There are two main categories of self-regulation failure: *underregulation* refers to a failure to exert control over oneself, and *misregulation* refers to exerting control in a way that fails to bring about the desired result, or particularly in a way that leads to some alternative result. Underregulation is more studied, although recently some evidence has accumulated about misregulation too. Accordingly we shall emphasize underregulation. In any case, the two are quite different and follow different processes, so it is necessary to analyze them separately.

Logically, one might suppose that something in the nature of *overregulation* would be a possible form of self-regulation failure. But overregulation presumably accomplishes its goal, even if it puts extra energy into the task or does more than is necessary, so it is not a form of failure. The only exception would be if overregulation produces some undesirable results, in which case it is a form of misregulation. For that reason, we will not have a separate treatment of overregulation.

The basic features and ingredients of self-regulation were covered in Chapter 1. These include having some standards, monitoring oneself in relation to these standards, and altering the self's responses so as to make them conform better to the standards. Self-regulation failure can occur with any of those: there can be a problem with knowing the standards, a problem with monitoring the self, or a problem with making the self conform to them.

CONFLICTING STANDARDS

The first sort of problem is one of the standards themselves. There could be a complete lack of standards, in which case one does not have any basis for self-regulation (e.g., Karoly, 1993). More common, though, is the problem in which one has multiple standards that are inconsistent, conflicting, or otherwise incompatible. If the person has several conflicting sets of standards, then it is very difficult to decide which one to use as the basis for self-regulation. Shakespeare's *Hamlet*, for example, depicted a young man torn between conflicting standards. On the one hand, he felt his duty as a prince to be loyal to his king, the man whom his mother had married and who had generally treated him well. On the other hand, he suspected the king to be a usurper who had murdered Hamlet's own father, and if these suspicions were correct it was his duty as a son to avenge his father's death. Caught between these incompatible obligations, Hamlet spent much of the drama paralyzed by indecision, ruminating about the proper course of action, misbehaving in various ways, and even seeming to lapse into madness.

Empirical evidence supports the view that self-regulation is severely hampered by conflicting standards. When people have multiple, conflicting goals, they become unable to manage themselves effectively. Paralysis, confusion, and other dysfunctional patterns result, just as they did for Hamlet. Emmons and King (1988) showed that conflicting goals tend to produce rumination rather than action, and in consequence the person fails to make progress toward any goals. Van Hook and Higgins (1988) showed that discrepant, conflicting self-guides (i.e., internal sets of standards) lead to muddled, indecisive, unsure, rebellious responses, confusion about identity, and emotional distress. They noted that these internal conflicts make self-assessment difficult, which contributes to self-regulatory difficulties.

Maphet and Miller (1982) provided similar evidence in a study with children that was based on the assumption that self-control derives from the internalization of instructions originating with an external, controlling agent. These researchers showed that children could effectively obey instructions that prohibited a certain behavior, even weeks after the prohibition was expressed. If the two authority figures (in this case, two experimenters) disagreed about the rules, however, the child was not likely to conform to their instructions.

REDUCTION OF MONITORING

A second prominent cause of self-regulation failure arises when the person ceases to monitor what he or she is doing. As we saw, effective self-regulation requires that the person frequently evaluates self and actions against the relevant standards, to see how one is measuring up. When the monitoring function breaks down, self-regulation becomes difficult if not impossible. In an authoritative overview of the problems that plague clinical, therapeutic efforts to improve self-regulation, Kirschenbaum (1987) concluded that clients' failure to monitor their behavior is a prominent and central cause of self-regulation failure.

A failure of monitoring may be central to one of the most discussed and controversial issues in all of social psychology, namely that of attitude-behavior consistency. For decades, social psychologists studied attitudes on the assumption that people's behaviors are based on their attitudes. Rather abruptly, however, the value of all that work came into question when researchers found that assumption to be false. Wicker (1969) compiled a large body of evidence to suggest that attitudes have at best a weak and inconsistent relationship to behavior. Over the following two decades, attitude researchers scrambled to establish a more compelling link between attitudes and behavior in order to justify the study of attitudes.

One important explanation for the frequent weakness of attitude-behavior correlations was that people often fail to monitor their behavior in relation to these attitudes. Ajzen and Fishbein (1977) pointed out that researchers often measured general attitudes and then sought links to very situationally specific behaviors; for example, a researcher might measure a general attitude about helping other people and then see if those who held the strongest pro-helping attitudes were also the most willing to give blood in response to a specific request. Studies like that often failed to find much of a relationship, partly because people failed to see the request to give blood as relevant to their broad general attitude about helping others. Instead, they may respond to that request in terms of squeamishness about needles, their own commitments or needs to have all their energy that evening, or other factors. Fazio, Powell, and Herr (1983) demonstrated that general attitudes can predict specific behaviors—but mainly when people think about these general attitudes and interpret the immediate situation with reference to them. When reminded of their broad feelings about helping others, for example, people might be more inclined to think of a request to give blood as a test of their helpfulness, and in such cases—that is, when they monitor their behavior against the relevant standards—their behavior does tend to become consistent with their attitudes.

The paradox of *deindividuation* is also related to issues of monitoring. Deindividuation means losing self-awareness and evaluation apprehension, especially as occurring when the person feels submerged in a group of people (e.g., Diener, 1979; Dipboye, 1977). The paradox was that the loss of individuality was often accompanied by behaviors that seemingly reflected the true feelings and impulses of the inner self. What is lost during deindividuation, however, appears to be very much a matter of the monitoring of self; people cease to attend to what they are doing and evaluate their actions against their own personal standards, with the result that ordinary restraints and inhibitions are suspended. Consequently, behavior may reflect impulses and feelings that would normally be held in check.

A familiar example of deindividuation is the lynch mob, that is, a group of people who take it upon themselves to punish and usually kill someone (usually someone accused of a crime). Mullen (1986) showed that factors conducive to a loss of individual self-awareness were associated with more severe, violent, and deadly behavior by lynch mobs. The implication is that when people stop monitoring their actions individually in relation to their personal standards and ideals, they become capable of performing dangerous and violent acts that lie beyond what they would normally do.

More generally, any loss of self-awareness may contribute to self-regulation failure, because attending to self is the essence of the monitoring function. Alcohol, for example, has been shown to reduce self-awareness (Hull, 1981). People lose the capacity to think about themselves, evaluate themselves, compare themselves to standards, and grasp the implications of current events for their future selves. It has long been known that under the influence of alcohol people will do things that they would not ordinarily do, and even things that they will later regret. One reason, apparently, is that alcohol reduces cognitive processing in relation to the self (Hull, 1981). Self-regulation may therefore be more likely to break down under alcoholic intoxication, allowing the person to perform actions that would normally be inhibited or stifled (e.g., Steele & Southwick, 1985).

Likewise, when the mind is preoccupied with other activities, the capacity to monitor the self may be reduced. And in some cases people want to escape from self-awareness, such as when it is unpleasant to think about the self (e.g., after a distressing failure experience), and the flight from self-awareness will often be accompanied by a reduction or cessation of monitoring and, consequently, by patterns of unusual and disinhibited behavior (e.g., Baumeister, 1991a; Heatherton & Baumeister, 1991).

INADEQUATE STRENGTH

We suggested in Chapter 1 that self-regulation involves a kind of strength, analogous to the common-sense concept of willpower. If that is correct, then self-regulation failure may occur when the person's strength is inadequate to the task. In an important sense, self-regulation involves a contest of strength: the power of the impulse and its resulting tendency to act, against the power of the self-regulatory mechanism to interrupt that response and prevent that action.

Strength failure is relevant to the third ingredient of self-regulation, namely the inability to make the self conform to the relevant standards. The problem is not an absence or disappearance of standards, nor is it a failure to monitor the self; indeed, the person may be quite acutely aware of the relevant standard and of his or her failure to live up to it. But the person feels unable to alter his or her responses to bring them into line with the desired, prescribed ones.

The nature of the "strength" that is needed for successful self-regulation can be illuminated by considering self-stopping, which we noted is probably the first and most basic form of self-regulation. Research suggests that self-stopping involves both mental and physical exertion, as suggested by multiple studies.

The cognitive aspect of self-stopping was studied directly by Gilbert, Krull, and Pelham (1988). These authors showed subjects a videotape of a social interaction, and the videotape contained a sequence of irrelevant and meaningless stimuli at the bottom. Subjects in the control condition simply watched the interaction on the film, and subsequent measures showed that they had processed the social information reasonably well. In the experimental condition, however, subjects were instructed to ignore those irrelevant and meaningless stimuli. This should have been easy enough; after all, the control subjects ignored that gibberish without being instructed to do so. The experimental subjects, however, felt they had to exert control over their gaze in order to prevent themselves from looking at the gibberish at the bottom of the screen, and this effort of self-control consumed some of their attention—with the result that they ended up with a more superficial and incomplete impression of what had happened in the interaction they watched. Self-regulation thus appeared to require some mental effort, to the extent that they were less able to attend fully to what they were watching and hence less able to understand its implications.

The link between self-stopping and physical exertion (usually measured in terms of physical arousal) has been suggested by several studies. Wegner, Shortt, Blake, and Page (1990) showed that suppressing thoughts about sex led to an arousal response that was higher than actually thinking about sex—thus, it is arousing to stop oneself from thinking about sex. Pennebaker and Chew (1985) required subjects to tell one lie mixed in with a series of truthful responses, and they found that the lie was associated with both the inhibition of incidental nonverbal behaviors (presumably as a means of stopping oneself from revealing one's untruthfulness) and increased psychophysiological arousal. Notarius, Wemple, Ingraham, Burns, and Kollar (1982) suggested that the inhibition of facial expression of emotion was marked by increases in physiological arousal. Waid and Orne (1982) found that levels of socialization moderated the tendency of inhibitory response conflict to generate high levels of electrodermal response; the implication is that arousal responses such as anxiety, guilt, and fear may be instrumental in enabling people to inhibit antisocial impulses. Thus, self-stopping often depends on those forms of emotional arousal.

Self-stopping thus appears to involve both mental and physical resources. To override an impulse, a habit, or some other tendency, one often has to exert oneself both mentally and physically. The resource that makes such exertion possible can thus be analyzed as a kind of strength. If a lack of strength makes the person unable to create the necessary cognitive or physical response, self-regulation may fail.

There are three main reasons that someone would have inadequate strength for successful self-regulation: one chronic, one temporary, and one external. The person may lack strength because he or she is a weak person who would probably never be able to override that same impulse. Alternatively, the person may be exhausted or tired, and so he or she is unable on some particular occasion to override a habit or impulse. Lastly, the impulse may be so strong that even someone with well-developed self-regulatory skills would be unable to conquer it. Let us consider each of these causes of weakness in turn.

The first is that of chronic weakness, and this is closest to the common-sense notion of willpower as a character trait. It is almost certainly true that some people have more self-discipline than others, are better able to

control their actions and feelings, are more capable of resisting temptation. If self-regulatory capacity is a kind of strength, then like a muscle one should be able to increase its capacity over time (by exercising it frequently). Conversely, it should be vulnerable to becoming weak and incapable if it is not challenged regularly. People who are not accustomed to controlling themselves should find it difficult to do so when it suddenly becomes necessary.

Self-regulatory strength has been studied by Funder and Block (1989) under the rubric of *ego control*. In their view, people differ on the trait of being able to control impulses, desires, and actions. Risk taking and a capacity to resist immediate temptations (in order to garner greater but delayed rewards) are related to this trait. Ego control holds similarities to what nonpsychologists might call the trait of willpower.

The second cause is temporary. Strength is a limited resource that can be depleted by multiple, simultaneous demands. Like a muscle, it may become tired if it is subjected to considerable exertions in a relatively short span of time, and so even if it is chronically strong it may lose its capacity to function effectively. At any given time, a person's strength is limited, and so when that is used up the person should become incapable of further self-regulation.

Hence factors that consume the person's strength should contribute to self-regulation failure. Physical tiredness should be one factor; the strength model will predict that people will be less effective at self-regulation when they are tired, such as late in the evening. Likewise, confronting stressful or other circumstances that are unusually demanding should also impair self-regulation. When going through divorce, or when coping with a busy season at work or final examinations in school, for example, people should be more likely to exhibit breakdowns in self-regulation (such as would be reflected in increases in smoking, drinking, or overeating). Even the demands of a new self-regulatory task, such as in setting out on a very tough diet, might consume so much of one's strength that one's self-regulatory capacity breaks down in other spheres (such as the capacity to prevent oneself from speaking crossly to others).

A particularly interesting implication is that people's capacity for self-regulation needs to be managed like any other limited resource. It will not be possible to regulate everything at once. Some months will be better than others to quit smoking, for example; one will be more successful at a time when other demands on one's self-control are relatively low.

The third factor is the strength of the impulse or other response that has to be controlled. If self-regulation depends on one response overriding another, then the strength of the competing response may prevent the override from occurring even if the person has a great deal of self-discipline. The notions of an "uncontrollable impulse" or an "unstoppable desire" reflect the belief that some responses are too strong to be regulated. Self-regulation failure is to be expected in such cases; in general, the stronger the impulse, habit, or desire (or other response), the greater the likelihood of self-regulation failure.

It is also important to remember that impulses and desires do not always remain at the same strength but may become stronger over time. Self-regulation may be initially successful but may eventually fail simply because the competing motivation becomes too strong to be stifled. A simple example of this is the desire to go to the bathroom. Most adults can resist that urge effectively for a period of time, but eventually the need will be too strong to resist, regardless of the person's resources of self-discipline and strength.

The fact that motivations change in strength over time, thereby making the self-regulatory process harder or easier, brings up the relevance of temporal change. The next section will examine an even more important way in which timing affects self-regulatory failure.

PSYCHOLOGICAL INERTIA

Because we have depicted self-regulation as a matter of one response process overriding another, the issue of timing is crucial. Two responses may compete in such a way that one will have precedence at one time but another will have precedence at another. As an example, consider the school pupil doing homework on a Saturday afternoon while tempted to go outside and play. Self-regulation is a matter of overcoming the impulse to go play, in order to make himself persist at his work. As the afternoon wears on, the competition between the two processes may shift repeatedly. Perhaps he was physically restless after lunch and the urge to play

was especially strong, but later in the day that may wear off, making it easier to continue working. Perhaps there was a rainstorm, in which case the urge to go outside was likely to vanish entirely. Meanwhile, his devotion to his homework might fluctuate as a function of his encouraging successes, his fatigue, or his frustration with it.

It is thus difficult to generalize about how timing will affect self-regulation. There is one general pattern, however, that in the absence of other fluctuations may prove decisive. This is the fact that response sequences apparently are easiest to override early in the sequence. There may be many actions that could easily be stopped early on but may become difficult to stop once they have gained a certain momentum.

This principle may be designated as psychological *inertia*. The term *inertia* refers to an obsolete and discredited concept in physics, namely that bodies in motion have a force that impels them to continue moving. Physical motion does not constitute or create any such force. Psychological processes, however, may indeed gain such a force. Thus, the longer someone is doing something, the more difficult it may be to get that person to stop.

The implications for self-regulation are important. Self-regulation will be most effective and will require the least strength when it overrides a response as early as possible. The longer one allows an objectionable response to go on, the harder it will be to stop it, just as a bad habit will be harder to break as it becomes more and more ingrained.

Illustrations of inertia are not difficult to find. Consider the example of self-stopping in terms of the person who is on a diet and gets an impulsive wish to have some ice cream. The diet would suffer a serious setback if the person were to go to the freezer, get out a carton of ice cream, and eat the entire carton. In principle, this outcome could be avoided by self-stopping at any point along the way, before the carton is emptied. In practice, however, we suspect it will be easiest to accomplish this early in the sequence. If the person can avoid getting up to walk over to the refrigerator, the diet is saved, and this might be relatively easy. In contrast, stopping may be much more difficult after the carton has been taken out and opened and the person is sitting at the table with the first spoonful of ice cream already in hand. And once the person has begun seriously eating the ice cream, interrupting the binge in progress may be even more difficult.

A similar argument can probably be made about most other instances of self-stopping. Consider illicit sex, for example. Anyone who has preserved his or her virginity through high school in recent decades probably has an implicit understanding of the principle of inertia. Refraining from sex is undoubtedly much easier if one backs away after (or even before) the first kiss than if one waits to intervene until after an hour of passionate necking and after garments have already been unbuttoned, unclasped, and unzipped. The longer one waits, the greater the effort of will that is required to override the sexual response.

The hypothesis of psychological inertia is hardly new or unique in our analysis. Indeed, versions of this hypothesis date back at least to the 1920s, when the Zeigarnik (1927) effect was first demonstrated. The Zeigarnik effect indicated that it is particularly difficult to interrupt a response sequence in the middle, and that as one approaches the fulfillment or conclusion of a sequence of actions, interruption brings increased rumination about the interrupted activity. Presumably there would be less rumination and less desire to resume if the response could be prevented from starting or, that failing, interrupted right away rather than later on.

Inertia should not be overstated. As already noted, it is not the only way in which timing is relevant to self-regulation. Sometimes things can lose their appeal, making self-regulation easier after some satisfaction has reduced the motivation. People do, after all, generally stop eating before they have consumed all the food in the house. Some grow tired of watching baseball games after seeing a couple hundred of them, and so they cease watching without having to exert themselves to override any desire. Even bulimic eating binges eventually come to an end. In short, there are multiple factors that can cause responses to stop after a period of time. But as one significant factor among several, inertia is important.

The implication of inertia is that self-regulation can be achieved most effectively if instigated as early as possible. Prevention will be easier and more effective than interruption. Self-regulation failure may therefore gradually snowball; the crucial thing is for the failure to get started, and once failure has begun, then regaining and reasserting self-control will become progressively more difficult.

But even the matter of snowballing is not as simple as it may seem. When self-regulation begins to fail, there are often other factors that come into play. These lapse-activated causes may be totally irrelevant to the onset of self-regulation failure, but they are decisive in transforming a minor failure into a major breakdown. The next section will examine these.

LAPSE-ACTIVATED CAUSAL PATTERNS

There has been a great deal of attention—not only in the research literature, but also in the popular press, in works of fiction, and even in everyday gossip—to the factors that conspire to bring a person to break the law, or a resolution, or a diet, or a promise, or some other commitment. That first step that crosses over the imaginary line is of considerable interest as well as drama. This is quite justified: After all, breakdowns in self-control do have to start with some signal failure, and the first step is undoubtedly a central event in that story.

But it is not the whole story. The one step across the line may be the only one, and the person can sometimes step back quickly—that is, reassert self-control. The first violation does not necessarily spell disaster. Sometimes, to be sure, the first step leads to another, and another, and another, until there is a full-blown breakdown of self-regulation, but other times it doesn't. Some researchers have focused their attention on just this issue of what causes some missteps to "snowball" into large-scale breakdowns while others remain minor, exceptional violations. The snowball metaphor is popular because it seems to capture the notion of something growing larger and larger as it continues on its way, just as a real snowball grows by picking up snow when it is rolled across a wintry field.

These lapse-activated snowballing patterns have been documented by some researchers under the rubric of *abstinence violation effects* (e.g., Marlatt, 1985). As the term implies, they have been mainly noted by researchers working with impulse control. When people break their diets or fall off the wagon or indulge in other activities that they have forbidden themselves, they often find that the initial lapse is quickly followed by a large-scale indulgence.

The key point here is that there are two sets of causes involved in self-regulation failure. One set consists of the factors that lead to the first lapse in self-control, that is, the first violation of one's program. The second set consists of factors that transform the initial lapse into a major binge. The second set only comes into play when the first set has finished causing the lapse.

The "snowball" metaphor for self-regulatory breakdowns is thus clearly inadequate, for two reasons. First, it leaves out the extremely important issue of what causes the initial lapse. In terms of the metaphor, it skips the question of where the initial, small snowball comes from. Second, not all lapses do end up snowballing into wholesale self-regulatory breakdowns.

An adequate explanation of self-regulation failure may therefore have to deal with two sets of causes which may be almost entirely separate. The first set of causes produces the initial lapse. The lapse, however, activates a second set of causes, which determine what happens next—in particular, whether there is a snowballing effect in which self-regulation breaks down extensively.

The recognition that two panels of causes may operate to cause failure is not new, even if theoretical models may change. Here is an account from Evagrius of Pontus, born in A.D. 345, whom Russell (1988) called "the greatest of the monastic psychologists." It is an elaboration of themes developed by the great theologian Origen:

> Our souls, having fallen from heaven and now being embedded in the body, are bent, their vision of God blurred. They are dominated by emotional turmoils they cannot shake off. … From turmoil arise worldly desires, which open gates for the demons lurking to attack us. Watching us carefully, Satan sees when we are weakened by a particular desire and then sends into the breach demonic troops suited and trained to exploit that particular temptation. Alert to each tiny breach, the demons pour through the hole and enlarge the beachhead. A desire for a woman may quicken in a man's heart, for example; the demons will rush in, flooding the mind with lewd images until his soul is a boiling cauldron. A woman may begin to dwell too much upon the investments she plans for her financial security; the demons will obsess her with money, turning need into greed and enslaving her to avarice. (quoted by Russell, 1988, p. 92)

Evagrius's explanation is especially relevant to a modern psychological approach if one can dismiss the supernatural forces as being merely metaphoric (which Evagrius himself probably would not have done, to be sure). He explains the initial lapse in terms of loss of strength as due to external stress and the mental and emotional overload of coping with the periodic difficulties of life. Amid all that turmoil, the person gives in to some temptation and indulges some impulse. That act of yielding sets in motion other forces (Satan's demons) that enter the picture after the initial breach of proper behavior and help transform the small misstep into a major breakdown.

As we shall find, emotion is often relevant to self-regulation failure—and not necessarily in the way Evagrius suggested, as a cause of the initial weakness, but rather as a factor that contributes to snowballing. In other words, emotions often enter the picture as lapse-activated causes. When a person violates a personal rule or goal or maxim, he or she may have an (often unexpected) emotional response. That emotion may influence subsequent behavior and contribute to the snowballing effect.

A vivid illustration of the role of emotion in lapse-activated causal patterns is provided in research on extramarital sex (see Lawson, 1988). Many people (particularly men, according to Lawson) reportedly commit their first act of infidelity in a desire for sexual novelty and adventure, and they firmly expect that the episode will remain a minor fling that will pose no threat to their marriage. Once they begin, however, some of them find themselves falling in love with the new sex partner. The affair ceases to be casual and can indeed lead to a breakup of the marriage. In short, the unexpected emotional reaction to the initial action helps produce a snowballing involvement that has serious consequences.

More generally, there are multiple ways in which emotional responses to an initial self-regulatory lapse can figure in lapse-activated causation and set the snowball in motion. Emotion involves arousal, and it consumes and manipulates attention; thus, it uses up both physical and mental strength that might otherwise be available for self-stopping. In addition, sometimes the emotion itself becomes a source of further motivations, such as a desire to continue to have sex or a need to escape guilt. Someone who has long abstained from alcohol or drugs, for example, may feel guilty after an initial lapse, and the desire to blot the guilt out of his or her mind may prompt the person to consume more of the forbidden substance.

One of the ironies of this duality of causal patterns is that certain factors that may support self-regulation in the initial phase can turn about and contribute to self-regulatory failure in the second phase. As an example, consider *zero-tolerance* beliefs, similar to the ones recently touted by American officials in response to drug use. The zero-tolerance view is that no misstep, no violation, can be allowed, because it will lead almost inevitably to disaster. There is no gray area, no allowance made for minor indulgences, no sympathy of occasional backsliding. Instead, all the attention and effort are focused on making certain that self-regulation is 100% effective at preventing any lapse at all.

Zero-tolerance beliefs are promoted on the not unreasonable assumption that if no one starts taking drugs, no one will become addicted. There is no danger of snowballing, of minor drugs serving as stepping stones to heavier, more dangerous drugs, of growing disregard for the risks or rising enjoyment of the newly discovered pleasures. As such, these beliefs may well contribute to help people avoid taking that first step across the line.

The problem with zero-tolerance beliefs, however, is that if a lapse does happen these beliefs may contribute to subsequent snowballing. And because people are not perfect and do not live absolutely by the rules 100% of the time, some of these lapses are likely to occur. Zero-tolerance beliefs catastrophize the first step in order to frighten people away from taking it. Once they do take it, however, the catastrophe has already seemingly occurred, so there is no particular reason to stop there. Some people may believe that what really matters, namely absolute compliance, has already failed with that first step (the first drug experience, the first cookie that violates the diet, the first cigarette after quitting, etc.),

and so one might as well do some more. Others may notice that no catastrophe occurred after all: One had sex, or smoked pot, or skipped church, and instead of the feared cataclysm life went on just as before. Such discoveries may serve to discredit the authoritative sources that warned one against such indulgences in the first place. The person may then feel some extra urge to explore or indulge further in this hitherto forbidden realm.

Thus, zero-tolerance beliefs can be compared to a military strategy of putting all one's defenses on the front line, with no reserves. The front line is defended maximally well; but if there is a breach, there is no fallback option, and catastrophe ensues.

There are of course other factors that contribute to snowballing effects; we have brought up the zero-tolerance beliefs here merely to illustrate how exactly the same cause, such as a commitment to perfect abstinence, can aid self-regulation and can also undermine and weaken it, depending on the phase of self-regulatory failure. Zero-tolerance beliefs contribute to lapse-activated causes by changing the meaning of an initial lapse. But this is getting ahead of the story. First we must take a more thorough and systematic look at what might cause the initial lapse.

RENEGADE ATTENTION

In reading the research literature on self-regulation, we were repeatedly struck by the central role of attention. In all spheres of self-regulation—controlling emotion, appetites and desires, performances, thought processes, and the rest—the management of attention emerged as a significant factor. Not only was it ubiquitous, but it also seemed widely effective. Managing attention is not only the most common technique of self-regulation, it may well be the most generally effective one (see also Kirschenbaum, 1987).

There are several good reasons for the preeminence of attention in successful self-regulation. In the first place, whatever is not noticed cannot have much in the way of consequences, whereas things that receive extensive attention tend to gain considerable power for producing psychological consequences.

The inertia principle furnishes another reason for the importance of attention. The inertia principle holds that response chains will be harder and harder to interrupt as they go on for longer amounts of time. The implication for self-regulation is that the easiest and most effective approach will be to intervene as early in the response process as possible. Attending to something—noticing it—is inevitably the first step in cognitive processing, and so there is relatively little inertia to overcome. In colloquial terms, attention management is the optimal strategy for nipping something in the bud.

Once the person loses control of attention, self-regulation becomes much more difficult. Any stimulus that manages to capture the person's attention will have a much improved chance of generating psychological reactions, such as impulses and desires, that will require ever greater exertions of self-regulatory strength to overcome. For that reason, the best strategy may be to prevent any dangerous or tempting stimulus to capture one's attention: It is probably easier and more effective to avoid temptation than to resist it. A reformed alcoholic may do quite well in a setting where drinking is neither done nor discussed, because there is little external cause to direct one's attention to the joys of the grape. In contrast, it may be far more difficult to stay on the wagon if the person resumes going to bars with his or her old friends who still drink.

The importance of managing attention leads to a seemingly paradoxical prediction, namely that being preoccupied can have opposite effects on self-regulation. On the one hand, if the person is seriously preoccupied with thinking about certain things, he or she may be less likely to notice tempting or threatening stimuli, and so there will be less difficulty resulting from conflicting impulses that need to be controlled. On the other hand, if such impulses do arise, being preoccupied may make it more difficult for the person to control them. We noted earlier that self-stopping apparently requires some mental resources, and so self-stopping should become more difficult when people are distracted, preoccupied, or operating under some other form of cognitive load.

Attending to the stimulus is not the only important attentional matter, however. One can also think more or less about the standard or goal that self-regulation is supposed to serve. Then, even when confronted with the threatening or tempting stimulus, one may still manage to retain control.

The key to this second attentional trick can be designated as *transcendence*. In essence, it involves seeing beyond the immediate stimulus environment. Other species, such as nonhuman animals, seem to find it very difficult to respond to anything beyond the immediate stimulus environment, but human beings can transcend their surroundings to an almost astonishing degree. Indeed, the history of Christian martyrdom records many examples of individuals acquiescing in their own certain death while singing hymns, which often made a deep impression on their executioners and onlookers. Such responses were possible because the martyrs were able to transcend the death-dealing stimuli in their immediate environment and focus instead on their anticipated rebirth and salvation in heaven.

At a more mundane level, the dieter who passes up the dessert, or the student who continues studying rather than stopping to play or rest, is engaging in transcendence too. One refuses to respond merely to the immediate stimulus and instead responds on the basis of more long-range, more abstract, or more distal goals and standards.

Transcendence too has important implications for self-regulation failure. Successful self-regulation often requires one to transcend the immediate stimulus environment. When, instead, the immediate stimulus environment floods awareness and the person is unable to look beyond it, self-regulation will be much more difficult. Thus, one important reason for losing control of attention—leading to self-regulation failure—occurs when the person becomes immersed in the immediate present. The transition from a long-term, broadly meaningful state of mind to a here-and-now, concrete focus is likely to accompany and even cause many significant patterns of self-regulatory breakdown.

The most likely mechanism of transcendence failure would involve cognitive shifts that reject broadly meaningful patterns of thought in favor of attending to immediate, concrete stimuli. Vallacher and Wegner (1985, 1987) provided an insightful and influential analysis of how any given act can be conceptualized at multiple levels, ranging from high levels (marked by long-range time spans and broadly meaningful implications) to low levels (marked by short-term immediacy and physical movement rather than meaning). Baumeister (1991b) has applied this idea broadly to explain a variety of patterns by which people seek to escape from self-awareness and unpleasant emotions. Emotion depends on a broadly meaningful understanding, so emotions exist mainly at high levels of thinking (see also Pennebaker, 1989). To escape from emotional distress, people may therefore shift toward more immediate and low-level styles of thinking.

Transcendence is linked to high levels of thinking, of course, so transcendence would fail whenever people escape into immediate, concrete forms of awareness. By the same token, inhibitions typically exist at highly meaningful levels, because inhibitions usually focus on a meaningful action (e.g., murder) rather than low-level acts (e.g., moving a finger in a way that would pull a gun's trigger). Inhibitions (and other forms of self-control) are thus weakened or even removed when awareness shifts down to low levels of meaning.

In general, therefore, we should find that transcendence facilitates self-regulation. When people are able to think beyond the immediate situation and interpret events with reference to long-range meanings and implications, they should be able to exert substantial control over themselves and override many impulses. In contrast, when they become immersed in the here and now and their awareness focuses on mere movements and sensations, self-control will cease to be effective.

ROLLING THE SNOWBALL

Thus far we have considered how self-regulation failures can begin, through loss of control of attention and through failure of strength. These are the things that cause people to step across the line and commit the first offense, first sin, first backslide, and so forth. The major instances of self-regulation failure, however, go far beyond the first step. Indeed, they often seem so extreme that one wonders how the same person could have maintained self-regulation so well up to that point and then lost control to such an extreme. The reason is that the first lapse may set off various reactions that escalate what might otherwise have been a minor lapse into a major breakdown. We turn our attention now to these other factors—in other words, to the lapse-activated causes and the resultant snowballing of self-regulation failure.

We have already mentioned two of the factors that can cause snowballing. First, we noted how zero-tolerance beliefs change their meaning and significance once a violation has occurred. These beliefs may support self-control as long as the person can live up to standards, but once a lapse has occurred, zero-tolerance beliefs tend to imply that the cause is already lost, and so they may foster a tendency to abandon further efforts at self-control. Second, we described the way emotional reactions to the initial lapse can interfere with subsequent self-regulatory efforts.

Another factor that may often contribute to snowballing of self-regulatory failure is a reduction of monitoring. We have already noted that successful self-regulation depends on monitoring oneself so as to compare one's actions and circumstances against the desired standards. Ceasing to monitor oneself can contribute to any phase of self-regulation failure, but there are reasons to think that in many cases it is especially relevant to lapse-activated patterns. More precisely, the person's reaction to the initial lapse may be to stop monitoring. For example, the person may feel guilty about the initial misstep and in order to prevent the feelings of guilt and remorse may make efforts to avoid self-awareness. Once people stop monitoring, it becomes essentially impossible to regulate themselves further.

Reduction of monitoring is actually common to several patterns that may produce snowballing of self-regulation failure. Indeed, zero-tolerance beliefs may even sometimes work by undermining the person's monitoring efforts, because they suggest that there is no longer any point in monitoring oneself.

Some byproducts of self-regulatory lapses may also weaken the tendency to monitor oneself. For example, if one consequence of self-regulatory failure is to drink alcoholic beverages, the person may become unable to monitor. One of the direct effects of alcohol consumption is a reduction in self-awareness (Hull, 1981): People lose the capacity to think about themselves, evaluate themselves, compare themselves to standards, and grasp the implications of current events for their future selves. It has long been known that under the influence of alcohol people will do things that they would not ordinarily do, and even things that they will later regret. One reason, apparently, is that alcohol reduces cognitive processing in relation to the self (Hull, 1981).

Without self-awareness—that is, without being able to reflect on one's actions and think through their implications for one's self—people cannot monitor themselves effectively (see Carver & Scheier, 1981, 1982). Therefore, alcohol use may directly reduce the effectiveness of self-regulation. A person such as a reforming alcoholic, who is trying to avoid drinking, may find that one small violation of being "on the wagon" may quickly snowball into a drunken binge. A reason for this is that the first drink already weakens the capacity to reflect on one's actions, and so the second drink is easier to take than the first, and quickly the person loses count.

Other forms of self-indulgence may also bring an immersion in immediate sensory pleasure that has the same effect, even without the psychophysiological basis, that alcohol has. Thus, the fanatical dieter may find that the first bite of cheesecake after a long period of bland, dull diet food tastes so wonderful that the mind becomes lost in the pleasing sensations and hence stops monitoring what one is doing. Again, the person may quickly lose count of how many bites have been had, until three pieces have been consumed and the person is bloated and suffering from indigestion.

Another, particularly interesting pattern is that of spiraling distress. In some cases, the first lapse of self-regulation may lead, not to pleasure, joy, or relaxation, but to emotional distress. The person may feel guilty, or worried, or disappointed with the self because of having lost self-control, however briefly. (Zero-tolerance beliefs may especially foster such reactions, because they magnify the supposed consequences of any misstep.) This distress is associated with attending to the self, and so it makes it doubly unpleasant to be aware of self. To be sure, some people may respond to this by stepping up their self-monitoring in order to make certain that this does not happen again, but undoubtedly there are many who will be less inclined to monitor themselves when every thought of self brings new distress. In these cases, a vicious cycle develops. Each violation of one's standards brings negative affect, which makes it unpleasant to be self-aware, so the person avoids monitoring his or her own behavior, which makes further violations possible. The longer this goes on, the more unpleasant it is to resume monitoring oneself, because one must recognize that one has severely violated one's desired patterns of behavior.

ACQUIESCENCE: LETTING IT HAPPEN

A theoretically elusive but very important issue is whether people actually acquiesce in their own self-regulation failures. We have analyzed self-regulation failure in terms of depletion of strength and other causes. These make it seem that such failure is something that happens to a person, something that the person is more or less powerless to prevent. On the other hand, some would argue that people allow themselves to fail, that they cooperate in their own failure to exert self-control.

Part of the interest in the issue of acquiescence comes from moral issues. If people cannot help what they are doing, then presumably they cannot be blamed for their self-regulatory failures. On the other hand, if the conscious self actively participates in abandoning self-control, then the person bears some responsibility for the results of his or her actions.

Given the moral (and legal) implications of this debate, there are powerful and outspoken voices in the national media taking sides. Alcoholics and drug addicts wish to be regarded as helpless and relatively innocent victims of genetic predispositions and of external, evil influences, rather than as irresponsible, self-indulgent pleasure seekers. Criminals wish their violent acts to be ascribed to "irresistible impulses" rather than to be regarded as deliberate choices.

Acquiescence is also important for the basic theoretical understanding of self-regulation failure. Thus, the strength model could be taken to imply that acquiescence has nothing to do with it; when the person's strength is gone, self-regulation will inevitably fail. Yet while that may be true, most self-regulation failures probably do not occur when the person's strength is completely gone. The person is merely tired, rather than fully exhausted; and in such circumstances, the person may choose to allow self-regulation to fail, because the tiredness makes the exertion of self-control that much more unappealing. The person does not wish to put forth the effort that would be required for successful self-regulation.

The issue of acquiescence has been in the background of several factors we have discussed. For example, one could object to our analysis of how people stop monitoring their behavior after an initial lapse occurred by saying that the person must be cooperating—acquiescing—in the cessation of monitoring. The dieter *could* count the number of bites, if necessary. The binge drinker is continuing to raise the glass to the lips and to pour or order another drink. The person is thus not a helpless, passive victim of being overwhelmed by forces that make self-regulation impossible; rather, in a sense the person *chooses* to stop keeping track of his or her own behavior and thus actively allows self-regulation to fail (see Peele, 1989).

Although it is very difficult to obtain decisive empirical data regarding the issue of acquiescence, we suspect that acquiescence is the norm, not the exception. It is rare that human behavior is the result of inner forces that the person is entirely helpless to stop or control. Going on a week-long drinking binge is not like the involuntary blinking of the eyes when a blast of hot air hits the face. In explaining self-regulation failure, therefore, the model of human behavior is less one of deterministic cause-and-effect than one of explaining why people allow themselves to lose control.

Often there are powerful factors that contribute to the person's acquiescence. In particular, many circumstances make people want to lose self-awareness, to escape from themselves and forget about the image of self they are projecting to the world (see Baumeister, 1991a). When people have had a bad day, or things have made them lose their sense of being a worthy person, or even when the stress of maintaining an acceptable public image becomes excessive, people may want to "let their hair down" and cease being self-aware. A small sensory indulgence such as a couple of drinks or some tasty dessert may often be part of such a relaxation. But these people will then be extra susceptible to the tendency to cease monitoring after the initial indulgence, because they are precisely wanting to escape from self-awareness.

There may indeed be some cases under which self-regulation is literally impossible and so it fails without any acquiescence by the individual. Undoubtedly there are other cases where people simply allow their self-control to lapse. In the subsequent chapters, we shall examine many forms of self-regulation failure, and these will offer some basis for addressing the question of whether people are to some extent responsible participants in these failures.

MISREGULATION

Our discussion thus far has focused on things that may prevent people from engaging in self-regulation. But this is not the only kind of self-regulation failure. It is also possible for people to engage in active efforts at self-regulation—but to do so in a way that is nonoptimal or counterproductive. In such cases, self-regulation failure may also occur—not because of a lack of trying, but because one used a technique or method that produced some result different from the desired one. In a word, it is *misregulation*, rather than underregulation.

It seems safe to say that the majority of misregulation patterns involve some kind of deficiency in knowledge, especially self-knowledge. The essence of misregulation is that the person tries to engage in self-regulation and knows what effect is wanted, but the regulatory methods produce the wrong effect. The methods must therefore be flawed in some way. If the person knew what the effects of these methods would actually be, he or she would not use them.

The knowledge flaws that lead to self-misregulation can have their origins in multiple places. After all, people are well stocked with beliefs that are simply false (see Gilovich, 1991). Future chapters will examine many ways in which false assumptions can originate, leading to misregulation of self. Let us just briefly review some of them here.

First, there is the problem of *overgeneralization*. People may assume that what works for one problem in one setting will work elsewhere. Thus, for example, many people feel better after consuming a small amount of alcohol, but in fact alcohol narrows attention, and so under some circumstances alcohol can simply focus the mind even more strongly on one's troubles (Steele & Josephs, 1990). When depressed people self-medicate by drinking heavily, they may end up feeling even more depressed (e.g., Doweiko, 1990).

Another factor may be the desire to believe that one can exert control even when one cannot, and so one intervenes with occasionally disruptive consequences. A good analogy is much of premodern medicine. Lacking valid techniques for curing illness, but feeling pressure to do something, premodern physicians resorted to various techniques (such as bleeding the patient or even cutting holes into the skull) that often did more harm than good. As we shall see, some major patterns of failure at task performance result from just such an attempt to control the uncontrollable.

A third source of distortion in self-knowledge is motivated. People want to have particular beliefs about themselves, and these may influence people's efforts to regulate themselves. In particular, people tend to exaggerate their abilities and other good points, and these exaggerations may lead to patterns of overcommitment.

Lastly, the culture may support various beliefs that can hamper optimal self-regulation. For example, American culture fosters the belief that persistence will eventually lead to success. Although persistence undoubtedly increases one's chances of success in many cases, it can also increase the danger of costly setbacks in others, because persistence in a failing or losing endeavor may compound a person's losses.

Misregulation also occurs in some cases because people focus their self-regulatory efforts on the wrong aspect of their behavior. There are two major patterns of this. First, people may sometimes try to control things that are not inherently controllable. Seligman (1994) has argued that people's efforts to control their lives and make themselves better are often thwarted by focusing on things that they cannot control. For example, nearly all researchers agree that most adult women cannot make themselves be as thin as the fashion models that appear on magazine covers. Indeed, the models themselves may often be unable to be that thin; some publications use computer image alteration techniques to stretch the pictures of models, thereby making the women seem thinner. Despite the impossibility of these ideals, and despite evidence that most men do not really want their wives and girlfriends to be so extremely thin, many women diet for years and do other things to try to make themselves conform to those ideals.

The second pattern involves focusing particularly on controlling one's emotions rather than on controlling whatever is the primary concern. Alcohol and drug problems may arise, for example, because people consume these substances as a way of making themselves feel better. Even though they know that excessive consumption may be bad for them, they focus their self-regulatory efforts on their emotional distress rather than on their substance abuse. In a similar vein, people may withdraw effort from a task in order to protect their feelings from the danger of failure, even though they would be better off in the long run to focus their self-regulatory efforts on making themselves persist in order to perform better.

SUMMARY AND CONCLUSION

In this chapter we presented some central concepts for understanding self-regulation failure. There are two main forms. Underregulation consists of a failure to control oneself. Misregulation consists of controlling oneself in a fashion that produces an undesirable or counterproductive outcome.

We began our analysis of underregulation with the three basic ingredients of self-regulation, as suggested in Chapter 1, namely standards, monitoring, and the capacity to alter behavior so as to bring it into line with the standards. A deficiency with any of those will tend to bring about self-regulation failure.

Standards are the conceptions of how one ought to act or be. When people lack standards, or when they have multiple and conflicting standards, self-regulation becomes difficult or even impossible.

Effective self-regulation also depends on monitoring oneself and one's behavior with respect to the standards. Accordingly, self-regulation failure will become more likely when people cease or fail to monitor themselves. When people stop keeping track of what they are doing or become unable (or unwilling) to pay attention to themselves, self-regulation will be impaired.

The most important aspect of the ability to alter one's behavior—the implementation aspect of self-regulation—is a form of strength. Even despite having clear standards and effective monitoring, people may fail at self-regulation because they lack the strength to alter their behavior in the desired fashion. Self-regulatory strength is akin to the colloquial concept of willpower, although it is necessary to remain cautious and skeptical about incorporating such concepts into psychological theory.

There are several main reasons that strength may be inadequate for effective self-regulation. There may be a chronic lack of strength, such as if the person is weak. This notion is closest to the conventional concept of willpower, and it suggests that certain people who lack self-discipline will tend to be vulnerable to many different forms of self-regulation failure at many times. In principle, however, people could build up their strength over time by practicing self-control or learning to regulate themselves effectively.

Alternatively, strength may be temporarily low, either because they are simply tired or because their strength has been depleted by recent exertions. Self-regulation failure may therefore occur when people are exhausted, such as late in the evening, or during times of stress, when there are many competing demands on one's self-regulatory capacity.

Lastly, strength may be inadequate simply because the impulse or behavior is itself too strong to overcome. Most people can control their appetites to some degree, for example, but if they are deprived of food for long enough the desire to eat may become overwhelming.

Several additional concepts are relevant to underregulation. *Inertia* refers to the principle that behaviors in progress are more difficult to override and overcome than behaviors that have not yet begun. Partly because of inertia, the management of attention is generally a crucial aspect of effective self-regulation, because it is the first step in information processing. Self-regulation failure will therefore tend to be marked by a loss of control over attention.

Effective self-regulation often requires adopting a long-range perspective that invokes distal outcomes and higher values—in other words, transcending the immediate situation. One particular form of loss of control of attention is therefore *transcendence failure*, in which the person loses the capacity to see beyond the immediate situation and begins responding mainly to immediate, salient environmental cues.

Unlike underregulation, misregulation occurs despite the fact that the person is successfully controlling his or her own behavior. The person is simply doing this in a counterproductive fashion. Misregulation often arises from faulty assumptions about the self, the world, or the consequences of certain actions. It also arises when people try to control things that cannot be effectively controlled or when they devote their self-regulatory efforts toward protecting their emotions and feelings instead of focusing on the task or problem itself.

Many serious instances of self-regulation failure involve two groups of causes. The first set of causes consists of what leads the person to begin the behavior. The second set, which may only become apparent after that point, transforms the initial behavior into a large-scale breakdown. We have chosen to designate this second set as *lapse-activated causes,* in order to indicate both the switching from one set of contingencies to another and the subsequent escalation (snowballing) of the self-regulatory failure. One example of a lapse-activated causal pattern would be that an initial misdeed creates an emotional reaction that leads to another misdeed, in a vicious cycle. Some causes can even facilitate self-regulation at one stage but hamper it in the other. For example, highly moralistic or absolutist beliefs that catastrophize any misdeed at all may help the person resist the temptation to commit the first misdeed, but if the first misdeed does nonetheless occur, such beliefs then imply that there is nothing left to lose and the person is a hopeless failure, which may then undermine any effort to stop the self-regulation failure from snowballing into a major breakdown.

What Is Addiction?

By George F. Koob and Michel Le Moal

OUTLINE

DEFINITIONS OF ADDICTION

Drug Use, Drug Abuse, and Drug Addiction

Drug addiction, also known as Substance Dependence (American Psychiatric Association, 1994), is a chronically relapsing disorder that is characterized by (1) compulsion to seek and take the drug, (2) loss of control in limiting intake, and (3) emergence of a negative emotional state (e.g., dysphoria, anxiety, irritability) when access to the drug is prevented (defined here as dependence) (Koob and Le Moal, 1997). The occasional but limited use of an abusable drug clinically is distinct from escalated drug use, loss of control over limiting drug intake, and the emergence of chronic compulsive drug-seeking that characterizes addiction. Modern views have focused on three types of drug use: (1) occasional, controlled or social use, (2) drug abuse or harmful use, and (3) drug addiction. An important goal of current neurobiological research on addiction is to understand the neuropharmacological and neuroadaptive mechanisms within specific neurocircuits that mediate the transition between occasional, controlled drug use and the loss of behavioral control over drug-seeking and drug-taking that defines chronic addiction (Koob and Le Moal, 1997).

The critical nature of the distinction between drug use, abuse and dependence has been illuminated by data showing that approximately 15.6 per cent (29 million) of the U.S. adult population will go on to engage in nonmedical or illicit drug use at some time in their lives, with approximately 3.1 per cent (5.8 million) of the U.S. adult population going on to drug abuse and 2.9 per cent (5.4 million) going on to Substance Dependence on illicit drugs (Grant and Dawson, 1998; Grant *et al*, 2005). For alcohol, 51 per cent (120 million) of people over the age of 12 were current users, 23 per cent (54 million) engaged in binge drinking, and 7 per cent (16 million) were defined as heavy drinkers. Of these current users, *7.7* per cent (18 million) met the criteria for Substance Abuse or Dependence on Alcohol (see *Alcohol* chapter). For tobacco, 30 per cent (71.5 million) of people aged 12 and older reported past-month use of a tobacco product. Also, 19 per cent (45 million) of persons in the U.S. smoked every day in the past month.

From the 1992 National Comorbidity Survey, 75.6 per cent of 15–54-year-olds ever used tobacco, with 24.1 per cent meeting the criteria for Dependence (Anthony *et al.,* 1994) (see *Nicotine* chapter).

The number of individuals meeting the criteria for Substance Dependence on a given drug as a function of ever having used the drug varies between drugs. According to data from the 1990–1992 National Comorbidity Survey, the percentage addicted to a given drug, of those people who ever used the drug, decreased in the following order: *tobacco > heroin > cocaine > alcohol > marijuana* (Anthony *et al.,* 1994) (Table 1.1, not shown). More recent data derived from the National Household Survey on Drug Abuse (Substance Abuse and Mental Health Services Administration, 2003) showed that the percentage addicted to a given drug, of those who ever used, decreases in the following order: *heroin > cocaine > marijuana > alcohol* (Fig. 1.1). These more recent data suggest unsettling evidence of an overall trend for a significant increase in Substance Dependence with marijuana (see *Cannabinoids* chapter).

The cost to society of drug abuse and drug addiction is prodigious in terms of both direct costs and indirect costs associated with secondary medical events, social problems, and loss of productivity. In the United States alone, it is estimated that illicit drug abuse and addiction cost society $161 billion (Office of National Drug Control Policy, 2001; see also Uhl and Grow, 2004). It is estimated that alcoholism costs society $180 billion per year (Yi *et al.,* 2000), and tobacco addiction $155 billion (Centers for Disease Control and Prevention, 2004). In France, the total cost of drug use is USD 41 billion (including $22 billion for alcohol, $16 billion for tobacco, and nearly $3 billion for illicit drugs) (Kopp and Fenoglio, 2000).

Addiction and *Substance Dependence* will be used interchangeably throughout this text and will refer to a final stage of a usage process that moves from drug use to abuse to addiction. Drug addiction is a disease and, more precisely, a *chronic* disease (Meyer, 1996). As such, it can be defined by its diagnosis, etiology, and pathophysiology as a chronic relapsing disorder (Fig. 1.2). The associated medical, social, and occupational difficulties that usually develop during the course of addiction do not disappear after detoxification. Addictive drugs are hypothesized to produce changes in brain pathways that

endure long after the person stops taking them. These protracted brain changes and the associated personal and social difficulties put the former patient at risk of relapse (O'Brien and McLellan, 1996), a risk higher than 60 per cent within the year that follows discharge (Finney and Moos, 1992; Hubbard *et al.,* 1997; McLellan and McKay, 1998; McLellan *et al.,* 2000). While much of the initial study of the neurobiology of drug addiction focused on the acute impact of drugs of abuse (analogous to comparing no drug use to drug use), the focus is now shifting to chronic administration and the acute and long-term neuroadaptive changes in the brain that result in relapse. Cogent arguments have been made which support the hypothesis that addictions are similar in their chronic relapsing properties and treatment efficacy to other chronic relapsing disorders such as diabetes, asthma, and hypertension (McLellan *et al.,* 2000). The purpose of current neuroscientific drug abuse research is to understand the cellular and molecular mechanisms that mediate the transition from occasional, controlled drug use to the loss of behavioral control over drug-seeking and drug-taking that defines chronic addiction (Koob and Le Moal, 1997).

Diagnostic Criteria of Addiction

The diagnostic criteria for addiction as described by the *Diagnostic and Statistical Manual of Mental Disorders,* 4th edition (DSM-IV) (American Psychiatric Association, 1994), also have evolved over the past 30 years with a shift from the emphasis and necessary criteria of tolerance and withdrawal to other criteria directed more at compulsive use. In the DSM-IV, tolerance and withdrawal form two of seven potential criteria. The criteria for Substance Dependence outlined in the DSM-IV closely resemble those outlined by the *International Statistical Classification of Diseases and Related Health Problems* (ICD-10) (World Health Organization, 1992) (Tables 1.2 and 1.3). The number of criteria met by drug addicts vary with the severity of the addiction, the stage of the addiction process, and the drug in question (Chung and Martin, 2001). For example, in adolescents, the most frequently observed criteria are *much time getting or recovering from use* (DSM-IV criteria #5 and #7), *continued use despite problems in social and occupational functioning* (DSM-IV criterion #6), and *tolerance or*

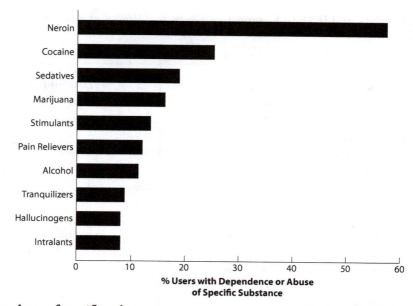

FIGURE 1.1 Dependence or abuse of specific substances among past-year users of substance (Substance Abuse and Mental Health Services Administration, 2003). Heroin: 57.4% (0.2 million), Cocaine: 25.6% (1.5 million), Marijuana: 16.6% (4.2 million).

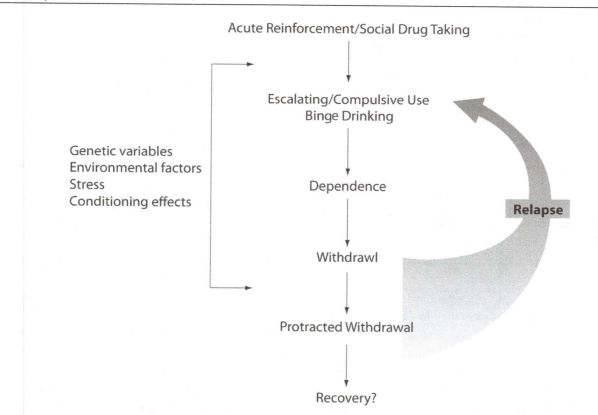

FIGURE 1.2 Stages of addiction to drugs of abuse. Drug-taking invariably begins with social drug-taking and acute reinforcement and often, but not exclusively, then moves in a pattern of use from escalating compulsive use to dependence, withdrawal, and protracted abstinence. During withdrawal and protracted abstinence, relapse to compulsive use is likely to occur with a repeat of the cycle. Genetic factors, environmental factors, stress, and conditioning all contribute to the vulnerability to enter the cycle of abuse/dependence and relapse within the cycle.

TABLE 1.2 DSM-IV and ICD-10 Diagnostic Criteria for *Alcohol and Drug Abuse/Harmful Use*

DSM-IV	ICD-10
Alcohol and drug abuse	**Harmful use of alcohol and drugs**
A. A maladaptive pattern of substance use leading to clinically significant impairment or distress, as manifested by one (or more) of the following occurring within a 12-month period:	A. A pattern of substance use that is causing damage to health. The damage may be physical or mental. The diagnosis requires that actual damage should have been caused to the mental or physical health of the user.
1. recurrent substance use resulting in a failure to fulfil major role obligations at work, school, or home.	B. No concurrent diagnosis of the substance dependence syndrome for same class of substance.
2. recurrent substance use in situations in which use is physically hazardous.	
3. recurrent substance-related legal problems.	
4. continued substance use despite having persistent or recurrent social or interpersonal problems caused or exacerbated by the effects of the drug.	
B. The symptoms have never met the criteria for substance dependence for the same class of substance.	

withdrawal (DSM-IV criteria #1 and #2) (Crowley *et al.*, 1998) (see *Cannabinoids* chapter).

Dependence View of Addiction

Historically, definitions of addiction began with definitions of dependence. Himmelsbach defined physical dependence as:

'... an arbitrary term used to denote the presence of an acquired abnormal state wherein the regular administration of adequate amounts of a drug has, through previous prolonged use, become requisite to physiologic equilibrium. Since it is not yet possible to diagnose physical dependence objectively without withholding drugs, the *sine qua non* of physical dependence remains the demonstration of a characteristic abstinence syndrome' (Himmelsbach, 1943).

Eventually this definition evolved into the definition for physical dependence or 'intense physical disturbances when administration of a drug is suspended' (Eddy *et al.*, 1965). However, this terminology clearly did not capture many of the aspects of the addictive process where no *physical* signs were observed, necessitating a second definition of *psychic dependence* to capture the more *behavioral* aspects of the symptoms of addiction: 'A condition in which a drug produces "a feeling of satisfaction and a psychic drive that require periodic or continuous administration of the drug to produce pleasure or to avoid discomfort" ...' (Eddy *et al.*, 1965). Modern definitions of addiction resemble a combination of physical and psychic dependence with more of an emphasis on the psychic or motivational aspects of withdrawal, rather than on the physical symptoms of withdrawal:

Addiction from the Latin verb "addicere", to give or bind a person to one thing or another. Generally used in the drug field to refer to chronic, compulsive, or uncontrollable drug

TABLE 1.3 DSM-IV and ICD-10 Diagnostic Criteria for *Alcohol and Drug Dependence*

	DSM-IV	ICD-10
Clustering criterion	A. A maladaptive pattern of substance use, leading to clinically significant impairment or distress as manifested by three or more of the following occurring at any time in the same 12-month period:	A. Three or more of the following have been experienced or exhibited at some time during the previous year:
Tolerance	1. Need for markedly increased amounts of a substance to achieve intoxication or desired effect; or markedly diminished effect with continued use of the same amount of the substance.	1. Evidence of tolerance, such that increased doses are required in order to achieve effects originally produced by lower doses.
Withdrawal	2. The characteristic withdrawal syndrome for a substance or use of a substance (or a closely related substance) to relieve or avoid withdrawal symptoms.	2. A physiological withdrawal state when substance use has ceased or been reduced as evidenced by the characteristic substance withdrawal syndrome, or use of substance (or a closely related substance) to relieve or avoid withdrawal symptoms.
Impaired control	3. Persistent desire or one or more unsuccessful efforts to cut down or control substance use. 4. Substance used in larger amounts or over a longer period than the person intended.	3. Difficulties in controlling substance use in terms of onset, termination, or levels of use.
Neglect of activities	5. Important social, occupational, or recreational activities given up or reduced because of substance use.	4. Progressive neglect of alternative pleasures or interests in favor of substance use; or A great deal of time spent in activities necessary to obtain, to use, or to recover from the effects of substance use.
Time spent	6. A great deal of time spent in activities necessary to obtain, to use, or to recover from the effects of substance used.	
Inability to fulfill roles	None	None
Hazardous use	None	None
Continued use despite problems	7. Continued substance use despite knowledge of having a persistent or recurrent physical or psychological problem that is likely to be caused or exacerbated by use.	5. Continued substance use despite clear evidence of overtly harmful physical or psychological consequences.
Compulsive use	None	6. A strong desire or sense of compulsion to use substance.
Duration criterion	B. No duration criterion separately specified. However, several dependence criteria must occur repeatedly as specified by duration qualifiers associated with criteria (e.g., 'often', 'persistent', 'continued').	B. No duration criterion separately specified.
Criterion for subtyping dependence	*With physiological dependence:* Evidence of tolerance or withdrawal (i.e., any of items A-1 or A-2 above are present). *Without physiological dependence:* No evidence of tolerance or withdrawal (i.e., none of items A-1 or A-2 above are present).	None

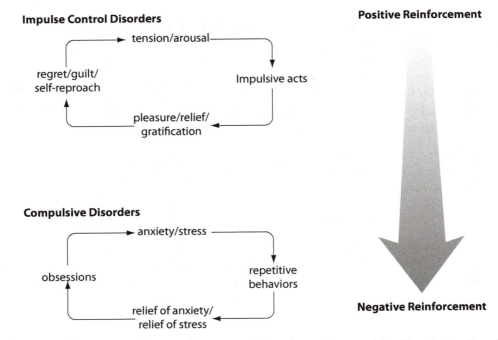

FIGURE 1.3 Diagram showing stages of impulse control disorder and compulsive disorder cycles related to the sources of reinforcement. In impulse control disorders increasing tension and arousal occur before the impulsive act, with pleasure, gratification, or relief during the act. Following the act there may or may not be regret or guilt. In compulsive disorders, there are recurrent and persistent thoughts (obsessions) that cause marked anxiety and stress followed by repetitive behaviors (compulsions) that are aimed at preventing or reducing distress (American Psychiatric Association, 1994). Positive reinforcement (pleasure/gratification) is more closely associated with impulse control disorders. Negative reinforcement (relief of anxiety or relief of stress) is more closely associated with compulsive disorders. [Reproduced with permission from Koob, 2004.]

use, to the extent that a person (referred to as an "addict") cannot or will not stop the use of some drugs. It usually implies a strong (Psychological) Dependence and (Physical) Dependence resulting in a Withdrawal Syndrome when use of the drug is stopped. Many definitions place primary stress on psychological factors, such as loss of self-control and over powering desires; i.e., addiction is any state in which one craves the use of a drug and uses it frequently. Others use the term as a synonym for physiological dependence; still others see it as a combination (of the two)' (Nelson *et al.,* 1982).

Unfortunately, the word *dependence* has multiple meanings. Any drug can produce dependence if dependence is defined as the manifestation of a withdrawal syndrome upon cessation of drug use, but meeting the DSM-IV criteria for *Substance Dependence* is much more than a manifestation of a withdrawal syndrome,

but rather is equivalent to addiction. For the purposes of this book, *dependence* with a lower-case 'little d' will refer to the manifestation of a withdrawal syndrome, whereas *Dependence* with a capital 'big D' will refer to Substance Dependence as defined by the DSM-IV or addiction. The words *Substance Dependence* (as defined by the DSM-IV), *addiction* and *alcoholism* will be held equivalent for this book.

Psychiatric View of Addiction

From a psychiatric perspective, drug addiction has aspects of both impulse control disorders and compulsive disorders. Impulse control disorders are characterized by an increasing sense of tension or arousal before committing an impulsive act—pleasure, gratification or relief at the time of committing the act—and there may or may not be regret, self-reproach or guilt following the act (American Psychiatric Association, 1994). In contrast, compulsive disorders are characterized by anxiety and stress before

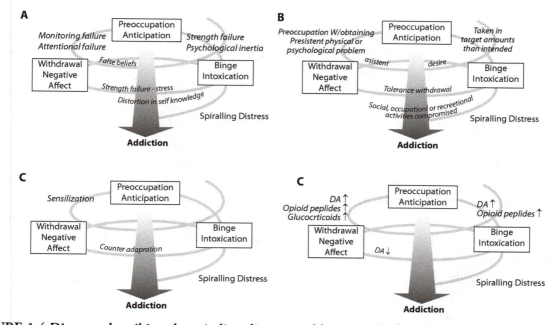

FIGURE 1.4 Diagram describing the spiraling distress—addiction cycle from four conceptual perspectives: social psychological, psychiatric, dysadaptational, and neurobiological. Note that the addiction cycle is conceptualized as a spiral that increases in amplitude with repeated experience, ultimately resulting in the pathological state known as addiction. (A) The three major components of the addiction cycle—preoccupation/anticipation, binge/intoxication, and withdrawal/negative affect—and some of the sources of potential self-regulation failure in the form of underregulation and misregulation. (B) The same three major components of the addiction cycle with the different criteria for substance dependence incorporated from the DSM-IV. (C) The places of emphasis for the theoretical constructs of sensitization and counteradaptation. (D) The hypothetical role of different neurochemical and endocrine systems in the addiction cycle. Small arrows refer to increased functional activity. DA, dopamine; CRF, corticotropin-releasing factor. [Reproduced with permission from Koob and Le Moal, 1997.]

committing a compulsive repetitive behavior and relief from the stress by performing the compulsive behavior. As an individual moves from an impulsive disorder to a compulsive disorder, there is a shift from positive reinforcement driving the motivated behavior to negative reinforcement driving the motivated behavior (Koob, 2004) (Fig. 1.3). Drug addiction has been conceptualized as a disorder that progresses from impulsivity to compulsivity in a collapsed cycle of addiction comprised of three stages: preoccupation/anticipation, binge/intoxication, and withdrawal/negative affect. Different theoretical perspectives ranging from experimental psychology, social psychology, and neurobiology can be superimposed on these three stages which are conceptualized as feeding into each other, becoming more intense, and ultimately leading to the pathological state known as addiction (Koob and Le Moal, 1997) (Fig. 1.4).

Psychodynamic View of Addiction

A psychodynamic view of addiction that integrates well with the neurobiology of addiction is that of Khantzian and colleagues (Khantzian, 1985, 1990, 1997) with a focus on the factors leading to vulnerability for addiction. This perspective is deeply rooted in clinical practice and in psychodynamic concepts developed in a contemporary perspective in relation to substance use disorders. The focus of this approach is on developmental difficulties, emotional disturbances, structural (ego) factors, personality organization, and the building of the self. It is important to note that this contemporary perspective contrasts with a classic but not abundant psychoanalytic literature on the subject which emphasizes the pleasurable aspects of drugs and the regressive aspects of drug use.

Two critical elements (disordered emotions and disordered self-care) and two contributory elements (disordered self-esteem and disordered relationships) have been identified, which have evolved into a modern self-medication hypothesis, where individuals with substance use disorders are hypothesized to take drugs as a 'means to cope with painful and threatening emotions.' In this conceptualization, addicted individuals experience states of subjective distress and suffering that may or may not be associated with conditions meeting DSM-IV criteria for a psychiatric diagnosis (American Psychiatric Association, 1994). Addicts have feelings that are overwhelming and unbearable and may consist of an affective life that is absent and nameless. From this perspective, drug addiction is viewed as an attempt to medicate such a dysregulated affective state. The suffering of the patient is deep-rooted in disordered emotions characterized at their extremes either by unbearable painful affect or by a painful sense of emptiness. Others cannot express personal feelings or cannot access emotions and are hypothesized to suffer from alexithymia, defined as 'a marked difficulty to use appropriate language to express and describe feelings and to differentiate them from bodily sensation' (Sifneos, 2000).

Such self-medication may be drug-specific in that patients may have a preferential use of drugs that fits with the nature of the painful affective states that they are self-medicating. Opiates might be effective in reducing psychopathological states of violent anger and rageful feelings. Others suffering from anhedonia, anergia, or lack of feelings, will prefer the activating properties of psychostimulants. Some flooded in their feelings, or cut off from feelings, will welcome repeated moderate doses of alcohol or depressants as medicine to express feelings that they are not able to communicate. Thus, in some cases, the subjects operate to relieve painful feelings, in others, the operative motive is to control or express feelings (Khantzian, 1995, 1997; Khantzian and Wilson, 1993). The common element to this hypothesis is that each class of drugs serves as an antidote to dysphoric states and acts as a 'replacement for a defect in the psychological structure' of such individuals (Kohut, 1971). The paradox is that the choice of drugs to self-medicate such emotional pain will later by itself perpetuate it, thereby continuing a life revolving around drugs.

Disordered self-care is hypothesized to combine with a disordered emotional life to become a principal determinant of substance use disorders. Self-care deficits reflect an inability to ensure one's self-preservation and are characterized by an inability to anticipate or avoid harmful and dangerous situations, and an inability to use appropriate judgment and feeling as guides in the face of danger. Thus, self-care deficits reflect an inability to appropriately experience emotions and appreciate the consequences of dangerous behaviors, and the core element of this psychodynamic perspective is a dysregulated emotional system or systems in individuals vulnerable to addiction.

This psychodynamic approach integrates well with a growing amount of evidence for a critical role of dysregulated brain reward and stress systems, from studies on the neurobiology of addiction using animal models that have developed from a physiological framework (see chapters that follow). However, from a neurobiological perspective, there is the additional insult to the personality produced by the direct effects of the drugs themselves to perpetuate, and actually *create,* such character flaws (Koob, 2003).

Social Psychological/Self-regulation View of Addiction

At the social psychology level, self-regulation failure has been argued as the root of the major social pathology in present times (Baumeister *et al.,* 1994). From this perspective there are important self-regulation elements that may be involved in the different stages of addiction to drugs, as well as in other pathological behaviors such as compulsive gambling and binge eating (Baumeister *et al.,* 1994). Such self-regulation failures ultimately may lead to addiction in the case of drug use or an addiction-like pattern with nondrug behaviors. Underregulation as reflected in strength deficits, failure to establish standards or conflicts in standards, and attentional failures as well as misregulation (misdirected attempts to self-regulate) can contribute to the development of addiction-like patterns of behavior (Fig. 1.4). The transition to addiction can be facilitated by lapse-activated causal patterns. That is, patterns of behavior that contribute to the transition from an initial lapse in self-regulation to a large-scale breakdown in self-regulation can lead to spiraling distress (Baumeister *et al.,* 1994). In some cases, the first self-regulation failure can lead to emotional distress which sets up a cycle of repeated failures to self-regulate and where each violation brings additional negative affect, resulting in spiraling distress (Baumeister *et al.*, 1994). For example, a failure of strength may lead to initial drug use or relapse, and other self-regulation failures can be recruited to produce an entrance to, or prevent an exit from, the addiction cycle.

At a neurobehavioral level, such dysregulation again may be reflected in deficits of information-processing, attention, planning, reasoning, self-monitoring, in-hibition, and self-regulation, many of which involve functioning of the frontal lobe (Giancola *et al.*, 1996a,b) (see chapters that follow). Executive function deficits, self-regulation problems, and frontal lobe dysfunctions or pathologies constitute a risk factor for biobehavioral disorders including drug abuse (Dawes *et al.*, 1997). Deficits in frontal cortex regulation in children or young adolescents predict later drug and alcohol consumption, especially for children raised in families with drug and biobehavioral disorders histories (Dawes *et al.*, 1997; Aytaclar *et al.*, 1999).

Vulnerability to Addiction

Drug abuse is a far more complex phenomenon than previously thought, and it is now recognized that drug abusers represent a highly heterogeneous group, and the patterns leading to dependence are diverse. Individual differences in temperament, social development, comorbidity, protective factors, and genetics are areas of intense research, and a detailed discussion of these contributions to addiction are beyond the scope of this book. However, each of these factors presumably inter-acts with the neurobiological processes discussed in this book. A reasonable assertion is that the initiation of drug abuse is more associated with social and environmental factors, whereas the movement to abuse and addiction are more associated with neurobiological factors (Glantz and Pickens, 1992).

Temperament and personality traits and some temperament clusters have been identified as factors of vulnerability to drug abuse (Glantz *et al.*, 1999) and include disinhibition (behavioral activation) (Windle and Windle, 1993), negative affect (Tarter *et al.*, 1995), novelty- and sensation-seeking (Wills *et al.*, 1994), and 'difficult temperament' (conduct disorder) (Glantz *et al.*, 1999).

From the perspective of comorbid psychiatric disor-ders, some of the strongest associations are found with mood disorders, anxiety disorders, antisocial personality disorders, and conduct disorders (Glantz and Hartel, 1999). Data from the International Consortium in Psychiatric Epidemiology (representing six different sites in the United States, Germany, Mexico, The Netherlands, Ontario, and Canada) and the National Comorbidity Study (United States; approximately 30,000 subjects) have revealed that approximately 35 per cent of the sample with drug dependence met lifetime criteria for a mood disorder. About 45 per cent met criteria for an anxiety disorder, and 50 per cent met criteria for either conduct or antisocial personality disorder (Merikangas *et al.*, 1998). More recent data on 12-month prevalence of comorbidity from the National Institute on Alcohol Abuse and Alcoholism's National Epidemiologic Survey on Alcohol and Related Conditions represents over 43,000 respondents and shows similar results (21–29 per cent for comorbidity of mood disorders; 22–25 per cent comorbidity for anxiety disorders; 32–70 per cent comorbidity for personality disorders) (Grant *et al.*, 2004a,b,c) (Table 1.4). The association of Attention Deficit Hyperactivity Disorder (ADHD) with drug abuse can be explained largely by the higher comorbid-ity with conduct disorder in these children (Biederman *et al.*, 1997). Independent of this association, there is little firm data to support a risk due to treatment of ADHD with stimulants (Biederman *et al.*, 1999), and no preference for stimulants over other drugs has been noted (Biederman *et al.*, 1997).

Developmental factors are important components of vulnerability, with strong evidence developing that adolescent exposure to alcohol, tobacco, or drugs of abuse leads to significant vulnerability for alcohol de-pendence and alcohol problems in adulthood. Persons first intoxicated at 16 or younger were more likely to drive after drinking, to ride with intoxicated drivers, to be injured seriously when drinking, to be more likely to become heavy drinkers, and to be 2–3 times more likely to develop substance dependence on alcohol (Hingson *et al.*, 2003) (Fig. 1.5). Similarly, persons who smoked their first cigarette during 14–16 years of age were 1.6 times more likely to become dependent than those who initiated at a later age (Breslau *et al.*, 1993; Everett *et al.*, 1999). Others have argued that regular smoking

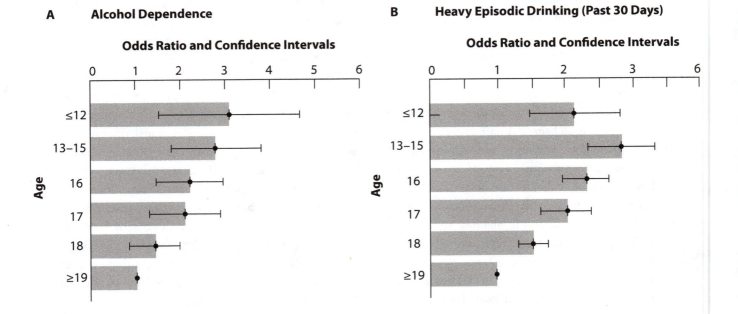

FIGURE 1.5 1999 College Alcohol Survey. (A) Alcohol Dependence according to age first intoxicated. (B) Past 30 days heavy episodic drinking according to age first intoxicated. After controlling for personal and demographic characteristics and respondent age, the odds of meeting alcohol dependence criteria were 3.1 times greater for those first drunk at or prior to age 12 compared with drinkers who were first drunk at age 19 or older. The relationship between early onset of being drunk and heavy episodic drinking in college persisted even after further controlling for alcohol dependence. Respondents first drunk at or prior to age 12 had 2.1 times the odds of reporting recent heavy episodic drinking than college drinkers first drunk at age 19 or older.

TABLE 1.4 12-Month Prevalence of Comorbid Disorders Among Respondents with Nicotine Dependence, Alcohol Dependence, or Any Substance Use Disorder

	Mood	Anxiety	Personality
Alcohol	27.6%	23.5%	39.5%
Nicotine	21.1%	22.0%	31.7%
Substance Dependence (including alcohol but not nicotine)	29.2%	24.5%	69.5%

[Data from Grant *et al.*, 2004a,b,c]

during adolescence raises the risk for adult smoking by a factor of 16 compared to nonsmoking during adolescence (Chassin *et al.*, 1990). Most smoking initiation occurs in the United States during the transition from junior high school to high school (14–15 years of age) (Winkleby *et al.*, 1993). The age at which smoking begins influences the total years of smoking (Escobedo *et al.*, 1993), the number of cigarettes smoked in adulthood (Taioli and Wynder, 1991), and the likelihood of quitting (Ershler *et al.*, 1989; Chassin *et al.*, 1990) (Fig. 1.6). When prevalence of lifetime illicit or nonmedical drug abuse and Substance Dependence was estimated for each year of onset of drug use from ages 13 and younger to 21 and older, early onset of drug use was a significant predictor of the subsequent development of drug abuse over a lifetime (Grant and Dawson, 1998) (Fig. 1.7). Drugs included sedatives, tranquilizers, opioids other than heroin, amphetamines, cocaine and crack cocaine, cannabis, heroin, methadone, hallucinogens, and inhalants. Overall, the lifetime prevalence of dependence among those who started using drugs under the age of 14 years was 34 per cent; this percentage dropped to 14 per cent for those who started using at age 21 or older (Grant and Dawson, 1998).

In adolescents, it has been proposed that there are stages and pathways of drug involvement (Kandel and Jessor, 2002). There is considerable support for the hypothesis that initiation begins with legal drugs, alcohol and tobacco, and involvement with illicit drugs occurs later in the developmental sequence, marijuana

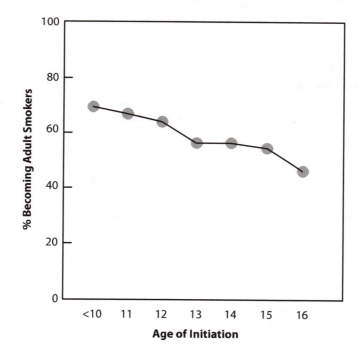

FIGURE 1.6 Percentages of adolescent regular smokers who became adult regular smokers as a function of grade of smoking initiation. Subjects consisted of all consenting 6th to 12th graders in a Midwestern county school system who were present in school on the day of testing. All 6th to 12th grade classrooms (excluding special education) were surveyed annually between 1980 and 1983. There was a potential pool of 5799 individuals who had been assessed at least once during their adolescence between 1980 and 1983. At the time of follow-up, 25 of these subjects were found to be deceased, and 175 refused participation, 4156 provided data (72%). The subjects were predominantly Caucasian (96%), were equally divided by sex (49% male; 51% female), and were on an average 21.8 years old. 71% had never been married, and 26% were currently married. 58% had completed at least some college by the time of follow-up. 32% were still students. 43% had a high school education. For nonstudents, occupational status ranged from 29% in factory, crafts, and labor occupations, to 39% in professional, technical, and managerial occupations. At follow-up, the overall rate of smoking at least weekly was 26.7%.

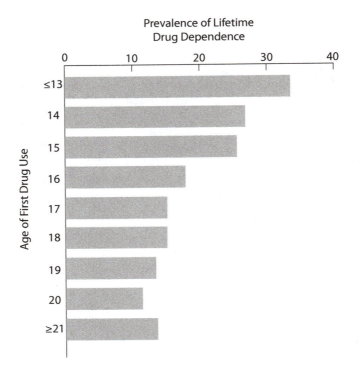

FIGURE 1.7 Prevalence of lifetime drug dependence by age at first drug use. The prevalence of lifetime depen-dence decreased steeply with increasing age of onset of drug use. Overall, the prevalence of lifetime dependence among those who started using drugs under the age of 14 years was about 34%, dropping sharply to 15.1% for those initiating use at age 17, to about 14% among those initiating use at age 21 or older.

often being the bridge between licit and illicit drugs. However, although this sequence is common, this does not represent an inevitable progression. Only a very small percentage of youths progress from one stage to the next and on to late stage illicit drug use or Dependence.

Genetic contributions to addiction have long been postulated and can result from complex genetic differ-ences that range from alleles that control drug metabolism to hypothesized genetic control over drug sensitivity and environmental influences. Complex genetic influences are those that are genetic but are not due to single-gene effects that produce Mendelian inheritance patterns, as stressed by Uhl and Grow (2004). The classical approach-es to complex trait genetics have been the examination of co-occurrence or comorbidity for the trait in monozy-gotic versus dizygotic twins, reared together or apart, and in analogous family studies with other sorts of biological relatives. Twin and adoption studies can provide research-ers with estimates of the extent of genetic effects, termed *heritability* (the proportion of observed variation in a particular trait that can be attributed to inherited genetic

factors in contrast to environmental factors). Using such estimates, genetic studies have demonstrated that genetic factors can account for approximately 40 per cent of the total variability of the phenotype (Table 1.5, not shown). Twin studies suggest significant overlap between genetic predisposition for Dependence on most classes of addic-tive substances (Karkowski *et al.,* 2000). Clearly, in no case is heritability 100 per cent, which argues strongly for gene-environment interactions, including the stages of the addiction cycle, developmental factors, and social factors.

It also should be emphasized that genetic and en-vironmental factors can convey not only vulnerability, but also protection against drug abuse. Certain Asian populations missing one or more alleles for acetaldehyde dehydrogenase show significantly less vulnerability to alcoholism (Goedde *et al.,* 1983a,b; Mizoi *et al.,* 1983; Higuchi *et al.,* 1995). There is also similar evidence developing for individuals with a genetic defect in me-tabolizing nicotine (Tyndale and Sellers, 2002; Sellers *et al.,* 2003). Clearly, there are also protective factors within the social environment that can promote competent adaptation and as a result prevent drug abuse (Dishion and McMahon, 1998).

NEUROADAPTATIONAL VIEWS OF ADDICTION

Behavioral Sensitization

Repeated exposure to many drugs of abuse results in a progressive and enduring enhancement in the motor stimulant effect elicited by a subsequent challenge. The phenomenon of *behavioral sensitization* has been thought to underlie some aspects of drug addiction (Vanderschuren and Kalivas, 2000). Behavioral or psychomotor sensitization, as defined by increased locomotor activation produced by repeated administration of a drug, is more likely to occur with intermittent exposure to drugs, whereas tolerance is more likely to occur with continuous exposure. This phenomenon was observed and characterized in the 1970s and 1980s for various drugs (Babbini *et al.*, 1975; Eichler and Antelman, 1979; Bartoletti *et al.*, 1983a,b; Kolta *et al.*, 1985). Another intriguing aspect is that it has been suggested that the sensitization grows with the passage of time (Antelman *et al.*, 1983, 1986, 2000). Moreover, stress and stimulant sensitization effects show cross-sensitization (Antelman *et al.*, 1980). Psychomotor sensitization is linked invariably to a sensitization of the activity of the mesolimbic dopamine system (Robinson and Berridge, 1993).

A conceptualization of the role of psychomotor sensitization in drug addiction has been proposed where a shift in an incentive-salience state described as *wanting*, as opposed to *liking*, was hypothesized to be progressively increased by repeated exposure to drugs of abuse (Robinson and Berridge, 1993) (Fig. 1.8, not shown). The transition to pathologically strong *wanting* or craving was proposed to define compulsive use.

The theory posits that there is no causal relationship between the subjective pleasurable effects of the drugs (drug *liking*) and the motivation to take drugs (drug *wanting*). The brain systems that are sensitized do not mediate the pleasurable or euphoric effects of drugs, but instead they mediate a subcomponent of reward termed *incentive salience* (i.e., motivation to take drug or drug *wanting*). It is the psychological process of incentive-salience specifically that is responsible for instrumental drug-seeking and drug-taking behavior (*wanting*) (Robinson and Berridge, 2003). When sensitized, this incentive-salience process produces compulsive patterns of drug use. By means of associative learning, the enhanced incentive value becomes oriented specifically toward drug-related stimuli, leading to escalating compulsion for seeking and taking drugs. The underlying sensitization of neural structures persists, making addicts vulnerable in the long-term to relapse.

The theory posits:

'... it is specifically sensitization of incentive salience attribution to representation of drug cues and drug-taking that cause the pursuit of drugs and persisting vulnerability to relapse and addiction ... Individuals are guided to incentive stimuli by the influence of Pavlovian stimulus-stimulus (S-S) associations on motivational systems, which is psychologically separable from the symbolic cognitive systems that mediate conscious desire, declarative expectancies of reward, and act-outcome representations' (Robinson and Berridge, 2003).

Counteradaptation–Opponent-Process

Counteradaptation hypotheses have long been proposed to explain tolerance and withdrawal and the motivational changes associated with the development of addiction. Here, the initial acute effect of the drug is opposed or counteracted by homeostatic changes in systems that mediate primary drug effects (Solomon and Corbit, 1974; Siegel, 1975; Poulos and Cappell, 1991). The origins of such counteradaptive hypotheses can be traced to some of the earlier work on physical dependence (Himmelsbach, 1943), and the counteradaptive changes associated with acute and chronic opioid administration on physiological measures.

Martin (1968) proposed a homeostatic and redundancy theory of tolerance and dependence to opioids that had a striking resemblance to what was to follow as a more general *opponent process* theory by other researchers (see below). Based on studies of acute tolerance and physical dependence produced in dogs by infusing 8 mg/kg of morphine per hour for 7–8 h, and subsequently precipitating abstinence with 20 mg/kg of the mixed agonist/antagonist nalorphine, a regular sequence of changes in physiological parameters such as temperature took place over time. Martin argued that the following sequence of events transpired in the development of *acute tolerance* (Fig. 1.9, left side, not shown). Morphine lowered the homeostat—that is, lowered the thermoregulatory set point (A). The difference between the homeostatic level and the level of the internal environment or existing state (B) gave rise to an error force (C) which in turn drove a physiological system (D) to rectify the error. In the case of a temperature change, this was effected by panting in the dog. As the error force was diminished, the level of function of the physiological system rectifying the error also diminished, and acute tolerance developed.

A similar scheme explained *acute physical dependence* except that initially, nalorphine rapidly reversed the effects of morphine on body temperature (A), restoring the homeostat to a control level. However, a new error force of the opposite valence was established by the nalorphine (C) which recruited heat-generating mechanisms (D) (Fig. 1.9, not shown). These error forces remained until a new equilibrium state was achieved (D).

Similar shifts in the homeostatic level of control were hypothesized for signs of withdrawal and precipitated abstinence in *chronically dependent subjects*. The mechanism involved was the same, except that with chronic physical dependence, chronic morphine elevated the homeostatic level above the pre-addiction level. In other words, at the time when morphine was administered, the animal was already in early abstinence and the homeostatic level was already slightly above the control level (E) (Fig. 1.9, not shown). When morphine was administered, the level to which the homeostat was depressed was smaller than it was in the nondependent state. Martin hypothesized that it proceeded from an elevated baseline and the absolute magnitude of the depression was smaller. As a consequence, the error force was smaller (G) (Fig. 1.9, not shown), and the level of function of the restorative system was lower (H) (Fig. 1.9, not shown). When nalorphine was administered, a very large error force was

generated (G) (Fig. 1.9, not shown) revealing the true level of the hypersensitized homeostat.

Martin (1968) went on to speculate that the changes observed in homeostatic set point could be explained by redundancy theory where two separate neurochemical systems mediate a given function (Martin and Eades, 1960). When applied to tolerance and dependence, it is assumed that morphine interrupts one of the redundant systems (pathway B) but does not disrupt the other (pathway A). Eventually, pathway A will develop hypertrophy and take over the previous function of pathway B. The tolerance that develops is a consequence of the hypertrophy of the redundant pathway A, not a decrement in the effect on pathway B. When the drug is withdrawn, pathway B returns to its normal level of excitability, but the total system functions at a much higher level because of the contribution of the hypertrophied pathway A. One means of integrating the redundancy theory with the original contra-adaptive theory of Himmelsbach (1942) was to argue that there exists a negative feedback mechanism on pathways A and B that is diminished when pathway A is hypertrophied.

The views of Martin (1968) significantly predate *opponent process* theory (Solomon and Corbit, 1974) and within-system (hypertrophy of pathway A) and between-system (decreased negative feedback of pathway A) neuroadaptations (Koob and Bloom, 1988), but certainly contained elements of both. In addition, as we will see later in the book, Martin's concepts of acute tolerance and acute dependence apply not only to temperature regulation but also to analgesia and the hedonic effects of drugs in humans and animals.

Opponent-process theory was developed during the 1970s by Solomon and colleagues (Solomon and Corbit, 1973, 1974; Hoffman and Solomon, 1974; D'amato, 1974). Since then, it has been applied by many authors to various situations such as drugs (opiates, nicotine, alcohol) to adjunctive drinking, fear conditioning, tonic immobility, ulcer formation, eating disorders, jogging, peer separation, glucose preference, and parachuting (Solomon and Corbit, 1973, 1974; Hoffman and Solomon, 1974; Solomon, 1980).

The theory assumes that the brain contains many affect control mechanisms, working as though they were affect immunization systems that counter or oppose all departures from affective neutrality or equilibrium,

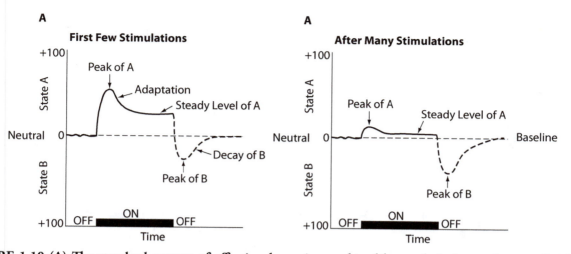

FIGURE 1.10 (A) The standard pattern of affective dynamics produced by a relatively novel unconditioned stimulus. (B) The standard pattern of affective dynamics produced by a familiar, frequently repeated unconditioned stimulus. [Reproduced with permission from Solomon, 1980.]

whether they be aversive or pleasant (Solomon and Corbit, 1974). The theory is a negative feed-forward control construct designed to keep affect in check even though stimulation is strong. The device is composed of three subparts organized in a temporal manner. Two opposing processes control a summator, which determines the controlling affect at a given moment. First, an unconditional arousing stimulus triggers a primary affective process, termed the *a-process*. It is an unconditional reaction that translates the intensity, quality, and duration of the stimulus (for example, a first opiate intake). Second, as a consequence of the *a-process,* and inherently linked to it on a biological basis, the *b-process* is evoked after a short delay, an opponent process. Empirically, the *b-process* feeds a negative signal into the summator, subtracting from the impact on the summator the already existing *a-process.* The two responses are consequently and temporarily linked (*a* triggers *b*) but were hypothesized to depend on different neurobiological mechanisms. The *b-process* has a longer latency, but some data show that it may appear soon after the beginning of the stimulus in the course of the stimulus action (Larcher *et al.,* 1998). The *b-process* also has more inertia, a slower recruitment, and a more sluggish decay. At a given moment, the pattern of affect will be the algebraic sum of these opposite influences and the dynamics reveal, with the passage of time, the net product of the opponent process (Solomon, 1980) (Fig. 1.10).

In this opponent-process theory from a drug addiction perspective, tolerance and dependence are inextricably linked (Solomon and Corbit, 1974). Solomon argued that the first few self-administrations of an opiate drug produce a pattern of motivational changes where the onset of the drug effect produces a euphoria that is the *a-process,* and this is followed by a decline in intensity. Then, after the effects of the drug wear off, the *b-process* emerges as an aversive craving state. The *b-process* gets larger and larger over time, in effect contributing to or producing more complete tolerance to the initial euphoric effects of the drug (Fig. 1.10).

What is important to understand is that the dynamics, with the repetition of the stimulus, is the result of a progressive increase in the *b-process*. In other words, the *b-process* sensitizes through drug use, appears more and more rapidly after the unconditional stimulus onset, lasts longer and longer (the conditional effect), and masks the unconditional effect (*a-process*), resulting in an apparent tolerance (Laulin *et al.,* 1999). Experimental data show that if the development of the *b-process* is blocked, no tolerance appears. The unconditioned effect of the drug does not change with repeated drug administration. The development of the *b-process* equals the development of a negative affective state and withdrawal symptoms, in opposition to the hedonic quality of the unconditioned stimulus. Importantly, the nature of the acquired motivation is specified by the nature of the *b-process*, that is, an aversive affect in the case of drug abuse. The subject

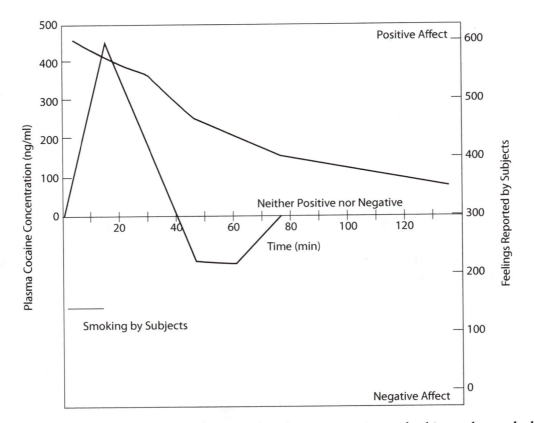

FIGURE 1.11 Dysphoric feelings followed the initial euphoria in experimental subjects who smoked cocaine paste, even though the concentration of cocaine in the plasma of the blood remained relatively high. The dysphoria is characterized by anxiety, depression, fatigue, and a desire for more cocaine. The peak feelings for the subjects were probably reached shortly before the peak plasma concentration, but the first psychological measurements were made later than the plasma assay. Hence, the temporal sequence of the peaks shown cannot be regarded as definitive. [Reproduced with permission from Van Dyke and Byck, 1982.]

will work to reduce, terminate, or prevent the negative affect.

Motivational View of Addiction

Rather than focusing on the *physical* signs of dependence, our conceptual framework has focused on *motivational* aspects of addiction. Emergence of a negative emotional state (e.g., dysphoria, anxiety, irritability) when access to the drug is prevented (defined here as dependence) (Koob and Le Moal, 2001), has been associated with this transition from drug use to addiction. Indeed, some have argued that the development of such a negative affective state can define dependence as it relates to addiction:

'The notion of dependence on a drug, object, role, activity or any other stimulus-source

requires the crucial feature of negative affect experienced in its absence. The degree of dependence can be equated with the amount of this negative affect, which may range from mild discomfort to extreme distress, or it may be equated with the amount of difficulty or effort required to do without the drug, object, etc.' (Russell, 1976).

A key common element that has been identified in animal models is the dysregulation of brain reward function associated with removal from chronic administration of drugs of abuse, and this observation lends credence to the motivational view (see subsequent chapters).

Rapid acute tolerance and opponent process-like effects to the hedonic effects of cocaine have been reported in human studies of smoked coca paste (Van Dyke and

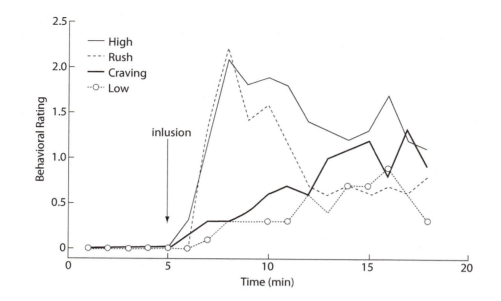

FIGURE 1.12 Average behavioral ratings after an infusion of cocaine (0.6 mg/kg over 30 s; *n* = 9). The rush, high, low, and craving ratings were averaged within each category for the subjects who had interpretable cocaine functional magnetic resonance imaging data after motion correction and behavioral ratings time-locked to the scanner. Both peak rush and peak high occurred 3 min post-infusion. Peak low (primary reports of dysphoria and paranoia) occurred 11 min post-infusion. Peak craving occurred 12 min post-infusion. No subject reported effects from the saline infusion on any of the four measures. Ratings obtained for rush, high, low, and craving measures were higher in subjects blinded to the 0.6 mg/kg cocaine dose compared to subjects unblinded to a 0.2 mg/kg cocaine dose. [Reproduced with permission from Breiter *et al.*, 1997.]

Byck, 1982) (Fig. 1.11). After a single smoking session, the onset and intensity of the 'high' are very rapid via the smoked route of administration, and a rapid tolerance is manifest in that the 'high' decreases rapidly despite significant blood levels of cocaine. Even more intriguing is that human subjects also actually report a subsequent 'dysphoria', again despite significant blood levels of cocaine. Intravenous cocaine produced similar patterns of a rapid 'rush' followed by an increased 'low' in human laboratory studies (Breiter *et al.*, 1997) (Fig. 1.12).

The hypothesis that compulsive use of cocaine is accompanied by a chronic perturbation in brain reward homeostasis has been tested in an animal model of escalation in drug intake with prolonged access. Animals implanted with intravenous catheters and allowed differential access to intravenous self-administration of cocaine show increases in cocaine self-administration from day to day in the long-access group (6 h; LgA) but not in the short-access group (1 h; ShA) (Ahmed and Koob, 1998; Deroche-Gamonet *et al.*, 2004; Mantsch *et al.*, 2004). The differential exposure to cocaine self-administration had dramatic effects on intracranial

self-stimulation (ICSS) reward thresholds. ICSS thresholds progressively elevated for LgA rats, but not for ShA or control rats across successive self-administration sessions (Ahmed *et al.*, 2002) (see *Psychostimulants* chapter). Elevation in baseline ICSS thresholds temporally preceded and was highly correlated with escalation in cocaine intake. Post-session elevations in ICSS reward thresholds failed to return to baseline levels before the onset of each subsequent self-administration session, thereby deviating more and more from control levels. The progressive elevation in reward thresholds was associated with the dramatic escalation in cocaine consumption that was observed previously. After escalation had occurred, an acute cocaine challenge facilitated brain reward responsiveness to the same degree as before but resulted in higher absolute brain reward thresholds in LgA when compared to ShA rats.

With intravenous cocaine self-administration in animal models, such elevations in reward threshold begin rapidly and can be observed within a single session of self-administration (Kenny *et al.*, 2003) (Fig. 1.13), bearing a striking resemblance to human subjective

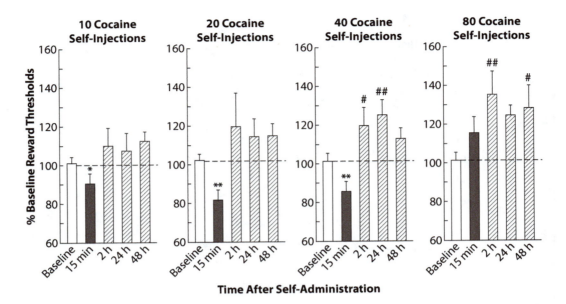

FIGURE 1.13 Rats (*n* = 11) were allowed to self-administer 10, 20, 40, and 80 injections of cocaine (0.25 mg per injection), and ICSS thresholds were measured 15 min and 2, 24, and 48 h after the end of each intravenous cocaine self-administration session. The horizontal dotted line in each plot represents 100% of baseline levels. All data are presented as mean + SEM percentage of baseline ICSS thresholds. *$p < 0.05$, **$p < 0.01$ compared to baseline; paired t-test. #$p < 0.05$, ##$p < 0.01$ compared to baseline; Fisher's LSD test after a statistically significant effect in the repeated-measures analysis of variance. [Reproduced with permission from Kenny *et al.,* 2003.]

reports. These results demonstrate that the elevation in brain reward thresholds following prolonged access to cocaine failed to return to baseline levels between repeated, prolonged exposure to cocaine self-administration (i.e., residual hysteresis), thus creating a greater and greater elevation in 'baseline' ICSS thresholds. These data provide compelling evidence for brain reward dysfunction in escalated cocaine self-administration that provide strong support for a hedonic allostasis model of drug addiction.

Allostasis and Neuroadaptation

More recently opponent process theory has been expanded into the domains of the neurocircuitry and neurobiology of drug addiction from a physiological perspective. An allostatic model of the brain motivational systems has been proposed to explain the persistent changes in motivation that are associated with vulnerability to relapse in addiction, and this model may generalize to other psychopathology associated with dysregulated motivational systems. Allostasis from the addiction perspective has been defined as the process of maintaining

apparent reward function stability through changes in brain reward mechanisms (Koob and Le Moal, 2001). The allostatic state represents a chronic deviation of reward set point that often is *not* overtly observed while the individual is actively taking the drug. Thus, the allostatic view is that not only does the *b-process* get larger with repeated drug taking, but the reward set point from which the *a-process* and *b-process* are anchored gradually shifts downward creating an allostatic state (Koob and Le Moal, 2001) (Fig. 1.14).

The allostatic state is fueled not only by dysregulation of neurochemical elements of reward circuits per se, but also by the activation of brain and hormonal stress responses (see *Neurobiological Theories of Addiction* chapter). From the perspective of a given drug, it is unknown whether the hypothesized reward dysfunction is specific to that drug, common to all addictions, or a combination of both perspectives. However, from the data generated to date, and the established anatomical connections, the manifestation of this allostatic state as compulsive drug-taking and loss of control over drug-taking is hypothesized to be critically based on dysregulation of specific

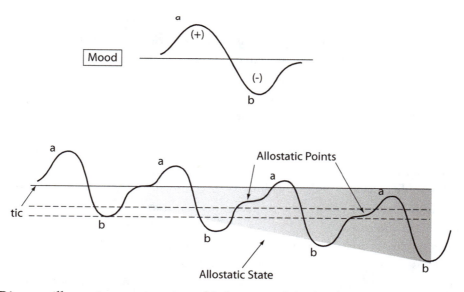

FIGURE 1.14 Diagram illustrating an extension of Solomon and Corbit's (1974) opponent-process model of motivation to outline the conceptual framework of the allostatic hypothesis. Both panels represent the affective response to the presentation of a drug. (Top) This diagram represents the initial experience of a drug with no prior drug history. The *a-process* represents a positive hedonic or positive mood state, and the *b-process* represents the negative hedonic or negative mood state. The affective stimulus (state) has been argued to be a sum of both an *a-process* and a *b-process*. An individual experiencing a positive hedonic mood state from a drug of abuse with sufficient time between re-administering the drug is hypothesized to retain the *a-process*. In other words, an appropriate counteradaptive opponent process (*b-process*) that balances the activational process (*a-process*) does not lead to an allostatic state. (Bottom) The changes in the affective stimulus (state) in an individual with repeated frequent drug use that may represent a transition to an allostatic state in the brain reward systems and, by extrapolation, a transition to addiction. Note that the apparent *b-process* never returns to the original homeostatic level before drug-taking is reinitiated, thus creating a greater and greater allostatic state in the brain reward system. In other words, the counteradaptive opponent process (*b-process*) does not balance the activational process (*a-process*) but in fact shows a residual hysteresis. While these changes are exaggerated and condensed over time in the present conceptualization, the hypothesis here is that even during post-detoxification, a period of protracted abstinence, the reward system is still bearing allostatic changes. In the nondependent state, reward experiences are normal, and the brain stress systems are not greatly engaged. During the transition to the state known as addiction, the brain reward system is in a major underactivated state while the brain stress system is highly activated. The following definitions apply: *allostasis,* the process of achieving stability through change; *allostatic state,* a state of chronic deviation of the regulatory system from its normal (homeostatic) operating level; *allostatic load,* the cost to the brain and body of the deviation, accumulating over time, and reflecting in many cases, pathological states and accumulation of damage. [Reproduced with permission from Koob and Le Moal, 2001.]

neurotransmitter function in the central division of the extended amygdala (a basal forebrain macrostructure comprised of the central nucleus of the amygdala, bed nucleus of the stria terminalis, and a transition area in the region of the shell of the nucleus accumbens) (Koob *et al.,* 1998) (see *Neurobiological Theories of Addiction* chapter). Decreases in the function of γ-aminobutyric acid, dopamine, serotonin, and opioid peptides, as well as dysregulation of brain stress systems such as corticotropin-releasing factor and neuropeptide Y are hypothesized to contribute to a shift in reward set point. Thus, a chronic elevation in reward thresholds as elaborated in Koob and Le Moal (2001) is viewed as a key element in the development of addiction and as setting up other sources of self-regulation failure and persistent vulnerability to relapse (protracted abstinence).

It is hypothesized further that the pathology of this neurocircuitry is the basis for the emotional dysfunction long associated with drug addiction and alcoholism in humans. Some of this neurocircuitry pathology persists into protracted abstinence, thereby providing a strong motivational basis for relapse. The view that drug addiction and alcoholism are the pathology that results from an allostatic mechanism that usurps the circuits established for natural rewards provides a realistic approach to identifying the neurobiological factors that produce vulnerability to addiction and relapse.

The neurobiological view of drug addiction presented in this book represents a neuroadaptational perspective that is shared by most current neurobiological theories. Controversies exist, however, over the importance of the phenomenon of psychomotor sensitization associated with the mesolimbic dopamine system (see *Neurobiological Theories of Addiction* chapter). According to the psychomotor sensitization conceptual framework, the *wanting* and *liking* of drugs are separate phenomena with separate neurobiological substrates, and a shift in an incentive-salience state described as *wanting* was hypothesized to be progressively increased by repeated exposure to drugs of abuse (Robinson and Berridge, 1993). However, the allostatic-neuroadaptational position is that locomotor sensitization may play a role in initial sensitivity to a drug, but that it disappears or becomes irrelevant with the development of motivational dependence. Intertwined with the psychomotor sensitization hypothesis is a prominent or even critical role for dopamine in the motivational effects of drugs of abuse. The allostatic-neuroadaptational position is that dopamine has a role in addiction, particularly for psychomotor stimulants, but is not critical nor sufficient for the development of addiction to many drugs of abuse such as opiates, alcohol, phencyclidine, and others. An extension of the psychomotor sensitization and dopamine theories of addiction is the dismissal of drug withdrawal as a motivating factor in drug addiction. The allostatic-neuroadaptational position is that drug withdrawal is largely misunderstood by the neurobiology of drug addiction research community. The focus should not be on *physical* withdrawal, which for the allostatic-neuroadaptational position is largely a marker for dependence, but rather on *motivational* withdrawal which allostatic-neuroadaptational hypotheses hold as one of the key elements of drug addiction

(see *Drug Addiction: Transition from Neuroadaptation to Pathophysiology* chapter).

SUMMARY

This chapter defines addiction as a chronic relapsing disorder characterized by compulsive drug seeking, a loss of control in limiting intake, and emergence of a negative emotional state when access to the drug is prevented. The definition of addiction is derived from the evolution of the concept of dependence and the nosology of addiction diagnosis, and a distinction is made between drug use, drug abuse, and drug addiction. Addiction affects overall a large percentage of society, including illicit drugs, licit drugs, alcohol, and tobacco, and has with it enormous monetary costs. Addiction is further conceptualized as a condition that evolves, moving from impulsivity to compulsivity, and ultimately being comprised of three major stages: binge/intoxication, withdrawal/negative affect and preoccupation/anticipation. Motivational, psychodynamic, social psychological, and vulnerability factors all contribute to the etiology of addiction, but the focus of the conceptualization for this book is placed on the neuroadaptational changes that occur during the addiction cycle. A theoretical framework is described that derives from early homeostatic theories and subsequent opponent process theories that provides a heuristic framework for understanding the neurobiology of addiction. This framework is followed in each subsequent major drug class, each covered by a separate chapter (*Psychostimulants, Opioids, Alcohol, Nicotine, and Cannabis*) and is tied together in the *Imaging, Neurobiological Theories of Addiction* and *Drug Addiction: Transition from Neuroadaptation to Pathophysiology* chapters.

REFERENCES

Ahmed, S. H., and Koob, G. F. (1998). Transition from moderate to excessive drug intake: Change in hedonic set point. *Science* 282, 298–300.

Ahmed, S. H., Kenny, P. J., Koob, G. F., and Markou, A. (2002). Neurobiological evidence for hedonic allostasis associated with escalating cocaine use. *Nature Neuroscience* 5, 625–626.

American Psychiatric Association (1994). *Diagnostic and Statistical Manual of Menial Disorders,* 4th ed. American Psychiatric Press, Washington DC.

Antelman, S. M., Eichler, A. J., Black, C. A., and Kocan, D. (1980). Interchangeability of stress and amphetamine in sensitization. *Science* 207, 329–331.

Antelman, S. M., DeGiovanni, L. A., Kocan, D., Perel, J. M., and Chiodo, L. A. (1983). Amitriptyline sensitization of a serotonin-mediated behavior depends on the passage of time and not repeated treatment. *Life Sciences* 33, 1727–1730.

Antelman, S. M., Kocan, D., Edwards, D. J., Knopf, S., Perel, J. M., and Stiller, R. (1986). Behavioral effects of a single neuroleptic treatment grow with the passage of time. *Brain Research* 385, 58–67.

Antelman, S. M., Levine, J., and Gershon, S. (2000). Time-dependent sensitization: the odyssey of a scientific heresy from the laboratory to the door of the clinic. *Molecular Psychiatry* 5, 350–356.

Anthony, J. C., Warner, L. A., and Kessler, R. C. (1994). Comparative epidemiology of dependence on tobacco, alcohol, controlled substances, and inhalants: Basic findings from the National Comorbidity Survey. *Experimental and Clinical Psychopharmacology* 2, 244–268.

Aytaclar, S., Tarter, R. E., Kirisci, L., and Lu, S. (1999). Association between hyperactivity and executive cognitive functioning in childhood and substance use in early adolescence. *Journal of the American Academy of Child and Adolescent Psychiatry* 38, 172–178.

Babbini, M., Gaiardi, M., and Bartoletti, M. (1975). Persistence of chronic morphine effects upon activity in rats 8 months after ceasing the treatment. *Neuropharmacology* 14, 611–614.

Bartoletti, M., Gaiardi, M., Gubellini, C., and Babbini, M. (1983a). Further evidence for a motility substitution test as a tool to detect the narcotic character of new drugs in rats. *Neuropharmacology* 22, 177–181.

Bartoletti, M., Gaiardi, M., Gubellini, G., Bacchi, A., and Babbini, M. (1983b). Long-term sensitization to the excitatory effects of morphine: a motility study in post-dependent rats. *Neuropharmacology* 22, 1193–1196.

Baumeister, R. F., Heatherton, T. F., and Tice, D. M. (Eds.), (1994). *Losing Control: How and Why People Fail at Self-Regulation,* Academic Press, San Diego.

Biederman, J., Wilens, T., Mick, E., Faraone, S. V., Weber, W., Curtis, S., Thornell, A., Pfister, K., Jetton, J. G., and Soriano, J. (1997). Is ADHD a risk factor for psychoactive substance use disorders? Findings from a four-year prospective follow-up study. *Journal of the American Academy of Child and Adolescent Psychiatry* 36, 21–29.

Biederman, J., Wilens, T., Mick, E., Spencer, T., and Faraone, S. V. (1999). Pharmacotherapy of attention-deficit/hyperactivity disorder reduces risk for substance use disorder. *Pediatrics* 104, e20.

Breiter, H. C., Gollub, R. L., Weisskoff, R. M., Kennedy, D. N., Makris, N., Berke, J. D., Goodman, J. M., Kantor, H. L., Gastfriend, D. R., Riorden, J. P., Mathew, R. T., Rosen, B. R., and Hyman, S. E. (1997). Acute effects of cocaine on human brain activity and emotion. *Neuron* 19, 591–611.

Breslau, N., Fenn, N., and Peterson, E. L. (1993). Early smoking initiation and nicotine dependence in a cohort of young adults. *Drug and Alcohol Dependence* 33, 129–137.

Carmelli, D., Swan, G. E., Robinette, D., and Fabsitz, R. R. (1990). Heritability of substance use in the NAS-NRC Twin Registry. *Acta Geneticae Medicae et Gemellologiae* 39, 91–98.

Centers for Disease Control and Prevention (2004). *Targeting Tobacco Use: The Nation's Leading Cause of Death,* Centers for Disease Control and Prevention, Atlanta.

Chassin, L., Presson, C. C., Sherman, S. J., and Edwards, D. A. (1990). The natural history of cigarette smoking: predicting young-adult smoking outcomes from adolescent smoking patterns. *Health Psychology* 9, 701–716.

Chung, T., and Martin, C. S. (2001). Classification and course of alcohol problems among adolescents in addictions treatment programs. *Alcoholism: Clinical and Experimental Research* 25, 1734–1742.

Crowley, T. J., Macdonald, M. J., Whitmore, E. A., and Mikulich, S. K. (1998). Cannabis dependence, withdrawal, and reinforcing effects among adolescents with conduct symptoms and substance use disorders. *Drug and Alcohol Dependence* 50, 27–37.

D'Amato, M. R. (1974). Derived motives, *Annual Review of Psychology* 25, 83–106.

Dawes, M. A., Tarter, R. E., and Kirisci, L. (1997). Behavioral self-regulation: correlates and 2 year follow-ups for boys at risk for substance abuse. *Drug and Alcohol Dependence* 45, 165–176.

Deroche-Gamonet, V., Belin, D., and Piazza, P. V. (2004). Evidence for addiction-like behavior in the rat. *Science* 305, 1014–1017.

Dishion, T. J., and McMahon, R. J. (1998). Parental monitoring and the prevention of child and adolescent problem behavior: a conceptual and empirical formulation. *Clinical Child and Family Psychology Review* 1, 61–75.

Eddy, N. B., Halbach, H., Isbell, H., and Seevers, M. H. (1965). Drug dependence: its significance and characteristics. *Bulletin of the World Health Organization* 32, 721–733.

Eichler, A. J., and Antelman, S. M. (1979). Sensitization to amphetamine and stress may involve nucleus accumbens and medial frontal cortex. *Brain Research* 176, 412–416.

Ershler, J., Leventhal, H., Fleming, R., and Glynn, K. (1989). The quitting experience for smokers in sixth through twelfth grades. *Addictive Behaviors* 14, 365–378.

Escobedo, L. G., Marcus, S. E., Holtzman, D., and Giovino, G. A. (1993). Sports participation, age at smoking initiation, and the risk of smoking among US high school students. *Journal of the American Medical Association* 269, 1391–1395.

Everett, S. A., Warren, C. W., Sharp, D., Kann, L., Husten, C. G., and Crossett, L. S. (1999). Initiation of cigarette smoking and subsequent smoking behavior among U.S. high school students. *Preventive Medicine* 29, 327–333.

Finney, J. W., and Moos, R. H. (1992). The long-term course of treated alcoholism: II. Predictors and correlates of 10-year functioning and mortality. *Journal of Studies on Alcohol* 53, 142–153.

Giancola, P. R., Moss, H. B., Martin, C. S., Kirisci, L., and Tarter, R. E. (1996a). Executive cognitive functioning predicts reactive aggression in boys at high risk for substance abuse: a prospective study. *Alcoholism: Clinical and Experimental Research* 20, 740–744.

Giancola, P. R., Zeichner, A., Yarnell, J. E., and Dickson, K. E. (1996b). Relation between executive cognitive functioning and the adverse consequences of alcohol use in social drinkers. *Alcoholism: Clinical and Experimental Research* 20, 1094–1098.

Glantz, M. D., and Hartel, C R. (Eds.), (1999). *Drug Abuse: Origins and Interventions*. American Psychological Association, Washington DC.

Glantz, M. D., and Pickens, R. W. (Eds.), (1992). *Vulnerability to Drug Abuse*. American Psychological Association, Washington DC.

Glantz, M. D., Weinberg, N. Z., Miner, L. L., and Colliver, J. D. (1999). The etiology of drug abuse: mapping the paths. In *Drug Abuse: Origins and Interventions* (M. D. Glantz, and C R. Hartel, Eds.), American Psychological Association, Washington DC, pp. 3–45.

Goedde, H. W., Agarwal, D. P., and Harada, S. (1983a). The role of alcohol dehydrogenase and aldehyde dehydrogenase isozymes in alcohol metabolism, alcohol sensitivity and alcoholism. In *Cellular Localization, Metabolism, and Physiology* (series title: *Isozymes: Current Topics in Biological and Medical Research*, vol. 8 (M. C Rattazzi, J. G. Scandalios, and G. S. Whitt, Eds.), pp. 175–193. Alan R. Liss, New York.

Goedde, H. W., Agarwal, D. P., Harada, S., Meier-Tackmann, D., Ruofu, D., Bienzle, U., Kroeger, A., and Hussein, L. (1983b). Population genetic studies on aldehyde dehydrogenase isozyme deficiency and alcohol sensitivity. *American Journal of Human Genetics* 35, 769–772.

Grant, B. F., and Dawson, D. A. (1998). Age of onset of drug use and its association with DSM-IV drug abuse and dependence: results from the National Longitudinal Alcohol Epidemiologic Survey. *Journal of Substance Abuse* 10, 163–173.

Grant, B. F., Hasin, D. S., Chou, S. P., Stinson, F. S., and Dawson, D. A. (2004a). Nicotine dependence and psychiatric disorders in the United States: results from the national epidemiologic survey on alcohol and related conditions. *Archives of General Psychiatry* 61, 1107–1115.

Grant, B. F., Stinson, F. S., Dawson, D. A., Chou, S. P., Dufour, M. C., Compton, W., Pickering, R. P., and Kaplan, K. (2004b). Prevalence and co-occurrence of substance use disorders and independent mood and anxiety disorders: results from the National Epidemiologic Survey on Alcohol and Related Conditions. *Archives of General Psychiatry* 61, 807–816.

Grant, B. F., Stinson, F. S., Dawson, D. A., Chou, S. P., Ruan, W. J., and Pickering, R. P. (2004c). Co-occurrence of 12-month alcohol and drug use disorders and personality disorders in the United States: results from the National Epidemiologic Survey on Alcohol and Related Conditions. *Archives of General Psychiatry* 61, 361–368.

Grant, B., Dawson, D., Stinson, F., Chou, P., Dufour, M., and Pickering, R. (2005). The 12-month prevalence and trends in DSM-IV alcohol abuse and dependence: United States, 1991–1992 and 2001–2002. *Drug and Alcohol Dependence*, in press.

Higuchi, S., Matsushita, S., Murayama, M., Takagi, S., and Hayashida, M. (1995). Alcohol and aldehyde dehydrogenase polymorphisms and the risk for alcoholism. *American Journal of Psychiatry* 152, 1219–1221.

Himmelsbach, C. K. (1942). Clinical studies of drug addiction: Physical dependence, withdrawal and recovery. *Archives of Internal Medicine* 69, 766–772.

Himmelsbach, C. K. (1943). Can the euphoric, analgetic, and physical dependence effects of drugs be separated? IV With reference to physical dependence. *Federation Proceedings* 2, 201–203.

Hingson, R., Heeren, T., Zakocs, R., Winter, M., and Wechsler, H. (2003). Age of first intoxication, heavy drinking, driving after drinking and risk of unintentional injury among U.S. college students. *Journal of Studies on Alcohol* 64, 23–31.

Hoffman, H. S., and Solomon, R. L. (1974). An opponent-process theory of motivation: III. Some affective dynamics in imprinting. *Learning and Motivation* 5,149–164.

Hubbard, R. L., Craddock, G., Flynn, P. M., Anderson, J., and Etheridge, R. M. (1997). Overview of 1-year follow-up outcomes in the Drug Abuse Treatment Outcome Study (DATOS). *Psychology of Addictive Behaviors* 11, 261–278.

Kandel, D. B., and Jessor, R. (2002). The gateway hypothesis revisited. In *Stages and Pathways of Drug Involvement: Examining the Gateway Hypothesis*, D. B. Kandel (Ed.), pp. 365–372. Cambridge University Press, New York.

Karkowski, L. M., Prescott, C. A., and Kendler, K. S. (2000). Multivariate assessment of factors influencing illicit substance use in twins from female–female pairs. *American Journal of Medical Genetics* 96, 665–670.

Kendler, K. S., and Prescott, C. A. (1998a). Cannabis use, abuse, and dependence in a population-based sample of female twins. *American Journal of Psychiatry* 155, 1016–1022.

Kendler, K. S., and Prescott, C. A. (1998b). Cocaine use, abuse and dependence in a population-based sample of female twins. *British Journal of Psychiatry* 173, 345–350.

Kendler, K. S., Neale, M. C., Sullivan, P., Corey, L. A., Gardner, C. O., and Prescott, C. A. (1999). A population-based twin study in women of smoking initiation and nicotine dependence. *Psychological Medicine* 29, 299–308.

Kenny, P. J., Polis, I., Koob, G. F., and Markou, A. (2003). Low dose cocaine self-administration transiently increases but high dose cocaine persistently decreases brain reward function in rats. *European Journal of Neuroscience* 17, 191–195.

Khantzian, E. J. (1985). The self-medication hypothesis of affective disorders: focus on heroin and cocaine dependence. *American Journal of Psychiatry* 142, 1259–1264.

Khantzian, E. J. (1990). Self-regulation and self-medication factors in alcoholism and the addictions: similarities and differences. In *Combined Alcohol and Other Drug Dependence* (series title: *Recent Developments in Alcoholism*, vol. 8), (M. Galanter Ed.), pp. 255–271. Plenum Press, New York.

Khantzian, E. J. (1995). The 1994 distinguished lecturer in substance abuse. *Journal of Substance Abuse Treatment* 12, 157–165.

Khantzian, E. J. (1997). The self-medication hypothesis of substance use disorders: a reconsideration and recent applications. *Harvard Review of Psychiatry* 4, 231–244.

Khantzian, E. J., and Wilson, A. (1993). Substance abuse, repetition, and the nature of addictive suffering. In *Hierarchical Concepts in Psychoanalysis: Theory, Research, and Clinical Practice* (A. Wilson, and J. E. Gedo, Eds.), pp. 263–283. Guilford Press, New York.

Kohut, H. (1971). *The Analysis of the Self* (series title: *The Psychoanalytic Study of the Child*, vol. 4), International Universities Press, New York.

Kolta, M. G., Shreve, P., De Souza, V., and Uretsky, N. J. (1985). Time course of the development of the enhanced behavioral and biochemical responses to amphetamine after pretreatment with amphetamine. *Neuropharmacology* 24, 823–829.

Koob, G. F. (2003). The neurobiology of self-regulation failure in addiction: an allostatic view [commentary on Khantzian, 'Understanding addictive vulnerability: An evolving psychodynamic perspective'], *Neuro-Psychoanalysis* 5, 35–39.

Koob, G. F. (2004). Allostatic view of motivation: implications for psychopathology. In *Motivational Factors in the Etiology of Drug Abuse* (series title: *Nebraska Symposium on Motivation*, vol. 50), (R. Bevins, and M.T. Bardo Eds.), pp. 1–18. University of Nebraska Press, Lincoln NE.

Koob, G. F., and Bloom, F. E. (1988). Cellular and molecular mechanisms of drug dependence. *Science* 242, 715–723.

Koob, G. F., and Le Moal, M. (1997). Drug abuse: Hedonic homeostatic dysregulation. *Science* 278, 52–58.

Koob, G. F., and Le Moal, M. (2001). Drug addiction, dysregulation of reward, and allostasis. *Neuropsychopharmacology* 24, 97–129.

Koob, G. F., Sanna, P. P., and Bloom, F. E. (1998). Neuroscience of addiction. *Neuron* 21, 467–476.

Kopp, P., and Fenoglio, P. (2000). *Le cout Social des Drogues Licites (Alcool et Tabac) et Illicites en France*, etude 22, Observatoire Francais des Drogues et des Toxicomanies, Paris.

Larcher, A., Laulin, J. P., Celerier, E., Le Moal, M., and Simonnet, G. (1998). Acute tolerance associated with a single opiate administration: Involvement of N-methyl-D-aspartate-dependent pain facilitatory systems. *Neuroscience* 84, 583–589.

Laulin, J. P., Celerier, E., Larcher, A., Le Moal, M., and Simonnet, G. (1999). Opiate tolerance to daily heroin administration: An apparent phenomenon associated with enhanced pain sensitivity. *Neuroscience* 89, 631–636.

Liu, I. C., Blacker, D. L., Xu, R., Fitzmaurice, G., Lyons, M. J., and Tsuang, M. T. (2004). Genetic and environmental contributions to the development of alcohol dependence in male twins. *Archives of General Psychiatry* 61, 897–903.

Mantsch, J. R., Yuferov, V., Mathieu-Kia, A. M., Ho, A., and Kreek, M. J. (2004). Effects of extended access to high versus low cocaine doses on self-administration, cocaine-induced reinstatement and brain mRNA levels in rats. *Psychopharmacology* 175, 26–36.

Martin, W. R. (1968). A homeostatic and redundancy theory of tolerance to and dependence on narcotic analgesics. In *The Addictive States* (series title: *Its Research Publications*, vol. 46), A. Wilder pp. 206–225. Williams and Wilkins, Baltimore.

Martin, W R., and Eades, C. G. (1960). A comparative study of the effect of drugs on activating and vasomotor responses evoked by midbrain stimulation: atropine, pentobarbital, chlorpromazine and chlorpromazine sulfoxide. *Psychopharmacologia* 1, 303–335.

McGue, M., Pickens, R. W., and Svikis, D. S. (1992). Sex and age effects on the inheritance of alcohol problems: a twin study. *Journal of Abnormal Psychology* 101, 3–17.

McLellan, A. T., and McKay, J. (1998). The treatment of addiction: what can research offer practice? In *Bridging the Gap Between Practice and Research: Forging Partnerships with Community-Based Drug and Alcohol Treatment*, S. Lamb, M. R. Greenlick, D. McCarty (Eds.), pp. 147–185. National Academy Press, Washington DC.

McLellan, A. T., Lewis, D. C., O'Brien, C. P., and Kleber, H. D. (2000). Drug dependence, a chronic medical illness: implications for treatment, insurance, and outcomes evaluation. *Journal of the American Medical Association* 284, 1689–1695.

Merikangas, K. R., Mehta, R. L., Molnar, B. E., Walters, E. E., Swendsen, J. D., Aguilar-Gaziola, S., Bijl, R., Borges, G., Caraveo-Anduaga, J. J., DeWit, D. J., Kolody, B., Vega, W. A., Wittchen, H. U., and Kessler, R. C. (1998). Comorbidity of substance use disorders with mood and anxiety disorders: results of the International Consortium in Psychiatric Epidemiology. *Addictive Behaviors* 23, 893–907.

Meyer, R. E. (1996). The disease called addiction: emerging evidence in a 200-year debate, *Lancet* 347, 162–166.

Mizoi, Y., Tatsuno, Y., Adachi, J., Kogame, M., Fukunaga, T., Fujiwara, S., Hishida, S., and Ijiri, I. (1983). Alcohol sensitivity related to polymorphism of alcohol-metabolizing enzymes in Japanese. *Pharmacology Biochemistry and Behavior* 18(Suppl. 1), 127–133.

Nelson, J. E., Pearson, H. W., Sayers, M., and Glynn, T. J. (Eds.), (1982). *Guide to Drug Abuse Research Terminology*, National Institute on Drug Abuse, Rockville MD.

O'Brien, C. P., and McLellan, A. T. (1996). Myths about the treatment of addiction. *Lancet* 347, 237–240.

Office of National Drug Control Policy, *The Economic Costs of Drug Abuse in the United States: 1992–1998*, Office of National Drug Control Policy, Washington DC, 2001.

Poulos, C. X., and Cappell, H. (1991). Homeostatic theory of drug tolerance: A general model of physiological adaptation. *Psychological Reviews* 98, 390–408.

Prescott, C. A., and Kendler, K. S. (1999). Genetic and environmental contributions to alcohol abuse and dependence in a population-based sample of male twins. *American Journal of Psychiatry* 156, 34–40.

Robinson, T. E., and Berridge, K. C. (1993). The neural basis of drug craving: An incentive-sensitization theory of addiction. *Brain Research Reviews* 18, 247–291.

Robinson, T. E., and Berridge, K. C. (2003). Addiction. *Annual Review of Psychology* 54, 25–53.

Russell, M. A. H. (1976). What is dependence? In *Drugs and Drug Dependence* (G. Edwards, Ed.), pp. 182–187. Lexington Books, Lexington, MA.

Sellers, E. M., Tyndale, R. F., and Fernandes, L. C. (2003). Decreasing smoking behaviour and risk through CYP2A6 inhibition. *Drug Discovery Today* 8, 487–493.

Siegel, S. (1975). Evidence from rats that morphine tolerance is a learned response. *Journal of Comparative and Physiological Psychology* 89, 498–506.

Sifneos, P. E. (2000). Alexithymia, clinical issues, politics and crime. *Psychotherapy and Psychosomatics* 69, 113–116.

Solomon, R. L. (1980). The opponent-process theory of acquired motivation: the costs of pleasure and the benefits of pain. *American Psychologist* 35, 691–712.

Solomon, R. L., and Corbit, J. D. (1973). An opponent-process theory of motivation. II. Cigarette addiction. *Journal of Abnormal Psychology* 81, 158–171.

Solomon, R. L., and Corbit, J. D. (1974). An opponent-process theory of motivation: 1. Temporal dynamics of affect. *Psychological Reviews* 81, 119–145.

Substance Abuse and Mental Health Services Administration (2003). *Results from the 2002 National Survey on Drug Use and Health: National Findings* (Office of Applied Studies, NHSDA Series H-22, DHHS Publication No. SMA 03–3836), Rockville MD.

Taioli, E., and Wynder, E. L. (1991). Effect of the age at which smoking begins on frequency of smoking in adulthood. *New England Journal of Medicine* 325, 968–969.

Tarter, R. E., Blackson, T., Brigham, J., Moss, H., and Caprara, G. V. (1995). The association between childhood irritability and liability to substance use in early adolescence: a 2-year follow-up study of boys at risk for substance abuse. *Drug and Alcohol Dependence* 39, 253–261.

Tsuang, M. T., Lyons, M. J., Eisen, S. A., Goldberg, J., True, W., Lin, N., Meyer, J. M., Toomey, R., Faraone, S. V., and Eaves, L. (1996). Genetic influences on DSM-III-R drug abuse and dependence: a study of 3,372 twin pairs. *American Journal of Medical Genetics* 67, 473–477.

Tyndale, R. F., and Sellers, E. M. (2002). Genetic variation in CYP2A6-mediated nicotine metabolism alters smoking behavior. *Therapeutic Drug Monitoring* 24, 163–171.

Uhl, G. R., and Grow, R. W. (2004). The burden of complex genetics in brain disorders. *Archives of General Psychiatry* 61, 223–229.

Van Dyke, C., and Byck, R. (1982). Cocaine, *Scientific American* 246, 128–141.

Vanderschuren, L. J., and Kalivas, P. W. (2000). Alterations in dopaminergic and glutamatergic transmission in the induction and expression of behavioral sensitization: a critical review of preclinical studies. *Psychopharmacology* 151, 99–120.

Wills, T. A., Vaccaro, D., and McNamara, G. (1994). Novelty seeking, risk taking, and related constructs as predictors of adolescent substance use: an application of Cloninger's theory. *Journal of Substance Abuse* 6, 1–20.

Windle, M., and Windle, R. C. (1993). The continuity of behavioral expression among disinhibited and inhibited childhood subtypes. *Clinical Psychology Review* 13, 741–761.

Winkleby, M. A., Fortmanm, S. P., and Rockhill, B. (1993). Cigarette smoking trends in adolescents and young adults: the Stanford Five-City Project. *Preventive Medicine* 22, 325–334.

World Health Organization (1992). *International Statistical Classification of Diseases and Related Health Problems,* 10th revision, World Health Organization, Geneva.

Yi, H., Williams, G. D., and Dufour, M. C. (2000). *Trends in Alcohol-Related Fatal Traffic Crashes,* United National Institute on Alcohol Abuse and Alcoholism, *10th Special Report to the U.S. Congress on Alcohol and Health: Highlights from Current Research,* National Institute on Alcohol Abuse and Alcoholism, Bethesda MD.

Neurobiology of Alcohol Dependence

Focus on Motivational Mechanisms

By Nicholas W. Gilpin and George F. Koob

Alcoholism is a debilitating disorder for the individual and very costly for society. A major goal of alcohol research is to understand the neural underpinnings associated with the transition from alcohol use to alcohol dependence. Positive reinforcement is important in the early stages of alcohol use and abuse. Negative reinforcement can be important early in alcohol use by people self-medicating coexisting affective disorders, but its role likely increases following the transition to dependence. Chronic exposure to alcohol induces changes in neural circuits that control motivational processes, including arousal, reward, and stress. These changes affect systems utilizing the signaling molecules dopamine, opioid peptides, γ-aminobutyric acid, glutamate, and serotonin, as well as systems modulating the brain's stress response. These neuroadaptations produce changes in sensitivity to alcohol's effects following repeated exposure (i.e., sensitization and tolerance) and a withdrawal state following discontinuation of alcohol use. Chronic alcohol exposure also results in persistent neural deficits, some of which may fully recover following extended periods of abstinence. However, the organism remains susceptible to relapse, even after long periods of abstinence. Recent research focusing on brain arousal, reward, and stress systems is accelerating our understanding of the components of alcohol dependence and contributing to the development of new treatment strategies.

Key words: Alcoholism; alcohol dependence; chronic alcohol and other drug effect (AODE); neurology; brain; animal models; animal studies; neurodegeneration; neuroadaptation; positive reinforcement; negative reinforcement; neural circuits; neurotransmitter; dopamine; opioids; γ-aminobutyric acid (GABA); glutamate; serotonin

Alcoholism, also called dependence on alcohol, is a chronic relapsing disorder that is progressive and has serious detrimental health outcomes. The development of alcoholism is characterized by frequent episodes of intoxication, preoccupation with alcohol, use of alcohol despite adverse consequences, compulsion to seek and consume alcohol, loss of control in limiting alcohol intake, and emergence of a negative emotional state in the absence of the drug (American Psychiatric Association 1994). According to the National Institute on Alcohol Abuse and Alcoholism (NIAAA), more than 17 million people in the United States either abuse or are dependent on alcohol (NIAAA 2007a), with a cost to U.S. society of over $180 billion annually (NIAAA 2004a).

Nicholas W. Gilpin, Ph.D., is a research associate, and GEORGE F. KOOB, Ph.D., is a professor in the Committee on the Neurobiology of Addictive Disorders, The Scripps Research Institute, La Jolla, California.

Nicholas W. Gilpin and George F. Koob, "Neurobiology of Alcohol Dependence," from *Alcohol Research and Health*, vol. 31, pp. 185–195. Copyright © 2008 by U.S. National Institute on Alcohol Abuse and Alcoholism. Permission to reprint granted by the publisher.

A major goal of basic research on alcoholism is to understand the neural underpinnings of alcohol use and the pathological progression to alcohol dependence (NIAAA 2007*b*). Preclinical research uses a wide array of techniques to assess the molecular, cellular, and behavioral events associated with the transition to alcohol dependence. These techniques are used in conjunction with animal models that mimic various components of alcohol dependence in humans. Chronic exposure to high doses of alcohol produces counteradaptive neural changes that affect the motivational properties of alcohol and drive subsequent alcohol-seeking behavior.

This article summarizes some basic neurobiological mechanisms associated with the motivational aspects of alcohol dependence. It briefly discusses the roles of brain reward and stress systems in alcohol dependence. Additionally, the article reviews the late stages of alcohol dependence, specifically the neurodegeneration associated with long-term alcohol exposure and the potential for relapse and recovery during long-term abstinence.

Reinforcement and the Transition From Alcohol Use to Dependence

Reinforcement is a process in which a response or behavior is strengthened based on previous experiences. Positive reinforcement describes a situation in which a presumably rewarding stimulus or experience (e.g., alcohol-induced euphoria) increases the probability that the individual exhibits a certain response (e.g., alcohol-seeking behavior). Negative reinforcement occurs when the probability of an instrumental response (e.g., alcohol-seeking behavior) increases if this response allows the individual to circumvent (i.e., avoidance response) or alleviate (i.e., escape response) an aversive stimulus. In alcohol dependence, the aversive stimulus often is composed of motivational/affective symptoms (e.g., anxiety, dysphoria, irritability, and emotional pain) that manifest in the absence of alcohol (i.e., during withdrawal) and which result from prior discontinuation of alcohol consumption. Thus, people may drink to prevent or alleviate the anxiety they experience during alcohol withdrawal. In conditioned positive and negative reinforcement, stimuli that become associated with either alcohol or withdrawal can motivate subsequent alcohol-seeking behavior.

Alcohol-drinking behavior is driven by both positive and negative reinforcement, although their relative contributions change during the transition from alcohol use to abuse to dependence.

One approach for the study of reinforcement in animal models of alcoholism is a procedure called operant conditioning. With this approach, animals are trained to perform a response (e.g., press a lever or nose-poke a hole) that results in delivery of a stimulus (e.g., a small amount of alcohol) that animals are motivated to obtain. Operant conditioning procedures can be fine-tuned to include different work requirements for stimuli with varying degrees of motivational value for the individual tested. This procedure models how humans exhibit varying degrees of willingness to work for alcohol and other drugs under many different conditions.

Positive Reinforcement

The positive reinforcing effects of alcohol generally are accepted as important motivating factors in alcohol-drinking behavior in the early stages of alcohol use and abuse. These effects most often are examined using animal models of self-administration. With different operant conditioning procedures, researchers can determine the time course, pattern, and frequency of responding for alcohol. For example, investigators can use progressive-ratio schedules of reinforcement, in which the number of responses (e.g., lever presses) required for subsequent delivery of the reinforcer (e.g., alcohol) gradually increases throughout a session. This procedure allows researchers to determine the maximum number of responses (i.e., the breakpoint) that animals are willing to perform to obtain a single reinforcer. Operant procedures most often are used to examine oral self-administration of alcohol, but they also can be used to assess self-administration of alcohol via other routes. For example, rats will respond for alcohol infusions directly into the stomach (Fidler et al. 2006), blood stream (Grupp 1981), or brain (Gatto et al. 1994).

An alternative to operant procedures, free-choice responding allows researchers to examine alcohol consumption and preference in rats in their home-cage environment. In this procedure, alcohol is available to the animals via normal drinking bottles in the home cage. Free-choice procedures incorporate a variety of experimental manipulations, such as offering multiple bottles with different alcohol concentrations, varying the schedules of when and for how long alcohol is available, and adding flavorants to available solutions. These manipulations provide valuable additional information about the preference for alcohol.

Another method for assessing the reinforcing properties of alcohol is intracranial self-stimulation (ICSS). In this procedure, rats are implanted with electrodes in discrete brain regions and then are allowed to self-administer mild electrical shocks to those regions via standard operant procedures. Rats readily self-administer shocks to brain regions that are important in mediating the rewarding properties of alcohol. The strength of the electrical stimulation needed for the animal to maintain responding reflects the reward value of the ICSS. Thus, if only mild electrical stimulation of a certain brain region is required to maintain responding, ICSS is said to have a high reward value; if, by contrast, a stronger electrical stimulation of a given brain region is required, then ICSS is said to have a lower reward value. Alcohol increases the reward value of ICSS because in the presence of alcohol, weaker electrical stimulation is required to maintain responding (e.g., Lewis and June 1990).

Finally, the reinforcing properties of alcohol can be assessed using a procedure called place conditioning. In this procedure, contextual cues repeatedly are associated with the presence or absence of alcohol availability—for example, rodents repeatedly are placed in a specific environment where they receive alcohol and in another environment where they receive no alcohol. Subsequently, the rodents are allowed to freely explore these environments. If the animal spends more time exploring the alcohol-paired environment, then this behavior is hypothesized to reflect the conditioned positive reinforcing effects of alcohol. Interestingly, this procedure is used primarily with mice because they exhibit a preference for alcohol-paired environments, whereas rats typically exhibit an aversion to environments that previously were paired with alcohol (Cunningham et al. 1993).

Some recently developed animal models mimic binge drinking in humans. This pattern of self-administration, defined in humans as an excessive pattern of alcohol drinking that produces blood alcohol levels greater than 0.08 percent within a 2-hour period, may be associated with dependence (NIAAA 2004b). Models of binge drinking have been developed for both adult (Ji et al. 2008) and adolescent (Truxell et al. 2007) rats and intend to mimic drinking behavior motivated primarily by the positive reinforcing effects of alcohol early in the transition to dependence. For example, sweeteners often are added to the alcohol solution in these models, a procedure that is thought to reflect the situation in humans because people tend to begin drinking alcohol in sweetened beverages (Gilbert 1978; Samson et al. 1996). Other approaches successfully have used genetic selection to produce animals that readily self-administer alcohol in a binge-like pattern (e.g., Grahame et al. 1999; Lumeng et al. 1977). For this approach, high- and low-alcohol–drinking rodents are selectively bred over generations to produce lines that are either highly prone or highly resistant to voluntary alcohol consumption. The resultant phenotypes* may provide models of specific subtypes of alcoholism.

Negative Reinforcement

As mentioned above, the early stages of alcohol use and abuse mainly are associated with alcohol's positive reinforcing effects. However, alcohols negative reinforcing effects may contribute to alcohol-drinking behavior at this stage in people who suffer from coexisting psychiatric disorders and use alcohol to self-medicate these disorders. Comorbidity of alcohol problems (i.e., abuse or dependence) with anxiety and depressive/bipolar disorders is high (44 percent and 50 percent, respectively) (Kushner et al. 1990; Weissman et al. 1980). Thus, these people may use alcohol to alleviate the symptoms of the coexisting disorders. Generally, however, the negative reinforcing effects of alcohol become a critical component of the motivation to drink alcohol during the transition to dependence, when withdrawal symptoms occur following discontinuation of alcohol use and the individual drinks to avoid those withdrawal symptoms.

In animal models, the negative reinforcing properties of alcohol often are studied during periods of imposed abstinence after chronic exposure to high doses of alcohol. Such studies have identified an alcohol deprivation

---

* For a definition of this and other technical terms, see the Glossary, pp. 279–283.

effect—that is, a transient increase in alcohol-drinking behavior following long-term alcohol access and a period of imposed abstinence (Sinclair and Senter 1967). Similarly, chronic inhalation of alcohol vapor can reliably produce large elevations in alcohol self-administration (Roberts et al. 1996, 2000a), an effect that is amplified when animals repeatedly are withdrawn from the alcohol vapor (O'Dell et al. 2004) and which lasts well into protracted abstinence (Gilpin et al. 2008b). Moreover, researchers can use nutritionally complete, alcohol-containing liquid diets to induce alcohol dependence (Frye et al. 1981). Again, symptoms of dependence are augmented when animals repeatedly are withdrawn from the alcohol diet (Overstreet et al. 2002). In general, studies using these approaches have demonstrated that the pattern of alcohol exposure (i.e., the frequency of withdrawals) appears to be as important as the cumulative alcohol dose in revealing alcohol's negative reinforcing properties.

In addition to these approaches, the negative reinforcing effects of alcohol can be examined using all the models described above (see the section entitled "Positive Reinforcement"), except that testing occurs during imposed withdrawal/abstinence from alcohol. For example, alcohol withdrawal decreases the reward value of ICSS because the threshold of electrical stimulation required to maintain responding is increased (Schulteis et al. 1995).

Neuroadaptation

Changes in the reinforcing value of alcohol during the transition from alcohol use and abuse to dependence reflect (counter) adaptive neural changes resulting from chronic exposure to high alcohol doses. As stated above, during the early stages of nondependent alcohol use, drinking behavior largely is motivated by alcohol's positive reinforcing effects, whereas in the dependent state it likely is driven by both the positive and negative reinforcing effects of the drug. Multiple processes contribute to the increased motivation to seek drugs during the development of dependence. Sensitization refers to an increase in the reinforcement value of drugs following repeated exposures. Tolerance refers to a decrease in the reinforcing efficacy of drugs following repeated exposures. Once neuroadaptation has occurred, removal of alcohol from the organism leads to a withdrawal syndrome.

Sensitization. The incentive sensitization theory of addiction posits that addictive drugs activate a common neural system responsible for attributing incentive salience to events and stimuli associated with the activation of that system (Robinson and Berridge 1993). As a result, the "liking" of alcohol's effects becomes closely associated with "wanting" the alcohol-associated incentive stimuli. Following repeated drug exposure, this wanting becomes stronger and transforms into pathological craving for the drug. The incentive sensitization theory of addiction most often is used to describe dependence on addictive drugs other than alcohol. However, alcohol stimulates locomotor activity in mice, an effect thought to correspond to alcohol-induced euphoria in humans, and mice become sensitized to this effect following repeated alcohol exposure (Phillips and Shen 1996), suggesting a role for sensitization in the development of alcohol dependence. This seems to be a species-specific effect, however, because alcohol-induced stimulation of locomotor activity rarely is observed in rats, and little evidence suggests that sensitization to this effect occurs in these animals.

Tolerance. An organism that is chronically exposed to alcohol develops tolerance to its functional (e.g., motor-impairing) effects (LeBlanc et al. 1975), metabolic effects (Wood and Laverty 1979), and reinforcing properties (Walker and Koob 2007). Once tolerance to the pleasurable (i.e., hedonic) effects of alcohol develops, the individual requires gradually higher doses of alcohol to produce the same effect previously experienced at lower doses. In animal experiments, this process is reflected by the fact that the animal will work harder to obtain alcohol on a progressive-ratio schedule. In a cyclical pattern, these gradually increasing alcohol doses produce even more tolerance to the hedonic effects of alcohol. Moreover, the clearance of alcohol from the body of an individual with high tolerance can produce a withdrawal syndrome defined by symptoms that are largely the opposite of the effects of alcohol itself.

Withdrawal. Following chronic alcohol exposure, the removal of alcohol reliably produces a constellation of withdrawal symptoms, some of which increase the motivation to seek and ingest alcohol (i.e., have motivational significance). Although alcohol withdrawal symptoms vary in severity according to the history of the individual, they are qualitatively similar across species.

The physiological aspects of withdrawal in humans and rodents usually last up to 48 hours following termination of alcohol exposure and include convulsions, motor abnormalities, and autonomic disturbances (e.g., sweating, higher heart rate, and restlessness) (Isbell et al. 1955; Majchrowicz 1975). Additionally, withdrawal is associated with a negative-affective state characterized by anxiety, dysphoria, and irritability that typically develops during early stages of withdrawal but can be very long lasting. Perhaps the most reliable of these disturbances across species is an increase in anxiety (Hershon 1977; Valdez et al. 2002). The allostasis theory of alcoholism posits that the negative-affective state produced by this withdrawal state is a major driving force in the propensity for relapse to alcohol-seeking behavior (Koob 2003).

Brain Circuits Mediating Alcohol Reinforcement

A neural circuit can be conceptualized as a series of nerve cells (i.e., neurons) that are interconnected and relay information related to a specific function. Within such a circuit, information is passed between neurons via electrochemical signaling processes. Activated neurons release chemical signaling molecules (i.e., neurotransmitters) that bind to specific proteins (i.e., receptors) on other neurons. Depending on the neurotransmitter involved, this binding leads to the electrical excitation or inhibition of subsequent neurons in the circuit. (For more information on nerve signal transmission, neurotransmitters, and their receptors, see the article by Lovinger, pp. 196–214.) Alcohol interacts with several neurotransmitter systems in the brain's reward and stress circuits. These interactions produce alcohol's acute reinforcing effects. Following chronic exposure, these interactions result in changes in neuronal function that underlie the development of sensitization, tolerance, withdrawal, and dependence. Research using pharmacological, cellular, molecular, imaging, genetic, and proteomic techniques already has elucidated details of some of these alcohol effects, and some of these findings will be discussed in other articles in this and the companion issue of *Alcohol Research & Health*. As a foundation for this discussion, the following sections briefly introduce some of the neural circuits relevant to alcohol

dependence, categorized by neurotransmitter systems; however, this discussion is by no means exhaustive. Figure 1 illustrates the changing role of positive and negative reinforcement circuits during the transition from the nondependent to the dependent state. The table summarizes the effects of interventions with these signaling systems on various aspects of positive and negative reinforcement.

Reward Circuits and Neurotransmitter Systems

Dopamine Systems. Dopamine is a neurotransmitter primarily involved in a circuit called the mesolimbic system, which projects from the brain's ventral tegmental area to the nucleus accumbens. This circuit influences how organisms orient toward incentive changes in the environment—that is, it affects incentive motivation.[†] Studies suggest that dopamine also has a role in the incentive motivation associated with acute alcohol intoxication. For example, alcohol consumption can be blocked by injecting low doses of a compound that interferes with dopamine's normal activity (i.e., a dopamine antagonist) directly into the nucleus accumbens (Hodge et al. 1997; Rassnick et al. 1992). Furthermore, alcohol ingestion and even the anticipation that alcohol will be available produce dopamine release in the nucleus accumbens as determined by increased dopamine levels in the fluid outside neurons (Weiss et al. 1993). However, lesions of the mesolimbic dopamine system do not completely abolish alcohol-reinforced behavior, indicating that dopamine is an important, but not essential, component of alcohol reinforcement (Rassnick et al. 1993). Finally, alcohol withdrawal produces decreases in dopamine function in dependent individuals, and this decreased dopamine function may contribute to withdrawal symptoms and alcohol relapse (Melis et al. 2005; Volkow et al. 2007).

Opioid Systems. Endogenous opioids are small molecules naturally produced in the body that resemble morphine and have long been implicated in the actions of opiate drugs and alcohol. There are three classes of endogenous opioids: endorphins, enkephalins, and

---

† More recently, incentive motivation also has been termed "incentive sensitization" or "incentive salience."

dynorphins. They all exert their effects by interacting with three subtypes of opioid receptors—μ, δ, and κ. Researchers have hypothesized that positive alcohol reinforcement is mediated at least in part by the release of endogenous opioids in the brain. This hypothesis is supported by numerous studies demonstrating that opioid antagonists acting either at all opioid receptor subtypes or only at specific subtypes suppress alcohol drinking in a variety of species and models (for a review, see Ulm et al. 1995). Moreover, complete inactivation (i.e., knockout) of the μ-opioid receptor blocks alcohol self-administration in mice (Roberts et al. 2000b). The agent naltrexone, a subtype-nonspecific opioid receptor antagonist, currently is approved as a treatment for alcoholism in humans and is particularly effective in reducing heavy drinking.

Opioid systems influence alcohol drinking behavior both via interaction with the mesolimbic dopamine system and also independent of the mesolimbic dopamine system, as demonstrated by alcohol-induced increases in extracellular endorphin content in the nucleus accumbens (see figure 2) (Olive et al. 2001). Opioid receptor antagonists interfere with alcohol's rewarding effects by acting on sites in the ventral tegmental area, nucleus accumbens, and central nucleus of the amygdala (Koob 2003).

γ-Aminobutyric Acid Systems.

γ-Aminobutyric acid (GABA) is the major inhibitory neurotransmitter in the brain. It acts via two receptor subtypes called $GABA_A$ and $GABA_B$. Alcohol can increase GABA activity in the brain through two general mechanisms:

- It can act on the GABA-releasing (i.e., presynaptic) neuron, resulting in increased GABA release; or
- It can act on the signal-receiving (i.e., postsynaptic) neuron, facilitating the activity of the $GABA_A$ receptor.

Alcohol drinking is suppressed by compounds that interfere with the actions of the $GABA_A$ receptor (i.e., $GABA_A$ receptor antagonists) as well as compounds that stimulate the $GABA_B$ receptor (i.e., $GABA_B$ agonists) in the nucleus accumbens, ventral pallidum, bed nucleus of

the stria terminalis, and amygdala (for a review, see Koob 2004). Of these, the central nucleus of the amygdala—a brain region important in the regulation of emotional states—is particularly sensitive to suppression of alcohol drinking by compounds that act on the GABA systems (i.e., GABAergic compounds) (Hyytia and Koob 1995). Indeed, acute and chronic alcohol exposure produce increases in GABA transmission in this brain region (Roberto et al. 2003, 2004a). Additionally, compounds that target a specific component of the $GABA_A$ receptor complex (i.e., the α_1-subunit)[‡] suppress alcohol drinking when they are injected into the ventral pallidum, an important region that receives signals from neurons located in the extended amygdala (Harvey et al. 2002; June et al. 2003).

Chronic alcohol exposure also leads to alterations in the GABA systems. For example, in some brain regions, alcohol affects the expression of genes that encode components of the $GABA_A$ receptor. This has been demonstrated by changes in the subunit composition of the receptor in those regions, the most consistent of which are decreases in α_1- and increases in α_4-subunits (for a summary, see Biggio et al. 2007).

The function of $GABA_A$ receptors also is regulated by molecules known as neuroactive steroids (Lambert et al. 2001) that are produced both in the brain and in other organs (i.e., in the periphery). Alcohol increases the brain levels of many neuroactive steroids (Van Doren et al. 2000). This increased activity of neuroactive steroids in the brain following alcohol exposure is not dependent on their production by peripheral organs (Sanna et al. 2004). Together, these findings suggest that neuroactive steroids are potential key modulators of altered GABA function during the development of alcohol dependence, perhaps by acting directly at $GABA_A$ receptors (Sanna et al. 2004).

Glutamate Systems.

Glutamate is the major excitatory neurotransmitter in the brain; it exerts its effects via several receptor subtypes, including one called the N-methyl-D-aspartate (NMDA) receptor. Glutamate systems have long been implicated in the acute reinforcing

---

‡ $GABA_A$ receptors consist of several proteins (subunits). There are several types of $GABA_A$ subunits, and the subunit composition of the receptors differs among different brain regions and may change in response to environmental changes.

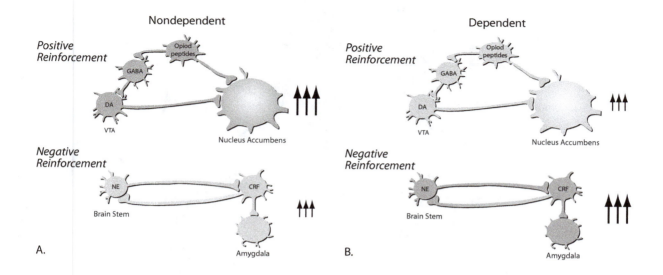

Figure 1 Changes in the activity of the reward circuit mediating the acute positive reinforcing effects of alcohol and the stress circuit mediating negative reinforcement of dependence during the transition from nondependent alcohol drinking to dependent drinking. Key elements of the reward circuit are dopamine (DA) and opioid peptide neurons that act at both the ventral tegmental area (VTA) and the nucleus accumbens and which are activated during initial alcohol use and early stages of the progression to dependence (i.e., the binge/intoxication stage). Key elements of the stress circuit are corticotropin-releasing factor (CRF) and norepinephrine (NE)-releasing neurons that converge on γ-aminobutyric acid (GABA) interneurons in the central nucleus of the amygdala and which are activated during the development of dependence.

SOURCE: Modified with permission from Nestler 2005.

Table Summary of Neurobiological Mechanisms of Alcohol During the Phases of the Addiction Cycle Dominated by Positive Reinforcement Versus Negative Reinforcement

"Light Side" of Addictioin: Positive Reinforcement

	Baseline alcohol self-administration	"Binge"-like alcohol self-administration	Progressive ratio/second-order reinforcement schedules	Alcohol priming-induced reinstatement	Alcohol-conditioned cue-induced reinstatement
Dopamine antagonist	↓	↓			↓
Opioid antagonist	↓	↓	↓	↓	↓

"Dark Side" of Addiction: Negative Reinforcement

	Baseline alcohol self-administration or place preference	Withdrawal-induced anxiety-like or aversive responses	Dependence-induced increases in self-administration	Stress-induced reinstatement
Corticatropin-releasing factor antagonist	——	↓	↓	↓
Neuropeptidu Y	——	↓	↓	

NOTE:- no effect, blank entries indicate not tested.

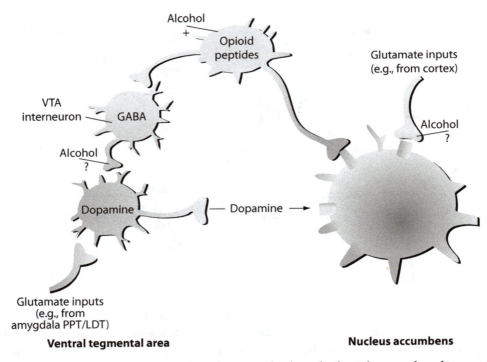

Figure 2 Alcohol's effects on neurotransmitter systems involved in the brain's reward pathways. Alcohol, by promoting γ-aminobutyric acid (GABA) subtype GABA$_A$ receptor function, may inhibit GABAergic transmission in the ventral tegmental area (VTA), thereby disinhibiting (i.e., activating) VTA dopamine. As a result, these neurons release dopamine in the nucleus accumbens, activating reward processes there. Similarly, alcohol may inhibit release of the excitatory neurotransmitter glutamate from nerve terminals that act on neurons in the nucleus accumbens. Many additional mechanisms (not shown) are proposed, through which alcohol may act on these pathways. Some evidence suggests that alcohol may activate endogenous opioid pathways and possibly endogenous cannabinoid pathways (not shown).

NOTE: PPT/LDT, peduncular pontine tegmentum/lateral dorsal tegmentum.

SOURCE: Modified with permission from Nestler 2005.

actions of alcohol, and alcohol effects perceived by an organism can be mimicked with NMDA receptor antagonists (Colombo and Grant 1992). In contrast to its effects on GABA, alcohol inhibits glutamate activity in the brain. For example, acute alcohol exposure reduces extracellular glutamate levels in a brain region called the striatum, which contains the nucleus accumbens, among other structures (Carboni et al. 1993). Acute alcohol administration also suppresses glutamate-mediated signal transmission in the central nucleus of the amygdala, an effect that is enhanced following chronic alcohol exposure (Roberto et al. 2004b). Alcohol affects glutamate transmission most likely by altering the functions of both NMDA receptors (Lovinger et al. 1989) and another receptor subtype known as metabotropic glutamate subtype 5 receptors (mGluR5) (Blednov and Harris 2008). The involvement of NMDA receptors in

alcoholism is especially interesting because they also play a role in neuroplasticity, a process characterized by neural reorganization that likely contributes to hyperexcitability and craving during alcohol withdrawal[§] (Pulvirenti and Diana 2001).

Compounds targeting the glutamate systems also are being used in the treatment of alcohol dependence. For example, the agent acamprosate modulates glutamate transmission by acting on NMDA and/or metabotropic glutamate receptors (for a review, see Littleton 2007).

---

§ Because alcohol normally reduces glutamate activity, the brain adapts to chronic alcohol exposure and maintains a "normal" state by increasing glutamate activity. When alcohol is withdrawn, heightened functionality of glutamate receptors makes neurons excessively sensitive to excitatory glutamate signals, resulting in hyperexcitability.

Thus, by dampening excessive glutamate activity, acamprosate blocks excessive alcohol consumption. This process appears to depend on the involvement of genes such as *Per2,* which typically is involved in maintaining the normal daily rhythm (i.e., the circadian clock) of an organism (Spanagel et al. 2005). Acamprosate's ability to suppress alcohol drinking has been observed across species, and the drug has been approved for the treatment of alcoholism in humans, primarily for its perceived ability to reduce alcohol craving and negative affect in abstinent alcoholics (Littleton 2007).

Serotonin Systems. The neurotransmitter serotonin (also known as 5-hydroxytryptamine or 5-HT) has long been a target of interest for potential pharmacotherapies for alcoholism because of the well-established link between serotonin depletion, impulsivity, and alcohol-drinking behavior in rats and humans (Myers and Veale 1968; Virkkunen and Linnoila 1990). Pharmacological compounds that target the serotonin system by inhibiting neuronal reuptake of serotonin,[§] thereby prolonging its actions, or by blocking specific serotonin receptor subtypes have been shown to suppress alcohol-reinforced behavior in rats (for a review, see Johnson 2008). However, some researchers are debating whether these compounds can affect alcohol-reinforced behavior without affecting consummatory behavior in general. During alcohol withdrawal, serotonin release in the nucleus accumbens of rats is suppressed, and this reduction is partially reversed by self-administration of alcohol during withdrawal (Weiss et al. 1996).

Stress Circuits and Neurotransmitter Systems

Corticotropin-Releasing Factor and Neuropeptide-Y Systems. Recent research has led to the hypothesis that the transition to alcohol dependence involves the dysregulation not only of neural circuits involved in reward but also of circuits that mediate behavioral responses to stressors. Alcohol-induced perturbation of the brains stress and antistress systems contributes to the negative emotional state characteristic of alcohol withdrawal. One stress system involves the signaling molecule corticotropin-releasing factor (CRF). CRF produced in and released from the hypothalamus activates the body's major stress system, called the hypothalamic–pituitary–adrenal (HPA) axis. However, activation of extrahypothalamic CRF systems also produces high anxiety-like states in animals. Several observations indicate that extrahypothalamic CRF contributes to the development of alcohol dependence. For example, alcohol-dependent rats exhibit increased extracellular CRF content in the central nucleus of the amygdala (Merlo-Pich et al. 1995). Moreover, CRF antagonists injected directly into this brain structure suppress both the anxiety-like behavior (Rassnick et al. 1993) and the increase in alcohol drinking (Funk et al. 2006) that are associated with alcohol dependence.

Another molecule involved in regulating the body's stress response is called neuropeptide-Y (NPY). It has a neural and behavioral profile that in almost every aspect is opposite to that of CRF. For example, NPY has powerful anxiety-reducing effects in animals. Moreover, alcohol-dependent rats exhibit decreased NPY content in the central nucleus of the amygdala during withdrawal (Roy and Pandey 2002), whereas, as stated above, CRF levels in this brain region are increased in alcohol-dependent animals. Furthermore, stimulation of NPY activity in this brain structure suppresses anxiety-like behavior (Thorsell et al. 2007) and dependence-induced increases in alcohol drinking (Gilpin et al. 2008*a*). The anatomical distributions of CRF and NPY are highly overlapping, suggesting that one might serve as a "buffer" for the effects of the other.

Emerging Stress-Related Targets.

Numerous other stress-related systems exist that may be important in the development of alcohol dependence, including those involving norepinephrine, orexin (hypocretin), vasopressin, dynorphin, nociceptin (orphanin FQ), neuropeptide-S, and neurokinin; an extensive overview of these systems can be found elsewhere (Koob 2008). Notable among these, recent work (George et

---

[§] One mechanism by which electrochemical signal transmission between neurons is terminated is by reuptake of the neurotransmitter into the signal-transmitting cell. When excess neurotransmitter remains in the synapse, receptors on the presynaptic terminal are activated to prevent the release of more neurotransmitter into the synapse. Some drugs target these presynaptic receptors by blocking this "termination" signal.

al. 2008) has identified neurokinin-1 and its receptors as potential targets for the pharmacological treatment of alcoholism. That study found that complete (but not partial) genetic knockout of neurokinin-1 receptors suppressed alcohol drinking in mice. Based on these results, pharmacological and neuroimaging approaches were used to demonstrate that antagonism of neurokinin-1 receptors reduces craving and neuroendocrine responses** to alcohol-related cues and negative-affective images in human alcoholics (George et al. 2008). This study provides an excellent example of the translational potential of basic research.

Late Stages of Alcohol Dependence

Neurodegeneration

Chronic exposure to high doses of alcohol can result in profound changes in the morphology, proliferation, and survival of neurons. For example, new neurons normally are constantly generated from neural stem cells throughout the life of an organism. In alcohol binge-drinking rats, however, both the proliferation of neural stem cells and the survival of neurons produced from the stem cells during alcohol exposure are decreased (Nixon and Crews 2002). Imaging studies also have revealed substantial reductions in the volumes of many brain structures in human alcoholics, particularly the prefrontal cortex and cerebellum, although prolonged periods of abstinence appear to promote at least partial recovery of these structural deficits (for a review, see Sullivan and Pfefferbaum 2005). The prefrontal cortex and, particularly, the orbitofrontal cortex†† have central roles in executive functions, such as decisionmaking. Accordingly, deficits in these brain areas may impact motivational circuits, impairing the ability of the organism to inhibit impulsive behavior

---

** A neuroendocrine response is the release of hormones into the bloodstream in response to a neural stimulus.

†† The prefrontal cortex is the outer layer of the brain at the front of the head, it can be divided into several regions, one of which is the orbitofrontal cortex. The prefrontal cortex is involved in high-level cognitive and executive functions, such as planning complex cognitive behaviors, decisionmaking, and moderating correct social behavior.

and thereby further contributing to pathological drug-seeking behavior Jentsch and Taylor 1999). More recently, imaging techniques were used to show that alcohol-dependent humans have smaller amygdala volumes than nondependent individuals and that smaller amygdala volume in alcohol-dependent humans is predictive of subsequent alcohol relapse (Wrase et al. 2008). This is an area of burgeoning research exploring the development, maintenance, and relapse to alcoholism in both preclinical and clinical studies.

Protracted Abstinence and Relapse

Abstinent human alcoholics typically relapse to alcohol drinking after acute withdrawal symptoms have subsided. The resilience of relapse behavior and, presumably, the alcohol craving that underlies it is highlighted by the observation that rodents given long-term free-choice alcohol access exhibit an alcohol deprivation effect after prolonged periods (up to 9 months) of imposed abstinence (Wolffgramm and Heyne 1995). Unfortunately, such longitudinal studies are not practical for high-throughput research. Accordingly, researchers more recently have started to condense the time scale required for such analysis by using specific procedures to induce dependence more rapidly (e.g., by exposing the animals to alcohol vapor). Chronic alcohol vapor inhalation results in enhanced alcohol-reinforced behavior that lasts well beyond the dissipation of acute withdrawal symptoms (Gilpin et al. 2008b; Roberts et al. 2000a; Sommer et al. 2008). Similarly, this approach leads to increased anxiety-like behavior in rodents that persists many weeks into abstinence (Zhao et al. 2007) and can be reinstated with exposure to a mild stressor (Valdez et al. 2002). One hypothesis is that this negative emotional state contributes to relapse behavior.

Another approach for examining relapse behavior uses reinstatement models. In these models, animals first are trained to respond (e.g., press a lever) for alcohol in an operant situation. That behavior then is extinguished—that is, the animal no longer receives alcohol for pressing a lever until the animal no longer attempts to press the lever at all. Researchers can then examine the propensity of animals to relapse to alcohol-seeking behavior under three conditions that mimic the human situation: (1)

following administration of a small "priming" dose of alcohol, (2) following exposure to environmental cues previously associated with alcohol, and (3) following exposure to stressors. Each of these three reinstatement models can be inhibited by different compounds (i.e., compounds that have different pharmacological profiles), indicating that they are mediated by different neural-circuits. For example, one elegant experiment showed that stressors and alcohol-paired cues, both individually and additively, reinstated previously extinguished responding on an alcohol-paired lever; however, the pharmacological basis of each situation was unique. Thus, the opioid antagonist naltrexone, but not a CRF receptor antagonist, blocked cue-induced reinstatement. Conversely, a CRF receptor antagonist, but not naltrexone, blocked stress-induced reinstatement. Finally, naltrexone and CRF receptor antagonists partially blocked the additive effect of stress and alcohol cues when administered individually but completely blocked the additive effect when administered together (Liu and Weiss 2002). These findings suggest that whereas stress-induced relapse may involve the CRF system, alcohol cue-induced relapse may be mediated by the endogenous opioid system. These observations may have important implications for the development of pharmacological therapies to prevent relapse in human alcoholics.

Conclusions

Alcohol dependence is a debilitating disease that worsens over time. New technologies are being combined with traditional approaches to identify and track the critical neural circuits in the transition from alcohol use and abuse to dependence. Substance dependence on alcohol, or alcoholism, is defined by neuroplasticity that is responsible for phenomena such as sensitization, tolerance, and withdrawal as well as for neuron survival, all of which contribute to the development and maintenance of the disorder. In addition to the extant literature on the importance of brain reward circuits in the development of alcohol dependence, recent research has focused on a new contingent of neural systems that play central roles in the regulation of stress and anxiety as well as mediate executive functions. This joint focus on brain arousal, reward, and stress systems, along with the integration of new technologies in the field, is accelerating our understanding of the components of alcohol dependence and contributing to the development of new treatment strategies.

Acknowledgments

This is manuscript number 19510 from The Scripps Research Institute. The authors thank Mike Arends for his excellent editorial assistance. This work was supported by the Pearson Center for Alcoholism and Addiction Research and NIAAA grants AA08459 and F32–AA016436.

References

American Psychiatric Association. *Diagnostic and Statistical Manual of Mental Disorders, 4th Ed.* Washington, DC: American Psychiatric Press, 1994.

Biggio, G.; Concas, A.; Follesa, P.; et al. Stress, ethanol, and neuroactive steroids. *Pharmacology and Therapeutics* 116(1):140–171, 2007. PMID: 17555824

Blednov, Y. A., and Harris, A. R. Metabotropic glutamate receptor 5 (mGluR5) regulation of ethanol sedation, dependence and consumption: Relationship to acamprosate actions. *International Journal of Neuropsychopharmacology* 11(6):775–793, 2008. PMID: 18377703

Carboni, S.; Isola, R.; Gessa, G.L.; and Rossetti, Z.L. Ethanol prevents the glutamate release induced by *N*-methyl-D-aspartate in the rat striatum. *Neuroscience Letters* 152(1–2): 133–136, 1993. PMID: 8100051

Colombo, G., and Grant, K.A. NMDA receptor complex antagonists have ethanol-like discriminative stimulus effects. *Annals of the New York Academy of Sciences* 654:421–423, 1992. PMID: 1385933

Cunningham, C.L.; Niehus, J.S.; and Noble, D. Species difference in sensitivity to ethanol's hedonic effects. *Alcohol* 10(2):97–102, 1993. PMID: 8442898

Fidler, T.L.; Clews, T.W.; and Cunningham, C.L. Reestablishing an intragastric ethanol self-infusion model in rats. *Alcoholism: Clinical and Experimental Research* 30(3):414–428, 2006. PMID: 16499482

Frye, G.D.; Chapin, R.E.; Vogel, R.A.; et al. Effects of acute and chronic 1,3-butanediol treatment on central nervous system function: A comparison with ethanol. *Journal of Pharmacology and Experimental Therapeutics* 216(2):306–314, 1981. PMID: 7193248

Funk, C.K.; O'Dell, L.E.; Crawford, E.F.; and Koob, G.F. Corticotropin-releasing factor within the central nucleus of the amygdala mediates enhanced ethanol self-administration in withdrawn, ethanol-dependent rats. *Journal of Neuroscience* 26(44):11324–11332, 2006. PMID: 17079660

Gatto, G.J.; McBride, W.J.; Murphy, J.M.; et al. Ethanol self-infusion into the ventral tegmental area by alcohol-preferring rats. *Alcohol* 11:557–564, 1994. PMID: 7865158

George, D.T.; Gilman, J.; Hersh, J.; et al. Neurokinin 1 receptor antagonism as a possible therapy for alcoholism. *Science* 319(5869):1536–1539, 2008. PMID: 18276852

Gilbert, R.M. Schedule-induced self-administration of drugs. In: Blackman, D.E., and Sanger, D.J., Eds. *Contemporary Research in Behavioral Pharmacology.* New York: Plenum, 1978, pp. 289–323.

Gilpin, N.W.; Richardson, H.N.; Lumeng, L.; and Koob, G.F. Dependence-induced alcohol drinking by alcohol-preferring (P) rats and outbred Wistar rats. *Alcoholism: Clinical and Experimental Research,* 32(9):1688–1696, 2008*a.* PMID: 18482158

Gilpin, N.W.; Misra, K.; and Koob, G.F. Neuropeptide Y in the central nucleus of the amygdala suppresses dependence-induced increases in alcohol drinking. *Pharmacology, Biochemistry, and Behavior* 90(3):475–480, 2008*b.* PMID: 18501411

Grahame, N.J.; Li, T.K.; and Lumeng, L. Selective breeding for high and low alcohol preference in mice. *Behavior Genetics* 29(1):47–57, 1999. PMID: 10371758

Grupp, L.A. An investigation of intravenous ethanol self-administration in rats using a fixed ratio schedule of reinforcement. *Physiological Psychology* 9:359–363, 1981.

Harvey, S.C.; Foster, K.L.; McKay, P.F.; et al. The GABA$_A$ receptor α_1 subtype in the ventral pallidum regulates alcohol-seeking behaviors. *Journal of Neuroscience* 22(9):3765–3775, 2002. PMID: 11978852

Hershon, H.I. Alcohol withdrawal symptoms and drinking behavior. *Journal of Studies on Alcohol* 38(5):953–971, 1977. PMID: 881849

Hodge, C.W.; Samson, H.H.; and Chappelle, A.M. Alcohol self-administration: Further examination of the role of dopamine receptors in the nucleus accumbens. *Alcoholism:*

Clinical and Experimental Research 21(6):1083–1091, 1997. PMID: 9309321

Hyytia, P., and Koob, G.F. GABA$_A$ receptor antagonism in the extended amygdala decreases ethanol self-administration in rats. *European Journal of Pharmacology* 283:151–159, 1995. PMID: 7498304

Isbell, H.; Fraser, H.F.; Winkler, A; et al. An experimental study of the etiology of rum fits and delirium tremens. *Quarterly Journal of Studies on Alcohol* 16(1):1–33, 1955. PMID: 14372008

Jentsch, J.D., and Taylor, J.R. Impulsivity resulting from frontostriatal dysfunction in drug abuse: Implications for the control of behavior by reward-related stimuli. *Psychopharmacology* 146(4):373–390, 1999. PMID: 10550488

Ji, D.; Gilpin, N.W.; Richardson, H.N.; et al. Effects of naltrexone, duloxetine, and a corticotropin-releasing factor type 1 receptor antagonist on binge-like alcohol drinking in rats. *Behavioural Pharmacology* 19(1):1–12, 2008. PMID: 18195589

Johnson, B.A. Update on neuropharmacological treatments for alcoholism: Scientific basis and clinical findings. *Biochemical Pharmacology* 75(1):34–56, 2008. PMID: 17880925

June, H.L.; Foster, K.L.; McKay, P.F.; et al. The reinforcing properties of alcohol are mediated by GABA$_A$1 receptors in the ventral pallidum. *Neuropsychopharmacology* 28(12):2124–2137, 2003. PMID: 12968126

Koob, G.F. Alcoholism: Allostasis and beyond. *Alcoholism: Clinical and Experimental Research* 27(2):232–243, 2003. PMID: 12605072

Koob, G.F. A role for GABA mechanisms in the motivational effects of alcohol. *Biochemical Pharmacology* 68(8):1515–1525, 2004. PMID: 15451394

Koob, G.F. A role for brain stress systems in addiction. *Neuron* 59(1):11–34, 2008. PMID: 18614026

Kushner, M.G.; Sher, K.J.; and Beitman, B.D. The relation between alcohol problems and the anxiety disorders. *American Journal of Psychiatry* 147(6):685–695, 1990. PMID: 2188513

Lambert, J.J.; Belelli, D.; Harney, S.C.; et al. Modulation of native and recombinant GABA$_A$ receptors by endogenous and synthetic neuroactive steroids. *Brain Research. Brain Research Reviews* 37:68–80, 2001. PMID: 11744075

Leblanc, A.E.; Gibbins, R.J.; and Kalant, H. Generalization of behaviorally augmented tolerance to ethanol, and its relation to physical dependence. *Psychopharmacologia* 44(3):241–246, 1975. PMID: 1239781

Lewis, M.J., and June, H.L. Neurobehavioral studies of ethanol reward and activation. *Alcohol* 7(3):213–219, 1990. PMID: 2184834

Littleton, J.M. Acamprosate in alcohol dependence: Implications of a unique mechanism of action. *Journal of Addiction Medicine* 1:115–125, 2007.

Liu, X., and Weiss, F. Additive effect of stress and drug cues on reinstatement of ethanol seeking: Exacerbation by history of dependence and role of concurrent activation of corticotropin-releasing factor and opioid mechanisms. *Journal of Neuroscience* 22(18):7856–7861, 2002. PMID: 12223538

Lovinger, D.M.; White, G.; and Weight, F.F. Ethanol inhibits NMDA-activated ion current in hippocampal neurons. *Science* 243(4899):1721–1724, 1989. PMID: 2467382

Lumeng, L; Hawkins, D.T.; and Li, T.K. New strains of rats with alcohol preference and nonpreference. In: Thurman, R.G., Ed. *Alcohol and Aldehyde Metabolizing Systems, Vol. 3.* New York: Academic Press, pp. 537–544, 1977.

Majchrowicz, E. Induction of physical dependence upon ethanol and the associated behavioral changes in rats. *Psychopharmacologia* 43(3):245–254, 1975. PMID: 1237914

Melis, M.; Spiga, S.; and Diana, M. The dopamine hypothesis of drug addiction: Hypodopaminergic state. *International Review of Neurobiology* 63:101–154, 2005. PMID: 15797467

Merlo-Pich, E.; Lorang, M.; Yeganeh, M.; et al. Increase of extracellular corticotropin-releasing factor-like immunoreactivity levels in the amygdala of awake rats during restraint stress and ethanol withdrawal as measured by microdialysis. *Journal of Neuroscience* 15(8):5439–5447, 1995. PMID: 7643193

Myers, R.D., and Veale, W.L. Alcohol preference in the rat: Reduction following depletion of brain serotonin. *Science* 160(835):1469–1471, 1968. PMID: 5690148

National Institute on Alcohol Abuse and Alcoholism. http://www.niaaa.nih.gov/Resources/DatabaseResources/QuickFacts/EconomicData/cost8.htm, 2004*a*

National Institute on Alcohol Abuse and Alcoholism. NIAAA Council approves definition of binge drinking. *NIAAA Newsletter* Winter (no. 3):3, 2004*b*.

National Institute on Alcohol Abuse and Alcoholism. http://www.niaaa.nih.gov/FAQs/General-English/default.htm#groups, 2007*a*.

National Institute on Alcohol Abuse and Alcoholism. *Five Year Strategic Plan FY08–13: Alcohol Across the Lifespan.* Bethesda MD: National Institute on Alcohol Abuse and Alcoholism, 2007*b*.

Nestler, E.J. Is there a common molecular pathway for addiction? *Nature Neuroscience* 8(11):1445–1449, 2005. PMID: 16251986

Nixon, K., and Crews, F.T. Binge ethanol exposure decreases neurogenesis in adult rat hippocampus. *Journal of Neurochemistry* 83(5):1087–1093, 2002. PMID: 12437579

O'Dell, L.E.; Roberts, A.J.; Smith, R.T.; and Koob, G.F. Enhanced alcohol self-administration after intermittent versus continuous alcohol vapor exposure. *Alcoholism: Clinical and Experimental Research* 28(11):1676–1682, 2004. PMID: 15547454

Olive, M.F.; Koenig, H.N.; Nannini, M.A.; and Hodge, C.W. Stimulation of endorphin neurotransmission in the nucleus accumbens by ethanol, cocaine, and amphetamine. *Journal of Neuroscience* 21(23):RC184, 2001. PMID: 11717387

Overstreet, D.H.; Knapp, D.J.; and Breese, G.R. Accentuated decrease in social interaction in rats subjected to repeated ethanol withdrawals. *Alcoholism: Clinical and Experimental Research* 26(8):1259–1268, 2002. PMID: 12198403

Phillips, T.J., and Shen, E.H. Neurochemical bases of locomotion and ethanol stimulant effects. *International Review of Neurobiology* 39:243–282, 1996. PMID: 8894850

Pulvirenti, L., and Diana, M. Drug dependence as a disorder of neural plasticity: Focus on dopamine and glutamate. *Reviews in the Neurosciences* 12(2):141–158, 2001. PMID: 11392455

Rassnick, S.; Pulvirenti, L.; and Koob, G.F. Oral ethanol self-administration in rats is reduced by the administration of dopamine and glutamate receptor antagonists into the nucleus accumbens. *Psychopharmacology* 109:92–98, 1992. PMID: 1365677

Rassnick, S.; Stinus, L.; and Koob, G.F. The effects of 6-hydroxydopamine lesions of the nucleus accumbens and the mesolimbic dopamine system on oral self-administration of ethanol in the rat. *Brain Research* 623(1):16–24, 1993. PMID: 8221085

Roberto, M.; Madamba, S.G.; Moore, S.D.; et al. Ethanol increases GABAergic transmission at both pre- and post-synaptic sites in rat central amygdala neurons. *Proceedings of the National Academy of Sciences of the United States of America* 100(4):2053–2058, 2003. PMID: 12566570

Roberto, M.; Madamba, S.G.; Stouffer, D.G.; et al. Increased GABA release in the central amygdala of ethanol-dependent rats. *Journal of Neuroscience* 24(45):10159–10166, 2004a. PMID: 15537886

Roberto, M.; Schweitzer, P.; Madamba, S.G.; et al. Acute and chronic ethanol alter glutamatergic transmission in rat central amygdala: An *in vitro* and *in vivo* analysis. *Journal of Neuroscience* 24(7):1594–1603, 2004b. PMID: 14973247

Roberts, A.J.; Cole, M.; and Koob, G.F. Intra-amygdala muscimol decreases operant ethanol self-administration in dependent rats. *Alcoholism: Clinical and Experimental Research* 20(7):1289–1298, 1996. PMID: 8904984

Roberts, A.J.; Heyser, C.J.; Cole, M.; et al. Excessive ethanol drinking following a history of dependence: Animal model of allostasis. *Neuropsychopharmacology* 22(6):581–594, 2000a. PMID: 10788758

Roberts, A.J.; McDonald, J.S.; Heyser, C.J.; et al. μ-Opioid receptor knockout mice do not self-administer alcohol. *Journal of Pharmacology and Experimental Therapeutics* 293(3):1002–1008, 2000b. PMID: 10869404

Robinson, T.E., and Berridge, K.C. The neural basis of drug craving: An incentive-sensitization theory of addiction. *Brain Research. Brain Research Reviews* 18(3):247–291, 1993. PMID: 8401595

Roy, A., and Pandey, S.C. The decreased cellular expression of neuropeptide Y protein in rat brain structures during ethanol withdrawal after chronic ethanol exposure. *Alcoholism: Clinical and Experimental Research* 26(6):796–803, 2002. PMID: 12068247

Samson, H.; Files, F.; and Brice, G. Patterns of ethanol consumption in a continuous access situation: The effect of adding sweetener to the ethanol solution. *Alcoholism: Clinical and Experimental Research* 20(1):101–109, 1996. PMID: 8651439

Sanna, E.; Talani, G.; Busonero, F.; et al. Brain steroidogenesis mediates ethanol modulation of GABA$_A$ receptor activity in rat hippocampus. *Journal of Neuroscience* 24(29):6521–6530, 2004. PMID: 15269263

Schulteis, G.; Markou, A.; Cole, M.; and Koob, G.F. Decreased brain reward produced by ethanol withdrawal. *Proceedings of the National Academy of Sciences of the United States of America* 92(13):5880–5884, 1995. PMID: 7597046

Sinclair, J.D., and Senter, R.J. Increased preference for ethanol in rats following alcohol deprivation. *Psychonomic Science* 8:11–12, 1967.

Sommer, W.H.; Rimondini, R.; Hansson, A.C.; et al. Upregulation of voluntary alcohol intake, behavioral sensitivity to stress, and amygdala *Crhr1* expression following a history of dependence. *Biological Psychiatry* 63(2):139–145, 2008. PMID: 17585886

Spanagel, R.; Pendyala, G.; Abarca, C.; et al. The clock gene Per2 influences the glutamatergic system and modulates alcohol consumption. *Nature Medicine* 11(1):35–42, 2005. PMID: 15608650

Sullivan, E.V., and Pfefferbaum, A. Neurocircuitry in alcoholism: A substrate of disruption and repair. *Psychopharmacology* 180(4):583–594, 2005. PMID: 15834536

Thorsell, A.; Repunte-Canonigo, V.; O'Dell, L.E.; et al. Viral vector-induced amygdala NPY overexpression reverses increased alcohol intake caused by repeated deprivations in Wistar rats. *Brain* 130:1330–1337, 2007. PMID: 17405766

Truxell, E.M.; Molina, J.C.; and Spear, N.E. Ethanol intake in the juvenile, adolescent, and adult rat: Effects of age and prior exposure to ethanol. *Alcoholism: Clinical and Experimental Research* 31(5):755–765, 2007. PMID: 17386073

Ulm, R.R.; Volpicelli, J.R.; and Volpicelli, L.A. Opiates and alcohol self-administration in animals. *Journal of Clinical Psychiatry* 56 (Suppl. 7):5–14, 1995. PMID: 7673105

Valdez, G.R.; Roberts, A.J.; Chan, K.; et al. Increased ethanol self-administration and anxiety-like behavior during acute withdrawal and protracted abstinence: Regulation by corticotropin-releasing factor. *Alcoholism: Clinical and Experimental Research* 26(10):1494–1501, 2002. PMID: 12394282

Van Doren, M.J.; Matthews, D.B.; Jams, G.C.; et al. Neuroactive steroid 3α-hydroxy-5α-pregnan-20-one modulates electrophysiological and behavioral actions of ethanol. *Journal of Neuroscience* 20(5):1982–1989, 2000. PMID: 10684899

Virkkunen, M., and Linnoila, M. Serotonin in early onset, male alcoholics with violent behaviour. *Annals of Medicine* 22(5):327–331, 1990. PMID: 2291840

Volkow, N.D.; Wang, G.J.; Telang, F.; et al. Profound decreases in dopamine release in striatum in detoxified alcoholics:

Possible orbitofrontal involvement. *Journal of Neuroscience* 27(46):12700–12706, 2007. PMID: 18003850

Walker, B.M., and Koob, G.F. The γ-aminobutyric acid-B receptor agonist baclofen attenuates responding for ethanol in ethanol-dependent rats. *Alcoholism: Clinical and Experimental Research* 31(1):11–18, 2007. PMID: 17207096

Weiss, F.; Lorang, M.T.; Bloom, F.E.; and Koob, G.F. Oral alcohol self-administration stimulates dopamine release in the rat nucleus accumbens: Genetic and motivational determinants. *Journal of Pharmacology and Experimental Therapeutics* 267(1):250–258, 1993. PMID: 8229752

Weiss, F.; Parsons, L.H.; Schulteis, G.; et al. Ethanol self-administration restores withdrawal-associated deficiencies in accumbal dopamine and 5-hydroxytryptamine release in dependent rats. *Journal of Neuroscience* 16(10):3474–3485, 1996. PMID: 8627380

Weissman, M.M.; Myers, J.K.; and Harding, P.S. Prevalence and psychiatric heterogeneity of alcoholism in a United States urban community. *Journal of Studies on Alcohol* 41(7):672–681, 1980. PMID: 7421256

Wolffgramm, J., and Heyne, A. From controlled drug intake to loss of control: The irreversible development of drug addiction in the rat. *Behavioural Brain Research* 70(1):77–94, 1995. PMID: 8519431

Wood, J.M., and Laverty, R. Metabolic and pharmacodynamic tolerance to ethanol in rats. *Pharmacology, Biochemistry, and Behavior* 10(6): 871–874, 1979. PMID: 482307

Wrase, J.; Makris, N.; Braus, D.F.; et al. Amygdala volume associated with alcohol abuse relapse and craving. *American Journal of Psychiatry* 165(9):1179–1184, 2008. PMID: 18593776

Zhao, Y.; Weiss, F.; and Zorrilla, E.P. Remission and resurgence of anxiety-like behavior across protracted withdrawal stages in ethanol-dependent rats. *Alcoholism: Clinical and Experimental Research* 31(9):1505–1515, 2007. PMID: 17760785

Nicotine

By N E Grunberg and A K Starosciak

Glossary

Abstinence/withdrawal—A syndrome of uncomfortable psychological and biological effects that result when the use of an addictive drug is discontinued.

Cigarette—French for small cigar (cigar+-*ette*). A manufactured product consisting of cured tobacco leaf and other additives that are rolled into a paper cylinder that may have a filter at one end. The product is ignited at the nonfiltered end and smoke is inhaled through the filtered end.

Cotinine—The primary chemical byproduct ($C_{10}H_{12}N_2O$) of nicotine metabolism that is often used as a marker of tobacco use because of its long half-life.

Drug addiction—A behavior pattern of psychoactive drug use that involves overwhelming involvement with use of the drug, securing its supply, and a high likelihood to relapse to drug use after abstaining from use. Addiction often is accompanied by tolerance and withdrawal effects.

Drug dependence—The highly controlled or compulsive use of a psychoactive drug that is reinforced by the effects of that drug. Drug dependence often is accompanied by drug tolerance and withdrawal.

Negative reinforcement—The increased likelihood that a behavior will be repeated when that behavior is followed by the removal of an unpleasant or aversive state.

Nicotiana tabacum—Genus and species name for the cultivated tobacco plant most commonly used to make commercial tobacco products.

Nicotine—A chemical alkaloid ($C_{10}H_{14}N_2$) that is found naturally in tobacco.

Nicotine replacement therapy (NRT)—Any of several medicinal nicotine-containing products intended to help a person abstain from tobacco use by offsetting withdrawal symptoms.

Nicotinic acetylcholine receptors (nAChRs)—Ligand-gated ion channels found in the cell membranes of various cell types, including neurons and muscles that open in response to the endogenous neurotransmitter acetylcholine and to nicotine.

Passive administration/involuntary smoking/ second-hand smoking—A mixture of the side-stream smoke from a burning cigarette, cigar, or pipe, and the smoke exhaled by a smoker, that is inhaled by a nonsmoker.

Positive reinforcement—The increased likelihood that a behavior will be repeated when that behavior is followed by a pleasant or rewarding consequence.

Sympathomimetic—The activation of the sympathetic nervous system branch of the autonomic nervous system.

Tobacco—An herbaceous plant native to North and South America, Australia, southwest Africa, and the South Pacific that contains nicotine, and is used to make consumer products such as cigarettes, cigars, pipe tobacco, chewing tobacco, and snuff.

Nicotine is a fascinating drug with a long history. It is highly addictive, can be arousing, as well as calming, but is usually self-administered through deadly tobacco products. The study of nicotine has

N.E. Grunberg and A.K. Starosciak, "Nicotine," from the *Encyclopedia of Behavioral Neuroscience*: *Volume 2*, George F. Koob, Michel Le Moal and Richard F. Thompson, eds. pp. 464–470. Published by Academic Press, 2010. Copyright by Elsevier Science and Technology Books. Permission to reprint granted by the rights holder.

revealed important information about receptor biology underlying drug actions in the body, neurochemical pathways in the brain, and mechanisms of positive and negative reinforcement. This primary drug of addiction in tobacco products also may be used or may inspire the development of new medications to treat anxiety, mood, thought, and skeletal muscle disorders.

History of Tobacco and Nicotine

Historical Use

Tobacco use and the self-administration of nicotine through tobacco products date back centuries. Mayan stone carvings (c. 600–900 AD) indicate tobacco use in the New World and other archeological evidence indicates tobacco use dating back several millennia earlier. European explorers to the New World in the late fifteenth and sixteenth centuries discovered native people of the American and Caribbean islands smoking or chewing dried tobacco leaves in spiritual practices, for medicinal reasons, and to achieve desired effects, including appetite regulation, energy enhancement, and relaxation. The word tobacco is derived from the Y-shaped tube (called a taboca or tobago) that was used to smoke tobacco leaves in the Caribbean islands. Several species of wild tobacco plant grew indigenously in North and South America, including *Nicotiana petunoides, Nicotiana rustica,* and *Nicotiana tabacum.* The tall, broad-leafed *N. tabacum* became the tobacco species that is primarily cultivated and sold for commercial use throughout the world. Today, tobacco is grown in over 100 countries worldwide, including the United States. In every country and culture where tobacco has been introduced, self-administration of tobacco products has become common and persistent.

Isolation and Synthesis

As tobacco use spread to Europe, interest in the plant and its actions grew. In the early 1800s, Cerioli and Vauquelin discovered that the major active ingredient in tobacco was an oily material which was named 'nicotianine' after Jean Nicot de Villemain, the French ambassador to Portugal who introduced tobacco to the French court as a universal cure-all herb. Several decades later, Posselt and Reimann at the University of Heidelberg isolated nicotianine from *N. tabacum* and changed the name to 'nikotin.' In the mid-1800s, Melsens determined the chemical formula for nikotin ($C_{10}H_{14}N_2$), and Schloesing determined its molecular weight (162.23 g mol^{-1}). In the late 1800s, Pinner discovered the structure of what became known as 'nicotine,' an Anglicized spelling of the German word. Also in the late 1800s, Langley and Dickinson discovered that nicotine acted to stimulate autonomic ganglia and investigations of these actions led to the idea that chemicals (including nicotine) act at specific sites or receptors on cells which, in turn, release chemicals that transmit information between neurons. Pharmacological study of nicotine became active in the mid-twentieth century and continues to the present day.

Physical Chemistry

Nicotine (3-(1-methyl-2-pyrrolidinyl)-pyridine) is a highly toxic liquid alkaloid found naturally in several plant species, including *N. tabacum,* and is the key addictive component of tobacco products. Nicotine is a bicyclic compound with pyridine and pyrrolidine rings. The compound possesses one asymmetric carbon and can exist in two enantiomeric forms. In nature, nicotine exists in the S-shape, or levorotary form. Nicotine is a colorless and odorless base, with a dissociation constant (pK_a) of approximately 8.0. It forms water-soluble solid salts when mixed with acids. Nicotine is hydrophilic and lipophilic and readily distributes throughout the body because it is absorbed through the skin, mucous membranes, lungs, and gastrointestinal tract. Free-base nicotine combusts at approximately 35 °C (95 °F), so much of the nicotine in a cigarette burns off when the cigarette is lit but the amount that is inhaled exerts powerful effects in the brain, nervous system, and at other sites in the body.

Forms of Nicotine and Their Use

Not only is nicotine most commonly self-administered through tobacco products, but it also is self-administered in an ever-increasing variety of nicotine replacement products.

Tobacco Products

Tobacco cigarettes are the most common nicotine-containing products. Most cigarettes are commercially produced, but some people continue to roll their own cigarettes. Smoking cigarettes is the most common way to self-administer nicotine and it is the most effective way to get nicotine to the brain. Tobacco also is smoked in pipes, cigars, flavored cigarettes, bidis, kreteks, and hookahs. Pipe and cigar smoking is more common among men than women, but cigar smoking is increasing in popularity among women. Flavored cigarettes are most common among teenage and young adult smokers. Flavored cigarettes usually have lower nicotine contents than conventional cigarettes, and have distinctive flavors such as cherry, mocha, or vanilla. Bidis are small, hand-rolled cigarettes primarily smoked in or imported from India and Southeastern Asian countries. Bidis may or may not be flavored. Kreteks are made from a mixture of tobacco, cloves, and other herbs. Bidis and kreteks deliver more nicotine than the standard tobacco cigarette. Hookah (also known as water pipe, nargeela, arghileh, and nargile) is a traditional Middle Eastern or Asian device that operates by water filtration and indirect heat to cool the tobacco smoke as it is inhaled by the smoker. Nicotine-containing tobacco products also include smokeless products, including chewing tobacco and snuff. Chewing tobacco is usually kept under the lip or in the cheek. Snuff can be inhaled through the nasal cavity.

Nicotine Replacement Products

In addition to tobacco products, nicotine is now available in various nicotine replacement products or nicotine replacement therapy (NRT). Nicotine polacrilex gum was developed by Ove Ferno and colleagues in Sweden in the 1970s to help people quit smoking tobacco cigarettes. Nicotine gum became available in the United States as a prescription medication in the 1980s to help alleviate withdrawal symptoms in abstinent smokers. By the twenty-first century several dosages and flavors of nicotine gum became available over the counter (OTC) and no longer required a prescription. Currently, nicotine is available in several other forms, including nicotine transdermal patches, nicotine vapor inhaler, nicotine lozenges, nicotine microtabs (small sublingual tablets that slowly dissolve under the tongue), nicotine nasal spray, and nicotine in water.

Epidemiology

Approximately 20% of adults (1.3 billion people) smoke cigarettes worldwide and more men than women smoke. Similarly, in the United States, 20.8% of adults (45.3 million people) currently smoke tobacco cigarettes, and prevalence is higher among men (23.9%) than among women (18.0%). In the United States, tobacco use by numbers and by percentage of the population has decreased over the past 20 years, but global numbers of smokers have increased. In the United States, it is estimated that 4000 children under the age of 18 try smoking each day, that about 2000 of them continue to smoke, and that almost 20% of high school students smoke cigarettes everyday.

Prevalence of smokeless tobacco use among adults in the US is about 3% (6% of men vs. 0.4% of women). About 8% of high school students in the US use smokeless tobacco (13.6% of males vs. 2.2% of females). Worldwide 11% of children use tobacco products other than cigarettes.

Administration, Absorption, and Distribution

The chemical and physical properties of nicotine allow it to be readily absorbed through the skin, mucous membranes, and the respiratory tract. These multiple sites of absorption and ready passage of nicotine allow it to be self-administered or administered medically through several different methods.

Self-Administration of Nicotine-Containing Tobacco Products

The most common way to self-administer nicotine is by smoking tobacco products, primarily commercially made cigarettes. When a person smokes a tobacco product, the inhaled smoked travels through the respiratory tract and is absorbed by the alveoli in the lungs. The absorbed nicotine passes from the alveoli through the capillary walls and into the bloodstream. The pulmonary circuit of the cardiovascular system carries nicotine directly to the brain within seconds of inhalation and the nicotine rapidly crosses the blood-brain barrier through passive diffusion because of its small size and lipophilicity and through active transport by the choroid plexus. As a result, the smoker receives a bolus of nicotine into the brain soon after taking a puff on the cigarette. That bolus infusion of nicotine sets off a cascade of neurochemical and neurophysiological events (discussed below under the section titled 'Actions') which result in reward, dependence, and other reinforcing effects.

Nicotine also is self-administered through smokeless tobacco products, but the time course for nicotine to reach the brain is much slower than with smoked tobacco products. Nicotine from smokeless tobacco either is absorbed in blood vessels in the mucous membranes of the mouth or travels to the stomach with saliva and enters the bloodstream through the digestive system. The amount of nicotine that reaches the brain from smokeless tobacco products is relatively small and some of it is metabolized in the liver before reaching the nervous system. The addiction liability to smokeless tobacco products is markedly less than the addiction liability to smoked tobacco products because of the slower time course and reduced quantities of nicotine that reach the brain.

Self-administration of Nicotine-Containing Medications

Nicotine is available in several products that are used as medications (NRT) to help smokers abstain from tobacco use and to attenuate withdrawal symptoms that accompany abstinence from regular tobacco self-administration. NRTs use several different routes of administration.

Nicotine polacrilex gum, or simply nicotine gum, was the first nicotine replacement product. Nicotine gum became available in Europe in the 1970s and seemed to be a valuable adjunctive pharmacological therapy to behavioral smoking cessation approaches. It was hailed as a new effective treatment to aid in smoking cessation but subsequent studies in the United States in the 1980s showed modest efficacy. Later in the 1980s and 1990s as nicotine addiction became better understood, comparison of nicotine gum clinical trials revealed that higher dosages were being used in the European versus American clinical trials. Now several dosages and flavors of nicotine gum are available. These gums are, indeed, useful ways to administer small amounts of nicotine and are valuable adjunctive therapies to behavioral and cognitive smoking cessation techniques.

Similar to nicotine gum, nicotine lozenges and nicotine microtabs administer nicotine orally. Some nicotine crosses the mucous membranes in the mouth and some nicotine travels through the gastrointestinal tract and is absorbed into the circulation. Much of this nicotine is metabolized in the liver, so reduced amounts of the drug reach the brain.

Nicotine can also be inhaled using an NRT vapor inhaler. Although the administration device is called a nicotine inhaler, most of the nicotine actually stays within the oral cavity and is absorbed through the oral mucosa rather than through the lungs. Similar to the gum, lozenge, and microtab, much lower plasma concentrations of nicotine are achieved from the NRT vapor inhaler than by smoking cigarettes, so many doses are necessary throughout the day to satisfy the smoker and to attenuate withdrawal.

Nicotine patches and nicotine nasal spray deliver nicotine through different routes than the other products. Nicotine skin patches are now available in several dosages and from several manufacturers. Nicotine is slowly absorbed across the skin over many hours (up to 24 h per patch). The nicotine nasal spray administers the drug intranasally and it is absorbed through the blood vessels in the mucous membrane of the nose. As with the other NRTs, dosages of nicotine are much lower and follow a slower time course than smoking tobacco products, which is why these products have a low addiction liability compared with smoking nicotine-containing tobacco.

Passive Administration

It is important to realize that nicotine can be administered unknowingly. Environmental tobacco smoke (also known as ETS, second-hand smoke, involuntary smoking, or passive smoking) from side-stream smoke of burning tobacco products and from exhaled smoke from tobacco smokers is absorbed by inhalation and transdermally by nonsmokers who are in the proximity of smokers. In fact, a nonsmoker who lives with a two-pack-a-day smoker can have urinary levels of cotinine (the primary metabolite of nicotine) equivalent to smoking several cigarettes per day. The amount of ETS exposure increases in spaces that are enclosed, poorly ventilated, or where the air is recirculated. That is why airplanes and many restaurants and enclosed public places have banned tobacco smoking. Children are at particular risk to develop smoking-related pulmonary health problems as a result of ETS.

Distribution

Following absorption, nicotine is rapidly distributed in many tissues and organs throughout the body because it is lipophilic and readily passes through cell membranes. In cigarette smokers and other tobacco users, nicotine reaches its peak plasma concentration within 30 min of administration, and then slowly declines during the next several hours. Smoking cigarettes delivers nicotine to the brain within seconds of inhalation. NRTs have different time courses for distribution of nicotine based on the specific route of administration. Nicotine nasal spray, gum, and lozenges deliver and distribute nicotine quickly to the peripheral bloodstream, but nicotine levels also decline quickly using these methods. In contrast, nicotine is delivered slowly by the nicotine transdermal patch. For the 24-h patch, plasma concentrations of nicotine rise slowly during the first 6–10 h, plateau after 8–12 h, and then decline slowly during the subsequent 6 h. The slow distribution and clearance of the patch allow for its once daily use, as opposed to the high dosing frequency of other NRTs.

Actions

Table 1 presents a summary of neural substrates underlying key actions of nicotine.

Nicotine Receptor Biology

Nicotine acts at chemical receptors located throughout the body which partially explains its wide-ranging

TABLE 1 Summary of neural substrates underlying key actions of nicotine

Nicotine action	Neural substrate
Reinforcing and rewarding effects	Mesocorticolimbic dopamine pathway (including PFC, NAcc
	and VTA) via α4β2
Increase attention, alertness, vigilance, and arousal	Decreased slow-wave EEG, increased fast-wave EEG
Enhance memory	Hippocampus via α7
Enhance movement	SNc
Sympathomimetic effects (including effects on respiration, heart rate,	Sympathetic and parasympathetic branches of the
and blood pressure)	autonomic nervous system
Mood modulator	Via increased serotonin release
Maintenance of self-administration and conscious urges	Insula and mesocorticolimbic dopamine pathway
Induce nausea and vomiting	Emetic trigger zone in area postrema
Induce vasopressin secretion	Supraoptic nucleus of hypothalamus

biological and psychological effects. Nicotine is an agonist at nicotinic acetylcholine receptors (nAChRs) in the central and peripheral nervous systems (nAChR$_N$), but has little or no effect at similar nicotinic acetylcholine receptors in the muscle (nAChR$_M$). The receptors are presynaptic ligand-gated ion channels which are composed of five subunits. There are several classes of subunits found in the nervous system (including α and β), each of which has several different subtypes (e.g., $\alpha2$–10 and $\beta2$–4). α-Subunits are differentiated from the β-subunits because they have two adjacent cysteine residues that are necessary for the binding of acetylcholine. There is growing evidence that the various effects of nicotine (e.g., addiction, appetite regulation, mood modulation, and attention effects) in humans and animals may be explained by activation of different nicotine receptor subunits and various combinations of these subunits.

Nicotine receptors are found on dopaminergic ($\alpha4\beta2$, $\alpha6\beta2$, and $\alpha6\beta3$), glutamatergic ($\alpha4\beta2$ and $\alpha7$), γ-aminobutyric acid (GABA)ergic ($\alpha4\beta2$), adrenergic ($\alpha3\beta2$ and $\alpha7$), and cholinergic ($\alpha3\beta4$) nerve terminals. The receptors are located in several areas of the brain relevant to reward, addiction, and psychoactive effects, including the substantia nigra pars compacta (SNc), ventral tegmental area (VTA), nucleus accumbens (NAcc), midbrain tegmentum, striatum, and various regions of the cerebral cortex. The receptors are located presynaptically in the brain. Nicotine binding increases depolarization of the nerve terminal, leads to an influx of Ca^{2+}, and enhances neurotransmission at that terminal. Stimulation of nAchRs in the VTA, for example, releases dopamine in the NAcc, an area responsible for the reinforcing effects of many drugs. Mice genetically bred with the $\alpha4$- or the $\beta2$-subunit knocked out do not exhibit increased dopamine release in response to nicotine, and do not maintain nicotine self-administration. Further, $\alpha4$ knock-in mice (which express a defective $\alpha4$-subunit) show reduced sensitization, reinforcement, and tolerance to nicotine. These data suggest that the $\alpha4\beta2$ receptor is necessary for dopamine release in the NAcc and is a key receptor underlying nicotine self-administration. The $\alpha7$-subunit seems to be involved in effects of nicotine on attention and memory and also may be involved in axogenesis and neuroprotection. Ongoing studies of nicotine subunits are focusing on the development of new medications to treat nicotine dependence and to treat other conditions that may be helped by nicotine agonists, including cognitive dementias; anxiety, mood, and thought disorders; and skeletomuscular problems.

Nervous System and Neurotransmitters

Nicotine acts at many sites in the brain, including the medial habenula, interpeduncular nucleus, SNc, and VTA. These sites are relevant to nicotine's physical (movement), cognitive (attention), motivational (reinforcement and reward), and therapeutic effects (e.g., to treat schizophrenia, dementia, or Parkinson's disease). Nicotine acts in the central nervous system (CNS) and peripheral nervous system (PNS). It is classified as a sympathomimetic pharmacological agent but it actually stimulates both the sympathetic and parasympathetic branches of the autonomic nervous system (ANS). Nicotine induces the release of norepinephrine in the sympathetic branch and acetylcholine in the parasympathetic branch of the ANS. Because the two branches have opposing actions, nicotine can exert differential effects depending on which branch has greater activation. These opposing effects may help explain why nicotine seems to be unique in that it can stimulate or relax, arouse, or calm. Colloquially stated, nicotine can bring people up when they are down and down when they are up. Although these opposite physiological effects have been well known to scientists and smokers for a century, psychologist Stanley Schachter (in the late 1970s) referred to this phenomenon as Nesbitt's paradox, based on research in his laboratory being conducted by Paul Nesbitt, and the nickname stuck.

Nicotine acts on mesolimbic and mesocortical dopaminergic pathways that are involved in reward and addiction. The major dopaminergic neurons of these pathways originate in the VTA and project to the NAcc, pallidum, hippocampus, amygdala, and medial prefrontal cortex (PFC) in the mesolimbic circuit, or to other areas of the frontal cortex in the mesocortical pathway. The mesocorticolimbic dopamine pathway is involved in reinforcing or rewarding effects of pleasurable experiences or activities including drug use. After smoking a cigarette, dopamine levels in the NAcc increase, which increases the likelihood that the person will smoke (self-administer nicotine) again in the future. Nicotine also increases release of serotonin, which may underlie nicotine's effects to help modulate mood. The insula, sometimes called the fifth lobe of the brain, is involved in conscious urges, and also may be involved in maintenance of nicotine self-administration and smoking. Nicotine increases the respiration rate through receptors in the carotid body and aortic arch, induces nausea and vomiting through receptors in the emetic trigger zone of the midbrain's area postrema (which is why first-time smokers often feel sick), and induces vasopressin secretion by acting in the supraoptic nucleus of the hypothalamus.

Physiology

Nicotine is considered a CNS stimulant or sympathomimetic because it increases heart rate, respiratory rate, blood pressure, and causes peripheral vasoconstriction. Increased arousal is evident in the electroencephalogram (EEG). Nicotine decreases slow-wave electrical activity in the brain; increases faster, high-voltage waves that are involved in conscious, active thought; and enhances responses to auditory and evoked potential responses reflecting increased attention and information processing. Nicotine decreases skeletal muscle tone as reflected by electromyogram (EMG) recordings, which may contribute to feelings of relaxation when smoking. Nicotine also decreases body weight by decreasing appetite and by increasing metabolism.

Behavior

Nicotine's ready passage into the CNS, especially when self-administered in tobacco smoke, produces marked central effects that increase subsequent self-administration of nicotine-containing products. The close temporal association between nicotine self-administration and central actions and the rewarding effects of nicotine (including increased arousal, attention and mood, and reduced anxiety, appetite, and body weight) increase the likelihood of nicotine self-administration.

Cognition

Nicotine increases selective attention, sustained attention, alertness, and vigilance. It also decreases distraction. Clinical studies suggest that nicotine can improve cognitive function in cases of senile dementia and Alzheimer's disease.

Motivation

Nicotine acts in several ways to alter motivation for nicotine self-administration. Nicotine decreases general and specific hunger (to sweet tastes) and increases desire for nicotine itself. It is likely that these motivational effects are related and that both involve mechanisms of the mesocorticolimbic dopamine pathway. These effects include alterations in hedonic tone, so it is likely that the limbic system also is involved in the pleasant experience associated with nicotine administration with repeated exposure. Further, it is likely that endogenous opioid systems and serotonergic mechanisms act in concert with the dopaminergic pathways to underlie reinforcement of nicotine self-administration. Both positive and negative reinforcement also contribute to motivation to self-administer nicotine. Nicotine's neurochemical actions (especially on dopamine, serotonin, and endogenous opioid peptides), appetite-controlling effects, and attention-enhancing effects, all act as positive reinforcers to increase the likelihood of nicotine self-administration. The unpleasant withdrawal effects following nicotine abstinence act through negative reinforcement to motivate nicotine self-administration to offset the abstinence effects (see the section titled 'Abstinence effects'). The fact that nicotine self-administration accompanies stress also may reflect a motivational effect and seems to involve the corticotropin-releasing factor (CRF) system.

Toxicity

Nicotine is a poisonous chemical and is used as a powerful pesticide. It is toxic at 60 mg for the average human adult and roughly 10 mg for a child. Exposures to toxic levels of nicotine are most common in tobacco farmers and in people exposed to high amounts of nicotine-containing pesticides. Symptoms of acute nicotine poisoning include nausea, vomiting, salivation, cold sweat, pallor, abdominal pain, diarrhea, and respiratory distress as a result of overstimulation of nAChRs in the ANS. Prolonged exposure to high dosages of nicotine results in severe CNS depression, muscle paralysis, and respiratory failure. The leading cause of death from nicotine poisoning is respiratory failure.

Metabolism

The liver is the major site of nicotine metabolism in the body, accounting for 80–90% of its metabolism. Approximately 70–80% of nicotine metabolized by the liver is converted to the nicotine imminium ion and 5′-hydroxynicotine by the cytochrome P450 (CYP) enzymes 2A6 and 2B6, and then to cotinine by aldehyde oxidase. Sixty percent of cotinine is further metabolized. Whereas it is clear that nicotine is an active drug, there is some evidence that cotinine also may have physiological and psychopharmacological actions. A small percentage of nicotine is converted to nicotine-1′-N-oxide (4%) by flavin-containing monooxygenase, nicotine glucuronide (4%) by N-glucuronidation, and nornicotine (<1%) by N-demethylation. Some nicotine is excreted unchanged. Minor sites of nicotine metabolism include the brain, lungs, and kidneys.

Elimination

Nicotine has an elimination half-life ($t_{1/2}$) of approximately 2 h in humans, but this value varies from 1 to 4 h among people. This relatively short $t_{1/2}$, and the relative pharmacological inactivity of nicotine's metabolites contribute to frequent smoking by people who are addicted to nicotine. The $t_{1/2}$ for cotinine is 17 h, and cotinine clearance is highly correlated with nicotine clearance. Concentrations of cotinine in the saliva, plasma, and urine are correlated, so salivary cotinine serves as a good biomarker for tobacco or nicotine exposure.

The major site of elimination for nicotine and its metabolites is in the urine, through the kidneys. Approximately 10% of nicotine and 10% of cotinine are excreted unmetabolized in the urine, although the process is pH dependent. When the pH of urine is acidic, then nicotine reabsorption from the kidney decreases which results in increased renal clearance of nicotine. Certain foodstuffs as well as physical and psychological stress can acidify the urine and may thereby contribute pharmacokinetically to increased nicotine intake through cigarette smoking.

Trace amounts of nicotine and its metabolites remain in other body fluids, such as the saliva. Nursing mothers also secrete nicotine in breast milk which can expose nursing children to nicotine.

Abstinence Effects

Abstinence from nicotine self-administration in a drug-dependent or addicted individual results in withdrawal effects. Symptoms of nicotine abstinence include craving for nicotine, irritability, difficulty concentrating and paying attention, sleep difficulties, dysphoria, impatience, increased appetite, and weight gain. Most of these symptoms begin within 24 h after nicotine abstinence, peak between 36 and 72 h, and gradually subside after several days. However, urges or craving for nicotine and increased appetite and weight gain can persist for 6 months to a year. The withdrawal symptoms, severity, and length of time symptoms last vary widely among people, and may be influenced by gender, age, ethnicity, duration of nicotine self-administration, and amount of nicotine self-administration.

Administration of nicotine will attenuate or offset the unpleasant withdrawal symptoms and will enhance dependence on nicotine via negative reinforcement. NRTs are used to offset withdrawal symptoms and to complement behavioral, cognitive, and motivational strategies and techniques to help people successfully give up tobacco use.

See also: Animal Tests for Anxiety; Cellular Plasticity in Cocaine and Alcohol Addiction; Depression; Drug Addiction; Drug Withdrawal—Motivational View; Ethanol and Nicotine Interactions; Feeding; Hallucinogens; Motivation; Neurobiology of Opioid Addiction; Parkinson's Disease; Psychostimulants; Schizophrenia.

Further Reading

Benowitz NL (ed.) (1998) *Nicotine Safety and Toxicity.* New York: Oxford University Press.

Feldman RS, Meyer JS, and Quenzer LF (1997) Nicotine. In: Feldman RS, Meyer JS, and Quenzer LF (eds.) *Principles of Neuropsychopharmacology,* pp. 591–611. Sunderland, MA: Sinauer.

Grunberg NE, Berger SS, and Starosciak AK (2009) Tobacco use: Psychology, neurobiology, and clinical implications. In: Baum A, Revenson T, and Singer JE (eds.) *Handbook of Health Psychology,* 2nd edn. Oxford: Psychology Press.

Grunberg NE and Phillips JM (2004) Nicotine addiction. In: Spielberger C (ed.) *Encyclopedia of Applied Psychology,* vol. 2, pp. 665–668. Oxford: Elsevier.

Heimann RK (1960) *Tobacco and Americans.* New York: McGraw-Hill.

Koob GF and LeMoal M (2006) Nicotine. In: Koob GF and Le Moal M (eds.) *Neurobiology of Addiction,* pp. 243–287. Oxford: Elsevier.

O'Brien CP (2006) Nicotine. In: Brunton LL, Lazo JS, and Parker KL (eds.) *Goodman and Gilman's The Pharmacological Basis of Therapeutics,* 11th edn., pp. 615–617. New York: McGraw Hill.

Rand MJ and Thurau K (1988) *The Pharmacology of Nicotine.* Oxford: The ICSU Press.

Taylor P (2006) Ganglionic stimulating drugs. In: Brunton LL, Lazo JS, and Parker KL (eds.) *Goodman and Gilman's The Pharmacological Basis of Therapeutics,* 11th edn., pp. 231–234. New York: McGraw Hill.

United States Department of Health and Human Services (1988) The health consequences of smoking: Nicotine addiction. *A Report of the Surgeon General* (DHHS Publication No. CDC 88-8406). Washington, DC: U.S. Government Printing Office.

Pathological Gambling

By W.A. Williams and M.N. Potenza

Glossary

Appetitive—Driven by a hedonic or pleasurable feeling or motivation.

Diagnostic and Statistical Manual—A book widely used in psychiatry that categorizes and defines mental health disorders.

Ego-dystonic—In opposition with the ego, or unpleasurable.

Ego-syntonic—In conjunction with the ego, or pleasurable.

Gambling—Placing something of value at risk in the hope of gaining something of greater value.

Microdialysis—A method for measuring levels of chemicals within the brain.

Pathological gambling—A mental health disorder characterized by excessive and interfering patterns of gambling.

Polymorphism—In genetics, a term used to describe a variant form of a gene, gene segment, or other segments of DNA.

Phenomenology

Of the formal group of impulse control disorders (ICDs) not elsewhere classified, which also includes intermittent explosive disorder, kleptomania, pyromania, trichotillomania, and ICDs not otherwise specified, pathological gambling (PG) arguably represents the disorder studied in greatest detail. ICDs have been characterized as obsessive–compulsive spectrum disorders and behavioral addictions, and diagnostically they are grouped in the *Diagnostic and Statistical Manual of Mental Disorders—Fourth Edition* (*DSM-IV*) as a heterogeneous cluster of disorders linked by failure-to-resist impulses to engage in harmful, disturbing, or distressing behaviors. Thus, a core set of clinical features characterize these disorders: (1) compulsive and repetitive performance of the problematic behavior despite adverse consequences; (2) diminished control over the behavior; (3) craving or appetitive urge states that precede the performance of the behavior; and (4) pleasure or release of tension derived from the behavior. These features are exhibited by individuals with PG who continue to gamble until financial resources are exhausted, and who do so with the knowledge that there is a high probability of severe social and economic consequences. This may be particularly true when aspects of tolerance develop, akin to and suggestive of drug tolerance in drug dependence.

One conceptual framework has been proposed in which impulsive features of PG are considered along an impulsive–compulsive spectrum similar to obsessive–compulsive disorder (OCD). In this framework, affected individuals are purported to experience an intense unpleasantness resulting in attendant neurophysiological compensation, and these processes, in turn, may promote an intense drive to perform the specific behavior, namely gambling. A key characteristic hypothesized to distinguish these obsessive–compulsive spectrum disorders is the degree to which an ego-syntonic component of PG is related to an underestimation of risk. By contrast, ego-dystonic feelings in OCD

W.A. Williams and M.N. Potenza, "Pathological Gambling," from the *Encyclopedia of Behavioral Neuroscience: Volume 3*, George F. Koob, Michel Le Moal and Richard F. Thompson, eds., pp. 29–34. Published by Academic Press, 2010. Copyright by Elsevier Science and Technology Books. Permission to reprint granted by the rights holder.

may lead to an overestimation of harm, risk aversion, and anticipatory anxiety. Alternate models consider the relationship between PG and mood regulation. Given the frequent co-occurrence of PG and depression and suicidal ideation and impaired judgment, as is also seen in bipolar disorder, PG has been conceptualized as an affective spectrum disorder. A third conceptual model posits PG as a non-substance-related addiction, consistent with its frequent co-occurrence with substance use disorders (SUDs).

Although the term addiction was not initially linked to excessive patterns of substance use, it has been specifically used to define 'impaired control over substance use behaviors.' However, recent arguments bolstered by biological data have been forwarded to consider non-substance-use illnesses such as PG as addictive disorders. One element proposed as a common characteristic has been loss of control or impaired control over a particular problem behavior with the attendant adverse consequences.

Case Example

James is a 43-year-old, married African-American man who suffers from compulsive thoughts of gambling, an inability to resist the urge to gamble, alcohol dependence, and high blood pressure. James began gambling and experimenting with drugs at age 16. Despite being a talented student-athlete, he frequently smoked pot on the weekends and drank beer with his friends, who would gamble and get involved in petty criminal mischief. When James went to college, his academic performance began to decline as he frequented a popular athlete-oriented, off-campus nightclub. He spent the majority of his time socializing, getting high, and skimping on his studies. After college, he married. Thereafter, his doctor sternly advised him to lose weight and cut down on alcohol intake, because of his positive family history of coronary artery disease and borderline hypertensive readings. Eventually, James resolved to get back into shape and was able to reduce his alcohol consumption and avoid gambling.

However, over the past 2 years, he has steadily become more engaged in high-stakes gambling activities, is preoccupied with gambling, always planning his next gambling excursion, and seeking ways to obtain money for gambling. He has begun to drink more heavily as the frequency of his gambling has escalated. His tolerance to alcohol has increased and he drinks daily to control symptoms of withdrawal, such as late-afternoon tremors.

James' drinking and gambling forays have left the family's finances in ruins and have had an impact on his job performance. Often, he arrives late for work and is exhausted due to gambling. He and his boss have clashed over the poor quality of his work. At home, he and his wife bicker constantly over their finances and the increasingly large cash withdrawals he makes before the weekend. At the time of his evaluation, James reported gambling about 3 times during the workweek and the entire weekend. When not gambling, he reports intense urges to gamble. When he is gambling, he reports alcohol cravings and a feeling of relief that comes over him when he has his first drink of the day, usually immediately after work at his favorite watering hole. When he goes to the casinos, he is mesmerized by the atmosphere and gambles up to 8 h continuously.

Over the past several months, his wife has become more resentful because of his worsening gambling and alcohol addiction, his lack of attention to his family, and his refusal to get help. This has left him feeling hopeless, guilty, anxious, and depressed. He fights these feelings by drinking more heavily, and resolving to hit it big the next time. He has borrowed money from his family, and as it became obvious that he had a gambling addiction, they refused additional loans. He insists that his behavior is not problematic but has become desperate, resorting to illegal activity, including placing bets with a local bookie. Recently, he started having an affair and justifies this behavior by stating that his wife is distant because "she is hung up on material possessions."

Diagnosis and Assessment

In 1980, PG was introduced into the *DSM*. Having undergone several revisions since its inception, a current listing of diagnostic criteria is included in **Table 1.** As the above case vignette illustrates, current diagnostic criteria for PG share similar features with substance dependence, including interference in major areas of life functioning, tolerance, withdrawal, and repeated unsuccessful attempts to cut back or quit. It is characterized by persistent and recurrent maladaptive patterns of gambling. Screening instruments include the South Oaks Gambling

Screen (SOGS) and symptom severity instruments include the Yale Brown Obsessive–Compulsive Scale for Pathological Gambling (PG-YBOCS) and Gambling-Symptom Assessment Scale (G-SAS).

Epidemiology

In surveys conducted throughout the United States and Canada, prevalence rates of PG ranged between 0.4% and 2.0%; in Australia, New Zealand, and Europe, 0.2–2.1%; and in Asian countries, 1–2%. A meta-analysis of prevalence studies performed in North America over several decades estimated the lifetime prevalence rates of problem gambling and PG at 3.9% and 1.6%, respectively. Hence, while a majority of people (86%) are thought to have engaged in some form of gambling activity, only a relatively small fraction develops gambling problems. In adolescents and young adults, higher lifetime prevalence rates of problem gambling and PG have been reported, 9.45% and 3.88%, respectively.

Males may represent a high-risk group, with most studies reporting a male-to-female ratio of approximately 2:1. However, the recently increased accessibility to legalized gambling, particularly, forms that appear more problematic for women such as slot machines, presages a decline in this ratio. Some studies have suggested that minority groups, particularly African-Americans, represent a high-risk group for PG. For example, African-Americans comprised 31% of problem gamblers as compared with 15% of recreational and 21% of nongamblers in the St. Louis Epidemiologic Catchment Study. The limited data on Hispanic, Asian-American, and Native American groups suggest that they may be at heightened risk for developing problem gambling or PG.

Psychiatric Comorbidity

An improtant factor in establishing effective treatment regimes is having reliable data on comorbidity of PG

TABLE 1 Diagnostic Criteria for Pathological Gambling

A. Persistent and recurrent maladaptive gambling behavior as indicated by five (or more) of the following:
1. is preoccupied with gambling (e.g., preoccupied with reliving past gambling experiences, handicapping or planning the next venture, or thinking of ways to get money with which to gamble)
2. needs to gamble with increasing amounts of money in order to achieve the desired excitement
3. has repeated unsuccessful efforts to control, cut back, or stop gambling
4. is restless or irritable when attempting to cut down or stop gambling
5. gambles as a way of escaping from problems or of relieving a dysphoric mood (e.g., feelings of helplessness, guilt, anxiety, depression)
6. after losing money gambling, often returns another day to get even (chasing one's losses)
7. lies to family members, therapist, or others to conceal the extent of involvement with gambling
8. has committed illegal acts such as forgery, fraud, theft, or embezzlement to finance gambling
9. has jeopardized or lost significant relationship, job, or educational or career opportunity because of gambling
10. relies on others to provide money to relieve a desperate financial situation caused by gambling
B. The gambling behavior is not better accounted for by a Manic Episode.

Reprinted with permission from the *Diagnostic and Statistical Manual of Mental Disorders,* 4th Edition. Text Revision, Washington, DC, American Psychiatric Association, 2000. p. 674.

and other psychiatric disorders. In a placebo-controlled, double-blinded, randomized, parallel-arm trial, lithium was superior to placebo in reducing symptoms of gambling and mania in individuals with PG and co-occurring bipolar spectrum symptomatology. Furthermore, in an independent trial in individuals with PG and co-occurring anxiety disorders using open-label escitalopram, followed by double-blind discontinuation, reductions in gambling and anxiety occurred during the open-label phase that persisted after double-blind discontinuation in the active condition but not the placebo one.

Individuals with SUDs have been reported to have 4- to 10-fold higher rates of PG (rates of 5–15% depending on the substance and the study). Studies have also found high rates of SUDs in PG cohorts, with rates as high as 45–55%, and nicotine dependence in the range of 70%. Some data suggest that PG and certain SUDs result from shared genetic factors representing a common etiologic basis. The presence of a co-occurring SUD may have a significant impact on clinical outcome. A study of individuals with alcohol dependence and a co-occurring nongambling disorder found that the presence of PG symptomatology was associated with a poorer treatment outcome. Therefore, it is important that concurrent treatment of gambling and comorbid disorders be tested further such that more precise treatment algorithms can be developed and validated.

Clinical Course, Pathophysiology, and Classification of Pathological Gambling

PG has been associated with impaired social functioning, bankruptcy, divorce, and incarceration. PG often begins early in the teen and young adult years, particularly among males. The progression of PG appears similar to that seen in SUDs, with high rates among youth, low rates among older adults, and periods of gambling interspersed with periods of abstinence. A 'telescoping' pattern, defined as a foreshortened time-period between initiation and problematic levels of behavioral engagement seen in women as compared to men, is observed in both PG and SUDs.

PG and other ICDs may go unrecognized in clinical settings. In one study that actively screened for ICDs following admission, over 30% of patients hospitalized for psychiatric care were found to have a current ICD, and this percentage contrasted with the less than 2% who were diagnosed with an ICD at the time of their hospitalization. Improved identification of ICDs with brief screening instruments may thus help to identify patients who could benefit from treatment of ICDs including PG.

Proposed Models of Addiction, Impulsivity, and Pathological Gambling

The core clinical features of addiction overlap with those for impulsivity. Impulsivity has been defined as "a predisposition toward rapid, unplanned reactions to internal or external stimuli with diminished regard to the negative consequences of these reactions to the individual or others." Thus, PG has been described as a "behavioral addiction" or an "addiction without the drug" because of shared similar features with substance dependence. Blum and colleagues have conceptualized a mechanism underlying impulsivity and addiction, using the term 'reward deficiency syndrome.' They hypothesize that diminished dopamine (DA) function in mesolimbic reward pathways renders affected individuals sensitive, potentially placing them at elevated risk for addictive, impulsive, and compulsive behaviors. Alternatively, the "impaired response inhibition and salience attribution" model of addiction and the allostasis addiction model proposed by Koob and Le Moal suggest that, among other aspects, there exist alterations in the DA reward pathways in people who are vulnerable to addiction. Each model incorporates important environmental and genetic contributions to the development of addictions.

Neurobiology

The DA neurotransmitter system represents an important component of the brain reward and reinforcement processes, particularly as related to drug addiction. DA neurons project from the ventral tegmental area (VTA) to the nucleus accumbens (NAcc). These neurons are important for reward reinforcement because interruptions in DA impulse trafficking along axonal routes or at the receptor level decrease the rewarding influences of VTA-related DA stimulation. This system may be perturbed in addictions wherein pleasurable sensation may be associated with DA release, and altered dopaminergic pathways may stimulate reward-seeking behavior. For example, acute ingestion of cocaine increases DA transmission in the basal ganglia, which may enhance the behavioral reinforcement and learned associations encoding the addictive behavior.

In addition to the DA system, other monoamine systems have been implicated in addictions. Serotonin (5-HT) has been proposed to be particularly relevant to the initiation and cessation of the problematic behavior, and norepinephrine (NE) appears particularly relevant to arousal and excitement. Abnormalities in DA, 5-HT, and NE neurotransmitter systems have been reported in PG. Hypotheses that drive the investigation of medications in the treatment of PG are typically based on the neurobiology of PG. Effective pharmacological treatments may also provide insights into the pathophysiology of PG.

Animal Models of Impulsivity and Neuronal Activation

Animal models have been used to assess impulse control. Preferred-choice paradigms of impulsivity may involve simultaneous measurements of real-time neurophysiological and neurochemical data. Such models suggest that ventral and dorsal prefrontal regions represent distinct neuroanatomical substrates of impulsive behavior related to specific aspects of monoamine neurotransmission. The discrete ventral and dorsal areas of frontal cortex implicated in impulse control have been further divided into functionally dissociable areas. DA, 5-HT, and their metabolite concentrations in rat medial prefrontal cortex (mPFC) and orbitofrontal cortex (OFC) were measured using *in vivo* microdialysis during a model of impulsive choice, with mPFC-related 5-HT efflux specifically implicated. By contrast, increased 3,4-di-hydroxyphenylacetic acid (DOPAC, a DA metabolite) levels were observed in OFC, suggesting a

double-dissociation, implicating fronto-cortical 5-HT and DA neuromodulation during impulsive decision making. In a similar experiment designed to measure DA release in PFC, Listar-hooded rats were tested on a visual attention task based on a behavioral disinhibition model of impulsivity. Compared to their pretask levels, DA and DOPAC efflux increased significantly (~100%) during performance runs. The increase in DA release observed in the PFC was associated with performance measures. Those animals demonstrating a greater tendency for impulsive behavior were noted to demonstrate a similar magnitude of DA response. Primate studies of impulsive decision making have also implicated medial PFC function. Together, these animal data complement those from human studies suggesting an important role for ventral and medial prefrontal cortical function in impulsive behaviors.

Brain Imaging

Relatively few brain-imaging studies have investigated the ways in which brain function in individuals with PG differs from that in those without PG. One early functional magnetic resonance imaging (fMRI) study found that during exposure to gambling videotapes, men with PG, as compared with control comparison men, show relatively diminished activation of cortical, basal ganglia, and thalamic brain regions. These findings contrast with cue provocation studies in OCD in which relatively increased activation of these regions was reported. During the period of most intense gambling stimulus presentation, subjects with PG were distinguished from those without by showing diminished activation of the ventromedial prefrontal cortex (vmPFC), a brain region implicated in emotional regulation and decision making. A separate study of cognitive control used the Stroop color–word interference task and found that subjects with PG were distinguished most from those without by showing less activation of vmPFC. Subsequent fMRI studies investigating simulated gambling and decision making have found that individuals with PG (with or without SUDs) show less activation of the vmPFC when compared with nonaffected control subjects. Thus, these studies indicate that PG subjects show less activation of the vmPFC during performance of multiple cognitive and behavioral processes. These findings extend data from stroke patients with vmPFC lesions, who demonstrated disadvantageous decision making. Another brain region implicated in PG is the ventral striatum, a region including the NAcc, wherein less activation was seen during a simulated gambling task. Taken together, these studies suggest an important role for ventral cortico-striatal function in the pathophysiology of PG.

Genetics

PG is heritable, with twin studies suggesting that over 50% of the variance for PG is related to genetic contributions. These findings are similar to those for drug addictions in which 30–60% of the contributing variance is estimated to be genetic in nature. There is also overlap in genetic and environmental contributions between PG and other comorbid disorders such as alcohol dependence and antisocial personality disorder. In comparison, a similar study found that the overlap between PG and major depression was accounted for predominantly by shared genetic factors.

Candidate genes have been proposed for PG and impulsivity in general. Genetic variations in the gene encoding the DA D4 receptor (DRD4) have been associated with novelty seeking and PG, and variations in the DRD2 allele have been associated with PG and drug addiction, albeit inconsistently. Preliminary data investigating influences of allelic variants of the DRD2 on reward processing have suggested differences in medial OFC, amygdala, hippocampus, and NAcc function. The extent to which such findings are observed in PG subjects requires further investigation.

While these results are intriguing, findings from genetic association studies should be viewed with caution. This is particularly true since there have been significant methodological limitations, such as the lack of definitive diagnoses or stratification by racial/ethnic identity. Perhaps given the preliminary nature and methodological limitations of early studies, some initial findings (e.g., an association between PG and DRD2 variation) have not been replicated in subsequent, controlled studies. Larger population-based studies using accurate diagnostic assessments and genome-wide interrogation should provide a framework for a more precise understanding of the genetic influences contributing to PG.

Treatment

Over the past decade, multiple pharmacotherapies have been tested in the treatment of PG. Placebo-controlled trials indicate frequent placebo responses so the findings from open-label trials should be interpreted cautiously. Serotonin reuptake inhibitors such as paroxetine and fluvoxamine have shown mixed findings, with some placebo-controlled trials observing superiority of active drug over placebo and others not. Preliminary data suggest that serotonin reuptake inhibitors may be particularly helpful for individuals with PG and co-occurring internalizing disorders (e.g., anxiety disorders). Mood-stabilizing drugs have been found to be helpful for some individuals. In one trial, lithium was found to be superior to placebo in diminishing gambling and manic symptoms in individuals with PG and co-occurring bipolar spectrum disorders (e.g., bipolar II disorder). Arguably, the most consistent findings have emerged from studies of opioid antagonists. In three separate placebo-controlled trials, the opioid antagonists nalmefene and naltrexone have been reported to be superior to placebo in the treatment of PG. Individuals with strong gambling urges at treatment onset or a family history of alcoholism appear to respond particularly well to opioid antagonists. The glutamatergic neutriceutical n-acetyl cysteine has been found to be superior to placebo in one controlled trial. Although encouraging, the majority of pharmacotherapy studies have limitations with respect to short-term durations, small sample sizes, and exclusion of subjects with co-occurring disorders. As such, more study is needed to identify treatments with long-term benefits and to understand who might respond best to specific treatments.

As with SUDs, behavioral therapies are currently a cornerstone of treatment for PG. Self-help approaches like Gambler's Anonymous have been associated with improved outcomes. Among formal therapies, imaginal desensitization, motivational approaches, cognitive behavioral therapy, and brief interventions have support in controlled studies. However, in some instances, long-term follow-up data have not been as encouraging as short-term data. More research is needed to investigate the possible predictors of treatment outcome and evaluate combinations of behavioral and pharmacological therapies.

Conclusions

PG and SUDs share features including tolerance, withdrawal, repeated attempts to quit or cut back, and impairments in life functioning. Phenomenological similarities exist, including age-related prevalence estimates and telescoping patterns in women. Multiple neurotransmitter systems (e.g., 5-HT, NE, DA, and opioids) appear to contribute to PG. Treatments targeting these neurotransmitter systems have demonstrated varying degrees of promise. Ventral cortico-striatal brain pathways appear particularly relevant to impulsive decision making and PG. The relationships between PG and SUDs, as well as those between PG and other psychiatric disorders, may be important considerations in the development of improved prevention and treatment strategies.

See also: Compulsive Buying; Impulsive–Compulsive Sexual Behavior; Problematic Internet Use.

Further Reading

Brewer JA, Grant JE, and Potenza MN (2008) The treatment of pathological gambling. *Addictive Disorders and Their Treatment* 7: 1–14.

Brewer JA and Potenza MN (2008) The neurobiology and genetics of impulse control disorders: Relationships to drug addictions. *Biochemical Pharmacology* 75(1): 63–75.

Cunningham-Williams R and Cottler L (2001) The epidemiology of pathological gambling. *Seminars in Clinical Neuropsychiatry* 6: 155–166.

Cunningham-Williams RM, Cottler LB, Compton WM, and Spitznagel EL (1998) Taking chances: Problem gamblers and mental health disorders—results from the St. Louis Epidemiologic Catchment Area Study. *American Journal of Public Health* 88: 1093–1096.

Eisen SA, Slutske WS, Lyons MJ, *et al.* (2001) The genetics of pathological gambling. *Seminars in Clinical Neuropsychiatry* 6: 195–204.

Petry NM, Stinson FS, and Grant BF (2005) Comorbidity of DSM-IV pathological gambling and other psychiatric disorders: Results from the National Epidemiologic Survey on Alcohol and Related Conditions. *Journal of Clinical Psychiatry* 66: 564–574.

Potenza MN (2006) Should addictive disorders include non-substance-related conditions? *Addiction* 101(supplement 1): 142–151.

Potenza MN (2008) The neurobiology of pathological gambling and drug addiction: An overview and new findings. *Philosophical Transactions of the Royal Society of London. Series B, Biological Sciences* 363: 3181–3189.

Shaffer HJ, Hall MN, and Vanderbilt J (1999) Estimating the prevalence of disordered gambling behavior in the United States and Canada: A research synthesis. *American Journal of Public Health* 89: 1369–1376.

Shah KR, Eisen SA, Xian H, and Potenza MN (2005) Genetic studies of pathological gambling: A review of methodology and analyses of data from the Vietnam Era Twin (VET) Registry. *Journal of Gambling Studies* 21: 179–203.

Welte J, Barnes G, Wieczorek W, Tidwell MC, and Parker J (2001) Alcohol and gambling pathology among US adults: Prevalence, demographic patterns and comorbidity. *Journal of Studies on Alcohol* 62: 706–712.

Compulsive Buying

By A. Mueller, J.E. Mitchell, J.M. Marino, and T.W. Ertelt

Glossary

Compulsive buying disorder (CBD)—Frequent buying episodes or impulses to buy that are experienced as irresistible or senseless. The spending behavior and impulses lead to personal distress, social, marital, or occupational dysfunction, and to financial or legal problems. The excessive buying behavior does not occur exclusively during episodes of mania or hypomania.

Compulsive Buying Scale (CBS)—A well-validated seven-item screening instrument for CBD. CBS-total scores can be calculated from the responses to the seven items through a regression formula. Lower scores on the scale indicate higher levels of compulsive buying. **Compulsive hoarding**—Acquisition of and failure to discard a large number of possessions that appear to be useless. Living places are cluttered. Hoarding causes significant distress or impairment in functioning.

Impulse control disorders—A group of impulsive behaviors that have been included in the *Diagnostic and Statistical Manual,* Fourth Edition, Text Revision (DSM-IV-TR). These disorders are characterized by an inability to resist the impulse to perform an action that is harmful to one's self or others. The diagnostic category consists of the following disorders: trichotillomania, intermittent explosive disorder, pathological gambling, kleptomania, and pyromania.

Impulse-control disorders, not otherwise specified (NOS)—The NOS category comprises impulse-control disorders that do not meet the criteria for any specific impulse-control disorder or for another mental disorder having features involving high impulsivity and low impulse control.

Compulsive buying disorder (CBD) is a culturally bound excessive behavior wherein affected individuals engage in excessive buying. Historically, about one century ago, Kraepelin and Bleuler described the phenomenon termed 'oniomania' as a clinical entity in their psychiatric textbooks. Although the phenomenon has received increasing attention in both consumer and psychiatric research, it has largely been ignored in clinical practice.

Phenomenology

Compulsive buying is characterized by shopping and spending behavior that seems out of one's control, wherein unnecessary items or large numbers of items are purchased. Individuals with CBD are preoccupied with buying impulses. They shop for longer periods of time and spend more money than intended. Repeated efforts to stop the excessive buying are unsuccessful, despite the negative consequences. The shopping episodes are typically preceded by negative feelings of tension, depression, anxiety, or boredom. Shopping typically leads to a short-term improvement in affect (i.e., a sense of relief, pleasure, well-being, and power), while the long-term negative consequences of the buying behavior are largely ignored. When the buying episode ends, most individuals experience guilt and shame. Typically, the purchased items are not used, but instead are hidden, hoarded, given away, or forgotten. These maladaptive patterns are at first minimized, then rationalized or dissimulated, and eventually produce further substantial negative psychological, social, occupational, and financial consequences. Sometimes, the pathological purchasing behavior also leads to legal problems. The extent of the shopping episode (i.e., amount of time spent shopping, amount of money spent during buying episodes), the negative consequences of the consumer behavior, and the stress individuals suffer from their behavior differentiate compulsive buying as a unique psychiatric entity when compared to occasional, unnecessary purchases. The excessive shopping behavior does not occur exclusively during periods of mania or hypomania. The following case example illustrates the behavioral excess.

Case Example

Anne, a 22-year-old student, suffers from repetitive, preoccupying thoughts of buying. Her debt has increased substantially because of her purchases of clothes, decorations, and cosmetics. Anne always enjoyed shopping and while buying her new purchases she imagined how attractive she would look wearing her new clothes and how other people would admire her. Her closets are overflowing with her purchases, which for the most part she does not use. In fact, many of the items are unwrapped and still have the sales tags on them. She cannot enjoy the purchases. Instead she feels depressed, ashamed, and angry with herself because of her uncontrolled shopping habits. It frightens her that she rarely uses what she buys and can hardly remember acquiring all of the items she had. Anne bought nearly the entire clothing line of one specific brand name. Her boyfriend and her parents, who have supported her financially in the past, are ashamed and refuse to offer financial help to her. Arguments are frequent between Anne and her family because Anne hides her purchases and lies to her family about her finances. In addition, she cannot pay the rent for her apartment because of her debts. Over the last few weeks, she has tried to stay at home and avoid shopping. However, she cannot resist the urge to visit the Internet homepage of different clothing companies several times daily.

Diagnosis and Assessment

Preliminary operational criteria for CBD were based on similar DSM-III-R criteria for impulse-control, obsessive-compulsive, and substance-use disorders.

Several questionnaires and diagnostic interviews have been developed to identify CBD (Table 1). The most widely used instrument in empirical studies is the Compulsive Buying Scale (CBS). For clarification purposes, a diagnostic interview should be administered in addition to a CBD questionnaire. To measure severity and clinical change in persons with CBD, the Yale-Brown Obsessive-Compulsive Scale-Shopping Version (Y-BOCS-SV) is recommended.

Epidemiology

Current research suggests that CBD is common in maturing consumer societies. Using the CBS in a national representative sample survey, researchers estimated the United States lifetime prevalence of CBD at 5.8%. German representative studies reported a point prevalence of CBD in Germany of about 7%. It should be noted that the use of only questionnaires is a limitation in these studies, and could result in an overestimation of CBD because of a response bias. Even so these findings demonstrate the high propensity to engage in compulsive buying in population-based samples.

There is also evidence that CBD has increased in prevalence in the past few decades. In Germany, two representative population-based surveys investigating CBD were conducted 10 years apart (1991 and 2001). In the first study, 1% of the East German population and 5.1% of the West German population were identified as having CBD. Ten years later the percentages had increased, with 6.5% of the population in East Germany and 8% of the population in West Germany reporting compulsive buying.

Clinical surveys suggest that women are more frequently affected by CBD than men, with the percentages of women in treatment-seeking samples being about 90%. However, population-based studies have not confirmed this gender difference. In fact, these population-based studies have found a near equal percentage of women and men in their surveys. Given these findings, it appears that CBD may not only affect women and that other gender-related

TABLE 1 Screening instruments for compulsive buying

	Screening instruments	Authors
Questionnaires	Compulsive Buying Scale	Faber & O'Guinn (1992)
	Edwards Compulsive Buying Scale	Edwards (1993)
	Canadian Compulsive Buying Measurement Scale	Valence *et al.* (1988)
	Buying Impulsiveness Scale	Rook and Fisher (1995)
	Compulsive Acquisition Scale	Frost *et al.* (2002)
Interviews	Minnesota Impulsive Disorder Interview (MIDI)	Christenson *et al.* (1994)
	Yale-Brown Obsessive-Compulsive Scale-Shopping Version (Y-BOCS-SV)	Monahan *et al.* (1996)
	SCID-I Impulse Control Disorders	First *et al.* (1996)
	SCID-I Obessive Compulsive Spectrum Disorders (SCID-OCSD)	du Toit *et al.* (2001)

For details on reference, see Further Reading section.

factors (e.g., in propensities for treatment seeking) may influence the composition of clinical samples.

Psychiatric Comorbidity

Previous research indicated that CBD may be associated with elevated rates of *Diagnostic and Statistical Manual, Fourth Edition, Text Revision* (DSM-IV-TR) Axis I disorders. Comparison of treatment-seeking individuals with CBD in Germany and the United States showed that almost all participants in both samples met criteria for at least one lifetime Axis I disorder. A few controlled trials were conducted comparing psychiatric comorbidity among individuals with and without CBD. Some researchers have reported elevated frequencies of lifetime mood disorders among those with CBD. Others have found higher frequencies of lifetime anxiety, substance-use, binge-eating, and impulse-control disorders. Another study described only substance dependence as occurring more frequently among patients with CBD. In a German study, treatment-seeking women with CBD showed significantly higher frequencies of affective, anxiety, and eating disorders compared to a nonclinical control group.

Two studies have assessed personality disorders among persons with CBD. One study found that 59% of 46 compulsive buyers met DSM-III-R criteria for at least one

personality disorder. The most frequently identified Axis II disorders were obsessive-compulsive, avoidant, and borderline personality disorders. A second study reported that, compared to community controls, individuals with CBD presented with a significantly higher frequency of any personality disorder (73%), most commonly avoidant, depressive, obsessive-compulsive, and borderline personality disorder. Further, 23% of the CBD sample described at least one further impulse-control disorder, most frequently intermittent explosive disorder.

A strong link has been observed between CBD and compulsive hoarding. Previous findings have indicated that many patients with CBD suffer from high levels of compulsive hoarding. In one investigation, it was observed that about two-thirds of a treatment-seeking CBD sample reported substantial hoarding. In addition, CBD patients exhibiting hoarding reported more severe compulsive buying and obsessive-compulsive symptoms and presented more frequently with psychiatric comorbidity, especially current affective, anxiety, and eating disorders.

Because of the high frequencies of psychiatric comorbidity, there exists some skepticism about the recognition of CBD as an independent psychiatric entity. Alternatively, CBD could be conceptualized as an epiphenomenon of other psychiatric disorders. Nonconsideration of CBD as an independent psychiatric condition may result in further neglect and minimization of this disorder in clinical

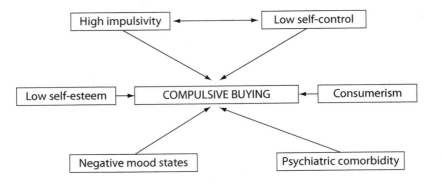

Figure 1 Proposed factors influencing CBD

practice. Clinical experiences suggest that CBT typically does not resolve with the successful treatment of comorbid disorders. Because of the psychiatric comorbidity, patients with CBD represent a very heterogeneous patient sample. In summary, these findings could be interpreted to support the idea that a subtyping approach might be useful in classifying CBD. The development of specific therapeutic interventions for those with CBD who also report comorbid psychiatric disorders may also be indicated.

Etiology

The etiology of CBD appears multifactorial, and models have been suggested based on psychological, social, neurobiological, and cultural influences. Patients with CBD report urges to buy, preoccupation with buying and shopping impulses, and in general increased impulsivity in the sense of acting without thinking. In addition, low self-regulatory resource availability and low self-control are associated with CBD. The negative consequences of CBD are often not considered by those affected. Furthermore, a close association between negative mood states and buying has been found. Using as a model short-term positive and negative reinforcement, compulsive buying is used as a way of escaping from problems and to relieve negative mood states. Individuals with CBD suffer from low self-esteem, and they often describe themselves mostly as socially anxious, depressed, and having decision-making problems.

Consumerism and money attitudes appear to play a key role in the development and maintenance of CBD. For example, younger age and higher materialistic values are associated with compulsive buying. The relationship between narcissism and compulsive consumption appears

to be mediated by both low impulse control and high materialism values, and credit card use moderates the effect of money attitudes on CBD. These considerations involving factors influencing the development and maintenance of CBD are schematized in Figure 1.

In addition to psychological, social, and cultural influences, the biological model posits serotonergic, dopaminergic, and opioidergic contributions and a role for the brain reward systems. Currently, there is no direct evidence to support these neurobiological hypotheses, and it should be noted that the high comorbidity could influence the specificity of future neurobiological findings.

CBD is probably a culture-specific excessive behavior that occurs in industrialized countries. Technological developments, including television and Internet shopping, allow individuals to buy a vast array of products rapidly. In this cultural context, some authors warn against the labeling and medicalization of the CBD. Indeed, such an approach minimizes the clinical observations that individuals with CBD may suffer significantly from their shopping and buying behaviors, and do not seem to be able to easily stop the behavior. To understand CBD, and to create and validate etiological models and disorder-specific treatment strategies, both the psychological and consumer-research approaches should be considered.

Considerations on Classification

The appropriate method of categorizing CBD continues to be debated. According to the preliminary diagnostic criteria, the inclusion of CBD in DSM-IV and ICD-10 as an "impulse control disorder not otherwise specified" is preferred. Some researchers have attempted to examine the link between CBD and obsessive-compulsive spectrum disorders (OCSDs) or addictive disorders. At present, there is a suggestion to create a category called 'behavioral and substance addictions' that would include both excessive behavioral disorders and substance-use disorders. The commonalities and a high comorbidity with substance-use disorders, the craving to buy, the sense of lack of self-control, the needs to spend increasing amounts of time shopping or spend increasing amounts of money in order to achieve the desired feelings (i.e., tolerance), and shopping-/buying-related withdrawal symptoms all support the categorization of CBD as an addiction. The similarities in phenomenological features, their courses, and their psychological and social consequences also cannot be ignored. In our experience, however, there exist crucial differences between substance addictions and excessive behaviors. A real dose-increase or tolerance ('more and more/more often/more expensive') is seen only in some of the CBD patients treated in our CBT studies. With regard to withdrawal symptoms, the patients describe negative feelings like depressive symptoms, pressure, and restlessness, if they begin to normalize their buying behavior. Detailed behavior analyses show, however, that these negative feelings are usually a matter of the emergence of negative mood states which had been suppressed through shopping behavior. The extent to which these reflect differences between CBD and substance-use disorders requires direct examination.

Treatment

Medication

A few case reports and successful open-label medication trials were reported using antidepressant, anxiolytic, mood stabilizer, anticonvulsant, and opioid antagonist drugs. Some smaller controlled trials examined the efficacies and tolerabilities of fluvoxamine, citalopram, and escitalopram. These trials have not found superiority for these selective serotonin-reuptake inhibitors over placebo. However, the results are limited by small sample sizes, high dropout rates, and placebo-response rates ranging up to 60%. In summary, data do not support the sole use of any one medication in the treatment of patients with CBD at this time.

Psychotherapy

Some authors have described successful individual psychodynamic psychotherapy treatment and cue exposure plus response prevention for patients with CBD. Moreover, several specific group therapy and self-help approaches have been described.

The effectiveness of disorder-specific, manualized, group CBT was supported in two controlled psychotherapy studies. In both studies, the treatment was specifically aimed at interrupting and controlling the problematic buying behavior, establishing appropriate purchasing patterns, identifying and restructuring maladaptive thoughts and feelings associated with shopping and buying, developing healthy coping skills and communication patterns, and implementing relapse-prevention techniques. In addition, more general sessions about self-esteem, stress management, and problem solving were included. Group participants were expected to complete homework assignments and read and review manual materials regularly as assigned. The psychotherapy treatment focused both on current factors that maintain the excessive buying behavior and on strategies for controlling buying problems. Treatment lasted 10–12 weeks with one 90-min group session per week. Groups were conducted with 5–8 participants. The treatment manuals have been described in detail elsewhere. Further research is needed to determine whether specific individual, group, or family interventions have the most substantial impact on helping individuals with CBD.

Conclusions

CBD is a relatively prevalent disorder, particularly in developed societies. Individuals with CBD often experience significant personal distress and interference in areas of life functioning, including within financial and interpersonal domains. More research is needed into the biological basis of the disorder and more effective preventive and therapeutic strategies.

See also: Depression; Drug Addiction; Impulsive–Compulsive Sexual Behavior; Intermittent Explosive Disorder; Kleptomania; Pathological Gambling; Problematic Internet Use; Pyromania; Trichotillomania (Compulsive Hair Pulling) and Compulsive Skin Picking.

Further Reading

Black DW, Gabel J, Hansen J, and Schlosser S (2000) A double-blind comparison of fluvoxamine versus placebo in the treatment of compulsive buying disorder. *Annals of Clinical Psychiatry* 12: 205–211.

Black DW, Repertinger S, Gaffney GR, and Gabel J (1998) Family history and psychiatric comorbidity in persons with compulsive buying preliminary findings. *American Journal of Psychiatry* 155: 960–963.

Christenson GA, Faber RJ, de Zwaan M, *et al.* (1994) Compulsive buying: Descriptive characteristics and psychiatric comorbidity. *Journal of Clinical Psychiatry* 55: 5–11.

du Toit PL, van Kradenburg J, Niehaus D, and Stein DJ (2001) Comparison of obsessive-compulsive disorder patients with and without comorbid putative obsessive-compulsive spectrum disorders using a structural clinical interview. *Comprehensive Psychiatry* 42: 291–300.

Edwards EA (1993) Development of a new scale for measuring compulsive buying behavior. *Financial Counseling and Planning* 4: 67–84.

Faber RJ and O'Guinn TC (1992) A clinical screener for compulsive buying. *Journal of Consumer Research* 19: 459–469.

First MB, Spitzer RL, Gibbon M, and Williams JBW (1996) *Structured Clinical Interview for DSM-IV Axis I Disorders (SCID).* Washington, DC: American Psychiatric Press.

Frost RO, Steketee G, and Williams L (2002) Compulsive buying, compulsive hoarding and obsessive compulsive disorder. *Behavior Therapy* 33: 201–214.

Koran LM, Faber RJ, Aboujoude E, Large MD, and Serpe RT (2006) Estimated prevalence of compulsive buying behavior in the United States. *American Journal of Psychiatry* 163: 1806–1812.

McElroy SL, Keck PE, Pope HG, Smith JMR, and Strakowski SM (1994) Compulsive buying: A report of 20 cases. *Journal of Clinical Psychiatry* 55: 242–248.

Miltenberger RG, Redlin J, Crosby R, *et al.* (2003) Direct and retrospective assessment of factors contributing to compulsive buying. *Journal of Behavior Therapy and Experimental Psychiatry* 34: 1–9.

Mitchell JE, Burgard M, Faber R, Crosby RD, and de Zwaan M (2006) Cognitive behavioural therapy for compulsive buying disorder. *Behaviour Research and Therapy* 44: 1859–1865.

Monahan P, Black DW, and Gabel J (1996) Reliability and validity of a scale to measure change in persons with compulsive buying. *Journal of Psychiatric Research* 64: 59–67.

Mueller A, Mueller U, Albert P, Mertens C, Silbermann A, Mitchell JE, and de Zwaan M (2007) Compulsive hoarding in a compulsive buying sample. *Behaviour Research and Therapy* 45: 2754–2763.

Mueller A, Mueller U, Silbermann A, Reinecker H, Bleich S, Mitchell JE, and de Zwaan M (2008) A randomized, controlled trial of group cognitive behavioral therapy for compulsive buying disorder: Posttreatment and 6-month follow-up results. *Journal of Clinical Psychiatry* 69: 1131–1138.

Neuner M, Raab G, and Reisch L (2005) Compulsive buying in maturing consumer societies: An empirical re-inquiry. *Journal of Economic Psychology* 26: 509–522.

Ninan PT, McElroy SL, Kane CP, *et al.* (2000) Placebo-controlled study of fluvoxamine in the treatment of patients with compulsive buying. *Journal of Clinical Psychopharmacology* 20: 362–366.

Rook DW and Fisher RJ (1995) Normative influences on impulsive buying behavior. *Journal of Consumer Research* 22: 305–313.

Schlosser S, Black DW, Repertinger S, and Freet D (1994) Compulsive buying. Demography, phenomenology, and comorbidity in 46 subjects. *General Hospital Psychiatry* 116: 205–212.

Valence G, d'Astous A, and Fortier L (1988) Compulsive buying: Concept and measurement. *Journal of Consumer Policy* 11: 419–433.

Impulsive–Compulsive Sexual Behavior

By A. Allen and E. Hollander

Glossary

Hyperactive sexual desire disorder—An interest or involvement in normative sexual activity that is so excessive as to cause distress or impairment in functioning.

Hyperphagia—Excessive appetite and excessive consumption of food.

Hypersexuality—Excessive interest or involvement in sexual activity. It is synonymous with hyperphilia.

Hypogonadism—Inadequate functioning of the testes or ovaries resulting in impaired sexual development or withdrawal effects (e.g., premature menopause) in adults and/or defective egg or sperm development leading to impaired fertility.

Nonparaphilic sexual addiction—Sexual thoughts, urges, and behaviors of normative content (but) that are unusually intense and persistent and are associated with distress or impaired functioning. Nonparaphilic sexual addiction (often simply referred to as sexual addiction) has been conceived of as a form of behavioral addiction.

Paraphilia—Powerful and persistent sexual urges, fantasies, or behaviors that involve: nonhuman objects; the suffering or humiliation of oneself or one's partner; or children or other nonconsenting individuals.

Sexual fetishism—Sexually arousing fantasies, sexual urges, or sexual behaviors focused on nonliving objects or on body parts not conventionally viewed as being sexual in nature, considered a paraphilia.

Impulsive–compulsive sexual behavior refers to sexual thoughts, urges, and behaviors that are extremely difficult to resist. These thoughts and behaviors are generally divided into two types, paraphilias (which involve socially deviant sexuality) and more conventional but excessive sexuality. The paraphilias are better researched and better understood; they involve sexual interests that focus on nonhuman objects, children, or other nonconsenting persons, or the suffering or humiliation of oneself or one's partner. Paraphilas are a recognized category of disorders in the current *Diagnostic and Statistical Manual of Mental Disorders,* Fourth Edition, Text Revision (DSM-IV-TR) and include disorders such as pedophilia, fetishism, exhibitionism, voyeurism, sexual sadism, and masochism among others.

The term impulsive–compulsive sexual behavior, the focus of this article, is more often used to refer to sexual thoughts, urges, and behaviors that are normative in content but occur with such frequency or intensity that they are distressing or cause impairment in functioning. Other terms used to describe this problem include nonparaphilia-related sexual disorders or nonparaphilic sexual addictions, to differentiate them from the paraphilias. Terms such as compulsive sexual behaviors, hyperactive sexual desire disorder, hyperphilia, hypersexuality, sexual addiction, and out-of-control sexual behavior have also been used to describe this disorder. We use the term impulsive–compulsive sexual behavior throughout this article. Although impulsive–compulsive sexual behavior, under one name or another, has been

A. Allen and E. Hollander, "Impulsive-compulsive sexual behavior," from the *Encyclopedia of Behavioral Neuroscience: Volume 2*, George F. Koob, Michel Le Moal and Richard F. Thompson, eds., pp. 94–99. Published by Academic Press, 2010. Copyright by Elsevier Science and Technology Books. Permission to reprint granted by the rights holder.

discussed in the scientific literature since the early 1800s, there has been little rigorous research on the topic, so our understanding is limited. This category is not designated as a specific disorder in the DSM-IV-TR; however, if an official diagnosis is needed, impulsive–compulsive sexual behaviors can be classified as impulse control disorders, not otherwise specified; or as sexual disorders, not otherwise specified.

Since it is not a formally recognized disorder, there are no official diagnostic criteria for impulsive–compulsive sexual behavior. However, there is some general agreement among experts. Impulsive–compulsive sexual behavior is operationally defined similarly to the paraphilias and to pathological gambling. The impulsive–compulsive sexual behavior diagnosis requires recurrent and intense sexually arousing fantasies, sexual urges, and sexual behaviors with a focus on normative sexual behaviors. It has been proposed that the behavior must have been present for a minimum duration of 6 months. The proposed diagnosis also requires standard DSM criteria of severity (frequency and/or intensity severe enough to cause clinically significant distress or impairment in social, occupational, or other important areas of functioning) and specificity (not due to a medical condition, medication or substance use, or better accounted for by another Axis I or II disorder).

Although the sexual behaviors themselves are normative, it is their excessive and poorly controlled nature that leads to serious problems such as exposure to human immunodeficiency virus and other sexually transmitted diseases, job loss, legal consequences, problems in maintaining romantic relationships or marriage, and unwanted pregnancies. Eli Coleman described seven subtypes of impulsive–compulsive sexual behavior: compulsive cruising and multiple partners, compulsive fixation on an unattainable partner, compulsive autoeroticism (masturbation), compulsive use of erotica, compulsive use of the Internet for sexual purposes, compulsive multiple love relationships, and compulsive sexuality in a relationship. Studies have shown that the most common impulsive–compulsive sexual behaviors are promiscuity, masturbation, pornography dependence, and phone sex, but the use of the Internet for sexual purposes certainly may be increasing.

Based on Alfred Kinsey's concept of total sexual outlet (TSO), the total number of orgasms achieved per week by any means is often used to indicate severity of impulsive–compulsive sexual behavior, with a TSO of 7 per week persistently for at least 6 months usually considered the minimum for the diagnosis. Although a TSO of 7 may seem low as a criterion for hypersexualty, a TSO of 1–3 is typical of males in the general population and most estimates place the percent of males having a TSO of 7 or more at 3–7.5%, though estimates have been as high as 15%. Recall that diagnostic clinical and research criteria also require that the sexual behavior, thoughts, and/or urges need to cause distress or functional impairment.

TSO or the total time spent in sexual activities overall are considered by many to be better measures to use to quantify impulsive–compulsive sexual behavior, as compared to the frequency or time spent in specific kinds of sexual behaviors; however, the amount of time spent seeking sexual activities can also be considerable and problematic. Studies of males with impulsive–compulsive sexual behavior or paraphilias found that the large majority of both groups have a TSO ≥7 per week and that the groups do not differ substantially from one another. Males with impulsive–compulsive sexual behavior spend 1–2 h a day occupied by their sexual urges, fantasies, or activities.

Most commonly, impulsive–compulsive sexual behavior is conceptualized either as an impulse control disorder, perhaps on the obsessive–compulsive spectrum, or as a behavioral addiction. Phenomenologically, at least initially, there is an impulsive component (pleasure, arousal, or gratification) at behavioral onset, and a compulsive component that leads to the persistence of the behavior, thus, the phenomenology can fit with either conceptualization. In the next version of the *Diagnostic and Statistical Manual of Mental Disorders* (the Fifth Edition; DSM-V), impulsive–compulsive sexual behavior may be recognized as a specific disorder. One new category under consideration for DSM-V into which impulsive–compulsive sexual behavior may be included is the behavioral and substance addictions. This category could include the disorders currently in the 'substance-related disorders' category as well as several putative impulse-control disorders (e.g., gambling addiction, sexual addiction, shopping addiction, and Internet addiction).

Epidemiology and Demographics

There have been no systematic epidemiological studies of impulsive–compulsive sexual behavior. Based on clinical samples, the estimate is that it affects 5–6% of the general population.

Impulsive–compulsive sexual behavior is believed to be approximately 3 times more common in males than females; the paraphilias are rarely diagnosed in females except for sexual masochism, which is about 20 times more common in males than females. Virtually all research on these disorders has been conducted among males and little is known about impulsive–compulsive sexual behavior in females. It may be that the disorder presents differently in males than in females. Some consider females who fantasize about sex and seem to be addicted to romantic relationships to be suffering from impulsive–compulsive sexual behavior, a difference being that males are focused on the physical aspects of sexuality, while females focus more on the relationship.

It seems likely that impulsive–compulsive sexual behaviors, such as paraphilias, begin by late adolescence and peak between ages 20 and 30. Although the severity may wax and wane, it may often be chronic. The typical outpatient in treatment for impulsive–compulsive sexual behaviors is a white, college-educated, employed man, with a middle-class income.

Individuals with impulsive–compulsive sexual behavior have a higher-than-expected rate of childhood sexual abuse; they differ from those with paraphilias in that the latter have a significantly higher rate of childhood physical abuse. Those with paraphilias have also often completed fewer years of education and are more likely to be unemployed or on disability.

Differential Diagnosis

Impulsive–compulsive sexual behavior may be a symptom of medical conditions (such as traumatic brain injury, stroke, epilepsy, and other conditions noted later in this article); in addition, substance intoxication, manic episodes, and schizophrenia may present with impaired judgment and diminished impulse control that may result in excessive sexual behavior. Onset in conjunction with an injury or change in health status, or at later than typical age, should be carefully evaluated for potential contributions from medical conditions.

Sexual obsessions can be a presentation of obsessive compulsive disorder (OCD) but can be distinguished from the obsessions that are part of impulsive–compulsive sexual behavior in several ways. Sexual obsessions in OCD are characterized by being ego dystonic and morally repugnant; the sexual thoughts induce anxiety and often include uncertainty as to whether the feared sexual behavior may have actually been committed without the patient knowing it. In OCD, the sexual behaviors are not carried out and the compulsive behaviors related to these obsessions are not generally sexual. Rather, OCD patients frequently avoid specific situations or people in order to prevent the feared sexual acts from occurring and they may also perform rituals that are repetitive behaviors of a nonsexual nature meant to prevent or undo the distressing sexual thoughts or fears (such as by confessing to acts that didn't actually occur).

In addition, OCD rituals are not pleasurable activities engaged in for their own sake; rather, they are neutral or often irritating and unpleasant behaviors that are engaged in to reduce anxiety. In contrast, impulsive–compulsive sexual behaviors generally have an element of pleasure, at least initially, although they may lose their pleasurable quality over time; in this regard, they are more similar to addictions and to impulse control disorders such as pathological gambling.

Comorbidities

Individuals with impulsive–compulsive sexual behaviors tend to have multiple additional Axis I disorders. A majority of these males have a lifetime diagnosis of depression, and substantial minorities have lifetime diagnoses of substance abuse, anxiety disorders (especially social phobia), and impulse control disorders (such as pathological gambling, compulsive buying, kleptomania, trichotillomania, pyromania, compulsive exercise, and intermittent explosive disorder). Interestingly, the major comorbidity difference between males with impulsive–compulsive sexual behavior and those with paraphilias is childhood attention deficit hyperactivity disorder (ADHD) (with corresponding ratios of approximately 1:6 vs. as many as 1:2, respectively).

By definition, those with impulsive–compulsive sexual behavior do not also have paraphilias; however, a majority of individuals with paraphilias also have impulsive–compulsive sexual behaviors; a majority report compulsive masturbation and notable minorities report promiscuity and pornography dependence.

Note that these individuals are not necessarily more ill than those with other psychiatric disorders; they simply differ from the general population in the pattern just described. Thus, patients with impulsive–compulsive sexual behavior should be screened for depression, anxiety disorders, other impulse control disorders, and substance abuse.

Neuroanatomical Features

Most knowledge of what brain structures may be involved in aberrant sexual behavior has come from animal research and from studies of traumatic brain injury and disease processes in humans. As with most complex human behavior, it has become clear from this and other research that neural circuits are as or more important than specific structures or locations. Two circuits most clearly implicated in human sexual behavior are the frontal-striatal and the temporo-limbic circuits. Some conditions can affect either circuit depending on the disease locus; these include traumatic brain injury, stroke, seizures, and dementias. Other conditions may primarily affect only one of these circuits.

Fronto-striatal abnormalities have been linked to increased sexual desire but this seems to be due to general disinhibition rather than sexuality specifically. For example, there are many reports of hypersexuality following traumatic brain injury to frontal regions. Although disinhibition is one common consequence of frontal lesions, not all frontal lesions will result in hypersexuality, and its occurrence cannot be predicted at this time based on the injury site or severity. Likewise, in multiple sclerosis, cases of hypersexuality have occurred with frontal lesions, but those patients may have also had lesions elsewhere. Similarly, hypersexuality may occur in dementias that affect this circuit or in epilepsy with frontal seizures. Striatal disease can also result in hypersexuality (e.g., Huntington's disease, although hyposexuality is more frequent in this disorder).

The frontal lobe is an interesting candidate for a role in impulsive–compulsive sexual behavior because, in addition to being involved in impulse control in general, the orbital frontal cortex is specifically implicated in social cognition, decision making, working memory, and emotional processing, particularly in deficits in recognition of emotional expressions and relative insensitivity to potential consequences. The prefrontal cortex is also critical to the acquisition of moral and social knowledge; injuries in this brain region during childhood have been associated with limitations in this knowledge and deficits in moral reasoning. Injuries that occur after this knowledge is acquired will generally leave the knowledge base intact, but the patient may be unable to behave in accordance with this knowledge.

The single condition most associated with hypersexuality, Kluver–Bucy syndrome, seems to be related to temporo-limbic circuit dysfunction. It results most often from lesions in the amygdala, a temporal lobe structure, but can also result if there is a disruption of the temporo-limbic circuits. Kluver–Bucy syndrome has many symptoms but two of particular interest here, hypersexuality and hyperphagia, may reflect a loss of the ability to discriminate appropriate objects rather than an increase in drive, *per se*. Kluver–Bucy syndrome can result from many different disease processes, including Alzheimer's disease, adrenoleukodystrophy, anoxia or ischemia, carbon monoxide intoxication, herpes simplex encephalitis, limbic encephalitis, multicentric glioblastoma multiforme, porphyria, progressive subcortical gliosis, Rhett's syndrome, systemic lupus erythematosus, trauma, and temporal lobectomies. Temporal lobe epilepsy and temporal lobe resection treatment of epilepsy have been related to changes in sexuality. The amygdala has been found to be a focal structure in emotion processing, that is where stimuli are given their emotional and motivational significance. Thus, if the amygdala is damaged, objects may lose their prior emotional significance.

It has been theorized that impulsive–compulsive sexual behavior may function similarly to substance addictions, that is, the intense, excessive sexual behavior may bring about changes to neural circuitry that may then perpetuate the behavior, just as the addictive substances may cause changes in neural circuitry.

Neurochemical Features

Strong biological influences are apparent in human sexual functioning, notably on the very basic phases: sexual desire, arousal, and orgasm. Endocrine, neurotransmitter, and neuropeptide influences on these phases have been specifically identified. However, there are also clear environmental/learned influences on sexual desire and behavior, and the relationship between these and biological factors is complex.

Among the endocrine factors that have been implicated, the androgens, in particular, play a role in sexual interest and activity in both males and females. Although there is a relationship between testosterone levels and the frequency of sexual thoughts in adolescent males, in adult males there seems to be no such relationship within a wide range of normal testosterone levels. In addition, hypogonadal and castrated males rapidly lose sexual interest, and this is reversed with testosterone administration. Similarly, females experience a decline in sexual interest as testosterone levels decrease, such as with natural or induced menopause. However, in females, estrogen has little effect on sexual interest while estrogens and progesterone seem to have an inhibiting effect on male sexual interest.

The monoamines (serotonin, dopamine, and norepinephrine) are considered important for human sexual functioning and there is reason to believe that hypersexuality may result from dysregulation of these monoamines. These neurotransmitters modulate sexual motivation. In that sexual side effects are associated with certain medications (antidepressants, psychostimulants, and neuroleptics), the neurotransmitter systems that they target influence sexual motivation and behavior. It has yet to be proven, however, that the monoamines are specifically involved in hypersexuality. Several relevant neurotransmitters are discussed below.

Serotonin

The role of serotonin in sexual functioning is complex and not yet fully understood. Activation of some receptors, such as 5-HT_2, may impair functioning while activation of other receptors, such as 5-HT_{1A}, may facilitate functioning. As noted earlier, medications that enhance central serotonin neurotransmission have dose-dependent side effects, including decreased desire and difficulties with arousal, although the most common sexual side effects are delayed ejaculation and delayed or absent orgasm. The importance of serotonin in sexual motivation and behavior is evident from animal research and records of human injury and disease. In addition, serotonin dysfunction has also been found in a number of other psychiatric disorders characterized by impaired impulse control (e.g., pathological gambling and substance abuse); this may reflect impaired frontal inhibition, which may result in a diminished ability to control desires. Impaired impulse control may result from overstimulated drive and/or impaired inhibition or reward processing.

Dopamine

Dopamine is important in several aspects of male sexuality ranging from basic sexual functioning (e.g., seminal emission and erectile function) to sexual arousal and motivation. The exact role of dopamine in female sexual behavior is less clear. In general, alterations in dopamine functioning may be associated with intense urges that override considerations of the consequences in impulse control disorders. As with serotonin, evidence for the role of dopamine in sexual interest and behavior comes from animal research as well as from observation of naturally occurring human injury and disease. For example, hypersexuality may result when Parkinson's disease is treated with dopaminergic medication. Dopamine is a key part of mammalian reward systems. Certain behaviors such as gambling and sexual arousal may result in a release of dopamine which may then lead to feelings of intense pleasure. Consequently, the dopamine system has been proposed as an important component of behavioral and chemical addictions.

Pharmacological Treatment

No pharmacological agents have been Food and Drug Administration (FDA)-approved for the treatment of impulsive–compulsive sexual behavior, and research on these treatments is limited with no convincing controlled trials in the literature. Given the absence of research and based on the knowledge regarding treatment of other impulse control disorders, it is important to consider prominent symptoms and comorbidities in choosing a pharmacological approach.

Considerable research has been performed investigating pharmacotherapy and medical treatments of the paraphilias; however, these treatments are not necessarily appropriate for impulsive–compulsive sexual behavior. Notably, surgical and pharmacological techniques to lower testosterone levels do reduce paraphilic preoccupations, urges, and activities, but may be too drastic and risky to be used in impulsive–compulsive sexual behavior treatment.

Although there are no definitive controlled trials, one placebo-controlled trial, open-label studies, and case reports suggest that serotonin reuptake inhibitors (SRIs) are effective in reducing the symptoms of impulsive–compulsive sexual behavior and/or paraphilias. The SRIs reported to be effective in impulsive–compulsive sexual behavior include citalopram, clomipramine, fluoxetine, sertraline, and venlafaxine; however, there is no evidence that the SRIs differ from one another in efficacy. In clinical practice, SRIs are one of the first-line treatments for both impulsive–compulsive sexual behavior and paraphilias. They were initially tried in the hope that their sexual side effects, especially decreased libido but also impaired sexual functioning, would be helpful in impulsive–compulsive sexual behavior. The results have been better than expected in that reduction in impulsive–compulsive sexual behavior symptoms may be a result of their anti-obsessional effects causing a decrease in thoughts and urges, rather than the sexual side effects, which seem to be independent. The best treatment would suppress disturbing and out-of-control sexual drives and behaviors, while leaving other aspects of sexuality intact.

The sexual side effects of selective SRIs (SSRIs) can sometimes be reduced by titrating the dose. In some cases, nefazodone may be worth trying since it has a lower rate of sexual side effects than other SSRIs and there are some reports that it is effective in ameliorating impulsive–compulsive sexual behavior; however, the possibility of liver abnormalities must be considered. In line with the notion of using comorbidities and symptoms to choose a treatment for impulsive–compulsive sexual behavior, SSRIs can be an excellent treatment because depression and anxiety disorders are common comorbidities and SSRIs are effective treatments for these disorders.

Although an open-label trial of divalproex sodium showed no change in paraphilic symptoms, there is some evidence for the use of mood stabilizers (such as carbamazepine, lamotrigine, topiramate, and valproic acid) in impulsive–compulsive sexual behavior. They have been shown to be effective in some other impulse control disorders, such as pathological gambling. These mood stabilizing agents should be considered in patients who are identified as bipolar or have prominent impulsivity. These drugs can also be used in combination with SRIs.

In line with the conceptualization of impulsive–compulsive sexual behavior as a behavioral addiction, if the SSRIs or mood stabilizers are not effective, opioid antagonists such as naltrexone and nalmafene may be helpful.

Case reports have noted other agents as successful in treating impulsive–compulsive sexual behavior or paraphilias; these include buspirone, tricyclic antidepressants, and atypical antipsychotics. Particular subgroups may benefit from adjunctive or other treatment. Patients with ADHD and impulsive–compulsive sexual behavior have been successfully treated with SSRIs augmented with the psychostimulant methylphenidate.

As noted, other agents widely used in the treatment of criminal sexual offenders, such as pedophiles, are often considered too drastic for most cases of impulsive–compulsive sexual behavior. These include anti-androgen treatment like medroxyprogesterone acetate and gonadotropin-releasing hormone. These agents may completely eliminate sexual interest.

Since benzodiazepines can be disinhibiting and increase impulsive behavior, they are generally not recommended for impulsive–compulsive sexual behavior, although they can be helpful in emergency situations.

In summary, when selecting a pharmacological treatment, it is probably best to refine the decision based on comorbidity and prominent symptoms. For individuals with depression or anxiety or prominent obsessive symptoms, an SSRI might be a good choice for a first trial. For those with a more addictive symptom profile, opiate antagonists might be tried. Those on the bipolar spectrum or with prominent impulsivity might be started on mood stabilizers. Patients with prominent ADHD symptoms might benefit from stimulants.

Psychological Treatment

Very little research has been conducted on psychological treatments for impulsive–compulsive sexual behavior. Most psychological treatments that have been studied in paraphilias might be appropriately applied to impulsive–compulsive sexual behavior. In addition, psychological treatment approaches used with behavioral and substance addictions show promise for impulsive–compulsive sexual behavior. Based on these two traditions, the most promising treatments might be 12-step programs, cognitive–behavioral therapy and motivational interviewing.

Treatments based on 12-step programs are widely used; these include Alcoholics Anonymous-type groups such as Sexaholics Anonymous, Sex Addicts Anonymous, Sex and Love Addicts Anonymous, Sexual Recovery Anonymous, and Sexual Compulsives Anonymous. As with Alcoholics Anonymous, there are also groups for partners and families of those with impulsive–compulsive sexual behavior (co-dependents of sex addicts and S-Anon international family groups). In addition, formal inpatient and outpatient treatment programs also incorporate this approach.

Cognitive behavioral therapy (CBT) is often used. CBT can help individuals identify the triggers for their sexual thoughts, urges, and behavior. It can be useful in training them to manage stress, improve their coping skills, and managing symptoms of depression and anxiety; all these applications of CBT can decrease patients' susceptibility to their impulsive–compulsive sexual behavior. In general, CBT may also be very useful in preventing relapse. There is some evidence that combinations of CBT and 12-step approaches are effective in reducing impulsive–compulsive sexual behavior.

Other similar disorders, such as pathological gambling and substance addictions, respond to 12-step, CBT and motivational interviewing approaches so these approaches seem promising for impulsive–compulsive sexual behavior.

Conclusions

Impulsive–compulsive sexual behavior may be a serious, chronic, and difficult-to-treat disorder with public health and societal consequences. It is similar in many ways to substance addictions and addiction-like disorders such as pathological gambling. Although there has been little research to date on its pathogenesis, some promising treatment options are currently available, including pharmacological and psychotherapeutic approaches. The condition can be difficult to treat and may be even more challenging than similar disorders mentioned since sex is a basic human drive.

See also: Compulsive Buying; Pathological Gambling; Problematic Internet Use.

Further Reading

Allen A and Hollander E (2005) Sexual compulsions. In: Hollander E and Stein DJ (eds.) *Clinical Manual of Impulse Control Disorders*, pp. 87–114. Arlington, VA: American Psychiatric Publishing.

Black D (2000) The epidemiology and phenomenology of compulsive sexual behavior. *CNS Spectrums* 5: 26–35; 72.

Coleman E, Raymond N, and McBean A (2003) Assessment and treatment of compulsive sexual behavior. *Minnesota Medicine* 86: 42–47.

Kafka MP (2000) Pharmacologic treatments for nonparaphilic compulsive sexual behaviors. *CNS Spectrums* 5: 49–59.

Kafka MP and Hennen J (1999) The paraphilia-related disorders: An empirical investigation of nonparaphilic hypersexuality disorders in outpatient males. *Journal of Sex and Marital Therapy* 25: 305–319.

Kafka MP and Hennen J (2002) A DSM-IV Axis I comorbidity study of males (n = 120) with paraphilias and paraphilia-related disorders. *Sex Abuse* 14: 349–366.

Kinsey AC, Pomeroy WB, and Martin CE (1948) *Sexual Behavior in the Human Male*. Philadelphia, PA: Saunders.

Martin PR and Petry NM (2005) Are non substance related addictions really addictions. *American Journal on Addictions* 14: 1–7.

Raymond NC, Coleman E, and Miner MH (2003) Psychiatric comorbidity and compulsive/impulsive traits in compulsive sexual behavior. *Comprehensive Psychiatry* 5: 370–380.

Stein DJ, Hugo F, Oosthuizen P, Hawkridge SM, and van Heerden B (2000) Neuropsychiatry of hypersexuality. *CNS Spectrums* 5: 36–46.

Sussman S (2007) Sexual addiction among teens: A review. *Sexual Addiction and Compulsivity* 14: 257–278.

Relevant Websites

http://www.mayoclinic.com—Mayo Clinic.

http://www.sa.org—Sexaholics anonymous.

http://sash.net—The Society for the Advancement of Sexual Health.

Problematic Internet Use

By T. Lin and M.N. Potenza

Glossary

Impulse-control disorders—As defined in the fourth-edition text revision of the *Diagnostic and Statistical Manual* (DSM-IV-TR), these are disorders of impulse control that are not categorized in groupings of other major psychiatric disorders. The essential feature of impulse-control disorders is the failure to resist an impulse, drive, or temptation to perform an act that is harmful to the person or to others. The individual with the disorder typically feels an increasing sense of tension or arousal before committing the act and then experiences pleasure, gratification, or relief at the time of committing the act.

Impulsivity—Impulsivity has been defined as a predisposition toward rapid, unplanned reactions to internal or external stimuli with diminished regard to the negative consequences of these reactions to the impulsive individual or to others.

Intermediary phenotype—A measurable characteristic, one that may not be immediately obvious (e.g., impulsivity), that may be closer to biological phenomena than other phenotypes (e.g., diagnostic categories used in mental healthcare settings). Intermediary phenotypes may facilitate the identification of clinically relevant genes and the elucidation of their functions. An intermediary phenotype can involve a simpler behavior or an underlying endocrine or neural mechanism.

Internet-enabled sexual behavior (IESB)—Alternatively termed Internet sex and cybersex, it encompasses a wide range of sexual behaviors expressed on the Internet, including Internet pornography (solitary), on-line sexually charged relationships (bidirectional), and their variants such as webcam strip-shows and role-playing sex games.

Massively multiplayer on-line games (MMOGs)—These encompass a genre of computer games in which hundreds or thousands of players can cooperate and compete with one another in the same game in real time. They typically feature at least one persistent virtual world, and typically require players to invest large amounts of time.

Problematic Internet use—Also termed Internet addiction, pathological Internet use, and compulsive-impulsive Internet-use disorder, this term describes poorly controlled or excessive use of the Internet that is associated with significant psychosocial and functional impairments.

Time distortion—It describes an individual's experience that time seems to pass slower or faster than it actually does. It is revealed by the discrepancy between the perceived length of time and the measured amount of time spent on a certain activity. It is often associated with computer and Internet uses, and with other pleasurable activities as well.

Introduction

The Electrical Numerical Integrator and Calculator (ENIAC), constructed in the United States (US) in 1946 by John Mauchly and John Presper Eckert, is widely regarded as the first functionally useful electrical

T. Lin and M.N. Potenza, "Problematic Internet Use," from the *Encyclopedia of Behavioral Neuroscience: Volume 3*, George F. Koob, Michel Le Moal and Richard F. Thompson, eds., pp. 104–111. Published by Academic Press, 2010. Copyright by Elsevier Science and Technology Books. Permission to reprint granted by the rights holder.

computer. It weighed almost 30 tons and covered 1800 square feet of floor space. The invention of the microprocessor in the 1970s made the development of consumer computers possible. By the 1990s, the computer became a common household appliance. It is estimated that at present over 70% of Americans own a personal computer. While computers may have been originally invented to be calculating machines, with the advent of the Internet the modern computer can now perform virtually unlimited varieties of functions and provide an unparalleled interactive experience. The significance of the computer and the Internet in human life has also assumed different dimensions. To many, the Internet enlivens the computer to much more than an inanimate device. The ways in which some individuals seem attached to or enslaved by computer activities, in particular Internet-based functions, led to the hypothesis of the addictive potential of such activities.

Internet addiction or problematic Internet use are two of the most commonly used terms for this behavioral syndrome. Both terms appear, in this article, to adhere to the terms used by different authors in describing their findings. Addiction is not a term used or defined in the current *Diagnostic and Statistical Manual of Mental Disorders,* Fourth Edition, Text Revision (DSM-IV-TR). Although the term problematic Internet use is widely used to characterize a variety of Internet-related behaviors, there exists no unified definition for the disorder. In this article, a descriptive approach is employed and the term problematic Internet use is used to describe poorly controlled or excessive use of the Internet that is associated with significant psychosocial and functional impairments. Computer activities are of a large variety and can be on- or off-line. Problematic patterns of computer use had been observed even before the Internet became widely available. However, since the advent of the Internet, it has been observed that the activities most typically associated with problematic use are Internet-based (e.g., Internet gambling, Internet-enabled sexual behavior (IESB), on-line gaming), and most existing research addresses problematic and compulsive use of the Internet.

Epidemiology

The true prevalence of problematic Internet use is not known. This is largely due to the lack of unified diagnostic criteria and assessment instruments, and the scarcity of epidemiological studies. One concern with regard to assessment instruments is that it is unclear how well they differentiate between normal and problematic uses, and their thresholds may greatly influence the prevalence estimates. Another problem is that most existing studies focus on children, adolescents, and college students based on the presumption that problematic Internet use is primarily a phenomenon of the younger population, although epidemiological evidence in support of this premise is largely lacking. Given the reports of problematic Internet use in people of different ages and professions, such as homemakers and working professionals, further study of the prevalence in the general population is needed.

The telephone survey conducted by Aboujaoude *et al.* in 2004 is probably the most methodological rigorous prevalence-estimate study to date. They conducted a nationwide, random-sample telephone survey of over 2500 US adults ($\geq$18 years) utilizing a structured interview that elicited responses to eight suggested measures of problematic Internet use, which were extrapolations from established diagnostic criteria for impulse-control disorders, obsessive-compulsive disorder, and substance abuse. Four sets of possible diagnostic criteria were generated, and the least restrictive one required that Internet use interferes with relationships; the respondent be preoccupied with the Internet when off-line; and, has either tried unsuccessfully to cut down on Internet use, or often stayed on-line longer than intended. Merely 0.7% of respondents endorsed all of these four criteria. However, considerably larger proportions (3.7–13.7%) endorsed one or more of the suggested measures. The study did not include people younger than 18 years of age and had a relatively small proportion of younger adults. As such, the study design might have biased the prevalence estimates downward. Nevertheless, the results suggest that potential markers of problematic Internet use are present in a sizeable proportion of the population.

Multiple observations can be made from the existing epidemiological studies of problematic Internet use. Studies have been performed in multiple geographical regions and significant prevalence rates have been reported in countries across multiple continents and countries (e.g., the United States, Korea, China, Norway, and Italy) indicating that the phenomenon is recognized worldwide. The disorder may be more prevalent among children, adolescents, and college students, with prevalence estimates from off-line studies of younger populations ranging approximately from 2% to 8%, higher than the <1% in adults reported by Aboujaoude *et al.* Problematic Internet use also appears to have a male preponderance, with most, but not all, off-line studies reporting higher prevalence rates and heavier computer use in male subjects. One possible explanation is that men are more likely to engage in computer activities that are associated with a strong emotional–motivational state that contributes to addictive behaviors, such as computer games, Internet pornography, and gambling. Given that multiple gender differences have been reported in other behavioral addictions such as pathological gambling, differences in computer-use patterns between the sexes are likely to be complex. In a sample of about 700 young people in Hong Kong, being a young female student, endorsement of being emotionally open on-line, and using Internet chat function heavily were all associated with problematic Internet use. Men and women may be attracted to, and experience problems with, different computer activities. The above-mentioned observations require replication in future studies of large, representative samples with the use of standardized criteria and assessment instruments and structured interviews.

Clinical Characteristics

Subjective Experiences and Behavioral Patterns

Individuals with problematic Internet use typically spend large amounts of time on Internet-related activities, in some cases objectively measured to be over 35 h a week. Time spent on the Internet is frequently longer than originally intended. Individuals may excessively participate solely in specific Internet activities, and may have made unsuccessful efforts to control or stop Internet use. Lying to family members or therapists to conceal the extent of Internet use is commonly reported—a behavior also seen in pathological gambling.

The above-mentioned study by Aboujaoude *et al.* found that the subjective experience of feeling preoccupied with the Internet when off-line was most highly associated with other suggested clinical markers for problematic Internet use. Consistent with the description of impulse-control disorders, individuals may report difficulty resisting an impulse to use the Internet, an increased tension prior to the desired activity, a release of the tension after the activity starts, and feeling stimulated and euphoric while engaging in the activity. Analogous to the phenomena of tolerance to and withdrawal from a chemical substance, individuals often report needing to use the Internet for increasing amounts of time in order to feel satisfied, and feeling restless, depressed, or irritable when Internet use is being cut down. Time distortion is also a common subjective experience, as documented by discrepancies between self-reported and measured amounts of time spent on the Internet. Subjects often report finding relief from dysphoric, unpleasant states through Internet activities, and thus may choose them as a way of coping or escaping.

Many of the above-mentioned clinical features are captured in proposed sets of Internet-addiction diagnostic criteria, and a commonly cited set was proposed by Young and modeled on the DSM-IV criteria for pathological gambling. The specificity and sensitivity of various symptoms and combinations of symptoms in differentiating normal versus problematic Internet use in the general population are yet to be established.

Physical Health Consequences

Problematic Internet use could potentially cause health problems secondary to the individual's general disregard of his or her health and reduction in physical activities. Poor personal hygiene, irregular eating and digestive system symptoms, declines in cardiovascular fitness, and sleep deprivation may occur in association with problematic Internet use. Other physical complaints related to excessive computer use may include musculoskeletal pain of the back and the wrist, eyestrain, and headache.

Psychosocial Impairments

Individuals with problematic Internet use may neglect family and friends outside the Internet world and thus may jeopardize significant relationships and work and educational opportunities. Individuals with problematic Internet use may be disciplined at work for nonproductive use of the Internet, and this may result in job loss. Other serious psychosocial problems, such as incurring debts and bankruptcy, academic failures, marital discord, and divorce, have also been associated with problematic Internet use.

Co-Occurring Disorders

As is the case in substance-dependence and impulse-control disorders such as pathological gambling, psychiatric disorders frequently co-occur with problematic Internet use. Common co-occurring psychiatric disorders appear to include mood disorders, attention deficit and hyperactivity disorder (ADHD), other impulse-control disorders, social phobia, and substance-use disorders. Comorbid psychotic disorders appear less common. Comorbidity might indicate causal relationships among two or more disorders—that they share common etiological factors, or some other relationship. The study of comorbidities in problematic Internet use may shed light on the underlying mechanisms and further inform prevention and treatment efforts.

Mood Disorders

The association between depressive disorders and problematic Internet use appears to be robust and has been observed in adolescents, college students, and adults. Approximately 10–25% of individuals with problematic Internet use have been reported to be depressed, but larger epidemiological studies are needed to determine the precise rate. Excessive Internet use could lead to stressful social circumstances, such as academic failures and marital discord, which could contribute to depression. Moreover, increased time devoted to the Internet means decreased time available for social engagement, which may lead to isolation and depression, as suggested by a longitudinal study by Kraut *et al.,* which gave randomly selected families Internet access and found higher levels of depression and loneliness in respondents who used the Internet as little as a few hours a week after a 2-year follow-up. On the other hand, depressed people may be drawn to computer games and the Internet for consolation. Precisely how the use of the Internet as a coping strategy may progress to become compulsive or excessive is not well understood. Irrespective of the nature of the relationship, it is important to effectively evaluate and treat depressive disorders in individuals with problematic Internet use.

With regard to the potential role of hypomania and mania, the case series by Shapira *et al.,* in 2000, found that 70% of subjects with Internet addiction had a lifetime diagnosis of bipolar affective disorder I or II, but all had a current or recent depressive or mixed episode, and none had current or recent mania. Poorly controlled Internet use could be a manifestation of hypomania or mania, but this does not seem to be the case in the majority of subjects encountered clinically.

Attention Deficit and Hyperactivity Disorder (ADHD)

ADHD has been associated with problematic Internet use in children and in adults. In a sample of over 500 Korean elementary-school students, over 20% of those identified as problematic Internet users had co-occurring ADHD. The majority of those children used the computer to play on-line games. Those with ADHD and problematic Internet use had more severe ADHD symptoms in that study, as reflected by reports by parents, teachers, and children. Further, in a college-student study with subjects older than 18 years of age, adult ADHD—as ascertained via diagnostic interviews—was the most significantly associated factor with Internet addiction in a logistic regression analysis. Since ADHD predated Internet use, Internet addiction may be a manifestation of ADHD or the two conditions may share common intermediary phenotypes such as a shortened delay gradient. This feature, which has been termed delay discounting and is related to impulsivity, manifests as the tendency to select an immediate reward over a larger but delayed reward. Immediate gratification is often a central experience of using the Internet, where objects of desire are just one-click away. ADHD patients may also have impaired impulse control and hence face difficulties restraining the urge to engage in activities like on-line games.

Obsessive-Compulsive Disorder (OCD) and Impulse-Control Disorders

Problematic Internet use has phenomenological similarities to OCD and impulse-control disorders, in particular pathological gambling. Impulse-control disorders and OCD have been proposed to lie along ends of an impulsive/compulsive spectrum. While obsessive-compulsive symptoms and the trait of harm-avoidance have been associated with excessive Internet use in some cases, patients typically report Internet use as more impulsive and ego-syntonic rather than ego-dystonic (as in OCD), and the remorse from losses secondary to problematic Internet use appears different from the irrational fears often present in OCD. In small case series in which clinical diagnoses were made, the frequencies of co-occurrence of OCD with problematic Internet use varied substantially (0–15%), but were low when compared to those of any non-computer-related impulse-control disorder (up to 50%). Multiple impulse-control disorders have been identified in association with problematic Internet use, and these include intermittent explosive disorder, kleptomania, pathological gambling, pyromania, compulsive buying, compulsive sexual behavior, and compulsive exercising.

Social Phobia

Shyness has been associated with heavy Internet use in college students. It has been contended that the anonymity of the Internet may draw socially fearful individuals to participate in low-risk social interactions via the web. In the case series of 20 patients reported by Shapira and colleagues (2000), concurrent social phobia was found in 40% of subjects, and social phobia was the most common anxiety disorder in the series. However, social phobia did not predict problematic Internet use in a large epidemiological study in Taiwan, nor in a sample of college students after depression and ADHD were controlled. It appears that social phobia, although it may contribute to heavier Internet use, may not fully explain or account for problematic Internet use.

Substance-Use Disorders

Given the phenomenological similarities between substance dependence and problematic Internet use, the co-occurrence of the two conditions might be anticipated. Moreover, pathological gambling, to which problematic Internet use has been likened, is commonly comorbid with substance-use disorders. However, epidemiological data are almost nonexistent in this regard, with one adolescent survey finding no association between Internet addiction and alcohol and nicotine dependence. On the other hand, small case series have found that up to 50% of subjects with Internet addiction have a lifetime diagnosis of substance abuse. Further epidemiological research is needed.

Internet Gambling, IESB, and On-Line Gaming

Internet gambling, IESB, and on-line gaming are behaviors most frequently associated with problematic patterns of use, although other computer-based behaviors such as on-line chatting and e-mailing may also become problematic. These forms of Internet use appear to share the propensity to alter mood states, a feature which has been proposed to contribute to addictive behaviors. Gambling, sexual behavior, and computer-gaming are not Internet-specific activities. However, certain distinctive properties of the Internet, including interactivity, accessibility, affordability, and anonymity, may potentially exacerbate or promote excessive involvement in specific individuals, although more research is needed to examine these possibilities. From the limited epidemiological data available, problematic forms of these behaviors appear to be more common in males than in females.

Internet Gambling

The majority of adults in the US have gambled within the past year, and epidemiological studies suggest that problem and pathological gambling occur in a small proportion of the population, probably up to 4.0%. The hypothesis that Internet gambling exacerbates the problem of pathological gambling because of the above-mentioned properties has not been confirmed by empirical studies. Two large-scale Internet gambling studies which recorded Internet betting activities from more than 4000 subscribers to an Internet gambling website over a 2-year period found that gambling behaviors were moderate at the population level, with 1–5% of subjects exhibiting behaviors that deviated markedly from the norm. However, Internet gambling may be a larger problem in subsets of the population such as college students. In one study, almost 25% of college subjects reported having wagered on the Internet at least once in their lives. The study also found that markedly more regular Internet gamblers than off-line gamblers were pathological gamblers (61.6% vs. 5.0%), and Internet gambling was associated with poorer mental health ratings. The question remains whether Internet gambling leads to problematic gambling behaviors, problem gamblers are drawn to Internet gambling, or some other relationship exists.

Internet-Enabled Sexual Behavior

Sex addiction, or nonparaphilic compulsive sexual behavior, is one of the proposed conditions currently subsumed under the DSM-IV-TR category of impulse-control disorder not otherwise specified. IESBs include pornography viewing, on-line sexual relationships, and their variants. It has been estimated that the Internet pornography industry is worth well over $1 billion, and most of the top word searches are related to Internet sex. Hence, IESBs appear to be very prevalent at the societal level. Internet sex replaces real-life intimacy in many cases, and has been related to reprimands at work, serious relationship problems, and divorce. However, given the secretive nature of the condition for the majority of individuals, the prevalence and extent of compulsive or problematic IESBs are difficult to determine. In a small outcome study of treatment for men involved in problematic IESBs, subjects with different co-occurring disorders responded differently to integrated group therapy—those with anxiety disorders responded best; those with depression showed a moderate response; and those with ADHD appeared to be most resistant to treatment, illustrating the heterogeneity of subjects with problematic IESBs.

On-Line Gaming

Computer gaming can be conducted on-line or off-line, but heavy or excessive playing is more frequently associated with on-line gaming modalities. Another observation repeatedly reported in multiple studies is that players and problematic players are predominantly males. Both quantitative and qualitative studies have shown that to socialize and interact with others is an important motivational factor in on-line gaming. This is consistent with the observation that excessive playing is most often associated with massively multiplayer on-line games (MMOGs). The design of MMOGs inherently promotes heavy gaming, since the competition runs continuously in real time, making devotion to gaming mandatory. A study of Korean adolescents found that role-playing game users had significantly higher Internet-addiction ratings than players of other genres, such as sports games. Although computer games are traditionally regarded as a leisure activity of children and adolescents, an on-line study of players of the popular online game Everquest found that almost 60% of players were between the ages of 18 and 31, indicating that on-line gaming may be gaining a wider audience. Whether the prevalence of compulsive gaming is increasing in the older age group is not known. In clinical practice, it is still most commonly encountered in children and adolescents, and underlying ADHD is implicated in some cases.

Neurobiological Features

Knowledge about the neurobiology of problematic Internet use is currently very limited. The theoretical models of substance-addiction and impulse-control disorders, to which problematic Internet use has been likened, are not mutually exclusive, and studies have shown multiple neurobiological and genetic similarities between the two groups of disorders. Pathophysiological mechanisms implicated in substance-addiction and impulse-control disorders may also contribute to problematic Internet use, but direct evidence is lacking.

Dopaminergic projections from the ventral tegmental area to the nucleus accumbens are considered to be important in the expression of goal-directed behaviors, and this pathway has long been implicated in drug addiction. A current hypothesis posits that low dopamine D2-receptor availability may mediate vulnerability to addiction. Multiple clinical observations suggest that the mechanism might also underlie problematic Internet use. The phenomenon of punding—characterized by an intense fascination with repetitive handling of technical equipments seen in relation to the use of psychostimulants (e.g., amphetamine and cocaine) and dopaminergic anti-Parkinsonian medications— has also involved compulsive use of the computer in some patients. Computer-use behaviors in punding and problematic Internet use in subjects not under the influence of dopaminergic medications share phenomenological features. A case report documented the successful treatment of compulsive IESB with naltrexone, the hypothesis being that a non-chemical stimulus such as Internet pornography causes the release of endogenous opiates which enhances dopamine release, and naltrexone works via blocking opioid receptors. As mentioned, further research with direct examination of the roles of dopaminergic and opioidergic systems in problematic Internet use is needed to examine these hypotheses.

A preliminary electroencephalographic study reported that as compared to nonaddicted computer-game players, addicted ones showed higher emotional arousal and stronger cortical reactivity in response to computer-game-related visual cues. In addicted computer-game players, game-related cues induced late positive complexes of significantly larger amplitudes. The findings are consistent with previous reports that individuals with Internet addiction may have a different Internet-use experience than do nonaddicted individuals, being more emotionally engaged with the Internet. Similar cue-induced responses had been described in alcohol- and drug-dependent subjects, as well as pathological gamblers confronted with related cues. Thus, problematic Internet use may share common pathophysiological processes with these other disorders.

Genetics

No genetic study has been published examining problematic Internet use. Genetic studies of pathological gambling showed that genetic factors contribute significantly, and pathological gambling shares genetic risk with alcohol dependence and antisocial behavior. All these conditions may be linked via common underlying pathways such as impulsivity. Hence, genetic study of problematic Internet use may help clarify its relationships with other impulse-control disorders and substance addictions.

Treatments

Given the recent recognition of problematic Internet use as a psychiatric problem, not much research has evaluated the efficacy of treatments for the disorder. No double-blind, controlled trials of pharmacotherapies or psychotherapies have been published. However, many patients seek help and the resulting treatment infrastructure is expanding. Multiple treatment centers and groups have emerged over time, both on- and off-line. For example, specialized outpatient treatment service is available at the Computer Addiction Study Center at McLean Hospital of Harvard Medical School. In some instances, patients have been admitted for inpatient rehabilitation. In China, a halfway house was recently opened for adolescents with problematic Internet use.

Since the Internet is an integral part of life for many, total abstinence may not be practical. Hence, many contend that moderated and controlled use is the most appropriate treatment goal. With regard to children and adolescents, the input of parents is essential. It has been found that although most parents appear open to buying computers because of perceived positive features, few may discuss with their children their appropriate use in detail or carefully supervise their use, unless or until the use becomes problematic.

Psychopharmacological Treatments

Selective serotonin-reuptake inhibitors (SSRIs) are effective in the treatment of OCD. Studies of the use of SSRIs in impulse-control disorders have shown mixed results. Problematic Internet use appears to have compulsive and impulsive qualities, and treatment with escitalopram, an SSRI, has been studied. An open-label study in 19 subjects by Dell'Osso, in 2006, showed that 10 weeks of escitalopram treatment (20 mg per day) was associated with significant decreases in weekly hours spent on-line (from a mean of 36.8 to 16.5 h) and in measures of impulsivity and compulsivity, as well as improvement in global functioning. After 10 weeks, subjects were blindly randomized to continue treatment with escitalopram or placebo. Following another 9 weeks of treatment, therapeutic gains achieved at week 10 were maintained in both treatment groups and no further gain was shown for either group. The medication was well tolerated. The most frequently reported side effects were drowsiness and nausea, which were modest and self-limited. In a case report, escitalopram successfully treated a depressed adult patient with compulsive on-line gaming. Another case study reported the successful use of an atypical antipsychotic (quetiapine) as augmentation for citalopram in the treatment of a subject with compulsive Internet use. This augmentation strategy has also been successfully used in treating OCD. Naltrexone has also been used with the reasoning that it may antagonize endogenous opiates that are induced by pleasurable stimuli, perhaps through modulation of dopamine pathways underlying motivated behaviors. A case report documented the successful use of naltrexone in the treatment of compulsive IESB. The patient's depressed mood initially responded to sertraline, but his urge to view Internet pornography was still uncontrolled until naltrexone was started. He reported complete control of his impulse at the dose of naltrexone 150 mg daily. Further clinical trials are needed to establish the efficacy and effectiveness of medication monotherapy and augmentation strategies.

Psychological Treatments

Cognitive behavioral therapy

Cognitive therapy is based on the underlying theoretical rationale that an individual's affective states and behaviors are largely determined by the way in which he or she structures the world on the basis of cognitions and assumptions. Recognition, examination, and correction of faulty cognitions and assumptions may then lead to changes in regulating affective states and controlling behaviors. Principles of cognitive therapy have been applied to the treatment of problematic Internet use. Studies suggest that compulsive Internet users may be more likely to expect positive outcomes and relief from negative affective states from Internet use, which may not be true given the psychosocial impairments they suffer from excessive use of the Internet. They may presume that the Internet is the most effective way to alleviate depressive feelings and meet truthful friends ("unlike my dishonest husband. …"). Such expectations represent potential targets for cognitive restructuring, as are other dysfunctional thoughts such as

"Just a few more minutes won't hurt" which may maintain the pattern of Internet use.

Cognitive therapy is typically combined with a behavioral component in the initial phase. Such therapies may initially start with a daily log to evaluate Internet-use behaviors and a focus on establishing and achieving reasonable goals such as decreasing the amount of time of use, abstaining from problematic applications, and developing alternative activities and coping skills. Such therapies may be combined with the use of software to restrict Internet access.

The outcome of CBT in the form of on-line counseling for problematic Internet use has been evaluated in a study conducted by Young. Overall, subjects reported incremental or continuous improvements in symptoms and functioning throughout the course of therapy of 12 sessions, and maintenance of benefits at 6-month follow-up. The moderate sample size (114 treatment-seeking subjects) and its highly educated composition may limit the generalizability of the results.

Motivational interviewing and stages of change

A transtheoretical model of behavioral change was proposed and developed by Prochaska and DiClemente. Based on this model, motivational interviewing has been successful in the treatment of substance addictions. The model has been adopted in the psychotherapy of problematic Internet use. The principle states that behavioral change goes through successive stages of precontemplation, contemplation, preparation, action, maintenance, and termination, and individuals at different stages have different needs and levels of readiness. A therapist should be sensitive to the motivational stage of the patient and respond to his or her needs accordingly. If the patient does not recognize any problem with his or her Internet use, it would not be therapeutic for the therapist to propose an action plan. The goal at this precontemplation stage is to help the patient overcome denial by discussing pros and cons of Internet use and overuse. If the patient is already trying to make behavioral changes, it may be unnecessary or inappropriate for the therapist to continue discussing negative ramifications of excessive Internet use. Support and educational materials are provided according to the patient's readiness to change. A small study of group therapy applying the principles of cognitive behavioral therapy (CBT), motivational interviewing, and stages of change showed improvements in quality of life and depression measures, but no significant changes in the subjects' computer-use behaviors.

Insight-oriented psychotherapy

While people have different motivations to use and overuse the Internet, qualitative studies and case reports illustrated common psychological themes in patients' stories. Internet activities may serve to fulfill some inherent psychological needs—the need for a sense of achievement, for interpersonal connectedness and a sense of belonging to a community, for entertainment, and to discharge frustration. The virtual self on-line can be an extension of the real self, or a compensatory identity to satisfy unfulfilled wishes. This interpretation may explain why role-playing games represent one of the most popular genres. Blogosphere may also provide a space to fulfill the wish to self-reveal. Insight-oriented psychotherapy aims to help patients understand the relationships among their anxieties, inner needs, motivations, and Internet-use behaviors so they can make their own choice to change behaviors and develop alternate ways of coping. Empirical data on this and other psychotherapeutic approaches for problematic Internet use are limited.

Conclusions

Problematic Internet use is a clinically recognizable behavioral syndrome that is associated with significant adverse psychosocial consequences. As is the case with substance-dependence and impulse-control disorders, comorbidity appears to be the rule rather than the exception. The study of the prevalence, phenomenology, pathophysiology, and treatment of problematic Internet use is hindered in part by the lack of standardized criteria and assessment instruments. This behavioral syndrome appears heterogeneous—people have different motivations to use the Internet to excess, and they have problems with different applications. Novelty-seeking individuals may be drawn to the Internet's incessant novelty, while people with harm-avoidance tendencies may find a sense of safety in the virtual world. Nonetheless, both types of individuals could develop problematic patterns of use. The study of

intermediary phenotype constructs, such as impulsivity, across diagnostic groups should facilitate further elucidation of neurobiological and genetic bases of problematic Internet use and other theoretically related conditions. Clinically, efforts in subtyping problematic Internet use may be performed in conjunction with understanding a patient's unique experience with the Internet, and helping him or her reflect on his relationship with the virtual world. Clinicians should be aware of the clinical features of problematic Internet use and its potential consequences, and be equipped to assess computer-use history in the clinical interview.

See also: Animal Models of Sexual Function; Cognition: Attention and Impulsivity; Brain–Machine Interfaces; Comorbidity–Depression; Compulsive Buying; Depression; Impulsive–Compulsive Sexual Behavior; Molecular Neurobiology of Addiction; Novelty; Pathological Gambling; Value of Animal Models for Predicting CNS Therapeutic Action.

Further Reading

Aboujaoude E, Koran LM, Gamel N, Large MD, and Serpe RT (2006) Potential markers for problematic internet use: A telephone survey of 2,513 adults. *CNS Spectrums* 11: 750–755.

Black DW, Belsare G, and Schlosser S (1999) Clinical features, psychiatric comorbidity, and health-related quality of life in persons reporting compulsive computer use behavior. *Journal of Clinical Psychiatry* 60: 839–844.

Block JJ (2008) Issues for DSM-V: Internet addiction. *American Journal of Psychiatry* 165: 306–307.

Brewer JA and Potenza MN (2008) The neurobiology and genetics of impulse control disorders: Relationships to drug addictions. *Biochemical Pharmacology* 75: 63–75.

Dell'Osso B, Altamura AC, Allen A, Marazziti D, and Hollander E (2006) Epidemiologic and clinical updates on impulse control disorders: A critical review. *European Archives of Psychiatry and Clinical Neuroscience* 256: 464–475.

Dell'Osso B, Altamura AC, Hadley SJ, Baker B, and Hollander E (2006) An open-label trial of escitalopram in the treatment of impulsive-compulsive internet usage disorder. *European Neuropsychopharmacology* 16: S82.

Kraut R, Patterson M, Lundmark V, Kiesler S, Mukopadhyay T, and Scherlis W (1998) Internet paradox. A social technology that reduces social involvement and psychological well-being? *American Psychologist* 53: 1017–1031.

Liu T and Potenza MN (2007) Problematic Internet use: clinical implications. *CNS Spectrums* 12: 453–466.

Shaffer HJ, Hall MN, and Bilt JV (2000) "Computer addiction": A critical consideration. *American Journal of Orthopsychiatry* 70: 162–168.

Shapira NA, Goldsmith TD, Keck PE, Jr., Khosla UM, and McElroy SL (2000) Psychiatric features of individuals with problematic internet use. *Journal of Affective Disorders* 57: 267–272.

Young KS (2007) Cognitive behavior therapy with Internet addicts: Treatment outcomes and implications. *Cyberpsychology and Behavior* 10: 671–679.

Failure to Control Emotions and Moods

By Roy F. Baumeister, Todd F. Heatherton, and Dianne M. Tice

One of the most successful and controversial movies of 1993 was *Falling Down.* Its success went beyond praise from critics and box-office sales; indeed, it was featured on the cover of *Newsweek,* which is a rare distinction for a film. Although the movie touched on several of the major social issues of contemporary America, there was at least one theme that ran throughout the movie: failure to control emotions.

The film begins by showing the mounting bad mood of the main character. He has been fired from his job because his knowledge and skills have become obsolete. His wife has left him and taken his child. Because of his economic situation, he is unable to make child support payments and therefore is not allowed to see his little girl on her birthday. He is stuck in an interminable traffic jam caused, he believes, by make-work projects invented by the highway crews to justify their outrageous budgets. He swelters in his car, but the air conditioning is broken, and he cannot even open the window because the handle is defective.

He tries to distract himself from his mounting anger over the traffic problem, but as he shifts his attention in various directions he is repeatedly reminded of his multiple dissatisfactions with the world. Finally he tries to escape the anger-producing situation by abandoning his car and heading off on foot. But in a convenience store he gets into a disagreement with the proprietor and ends up madder than ever. Seeking to recover his peace of mind by sitting alone and thinking through his situation, he is accosted by some teenagers who try to

rob him, and so again he is unable to feel better. He tries at one point to stop the escalating hostility between him and the teenagers and to speak in a friendly and rational fashion, but this too is to no avail, and again violence is the outcome. Throughout the film, his efforts at emotional control meet with frustration and failure, and it is only through violent and aggressive outbursts that he ever gets what he wants.

Like the protagonist of this movie, many people find themselves unable to escape from aversive emotional states and bad moods. The topic of controlling moods and emotions (*affect regulation*) has emerged in recent years as an important focus of research efforts. This chapter will examine one part of that literature, specifically that of failure at affect regulation. How, when, and why do people fail to regulate their emotional states?

Given the state of knowledge in the field, it will be necessary to narrow the focus of this chapter even further. We shall emphasize the failure to escape from a bad or unpleasant emotional state. In principle, there are at least six main types of emotion control tasks: A person could be trying to get into, get out of, or prolong either a good or a bad mood (Parrott, 1993; Tice, Muraven, & Baumeister, 1994; see also Clark & Isen, 1982; Wegner & Erber, 1993; Morris & Reilly, 1987). At first glance, one might ask when would someone ever desire to get into a bad mood, but such cases do arise and are important. For example, a politician might seek to work up a state of anger in preparation for giving a speech about injustice, a physician might need to put herself into a somber mood when it is necessary to tell a patient that he is dying, and a parent might have to get into a disappointed or outraged mood when discussing failing grades with a child.

Still, the most common attempt to control moods involves getting out of various bad moods (Tice & Baumeister, 1993; Tice et al., 1994), and so research interest has understandably emphasized those attempts. Accordingly, the evidence about self-regulation failure is also concentrated on that topic, and that is the one that will receive most attention here. Like the other self-regulation failures discussed in previous chapters, failure to control one's moods and emotions can result either from underregulation (i.e., not managing to exert sufficient control over these states) or from misregulation (i.e., using ineffective or inappropriate techniques for regulating affect).

Some writers distinguish between mood, affect, and emotion, whereas others use them interchangeably. Although we recognize that greater specificity is often useful, the distinctions are not important for our purposes, and so we shall follow the latter practice.

UNDERREGULATION AND THE MYTH OF VENTING

Although we shall turn shortly to the central problem of unrestrained emotional expression or venting, it is necessary to begin with a more fundamental reason for lack of emotional control: a belief that one should never control emotions. Some people simply believe that they should never try to control their moods.

In a series of surveys about emotion and mood control, Tice and Baumeister (1993) found that up to 4% of adults report that they never consciously attempt to alter their affective states. They typically explain this on the basis of some belief that it is morally wrong or psychologically damaging to alter emotions. Thus, one respondent wrote that "it might be bad for me/for my health to stifle or control my emotions," and another responded that "emotions are a natural part of life and should be experienced naturally." Steinmetz (1977) found that most adults in his sample believed that stifling anger is both harmful and futile. They believed that instead of controlling one's anger, one should

express it for cathartic reasons. Tavris (1989) likewise suggested that it is common for people to view the expression of anger as healthful and to believe that it is wrong, useless, and harmful to try to control anger. In Tavris's opinion, this popular misconception has multiple sources, including a bastardized popular version of Freudian theory, which characterized repression as both harmful and ultimately futile, as well as a cultural quest for excuses to enable people to indulge themselves irresponsibly.

Likewise, Averill (1980, 1982) has argued that the cultural construction of emotion as passive (hence the related term "passion") is a deliberately fostered illusion that is designed to allow people to behave in wild or aggressive ways without accepting responsibility. As a prominent example of his approach, Averill cited evidence that juries give lighter sentences for crimes committed in the heat of passion (especially anger) because they believe that people are unable to control their emotions and that strong emotions make people unable to control their actions (Averill, 1979, 1982).

It is worth noting that people may sometimes fail at *not* controlling their emotions. In other words, despite their beliefs that they should allow emotions to proceed without regulation, many people end up using automatic or semiautomatic processes that regulate their moods, even if the people are not conscious of doing so or even if they think that they are unable to exert such control. For example, Gelles (1979) described a man who beat his wife and justified his actions on the basis of the alleged uncontrollability of anger when he was drinking. Yet the man refrained from shooting or stabbing her, and when this control of his behavior was pointed out to him by the therapist he began to realize that his "uncontrollable" angry aggression might indeed be controllable. Likewise, the Malay people long sustained the practice of *running amok,* in which individuals completely lost control of their actions and became wildly destructive. However, when social changes instituted severe punishments for running amok, the Malay discovered suddenly that they could control it after all, and the practice decreased dramatically (Carr & Tan, 1976). Thus, many people do in fact control their emotions and emotional actions even if they seem to insist and believe that such control is not possible for them.

Venting as Underregulation

Venting may be defined as the unrestrained expression of emotions, ranging from mere disclosure of emotional states to outrageous or wildly inappropriate behavior stimulated by emotions. If an entire society were to adopt the minority view mentioned in the previous section, namely that it is wrong and harmful to control emotions and so people should freely vent all emotions that they experience, human social life would be radically different from what it is now: Almost every human encounter would be marked by laughing, weeping, screaming, hitting, or other emotional outbursts. Some would argue that such a society would be more natural and authentic in its behavior. In our view, however, a widespread failure to control emotions (especially anger) would greatly increase the problems, stresses, and hazards of human interaction.

Modern adherents of venting often cite a *hydraulic view* of emotion. Such views depict the human psyche as similar to a container of water, and in that view emotions resemble increases in water pressure—which need to be allowed to discharge periodically, or else the system will explode and be destroyed. The most famous hydraulic model was proposed by Breuer and Freud (1982) (drawing heavily on Helmholtz's principle of the conservation of energy), who used the term *catharsis* to describe the discharge of emotional impulses. In their view, emotional impulses do not go away until they are discharged, and indeed preventing their discharge may actually increase their pressure. They developed the notion of catharsis as a therapy technique: Patients with allegedly "pent up" emotions could vent these feelings in the safety of the therapist's office. However, Freud did not find therapeutic catharsis to be effective, and so he and his colleagues moved on to focus their therapeutic efforts on thoughts and on talking rather than on emotional expressions such as crying.

Although Freud may have gradually discarded catharsis as a major therapeutic technique, the public at large did not. Freud's discourses on the supposedly harmful effects of repressed feelings have influenced several generations of people to think that failing to express one's feelings must invariably be dangerous and unhealthy. The idea that people need to "vent" their emotions has remained ingrained in the public and

therapeutic literature (see Tavris, 1989, for a discussion of the harmful consequences of such societal beliefs).

A great deal of research has demonstrated that venting is ineffective at decreasing or eliminating the mood state. In fact, venting is often shown to *prolong* the negative affect, mood, or emotion, rather than reduce it. For example, Gondolf (1985), in his book on spouse abuse, disputed the hypothesis that venting (or "letting it all out short of violence") is a good way to defuse angry hostility. Rather, he cited evidence that "physical abuse by the man is shown to be marked by escalating verbal and physical aggression between the partners" (p. 31). In other words, domestic violence often follows from the venting of anger between spouses.

Gondolf interviewed a number of men who had admitted to battering their wives. These men frequently claimed that the venting of negative feelings was instrumental in beginning the cycle of violence. According to one of the men interviewed, "the anger leads to violence before you know it. ... It just takes over and you become a different person."

Straus (1974), Straus, Gelles, and Steinmetz (1980), and Steinmetz (1977) likewise provided evidence that venting is likely to lead to more angry aggression, not less. When one member of a couple angrily "vents" his or her negative feelings to the partner, the partner frequently responds in an angry fashion, leading to an escalation of angry exchanges that frequently ends in physical aggression.

To understand why venting is ineffective, it is important to consider some of the details about what venting does. Venting may often fail to reduce anger or other emotions because the components of venting are directly incompatible with other self-regulatory responses. For example, venting involves focusing on one's feelings of anger or sadness in order to express them in detail—but research has demonstrated that focusing on one's negative feelings is ineffective for escaping from the negative mood (e.g., Carver, Scheier, & Weintraub, 1989; Lyubomirsky & Nolen-Hoeksema, 1993; Morrow & Nolen-Hoeksema, 1990). In contrast, *distracting oneself* from the negative thoughts or emotions is an effective way of getting out of a mood (e.g., Miller, 1987; Nolen-Hoeksema, 1990, 1993; Wegner, 1989; Wenzlaff et al., 1988), but venting prevents people from distracting themselves. Indeed, we have seen throughout this work that distraction is often a powerful and effective means of managing attention. Venting directs attention to precisely the wrong place, namely to one's distress and to what is causing it.

Emotional Expressivity

Many researchers have demonstrated that when one expresses an emotion, one is likely to experience that emotion; this effect is known as the *emotional expressivity effect*. James (1890/1950), Allport (1924), and Jacobson (1929) all described early scientific theories of controlling emotions through the self-control of expressive facial behavior. Izard (1990) claimed that the idea that naturally occurring emotion feelings can be influenced by self-managed expressive behavior "may be at least as old as written records," (p. 489), and he quoted Shakespeare's Henry V's beliefs that altering the outward expression of emotion can alter the inward experience of that emotion:

> Then imitate the action of the tiger;
> Stiffen the sinews, summon up the blood,
> Disguise fair nature with hard-favour'd rage.
> Then lend the eye a terrible aspect;
> Let it pry through the portage of the head,
> Like the brass cannon; let the brow o'erwhelm it,
> As fearfully, as doth a galled rock
> O'erhand and jutty his confounded base,
> Swill'd with the wild and wasteful ocean.
> Now set the teeth, and stretch the nostril wide;
> Hold hard the breath, and bend up every spirit
> To his full height!
> —Act III, Scene 1

Multiple studies have provided evidence of the emotional expressivity effect, by demonstrating that facial feedback is an important determinant of how people experience emotion and that such feedback plays an important role in regulating emotions (e.g., Cacioppo, Petty, Losch, & Kim, 1986; Cupchick & Leventhal, 1974; Gellhorn, 1964; Kleinke & Walton, 1982; Kraut, 1982; Leventhal & Mace, 1970). Arranging someone's face to conform to an emotional expression seems to cause the person to begin to feel that emotion (e.g., Lanzetta, Cartwright-Smith, & Kleck, 1976; Laird, 1974, 1984; Strack, Martin, & Stepper, 1988). By the same token,

putting someone's face into an inexpressive pattern that might conceal emotion seems to cause that person to feel less emotion. Izard's (1990) review of the facial feedback literature concluded that "patterns of expressive behavior can be effectively used in the management of emotion experience" (p. 496), and that *self*-management or spontaneous use of the technique (of controlling facial expression to regulate emotion) is even more effective than experimentally manipulated use of the technique. Other researchers have demonstrated that not just facial expressiveness, but other bodily expressive cues such as posture, can also affect mood and emotion (Riskind, 1984; Riskind & Gotay, 1982; see also Weisfeld & Beresford, 1982).

These studies suggest one mechanism by which venting will fail. Expressing an emotion tends to make that emotion stronger, not weaker. Hence, if people seek to reduce their anger by expressing it, their expressions are likely to increase the anger, which is the opposite of the desired effect.

Relaxation and Physiological Reactivity

Another reason venting may be ineffective in reducing some emotions is that it strengthens or increases arousal—whereas escaping from distress may often be best served by getting rid of arousal. Relaxation and meditation have been shown to be effective techniques for reducing the high-arousal states associated with negative emotions and moods like fear and anger (e.g., Feindler, 1989; Feindler & Ecton, 1986; Novaco, 1975). Giving vent to one's fear and anger will most likely produce the opposite result. A large number of researchers have found that venting, or outwardly expressing one's anger, has been positively associated with greater heart rate and blood pressure reactivity (e.g., Dembroski, MacDougall, Shields, Petitto, & Lushene, 1978; Diamond et al., 1984; VanEgern, Abelson, & Thornton, 1978), which constitute a physiological component of emotion. If venting leads to greater physiological reactions, which most researchers consider an important or even necessary component of emotion and mood (e.g., Schachter & Singer, 1962; Thayer, 1989), then venting (which leads to an increase in physiological states) should be incompatible with a reduction in the mood one is trying to control. This physiological reactivity associated with venting can be so pervasive that venting is found to be positively associated with coronary heart disease (e.g., Hecker, Chesney, Black, & Frautschi, 1988; Mathews, Glass, Rosenman, & Bortner, 1977) and hypertension (e.g., Harburg et al., 1973).

Silent Seething

It must be acknowledged that some researchers have found what seems at first to be an opposite result, namely that *refraining* from expressing one's anger produces harmful effects. In particular, holding one's anger in (as opposed to venting it) is positively associated with greater heart rate and blood pressure reactivity, coronary heart disease, and hypertension (Funkenstein, King, & Drolette, 1954; Harburg et al., 1973; Haynes, Feinleib, & Kannel, 1980; Holroyd & Gorkin, 1983; MacDougall, Dembroski, Dimsdale, & Hackett, 1985; MacDougall, Dembroski, & Krantz, 1981; Schalling, 1985).

Thus we have seemingly contradictory sets of findings. On the one hand, venting anger ("anger-out," as it is sometimes called) appears to have harmful effects. On the other hand, similarly harmful consequences have been linked to *not* venting, in the sense of keeping one's anger inside ("anger-in"). Which is correct?

One attempt to resolve this controversy was undertaken by Engebretson, Mathews, and Scheier (1989), who proposed that it is simply a matter of individual differences. Perhaps some people are better off expressing their anger, while others are better off keeping it inside. In their study, some subjects were allowed to express their anger at a confederate in their preferred or habitual manner (either anger-in or anger-out), whereas others were required to deal with the anger in the manner opposite to their preferred one. These researchers hypothesized that subjects who were allowed to express their anger at a confederate in their preferred manner would have less cardiovascular reactivity than subjects who were forced to deal with their anger in the opposite mode. Some of their results fit that hypothesis, but they also reported that "individuals who characteristically express their anger outwardly exhibited elevated heart rate during harassment and elevated systolic blood pressure, which persisted even after being harassed and writing a negative story about the confederate" (i.e., aggressing

against the harasser; p. 519). In other words, the arousal did not subside after venting, even among people who preferred to vent their anger.

Thus, Engebretson et al. (1989) have shown that individual differences are an important factor in deciding whether anger-in or anger-out is worse. The fact that people who prefer to vent remain aroused after venting complicates the issue, however, and so their findings are not a complete resolution of the inconsistency in previous findings.

What is destructive may be *staying angry*, regardless of whether it is associated with anger-in or anger-out (see Tice, 1994). In this view, venting is bad because it rekindles and strengthens the angry state, leading to increased arousal and increased attention to the problem that caused the anger. Keeping one's anger from being expressed is also bad, however, if it means that the person seethes with anger in silence. Thus, what is common about anger-in and anger-out is that the anger persists; and it is the continued anger that has the destructive effects.

This conclusion fits with several comments made by Engebretson et al. (1989) regarding their unpredicted finding about the persistence of high arousal among the subjects who vented their anger. These authors speculated that the continued arousal levels may have been due to continued rumination about the negative experience with the confederate. Continuing to ruminate typically means that one remains angry—and as long as one remains angry, it is hardly surprising that one's heart rate and other signs of arousal remain high.

More generally, we think that the inconsistent findings in the literature regarding anger-in and anger-out reflect the destructive consequences of staying angry, in part because measures have sometimes confounded anger-in with simply not expressing anger (Tice, 1994). Measures of anger-in may thus combine two kinds of people: those who refuse to show anger while continuing to seethe inwardly, and those who simply manage to exert self-control until the anger goes away.

Thus, the seeming contradictions among past findings may not properly bear on the issue of whether it is a good idea to express one's anger or not; rather, the decisive issue is whether the person stays angry or not. Venting one's anger is likely to lead to staying angry, because of the emotional expressivity effect, attending to the provocation, maintaining arousal, and the like. Refusing to vent one's anger, however, may lead to two quite different outcomes. Some people may stop feeling angry when they hold their tongues (possibly aided by relaxation or self-distraction techniques), and they may end up feeling better; but other people will simply continue to seethe with anger inwardly, which is not likely to be much better than venting.

When Does Expressing Feelings Help?

If venting negative affect is an ineffective strategy for controlling moods as well as being bad for health, how should people communicate their dissatisfaction or unhappiness when someone has wronged them? Without venting one's anger, how can someone prevent the anger-producing event from recurring?

Most current anger therapies (e.g., Feindler, 1989; Feindler & Ecton, 1986; Goldstein & Glick, 1987; Lochman, 1984; Novaco, 1975, 1979) recommend avoiding venting, but they also recommend considering the possibility of discussion after the anger of all parties involved has subsided. An emotion-laden confrontational debate is likely to escalate into an argument and therefore is unlikely to yield constructive resolutions to conflict (e.g., Wilson, 1982; Zillman, 1993). If an individual becomes angry and vents the anger at another, the person listening to the angry individual is likely to become angry as well, and the anger of the dyad or group is highly likely to escalate (e.g., Gondolf, 1985; Straus, 1974; Straus et al., 1980; Steinmetz, 1977).

However, if you wait until the anger has subsided and then attempt to make your feelings known to the others involved, you are less likely to say things that you do not mean or will be sorry for later (which constitutes a very unfortunate case of lapse-activated causation!). Averill (1982) refers to a "cooling time" in which confrontational debate is avoided, which can be followed by rational discussion if the previously angry individual still feels that the issue is worthy of discussion after he or she has "cooled off." This waiting period will only work to help avoid angry confrontation if the parties actually try to control their anger (perhaps through pleasant distraction) during the cooling time. If the parties use the period between the anger-provoking event and the confrontation to rehearse their grievances and brood

over their perception of events, then the likelihood of angry aggression and argument is just as strong as if no waiting period had taken place (e.g., Zillman, 1993). In addition, stating one's feelings, such as saying, "I am feeling ..." is a much more effective means of discussing the emotion-producing event without escalating the anger than is making statements blaming the other, such as saying, "You always ..." (e.g., Lochman, 1984; Tavris, 1989).

This advice applies to a variety of bad moods and emotions in addition to anger. Many researchers have suggested that one highly effective means of regulating negative affect is to directly confront the problem and make instrumental progress at trying to change the state of affairs that led to the negative feelings (e.g., Billings & Moos, 1984; Morrow & Nolen-Hoeksema, 1990; Parker & Brown, 1982; Rippere, 1976, 1977; Rohde, Lewinsohn, Tilson, & Seeley, 1990). However, waiting until the negative mood has lifted (which one can induce by using effective mood control techniques such as distraction) before attempting to confront the emotion-inducing event or person may be much more effective than venting.

Venting Other Emotions

In the Freudian conception, catharsis technically applied to any negative emotion that was pent up, and Freud in fact was interested in pent-up anxiety, fear, and sadness, as well as anger. Most of the popular interpretation of venting, as well as the scientific research, has focused on the venting of anger. Any conclusions about the efficacy of venting other emotions must remain primarily speculative.

As we have seen, the evidence is quite clear that venting anger is not an effective mood control strategy. The data on venting sadness are not as straightforward, however, perhaps because venting sadness (e.g., through crying, talking about the sadness) has not been as well researched as venting anger. Some researchers think that crying may help to alleviate sad moods, because as tears leave the body they carry with them some of the neurotransmitters that increase feelings of sadness and depression. These findings are far from conclusive, however, and it may be that crying actually increases the total quantity of those transmitters in the brain; it is possible that those neurotransmitters are actually produced in response to crying (see, for instance, Kraemer & Hastrup, 1988, for evidence that crying does not have a cathartic effect and does not reduce sadness).

Meanwhile, there is a fair amount of evidence that continuing to focus attention on one's sadness can lead to depressive episodes, and one effective way to avoid depressed moods is to distract oneself from sad thoughts (e.g., Billings & Moos, 1984; Morrow & Nolen-Hoeksema, 1990; Nolen-Hoeksema, 1990, 1993; Wenzlaff et al., 1988). These findings suggest that self-distraction may be much more effective than venting for escaping from sadness.

Ultimately, it may well be that the conclusion about venting sadness and other aversive mood states parallels the one we have proposed for anger, namely that it is the persistence of the bad mood that is the crucial issue. Venting may typically fail to alleviate the bad mood, but continuing to ruminate silently about the problem may be just as bad. Merely stifling outward expression of distress is inadequate. Instead, people need to use techniques that actually work to remove themselves from persisting in bad moods.

MISREGULATION

In the previous section, we saw that people may fail to control their emotions because they simply do not try to control them. Alternatively, however, people may fail because they resort to methods that backfire or are simply ineffective. As with the misregulation patterns shown in other chapters, a central cause of affect misregulation is people's misconceptions about what will be effective. Inadequate understanding of self, of the nature of emotion, or of the consequences of certain techniques can cause people to exert control over their moods and emotions in a destructive or counterproductive fashion.

Indeed, venting may sometimes be an example of misregulation deriving from faulty knowledge. We covered venting as a form of underregulation, but in some cases people may deliberately vent their emotions because of the mistaken belief that venting is an effective means of bringing these feelings under control or bringing them to an end. Tavris (1989) has described how debased versions of Freudian concepts and misreported

research findings have created a popular belief that trying to exert self-control over anger is wrong, useless, and ultimately harmful to one's health. The prevalence of that view, despite the plethora of information contradicting it, may reflect a cultural self-indulgence with finding excuses to behave in a self-gratifying manner, even if it is harmful to others (e.g., Tavris, 1989).

Thus, although some people may engage in the ineffective mood control strategy of venting emotion because they do not want to bother exerting control over their moods, others may engage in the same strategy because of the mistaken belief that venting is an effective form of mood control (based on their very limited and distorted knowledge of the scientific findings). For whichever reason one engages in venting, it is still unlikely to be effective.

Cognitive Suppression

Many people try to regulate their negative feelings by avoiding or suppressing the thoughts that cause them to feel bad (e.g., Billings & Moos, 1984; Morrow & Nolen-Hoeksema, 1990; Rachman & de Silva, 1978; Rohde et al., 1990; Wegner, 1992). In fact, there is even a form of psychological therapy that advocates suppressing thoughts as a means of achieving mental health. Most empirical studies, however, have found that suppressing or avoiding unwanted thoughts or feelings (or suppressing thoughts about the problems that cause these unwanted feelings) is an ineffective method of reducing the unwanted feelings (e.g., Billings & Moos, 1984; Morrow & Nolen-Hoeksema, 1990; Rachman & de Silva, 1978; Rohde et al, 1990; Wegner, 1992).

The preceding chapter covered the inefficacy of simple thought suppression, and that same inefficacy applies to attempts at affect regulation that rely on thought suppression. Wegner's (1989; see also Wegner et al., 1987) work has provided a rather thorough explanation of why thought suppression might be an ineffective manner of controlling moods. When subjects in those studies were asked not to think about something, they were eventually with practice able to suppress thoughts about the forbidden item. However, these subjects later showed a rebound effect in which they thought about the forbidden item even more than people who had not been trying to suppress the thought earlier (or even more than people who had been focusing on the thought earlier!). Thus, ironically, people who try to suppress thoughts often end up actually obsessing about the things they are trying to suppress.

People are less able to suppress the thought under cognitive load (Wegner, 1994; Wegner, Erber, & Zanakos, 1993), so when people are under stress (such as from being tired or from attempting to do several things at once) they are more likely to show the intrusions of the thoughts they are trying to suppress. This is similar to the idea of *strength failure* discussed elsewhere in this book. Under conditions of fatigue, weakness, or competing demands on strength, people are less likely to be able to suppress their mood-relevant thoughts.

Several studies have been directly concerned with the affective implications of thought suppression. Wegner et al. (1990) showed that trying to suppress thoughts about an exciting or arousing topic (like sex) can even lead to greater physiological arousal than trying to think about the topic! In another study, a different version of misregulation through thought suppression was shown. Wenzlaff et al. (1988) found that depressed subjects undertook self-distraction to escape from a sad, distressed mood. Normally, self-distraction is a fairly effective technique, but in this case depressed subjects chose distractors that were themselves unpleasant and sad. Hence, although they may have succeeded in taking their minds off of the initial cause of their distress, they continued to feel bad.

Rumination and Perseveration

If the attempted suppression of unhappy thoughts is ineffective for overcoming a bad mood, it is not surprising that some people will try the opposite technique, namely focusing their thoughts on precisely what is bothering them. It is quite clear that many people spend a great deal of time ruminating about things that have upset them. Many individuals report that they try to control their moods by focusing on their feelings or ruminating about the events or issues that caused the negative moods, although they do not for the most part rate this as a highly effective means of changing their mood (Tice & Baumeister, 1993). Sometimes obsessing over feelings can be inadvertent, such as when one is trying to suppress a thought and the rebound occurs, with numerous and frequent intrusions of the previously suppressed thought (Wegner, 1989).

Ruminating about a bad mood or brooding about what caused a bad mood is not likely to result in mood change (e.g., Billings & Moos, 1984; Lyubomirsky & Nolen-Hoeksema, 1993; Morrow & Nolen-Hoeksema, 1990; Nolen-Hoeksema, 1990, 1993). Indeed, it may be just as ineffective as trying to suppress the thoughts.

There are several reasons that rumination fails to improve affect. When people engage in ruminative, emotion-focused thoughts and behaviors, they are less likely to engage in active problem-solving thoughts and behaviors (Carver et al., 1989; Klinger, 1993; Nolen-Hoeksema, 1993). In other words, one reason brooding about one's emotional state or problems is an ineffective mood control strategy is because it seems to interfere with active problem solving. Rumination may also thwart mood regulation by interfering with instrumental behavior, such as work-related tasks (e.g., Carver et al., 1989). Instrumental tasks are an opportunity for positive reinforcement, so interfering with instrumental behavior reduces one's chances of positive outcomes. In addition, instrumental behavior is a good source of pleasant distraction, so reducing instrumental behavior reduces the set of possible valuable distractors (Nolen-Hoeksema, 1993). Rumination decreases the likelihood of engaging in pleasant behaviors, and engaging in pleasant activities is likely to improve mood (Cialdini, Darby, & Vincent, 1973; Morris & Reilly, 1987; Underwood, Moore, & Rosenhan, 1973). A third reason rumination is ineffective at reducing bad moods is because it may increase the impact of moods on information processing. Nolen-Hoeksema cited a study by Needles and Abramson (1990, in Nolen-Hoeksema, 1993) that suggests that rumination increases the accessibility of negative cognitions, making further negative thoughts more likely.

Rumination fits one pattern we have repeatedly seen in self-regulation problems that are associated with serious, even clinical disturbances, namely the inability to stop oneself from perseverating in a distressful matter. In the preceding chapter, we saw that the core of obsessive-compulsive disorder appears to be an inability to stop the thought (as opposed to being troubled by an exceptionally powerful thought). Several other clinical patterns are marked by the inability to stop ruminating. For example, incest victims continue to think about and ruminate about their trauma even decades after the event (Silver et al., 1983). No practical or beneficial purpose is served by this quixotic quest for meaning, but the rumination does appear to be linked to increased and prolonged distress.

Depression may involve yet another failure at self-stopping, according to Pyszczynski and Greenberg (1987). Sooner or later, everyone suffers failure, rejection, or other losses that threaten one's self-esteem. Most people become self-focused at this time; indeed, self-awareness may arise precisely because falling short of standards is an occasion for self-assessment in order to appraise one's projects and progress (Carver & Scheier, 1981). Moreover, this self-focused state will tend to be an unpleasant one when it follows a serious failure or rejection experience, because it draws attention to something bad about the self.

Most people, however, pull themselves out of this self-focused state in a fairly short time. In particular, if the failure or rejection or other loss is something that cannot be rectified, then there is no point in continuing to dwell on it. Depressed people, however, seem to be unable to let go. Their attention remains focused on themselves and their shortcomings, and when there is no chance to make the situation better they end up dwelling on this tragedy and its implications. Perseverating in this state amplifies their emotional distress and their tendencies to derogate themselves. Subsequent failures or losses are then magnified, because they seem to confirm the unhappy thoughts about the self.

Distractors That Backfire

Although trying to merely suppress thoughts can be difficult, especially in the long run, the use of distractions to take one's mind off of the distressing problems does appear to be a useful means of regulating cognitions and emotions (e.g., Billings & Moos, 1984; Miller, 1987; Morrow & Nolen-Hoeksema, 1990; Nolen-Hoeksema, 1993; Wegner, 1989; Wenzlaff et al., 1988; Zillman, 1988, 1993).

Distraction is not infallible, however. In particular, if the distractors are themselves distressing, then the person may end up merely exchanging one source of distress for another. As already noted, Wenzlaff et al. (1988) found that depressed individuals were more

likely than nondepressed individuals to try to use other negative thoughts to distract themselves from a depressing thought. Depressed individuals were less effective at regulating their bad moods because of their use of this ineffective form of distraction. Similarly, in the example cited at the beginning of this chapter, the main character in *Falling Down* tried to distract himself from the irritating traffic jam by looking around at his surroundings, but the objects that caught his attention when he was trying to distract himself were other things that made him angry, and so he was unable to get out of the bad mood that way.

Zillman and colleagues (e.g., Bryant & Zillman, 1984; Zillman, Hezel, & Medoff, 1980) have examined the use of entertainments and communications media for controlling bad moods. They found that characteristics of the entertainment, such as its pleasantness, its ability to produce arousal or calm, and its tendency to absorb attention, were critical for mood management. Angry individuals, for example, were most likely to reduce their anger if they watched highly absorbing, highly pleasant, but very nonarousing, even calming, movies. Unfortunately, sometimes people choose movies that will be distressing, upsetting, or arousing, and these tend to be very ineffective means of escaping from bad moods (see Zillman, 1988, for a review of this literature).

Another ineffective use of distraction involves using reckless, violent, or dangerous activities to distract oneself from a bad mood. Nolen-Hoeksema (1993; also Nolen-Hoeksema & Morrow, 1991) has shown that people who brood and ruminate about their mood and problems are likely to engage in reckless, dangerous or violent activities, perhaps in a desperate attempt to disengage from the bad mood. Rohde et al. (1990) suggested that subjects who endorse reckless and dangerous coping strategies, such as "Do something reckless (like drive a car fast)" or "Do something rather dangerous" were more likely to be depressed both at the time of assessment and in the future than were subjects who did not endorse these items (see also Parker & Brown, 1979). In other words, using risk-taking or dangerous distractors to distract oneself from one's problems seems to cause or at least increase the chances of depression.

Some current studies in our own laboratories have shed preliminary light on how emotional distress leads to risky behavior. Apparently, bad moods increase a preference for high-risk, high-payoff options. Baumeister and Stillwell (1992) offered subjects a choice between two lotteries. One was a fairly safe bet with a small reward: Subjects had a 60% chance of winning $2. The other lottery was a long shot, offering a 5% chance of winning $20. In both cases, losing the lottery meant that one received no money and would have to undergo an unpleasant experience involving exposure to noise stress (i.e., an amplified recording of the sound of fingernails scratching on a blackboard). Statistical rationality would predict that the safe bet lottery is the better choice, because it yields a higher expected value (calculated by multiplying the chances of winning times the amount one would win).

We found that subjects who were in a bad mood (which was stimulated by an embarrassing experience) were more prone to choosing the long shot. Subjects in good or neutral moods tended to be about evenly divided in their preferences.

Thus, being in a bad mood tended to cause a preference for a long-shot lottery. In a sense, this preference is understandable, because winning a mere $2 might be inadequate to cure the person's bad mood, whereas winning $20 could be sufficient to accomplish that. The bad mood thus increases the attractiveness of the big score. However, consider what would be most likely to happen under such circumstances. The person feels bad and so chooses the high-risk option. Unfortunately, 95% of the time, the outcome will be bad, and so the person will end up with one more reason to feel bad. In that way, the bad mood can be self-perpetuating, even though the person chose the long shot with the hope of escaping from those feelings.

The use of emotionally similar distractors or dangerous distractors when trying to escape from a bad mood is likely to result in what we have called *psychological inertia*. The mood state itself may create conditions that make it more difficult to escape from the mood. Depression may make it more likely that distraction attempts will employ negatively valanced distractors, perpetuating the depressed mood. Anger may make irritating distractors more salient, perpetuating the angry mood. Anxiety may make fearful distractors more accessible, thus perpetuating the anxious mood, in all these cases, there appears to be a loss of control of attention. Angry people do

not seem to control their attention toward nonirritating distractors. Wenzlaff et al. (1988) demonstrated that if researchers give depressed individuals pleasant distractors, they are able to make use of them and decrease their depressed mood. However, the normal attentional path of depressed individuals is toward negative distractors, which perpetuate the depression.

Thus, although distraction is normally a highly effective means of controlling bad moods, distractors have to be of a certain type in order to work well. Nolen-Hoeksema (1993) has proposed that in order to be successful at reducing a bad mood, distractors must be engrossing and must have a high probability of positive reinforcement. Doing things with friends, working on an enjoyable hobby, or concentrating on work are examples of distractors recommended by Nolen-Hoeksema (1993) for escaping from depression. Zillman (1993) recommends highly engaging and pleasant stimuli to reduce bad moods. Using distractors that are emotionally similar to the bad mood one is in (such as distracting oneself with different sad thoughts when one is depressed, or arousing media events when one is angry) and use of dangerous, reckless, or risky distractors are not effective at reducing bad moods. If anything, they may be counterproductive.

Consumptive Behaviors

A very different class of affect regulation strategies involves consumptive behaviors: eating, drinking, taking drugs, and the like. Undoubtedly these behaviors have mood-altering effects, and sometimes they may even help people to feel better. In other circumstances, however, they tend to backfire, thereby qualifying as forms of affective misregulation.

Many people, especially women, report eating favorite foods to control their moods, and they report that this strategy is fairly effective for reducing sad moods if they do not overuse it (Tice & Baumeister, 1993). Food may serve to improve a minor sad mood because it serves as a pleasant distractor. Eating may also backfire, however, especially when one considers that most women in modern America are chronic dieters. When people are in a bad mood and want to eat something to make themselves feel better, they may focus on the pleasures of tasting and swallowing or on the feeling of satiety. After having eaten, however—especially if the food was high in fat and calories, like most of the treats people choose to cheer themselves up—people may focus instead on the caloric threat or the violation of one's diet, particularly if they are concerned about weight and body image, and this focus may bring back (or regenerate) a bad mood (Larsen, 1993).

A number of researchers have examined whether eating helps control moods (e.g., Billings & Moos, 1981, 1984; Frost, Goolkasian, Ely, & Blanchard, 1982; Larsen, 1993; Morris & Reilly, 1987; Thayer, 1987, 1989; Tice & Baumeister, 1993). Most of the findings have suggested that eating favorite foods is not an effective way to reduce negative moods (e.g., Billings & Moos, 1984; Larsen, 1993), but a more detailed examination of the data suggests that there may be certain conditions under which mood is improved after eating. Although Thayer (1987) found that a sugary snack could improve mood and energy level in the short run, he found that brief exercise (a brisk 10-min walk) was more effective in the longer run, such as one or two hours later. Tice and Baumeister (1993) suggested that eating does serve to temporarily reduce sad moods, but it does not have an effect on reducing anger. Likewise, although they found that it reduced sad moods produced by minor daily events, other evidence suggests that eating does little to improve long-term, clinical depression, and it may serve to worsen the depressed mood (Billings & Moos, 1984).

Thus, eating may serve to improve mood only in very specific, limited conditions. If the bad mood is sadness, not anger or clinical depression, if the person is not overly concerned with weight or body image (and the loss of control that the eating to improve mood signifies), if the food eaten is consumed in reasonable quantities, and if the strategy is not used too frequently, eating may improve mood.

Similar patterns of misregulation can be found with alcohol consumption. Many people, especially men, report drinking alcohol to reduce bad moods (Larsen, 1993; Morris & Reilly, 1987; Parker & Brown, 1982; Pearlin & Radabaugh, 1976; Rippere, 1977; Tice & Baumeister, 1993; see also Marlatt, Kosturn, & Lang, 1975). Like the data reported above for eating to control bad moods, drinking alcohol may work only if it is an infrequent strategy used in moderation. Otherwise it may backfire.

Alcohol is often associated with parties, celebrations, and other good times, and so people may unfortunately think that getting drunk will be a generally effective way of feeling better. As a result, people may use alcohol in ways that will end up making them feel worse. Billings and Moos (1984) showed that drinking alcohol is an ineffective strategy for combating clinical depression—in fact, alcohol tends to intensify depressive symptoms. The unfortunate consequence of this pattern may be a vicious cycle, in which a person feels depressed, tries to "self-medicate" by consuming alcohol, ends up feeling worse, and therefore consumes even more alcohol.

Attentional factors may be one reason for the ineffectiveness of alcohol as an affect regulation strategy. As described elsewhere in this book, Steele and Josephs (1990) portrayed the effects of alcohol intoxication as a kind of "myopia": a narrowing of attention. The drunk person can only focus on one or two things at a time. If alcohol use is combined with compelling distractors, such as watching a ball game or engaging in conversation at a cocktail party, it may indeed improve one's mood. But if a depressed person simply consumes alcohol and then thinks about his or her problems, the narrowed focus will make the problems seem even more pervasive than they did before getting drunk. Attention will thus end up being riveted to the distressing issues, and the mood will get worse instead of better.

In a sense, alcoholic myopia contributes to transcendence failure. Transcendence—seeing beyond the immediate situation—is often effective for regulating affect. One can say that one's problems may seem small in a broad context or that things may not be as bad as they seem at the moment. The narrowed focus of alcoholic intoxication makes it harder, however, to take the broad view. One's attention remains immersed in the immediate situation, and so the source of one's distress looms large.

Similar processes apply to people who turn to drink to regulate anger. Angry and irritated men sometimes report choosing to drink in order to "calm down." However, alcohol-intoxicated individuals respond more aggressively to the same provocation than sober people (Taylor & Leonard, 1983; Zillman, 1993), perhaps because they are less sensitive to their opponents' desire to stop fighting (Leonard, 1989). Thus, in the presence of continued irritating stimuli, angry people who drink alcohol are likely to respond more aggressively and therefore remain angrier than angry people who do not drink. Given the tendency of alcohol intoxication to narrow attention to immediate stimuli and to intensify aggressive responses to provocations, it is hardly surprising that many violent crimes are committed by intoxicated people (e.g., Gottfredson & Hirschi, 1990). The alcoholic myopia makes it harder to see beyond the immediate situation—such as thinking that one's pride and honor will not really be tarnished by the disrespectful remarks of another bar patron, or by reflecting that avenging some insult is not worth risking arrest and imprisonment. Without such transcendence, the drunk person's consciousness becomes saturated with the immediate provocation, and violent responses become more likely. (Indeed, according to Gottfredson and Hirschi [1990], many perpetrators of homicide are scarcely able to recall the next day what made them angry enough to kill.) Drink is a poor cure for anger, unless one is surrounded by peaceful and pleasant distractors that are quite compelling.

Other drugs are also implicated in patterns of affect misregulation. People report smoking cigarettes, using tranquilizers, and using illicit drugs in an effort to improve their moods (Tice & Baumeister, 1993), although even self-reported success with these methods is not very high. Billings and Moos (1984) found that smoking and drug use are often associated with intensified depression.

Thus, although there is quite a bit of folk wisdom suggesting that eating favorite foods to be nice to oneself, drinking alcohol, or smoking a cigarette will help one to calm down or to cheer up, there is little empirical support for these beliefs. In fact, as detailed above, there is even considerable evidence suggesting that these efforts at cheering oneself up or calming oneself down will actually serve to worsen one's bad mood. To be sure, they can be effective under very limited and specific circumstances, but for the most part consumptive strategies are not to be recommended as ways of regulating affect.

OVERGENERALIZATION: MISMATCHING MOODS AND STRATEGIES

Not all mood regulation strategies work equally well for all moods. Although a strategy such as socializing with others (e.g., calling family members on the phone, visiting friends, engaging in pleasant activities with companions) might work well for one kind of bad mood like sadness, it might backfire when used to control other kinds of bad moods such as anger (Tice & Baumeister, 1993). Thus, mood control might fail because people have used a strategy successfully in the past to control one bad mood and so are likely to use it again when they feel bad, even if they are experiencing a different unpleasant emotion. This form of misregulation may be especially confusing to people, because a strategy that worked many times in the past suddenly is not effective.

Like socializing with others, social isolation can effectively reduce some bad moods, but it makes other worse. Many angry people report that social isolation, particularly if combined with a pleasant activity, helps to reduce feelings of anger (Tice & Baumeister, 1993). However, sad or depressed people are likely to worsen their sad or depressed mood if they choose to withdraw from others (e.g., Rohde et al., 1990). Even if people are aware that it is effective to be alone when one is angry and be with people when one is sad, they may still misregulate and worsen their bad mood if they spend their solitary time brooding. Social isolation helps to alleviate anger if one engages in a pleasant and distracting activity, but not if one uses the time alone to rehearse one's grievances (e.g., Zillman, 1993; Tice & Baumeister, 1993; Tice, 1994). Likewise, interacting with friends or others helps to reduce sadness only if one engages in pleasant conversation or activities with friends—not if one monopolizes the conversation with discussions of one's problems. Although it may be useful to consult a trusted friend or relative occasionally about one's problems in order to get a fresh approach or even just some sympathy, this backfires if the technique is overused.

One of the reasons that interacting with others can fail to improve a bad mood is that the other people may end up sharing the bad mood after listening to the person's problems. The sad person may hope that after talking with a happy person both people will be happy, but sometimes the outcome may be bilateral sadness (e.g., Pennebaker, 1993).* For example, Strack and Coyne (1983) demonstrated that people who talked with a depressed person for only 15 min subsequently reported feeling depressed, anxious, and hostile themselves, and talking to an angry person about one's angry feeling can create anger in the listener (e.g., Tavris, 1989). Living with a depressed person leads to greater depression (Coyne et al., 1987), perhaps because the depressed person communicates his or her sad thoughts and feelings to the roommate.

Another fact that raises problems for some affect regulation efforts is that being together with other people is arousing. Social psychologists have long acknowledged that the presence of members of one's own species tends to produce arousal, dating back at least to Zajonc's (1965) social facilitation theory. This arousal may contribute to a variety of emotional reactions, including excitement, nervousness, anxiety, sexual attraction, and many others. At bottom, many of these reactions are simply due to the fact that people are more readily, easily, and strongly aroused when they are with others.

Because people tend to become aroused when others are there, seeking out other people may often help to overcome feelings of dejection, sadness, or apathy, or indeed any unpleasant mood that is characterized by a lack of arousal. People may overgeneralize the benefits of being with others, however, and so may try to use the same strategy to cure bad moods that are marked by high arousal or agitation. This can easily backfire.

Anger, in particular, is typically marked by high levels of arousal. In order to escape from an angry state, it is generally necessary to calm down. Being together with other people may create further arousal, however, and as a result it becomes that much harder to calm down. There may be exceptions, of course; certain companions may have a strongly calming influence on others, and so being together with them could be helpful. But in general the presence of other people has an arousing effect and is thus counterproductive for overcoming anger.

Being with others can be counterproductive for escaping anger for other reasons too. An angry person will tend to be irritable. In the normal give and take of social interaction, an angry person may therefore be prone to respond irritably, such as to say something sarcastic or nasty. A stray nasty remark can easily elicit an angry response from someone else, leading to a disagreement or argument, and the result may be that the angry person now has yet another reason to feel angry. The escape from anger has thus gotten even more remote.

The same goes for someone who is feeling upset because of stress. Repetti (1989) found that people in stressful occupations tended to find that a brief period of social withdrawal improved their relationships with their families. If they went straight from a stressful workday to interacting with their families, they were prone to get into arguments and disputes. But spending part of an hour by themselves enabled them to calm down, and subsequent family interactions were therefore much more pleasant for everyone.

Thus, social interaction may produce failure to regulate anger because it is arousing. Other arousing activities have the same pitfall. People may do things that they normally enjoy but find that they fail to overcome an angry state. In a recent summary of research on using the media to control moods, Zillman (1988) reviewed work done by him and his colleagues (Bryant & Zillman, 1984; Zillman et al., 1980) that suggests that arousing stimuli, even if they are absorbing and pleasant, are not as effective at reducing anger as are calming or at least nonarousing stimuli. A fan of exciting action movies may find, for example, that watching such a movie will fail to cure an angry mood. Although most of Zillman's work was done with media distractors such as films and

---

* Although normally people should not communicate everyday problems and bad moods to others in order to improve their moods, Pennebaker (1990, 1993) has demonstrated that people may be healthier and happier if they can confide their deepest traumas to another person. Pennebaker does not suggest that it is helpful to discuss these traumas continually with friends or with everyone one meets; rather, his point is that the process of organizing one's thoughts, and the reactions of the confidant, may be beneficial enough to justify a one-time, full, detailed confession.

books, other distractors such as games and discussions should operate by the same principles. Even though a rousing game of checkers made you feel better when you were depressed, it may not help at all and may even make you feel worse when you are angry.

Shopping may be another form of mood control that is prone to backfire when overgeneralized. Many people report going shopping when they are sad, but they report that this strategy is not very effective for overcoming anger or irritation (Tice & Baumeister, 1993). It may be that imagining oneself owning the pleasingly displayed items offered for sale, having a successful experience getting a good bargain, finding just the right item for oneself or for a gift, and interacting with others all help to cheer up a sad person, but these positive experiences may not make up for the frequently irritating aspects of the shopping experience: having to wait in line, not being able to find what one came for, dealing with preoccupied or uncooperative salespeople, or having another driver take the parking spot one wanted.

Another similar misregulation of mood control strategies is to use relaxation strategies when one is feeling depressed. Seligman (1994) states that a major misregulation of depression occurs when sad or depressed people try to use relaxation strategies and make themselves even sadder. Popular wisdom, friends and family members, talk show hosts and guests, and others teach people how to relax and calm down when they are feeling "uptight." The problem for people is that they sometimes misapply these strategies to times when they are feeling depressed rather than anxious. Because depression and anxiety tend to co-occur at high rates (e.g., Polivy, 1981), sufferers may focus on one component of the emotion-complex and ignore other components. If a person is suffering primarily from depression but is more aware of or concerned about the concomitant anxiety, then he or she may attempt to use relaxation strategies that worsen the depression. One reason relaxation strategies may not work well for depression is that they frequently require social isolation, and the isolation might interfere with effective coping with the depression.

The problem of dealing with both depression and anxiety brings up one additional, broader problem for affect regulation. Most mood states are not single, discrete moods, but rather a combination of multiple moods (e.g., Izard, 1972, 1977; Polivy, 1981). Thus, even a person who had careful and thorough knowledge of which techniques cure which moods might become perplexed at how to deal with certain mixtures of bad moods. For example, most researchers are familiar with the mixture of depressed sadness, nervous anxiety, and anger that often accompanies having one's work rejected by scientific journals. Few affect regulation strategies seem likely to succeed at ending such a mix of distress. Trying to calm down may help overcome the anger—but may intensify the sadness. Meanwhile, doing something exciting may help overcome the sadness but intensify the anger. The persistence of that particular form of distress—indeed, at any scientific conference one can hear researchers still telling bitter stories about their most upsetting rejections many months and even years after the fact—may be due to the difficulty of finding any strategy that can address all parts of such a blend of bad moods.

Thus, many mood control strategies are best suited to particular moods. When people try to use them to escape from other bad moods, they may backfire. The evidence currently available suggests that overgeneralization problems are mainly associated with the arousal dimension: Exciting activities (even pleasant ones) may fail to cure bad moods marked by high arousal, and calming activities may be counterproductive for overcoming bad moods marked by low arousal.

OVERGENERALIZATION ACROSS CIRCUMSTANCES

A second route into self-regulation failure by way of overgeneralization consists of neglecting the fact that circumstances may thwart techniques that work at other times. If a person discovers that a certain method cures a certain bad mood once, he or she may (not surprisingly) use that technique again, even under conditions that undermine its effectiveness.

Going for an automobile drive is a good example of this. A number of people report that going for a drive is an effective way to reduce anger (Tice & Baumeister, 1993). Driving not only gets the angry person away from friends and family members before he or she says something regrettable; it can also provide a pleasant "flow experience" (Csikszentmihalyi, 1990) that may improve a bad mood. Not all driving experiences are the same, however. Taking a peaceful, unhindered drive down a lonesome country road may help calm one down and allow anger to dissipate. But driving through heavy city traffic, especially where one may get caught in an annoying traffic jam or be subjected to the frustrations of being cut off by rude fellow motorists, is not likely to allow anger to dissipate.

Indeed, we suspect that some of the hostilities currently seen between motorists on American highways (ranging from obscene gestures to gunplay) may derive from just such failed efforts at affect regulation. An angry person may storm out of the house after a dispute and go for a drive, consistent with self-reports that people go driving in order to control their anger. If such a driver objects to the driving practices by another motorist, however, a resort to hostility would not be surprising.

Exercise is another form of mood control that can backfire under some circumstances. Exercise has been proven highly beneficial in reducing both sad moods and long-term, even severe depression (e.g., Bahrke & Morgan, 1978; Doyne, Chambless, & Beutler, 1983; Greist et al., 1979; McCann & Holmes, 1984), and a number of people even report that it is effective in reducing anger (Tice & Baumeister, 1993). Because sadness and depression are states associated with lower than optimal arousal (e.g., Thayer, 1989), it makes sense that getting oneself aroused through exercise would help overcome such moods. Ironically, however, some people report using exercise to overcome anger, which is an aroused emotion. They say that exercise works sometimes but not other times. The discrepancy may be the result of overgeneralization. Whether exercise helps overcome anger may depend on the circumstances.

To understand why exercise may sometimes fail, it is necessary to appreciate how it can affect an angry state. Unfortunately, at present there are several competing hypotheses about the effects of exercise. One view is that exercise makes the person tired, which thus removes arousal and hence precludes a continuation of the angry state (Tice & Baumeister, 1993; see also Thayer, 1989). In that view, the initial, arousing stage of exercise might even magnify the anger. The eventual fatigue would be effective at reducing anger, but it is of course necessary for the person to continue the exercise until that point is reached. If the person interrupts the exercise before

becoming tired, the added arousal may leave him or her more angry than ever.

A second hypothesis is that exercise may serve as a misattribution for the arousal caused by anger. If angry people exercise, they may attribute their subsequent arousal to the exercise and not perceive themselves to be as angry as people who had not exercised (see Zillman's work on excitation transfer, e.g., Zillman, 1978, 1979; Zillman, Johnson, & Day, 1974; Zillman, Katcher, & Milavsky, 1972). The danger with such a misattribution strategy is that it could just as well work in the opposite direction. For anger to be misattributed to exercise, the person would presumably have to have not yet labeled the arousal as anger. This may be unlikely; most people seem to know soon enough when they are angry. In contrast, the excitation from the exercise could easily be misattributed to the anger, leading the person again to think that he or she is angrier than ever.

The third hypothesis is that exercise serves as a distraction (e.g., Morgan, 1985; Morrow & Nolen-Hoeksema, 1990). We have repeatedly emphasized the potential effectiveness of self-distraction strategies for self-regulation in general. Still, under some circumstances exercise may fail or even backfire as a distraction. Some forms of exercise are less distracting than others. Jogging, for example, makes few demands on the mind, and so the person may find himself or herself ruminating about what caused the anger, with the result that the exercise session turns into a period of concentrated brooding (leading to increased anger). Moreover, we have already noted the fallacy of using aversive distractors to overcome bad moods, and there is no denying that sport activities can produce frustration, annoyance, discomfort, and other sources of distress. An angry person may resort to a cognitively demanding sport such as tennis or racquetball in order to distract himself or herself, only to find that new irritations such as having to wait for the court, an opponent's self-serving bad calls, or the failure of one's own seemingly unlucky shots, end up producing more anger.

In short, there are many affect regulation strategies whose effectiveness is limited to certain emotions *and* to certain types of circumstances. Self-regulation may fail when people overgeneralize and use these strategies when they are not effective.

IGNORING LONG-TERM CONCERNS

A final set of mood misregulation strategies involves focusing on short-term rather than long-term concerns, with the result that short-term improvements may effectively be obtained but the distress soon returns. Overconcern with immediate concerns has been treated throughout this work under the rubric of *transcendence failure*, and this final set of affect misregulation patterns is related to transcendence failure. Some of them also invoke the kind of counterproductive self-management patterns that we covered in Chapter 4 on self-management.

There are a number of strategies that people use to control their moods that work in the short term but do not seem to have long-term effects, including eating favorite foods, interacting with friends or family members, listening to music, and use of drugs or alcohol (e.g., Aneshensel & Huba, 1983; Larsen, 1993; Morris & Reilly, 1987; see also Thayer, 1987, 1989). Indeed, some of these can produce worse problems in the long run.

If people are in a bad mood because of something that is not able to be changed and is not likely to recur, than focusing on the short term may be helpful. For instance, if one is in a bad mood because a stranger cut ahead in line at the supermarket, doing something that would be a pleasant distraction from the event is likely to make one feel better in the present. (This assumes that the problem is an isolated case of stranger rudeness rather than a reflection of chronic lack of assertiveness.) Because this event is unlikely to recur, just getting out of the bad mood temporarily is enough: once out of the bad mood one is likely to continue feeling good.

However, if focusing on the short-term mood change prevents long-term coping with the event causing the bad mood, then the bad mood is likely to come back. For example, if a person with money problems is sad because he is receiving disconnection notices from the utilities because he has neglected to pay his bills, then trying to cheer himself up by going out drinking with his buddies is not likely to make him feel much better tomorrow. Likewise, if a dieter feels bad because her clothes no longer fit since she gained weight, then cheering herself up by eating a sundae is not likely to create lasting mood improvement.

Seeking out social companionship may be another strategy that may sometimes be counterproductive in the long run because it fails to address the basic causes of the bad moods. We have already noted that being with friends is effective for bringing about an immediate improvement in many moods (e.g., Billings & Moos, 1984; Rohde et al., 1990; Tice & Baumeister, 1993; Zillman, 1993). Yet Larsen (1993) found that the affective benefits of social interaction tended to be temporary at best. One reason may be that using social interaction as an escape from one's problems leaves one vulnerable to future distress when the problem returns. For example, if a student feels bad because he received a D in chemistry, and he attempts to make himself feel better by hanging out with his friends at the student center rather than doing chemistry homework and readings, then he is not working at solving the problem that caused the bad mood in the first place. He may feel better on that particular day, but it seems likely that more Ds, and more bad moods, lie ahead.

Not all problems can be solved, and so some bad moods can be improved by interacting with others. For instance, if in the example above the student had felt bad about not getting selected by the fraternity of his choice, then interacting with his friends might have proved to be an effective mood control strategy, because his friends provide reassurance that he is a likable fellow, and besides there is nothing he can do now to reverse the fraternity's rejection. But when social interaction interferes with effective problem solving, then it may result in continued bad mood in the long term.

Thus, if the mood arises from a temporary event that could not be solved by focusing on the problem, then focusing on the short term may be the best one can do. If getting out of the bad mood temporarily is likely to result in our staying in a neutral or positive mood, then escaping from the bad mood by using temporary mood improvement strategies is likely to be effective. On the other hand, if coping with the short-term effects prevents active problem solving so that the problem causing the bad mood is likely to recur, then a short-term focus is problematic.

The self-regulation problem of procrastination (which we covered in the chapter on self-management) may often be traced to a similar overconcern with short-term affective improvement at the expense of long-term self-management. One of the several reasons that people procrastinate is that they wish to avoid the anxiety or other emotional distress that the work gives them. For example, as the would-be novelist sits down at the typewriter to work on her first novel, anxiety about producing a mediocre product and about unclear standards for success may create negative affect that impels her to put off working on the manuscript and avoid the anxious mood. In the short run, she is better off, because the anxiety is in fact prevented. In the long run, however, postponing important work tasks is a recipe for career failure.

INDIVIDUAL DIFFERENCES IN SKILL

A number of researchers have investigated the possibility that some people just have more skill than others at regulating their emotions. Salovey and Mayer (1990) identified the concept of *emotional intelligence,* which they defined as "the ability to monitor one's own and others' feelings and emotions, to discriminate among them, and to use this information to guide one's thinking and actions" (Salovey & Mayer, 1990, p. 189; see also Salovey, Hsee, & Mayer, 1993), and they suggested that people with higher emotional intelligence would be better able to regulate their own emotions as well as produce desired emotional responses in others. Mayer and Gaschke (1988; see also Mayer, Salovey, Gomberg-Kaufman, & Blainy, 1991) have developed a scale to discriminate among people's experience and meta-experience of mood, including the ability to regulate emotions. Catanzaro and Mearns (1990; see also Kirsch, Mearns, & Catanzaro, 1990; Mearns, 1991) have focused on individual differences in expectancies for regulating negative moods, whereas Campos, Campos, and Barrett (1989) and Kopp (1989) have examined the developmental aspects that affect one's ability to regulate emotion. Larsen and Ketelaar (1989, 1991) have examined the effects that neuroticism and extraversion have on susceptibility to positive and negative emotional states. Larsen has also demonstrated that some individuals are likely to experience their emotional life much more intensely than others (Larsen, 1984; Larsen, Diener, & Emmons, 1986), and those individuals may have more need to regulate and more difficulty regulating their emotions than people who experience their moods less intensely. Together, these findings suggest that because

of differences in background, prior experiences, intelligence, personality, and other individual differences, some people are better able to understand and regulate their emotional experiences than others.

SUMMARY AND CONCLUSION

Self-regulation of mood and emotion is often unnecessary and often unsuccessful. In many cases, emotions serve valuable functions such as to motivate adaptive actions, and suppressing the emotion might therefore prevent helpful actions. Also, as we have noted in many other chapters, a broad variety of self-regulation failures arise when people focus on controlling their feelings and leave the more fundamental and serious problems unresolved.

Emotions contain many automatic components, and therefore they are especially difficult to control directly. Affect regulation is thus limited in what it can accomplish. Many failures are therefore simply attributable to the fact that the person was trying to control something that could not be controlled.

Still, people do have some effective ways of controlling their moods and emotions. Although in theory there are many different types of affect regulation tasks, by far the most common is the attempt to escape from a bad mood or aversive emotional state, and so we have emphasized that one.

Some affects fail to be regulated because of simple underregulation patterns. Two reasons for underregulation are important. First, people sometimes believe that they should not try to control their emotions. Second, many people believe that it is best to vent all their feelings whenever they arise, and so they act out all emotional reactions (particularly anger) rather than trying to exert self-control. The evidence suggests that venting is not helpful and may be counterproductive for reducing anger. (On the other hand, keeping one's anger in can also be harmful; the only beneficial response is to try to bring one's anger to an end.) These beliefs may encourage people to acquiesce in not controlling their emotions.

Misregulation of moods and emotional states occurs for a variety of reasons. Overgeneralization is particularly common as a source of misregulation: People apply strategies that work for one mood to another mood, such as when they seek out companionship of others (which does alleviate sadness and fear) when angry but then make themselves angrier as they tell these other people all their grievances. They also may seek out arousing entertainments when they are already too aroused by some emotional reaction. Others keep using strategies that may have worked once, even though circumstances have now changed and those strategies are no longer advisable or effective.

Misregulation also occurs when people try strategies that simply do not work. They may try to suppress thoughts that are linked to the bad mood, but often people cannot simply block an upsetting matter out of their minds. They also may use distractors that compound the problem by generating other bad moods, such as when people may go to a depressing or upsetting movie in order to take their mind off their own troubles.

Transcendence failure is also a frequent source of failure to regulate affect. The more the person becomes immersed in the immediate situation, the harder it is to escape from the emotional reactions that it engenders. Emotions appear to engender a short-term focus, which may be one reason that moods and emotions acquire inertia and are difficult to overcome.

Many emotions are automatic reactions to circumstances, so the emotions cannot be prevented from arising. On the other hand, when people do things that prolong their exposure to those same circumstances or (indeed) that make things worse, they may be accused of acquiescing in their failure to control emotions. The social context of emotion must always be considered, however, because it often imposes severe limits on the person's ability to control his or her emotional state. The social context also encompasses the reactions of other people to how one deals with one's emotions. Lapse-induced causes may even be invoked, such as when an angry person says something that provokes an angry response from another person, thereby creating a new reason to continue being angry.

Kleptomania

By J.E. Grant and B.L. Odlaug

Glossary

Antisocial personality disorder—A psychiatric condition characterized by persistent disregard and violation of the rights of others and what society considers right and wrong.

Escitalopram—A drug in the selective serotonin reuptake inhibitor (SSRI) class which is an isomer of citalopram and is used to treat depression and anxiety.

Opioid antagonist—A class of medications which bind to the opioid receptors in the brain, effectively blocking the effects of opiates (e.g., heroin and morphine). Examples of this class of medication include naloxone hydrochloride and naltrexone hydrochloride.

Serotonergic dysfunction—Problems in the neurotransmission of serotonin.

Ventromedial prefrontal cortex—A brain region that contributes to decision-making and risk-taking.

White matter—Brain tissue consisting of myelinated nerve fibers (e.g., axons).

Introduction

Kleptomania is a psychiatric disorder characterized by persistent and recurrent patterns of stealing. The *Diagnostic and Statistical Manual* (Fourth Edition) defines kleptomania by the following criteria: (1) recurrent failure to resist impulses to steal objects that are not needed for personal use or for their monetary value; (2) increasing sense of tension immediately before committing the theft; (3) pleasure, gratification, or relief at the time of committing the theft; (4) the stealing is not committed to express anger or vengeance and is not in response to a delusion or a hallucination; and (5) the stealing is not better accounted for by conduct disorder, a manic episode, or antisocial personality disorder. Psychosocial problems are common among individuals with kleptomania and include significant legal consequences, reduced quality of life, and impaired functioning. Suicide attempts are also common and have been reported in 25–30% of persons in treatment for kleptomania.

Estimates of more than $13 billion of retail sales lost due to shoplifting have been documented by the National Association for Shoplifting Prevention in 2009. Recent data provided through the National Epidemiologic Survey on Alcohol and Related Conditions (NESARC) illustrate rates of lifetime shoplifting of 11.3% in the United States. Historically, the terms 'shoplifting' and 'kleptomania' have been used interchangeably but significant differences separate someone with kleptomania from one who shoplifts. Shoplifting is defined as stealing items from a store without a specific motivating factor. Kleptomania, on the other hand, is defined as a psychiatric diagnosis characterized by a diminished ability to resist recurrent impulses to steal objects that are not needed for their monetary or personal use. Although kleptomania has been documented for almost two centuries, it remains a poorly understood disorder with limited data regarding neurobiology or treatment. This article details what is currently known about the clinical characteristics, neurobiology, and treatment of kleptomania.

J.E. Grant and B.L. Odlaug, "Kleptomania," from the *Encyclopedia of Behavioral Neuroscience: Volume 2*, George F. Koob, Michel Le Moal and Richard F. Thompson, eds. pp. 118–122. Published by Academic Press, 2010. Copyright by Elsevier Science and Technology Books. Permission to reprint granted by the rights holder.

History

Reports of uncontrolled, impulsive shoplifting behavior date back centuries and gained notoriety in the nineteenth century with the advent of the department store which made a variety of goods available in a concentrated area. Upper-middle-class women were caught stealing from these stores, creating a media-frenzy in the newspapers of both North America and Europe describing unbridled shoplifting behavior. It was at this time that the medical community began attempts to explain this behavior.

First coined in 1816 by the Swiss physician Andre Matthey, the term 'klopemanie' was derived from the Greek words 'kleptein' (to steal) and 'mania' (insanity) to describe a person who could not or did not control their stealing behavior. In 1838, Jean-Etienne Esquirol wrote the first detailed description of this seemingly nonvolitional and irresistible behavior. This article on kleptomania was important as it distinguished a person with this disorder from those who steal due to a lack of moral character.

Because of the extensive newspaper reports in the nineteenth century depicting women stealing, the medical community initially attributed this 'exclusively female' behavior to the female reproductive system, specifically uterine diseases and premenstrual tension. Following the dismissal of this explanation in the early twentieth century, partially due to the observation that more men were presenting with similar behavior, nearly all research pertaining to kleptomania ceased. The first *Diagnostic Manual of Mental Disorders* (DSM-I) in 1952 did not include kleptomania as a formal diagnostic illness but rather as a supplementary term. Kleptomania was not included in DSM-II. In 1980, DSM-III categorized kleptomania as an impulse control disorder not elsewhere classified, the same clinical diagnostic category it currently holds in the DSM-IV-TR.

Epidemiology

Although kleptomania has been documented in case studies and newspaper articles for centuries, relatively little is known about its prevalence in the general population. In the only study assessing rates in a general community sample using DSM-IV criteria, researchers examined 791 college students and found that although 28.6% reported having stolen an item in his/her lifetime, only 0.4% met criteria for kleptomania.

Other studies have examined the rates of kleptomania in treatment samples. An adult psychiatric inpatient study ($n = 204$) revealed lifetime rates of 93% ($n = 19$) while 7.8% ($n = 16$) had symptoms consistent with a current diagnosis of kleptomania. In a recent study of 102 adolescent psychiatric inpatients, researchers noted that 9 (8.8%) met diagnostic criteria for current kleptomania.

The prevalence of kleptomania in specific psychiatric populations has also been assessed. A study of 79 patients with alcohol dependence found that 3.8% ($n = 3$) endorsed symptoms consistent with kleptomania while a study of 107 depressed patients found that 3.7% ($n = 4$) suffered from kleptomania. In two studies of individuals with pathological gambling, rates of co-occurring kleptomania were 2.1% and 5%.

A Comparison of Kleptomania and Shoplifting

Individuals with kleptomania differ from 'ordinary' shoplifters in that they do not steal for personal gain, but rather for symptomatic relief. It is estimated that more than $13 billion worth of goods are stolen from retailers each year, which translates into more than $35 million per day. Vast majority of shoplifters are described as amateurs with sporadic activity and no known history of criminal activity who steal for their own consumption rather than for resale. Studies involving apprehended, legally referred shoplifters indicate that shoplifting may be more common in women (ranging from 52% to 100%) than in men. However as with kleptomania, these rates may be falsely elevated because women may be more likely to be referred for psychiatric evaluation or seek psychiatric treatment than are men. Male shoplifters are more likely to be apprehended during adolescence and early adulthood, whereas women shoplifters are more likely to be apprehended during puberty/early adulthood and around the age of menopause. Some of these same studies also revealed that shoplifting was not related to lower socioeconomic level and that most stole for personal gain. Rates of kleptomania among people who are arrested for shoplifting have ranged from 0% to 8%. A study that compared individuals with kleptomania to shoplifters interviewed directly after apprehension found that 58% of the shoplifters were male compared to only 32.4% of kleptomania patients. The mean age among shoplifters was 27 years and among the kleptomaniacs, 41 years. Although none of the shoplifters met DSM criteria for kleptomania, approximately one-fifth had not stolen for personal use and had eventually discarded the object. The study also found that both groups reported the same degree of impulsivity and 'a feeling of not being oneself.' On the other hand, individuals with kleptomania reported a relatively greater number of previous thefts compared to shoplifters, a finding consistent with a compulsive aspect of kleptomania.

Childhood and Adolescent Stealing

Both typical shoplifting and kleptomania may start at a relatively early age. A young child generally has little, if any, concept of stealing—for him or her, desiring or wanting means possession of the object. By the age of 6 or 7, children begin to realize they are doing something wrong when they take something that does not belong to them. Children may steal because they are unhappy, lonesome, jealous, fearful, or craving attention. For older children and adolescents, stealing can be used to gain acceptance from a group, but is also a strong predictor of future delinquency and a marker for families lacking in warmth and personal stimulation. A strong attachment to parents decreases involvement in shoplifting.

Overall, studies have shown that roughly 40% of apprehended shoplifters are adolescents. A study involving almost 1700 adolescents found that 37% reported shoplifting at least once in the prior 12 months. The percentage of subjects acknowledging shoplifting peaked around the 10th grade and then declined, consistent with official crime statistics. One hypothesis for adolescent theft involves multiple, non-mutually-exclusive factors involving a function of immaturity during a stressful transition to adulthood, an inability to purchase certain items, and an increased opportunity (the steepest gain of independence occurs around age 16 when most adolescents are allowed to drive and work). On the other

hand, adolescents report that they shoplift because of the associated novelty and risk, for social reasons, and because they desire for the stolen items. Additionally, no relationship has been found between family occupational status and adolescent shoplifting. How many of these adolescent shoplifters currently suffer from, or will develop a problem with, kleptomania is not clear. Longitudinal studies of this nature, to help clinicians better assess who should receive treatment, are needed.

Clinical Characteristics of Kleptomania

Case Vignette

Jennifer, a 54-year-old married female, described a history of uncontrollable shoplifting beginning at about age 16 years of age. She started by stealing a scarf 'in a dare' from a friend but found the 'high' was intense and overwhelming. Over the course of about 1 year, she reports that she progressed from occasional theft to being unable to control herself when she entered a store. Although she has had periods of a year or two without any shoplifting, Jennifer reports that she currently shoplifts once or twice a week. She describes a 'rush' each time she steals. In fact, the 'rush is short-lived' and when she leaves the store she usually throws away the stolen item or leaves it outside the store. Although she usually steals clothing, she denies really wanting the items and she could easily afford to buy them. Jennifer also describes daily thoughts and urges to shoplift that interfere with her ability to concentrate at work. In addition, she has never told her husband about her behavior. The behavior and the lying cause significant depression and feelings of worthless. Jennifer tried to commit suicide on one occasion, never telling anyone the reason behind her suicide attempt. She also reports drinking in the evening to 'deaden' the pain and guilt over her shoplifting.

Kleptomania usually begins in adolescence or early adulthood, with males tending to start at an earlier age, though kleptomania has been documented in patients as young as 4 years old and as old as 77 years old. Although prospective studies are largely lacking, kleptomania appears to follow a similar trajectory as substance dependence, with high rates in adolescent and young adult groups, lower rates in older adults, and periods of abstinence and relapse.

One study found that individuals with kleptomania stole, on average, twice or thrice a week. The places from which items are stolen and the value of those stolen items generally change over time for those with kleptomania. Although stealing from stores is the most common place of theft, stealing from friends, relatives, and work is not uncommon. The objects stolen by the individual are usually affordable and are typically discarded, hoarded, thrown away, discreetly returned to the store, or given away. Most individuals with kleptomania report that the value of a stolen item increases over time. Examples of commonly stolen objects include sweets, newspapers, food, books, and clothes. The excitement and rush associated with the act of committing the theft and getting away with it are typically immediately followed by feelings of shame and remorse.

Gender Differences

Clinical samples of patients have reported that two-thirds of patients with kleptomania are female. Women with kleptomania are more likely to be married, tend to have a later onset of shoplifting, are more likely to steal household items, and hoard the items stolen. They are also more likely to have a comorbid eating disorder. Men with kleptomania are more likely to steal electronic goods and more likely to have another co-occurring impulse control disorder (most commonly intermittent explosive disorder or compulsive sexual behavior).

Quality of Life Issues and Legal Consequences

Individuals with kleptomania endorse a significant amount of impairment in their daily lives. Independent of comorbidity, they report significantly poorer life satisfaction compared to a general, nonclinical adult sample. Perhaps because many individuals with kleptomania report significant amounts of shame and embarrassment, patients may not tell their significant other about the behavior or endorse kleptomania symptoms until after being arrested or after responding to treating for a co-occurring psychiatric condition.

Along with impairment in the social and occupational realms, legal repercussions are common for individuals with kleptomania. Among clinical samples of patients who meet criteria for kleptomania, a majority have been arrested. In fact, many individuals with kleptomania have been apprehended multiple times. Because kleptomania often goes undiagnosed for years, it is important upon initial presentation to consider the involvement and education of psychiatric, psychological, and legal professionals.

Psychiatric Comorbidity

Comorbid Axis I psychiatric conditions are common in kleptomania. Substance use (15–50%), eating (9–25%), impulse control (20–47%), and mood (45–100%) disorders are frequently observed. Suicidal ideation among individuals with kleptomania is common.

Personality disorders also appear to be common in kleptomania. High frequencies of paranoid (17.9%), schizoid (10.7%), and borderline (10.3%) personalities have been reported in individuals with kleptomania.

Family History

Few family history and genetics studies of kleptomania have been performed. In the only study to use a control group, the first-degree relatives of subjects with kleptomania had a significantly higher frequency of alcoholism (15.1%) as compared to healthy controls (5.1%). Other studies have reported frequent depression, bipolar, and obsessive-compulsive disorder in the first-degree relatives of individuals with kleptomania.

Neurobiology

Although the etiology of kleptomania is unknown, serotonergic dysfunction in the ventromedial prefrontal cortex has been suggested as one contributing factor underlying the poor decision making seen in individuals with kleptomania. One study examining the platelet serotonin transporter in patients with kleptomania found that the number of platelet 5-HT transporters, evaluated by means of binding of 3H-paroxetine, was lower in kleptomania subjects compared to healthy controls, thereby suggesting some nonspecific serotonergic dysfunction.

Neurocognitive assessment of women with kleptomania revealed, as a group, no significant deficits in tests of frontal lobe functioning when compared to normative values. Those individuals with greater kleptomania symptom severity, however, had significantly below-average scores on at least one measure of executive functioning. Significantly higher rates of cognitive impulsivity were found in kleptomania subjects compared to a control group of psychiatric patients without kleptomania.

Damage to the orbitofrontal–subcortical circuits of the brain has been reported to result in kleptomania. Neuroimaging techniques have demonstrated decreased white matter microstructural integrity in the ventral–medial frontal brain regions of individuals with kleptomania compared to controls. These findings are consistent with reports of increased impulsivity in individuals with kleptomania. These studies also support the hypothesis that specific brain-based differences contribute to some individuals with kleptomania demonstrating a diminished ability to control their impulses to steal.

Treatment

There are limited data regarding effective treatments for kleptomania. Most available data are confined to case reports and case series with small samples of subjects. Although there are no medications approved by the Food and Drug Administration in the United States to treat kleptomania, pharmacotherapy and psychotherapy have shown some early promise in treating this disorder.

Pharmacotherapy

Case series and case reports have suggested a benefit of mono- or combination pharmacotherapy in the treatment of kleptomania. In the case of monotherapy, the following medications have shown preliminary benefit: topiramate, naltrexone, escitalopram, paroxetine, fluoxetine, valproic acid, and fluvoxamine.

In terms of combination therapy the following have been preliminarily reported as successful in treating kleptomania: paroxetine plus valproic acid plus naltrexone; topiramate plus paroxetine; naltrexone plus venlafaxine; lithium plus fluoxetine; trazodone plus tranylcypromine; sertraline plus methyphenidate; and imipramine plus fluoxetine.

To date, there are only two published trials of pharmacotherapy for the treatment of kleptomania. In the first of these trials, 24 subjects received open-label escitalopram. After 7 weeks of treatment, escitalopram was shown to reduce shoplifting urges in 19 (79%) of the participants. Responders were then randomized to a double-blind discontinuation phase where patients either received active medication or placebo. At the end of this portion of the study, no significant differences were seen between active medication and placebo as 50% of those on placebo and 43% on active medication maintained their improvement from the open-label portion of the study.

The other open-label study involved the use of the opioid antagonist naltrexone in the treatment of kleptomania. After 12 weeks, at a mean dose of 145 mg/day, 20% of subjects reported full remission of symptoms and 80% overall had significant improvement in their shoplifting urges and behavior.

A naturalistic study of naltrexone produced similar results. Seventeen subjects were followed over a 3-year period while being treated with naltrexone (mean dose of 135.3 mg/day). The study showed that 41% of subjects reported complete abstinence from stealing and 76% of subjects reported significant reductions in their urges to steal.

Pharmacotherapy and Combination Treatments

Although there have been no studies evaluating the efficacy of psychotherapy for kleptomania, case reports have illustrated the benefit of combining medication with cognitive-behavioral therapy (CBT). Aversion therapy, covert sensitization, and systematic desensitization are CBT techniques shown in case reports to benefit patients with kleptomania. In addition, techniques such as a self-imposed ban on shopping appear to be the most common intervention which allows the patient to treat the behavior without seeking help from a medical professional.

Promising examples of combined psychotherapy and pharmacology for the treatment of kleptomania include: fluoxetine 40 mg/day combined with supportive psychotherapy; fluoxetine 40 mg/day combined with problem-oriented psychotherapy; fluoxetine 20 mg/day plus cognitive therapy; combination of CBT, sertraline 50 mg/day, and a self-imposed shopping ban; and a combination of CBT and citalopram 40 mg/day.

Conclusions

Kleptomania, a disorder currently receiving scant attention from the psychiatric community, may present as a chronic illness for many individuals and cause significant psychological, social, and legal repercussions. Since presentation specifically for kleptomania is rare, it is important that clinicians recognize the disorder and screen patients appropriately. Various treatments have been helpful in case studies and small treatment studies but more research examining etiology and treatment is needed.

See also: Compulsive Buying; Impulsive–Compulsive Sexual Behavior; Intermittent Explosive Disorder; Obesity and Binge Eating Disorder; Pathological Gambling; Problematic Internet Use; Pyromania.

Further Reading

Abelson ES (1989) *When Ladies Go A-Thieving: Middle-Class Shoplifters in the Victorian Department Store.* New York: Oxford University Press.

Bayle FJ, Caci H, Millet B, Richa S, and Olie JP (2003) Psychopathology and comorbidity of psychiatric disorders in patients with kleptomania. *American Journal of Psychiatry* 160(8): 1509–1513.

Blanco C, Grant J, Perry NM, Simpson HB, Alegria A, Liu SM, and Hasin D (2008) Prevalence and correlates of shoplifting in the United States: Results from the National Epidemiologic Survey on Alcohol and Related Conditions (NESARC). *American Journal of Psychiatry* 165: 905–913.

Goldman M (1991) Kleptomania: Making sense of the nonsensical. *American Journal of Psychiatry* 148(8): 986–996.

Grant JE (2008) *Impulse Control Disorders: A Clinician's Guide to Understanding and Treating Behavioral Addictions.* New York: Norton Press.

Grant JE and Kim SW (2002) An open label study of naltrexone in the treatment of kleptomania. *Journal of Clinical Psychiatry* 63(4): 349–356.

Grant JE and Kim SW (2002) Clinical characteristics and associated psychopathology of 22 patients with kleptomania. *Comprehensive Psychiatry* 43(5): 378–384.

Grant JE, Correia S, and Brennan-Krohn T (2006) White matter integrity in kleptomania: A pilot study. *Psychiatry Research: Neuroimaging* 147(2–3): 233–237.

Grant JE, Levine L, Kim D, and Potenza MN (2005) Impulse control disorders in adult psychiatric inpatients. *American Journal of Psychiatry* 162(11): 2184–2188.

Grant JE, Odlaug BL, and Wozniak JR (2006) Neuropsychological functioning in kleptomania. *Behaviour Research and Therapy* 45(7): 1663–1670.

Grant JE and Potenza MN (2008) Gender-related differences in individuals seeking treatment for kleptomania. *CNS Spectrums* 13(3): 235–245.

Koran LM, Aboujaoude EN, and Gamel NN (2007) Escitalopram treatment of kleptomania: An open-label trial followed by double-blind discontinuation. *Journal of Clinical Psychiatry* 68(3): 422–427.

McElroy SL, Pope HG, Jr., Hudson JI, Keck PE, Jr., and White KL (1991) Kleptomania: A report of 20 cases. *American Journal of Psychiatry* 148(5): 652–657.

Presta S, Marazziti D, Dell'Osso L, *et al.* (2002) Kleptomania: Clinical features and comorbidity in an Italian sample. *Comprehensive Psychiatry* 43(1): 7–12.

Segrave K (2001) *Shoplifting: A Social History.* Jefferson, NC: McFarland.

Relevant Websites

http://www.shopliftersanonymous.com—Cleptomaniacs and Shoplifters Anonymous (CASA).

http://shopliftingprevention.org—National Association for Shoplifting Prevention (NASP).

http://www.impulsecontroldisorders.org—University of Minnesota Impulse-Control disorders Clinic.

Pyromania

By J.E. Grant, N. Thomarios, and B.L. Odlaug

Glossary

Affective disorder spectrum—A grouping of psychiatric disorders characterized by alterations in mood that share clinical and treatment-related characteristics.

Arachnoid cyst—A sac, filled with cerebrospinal fluid, that forms around the cranial base in the surface region of the brain, or on the arachnoid membrane.

Cerebellar vermis—A midline part of the cerebellum.

Ego-dystonic—The aspects of a person's thoughts, mood, impulses, and behavior which are repugnant and inconsistent with how the person normally views his or herself (opposite of ego-systonic).

Nucleus accumbens—A brain region where dopamine-secreting neurons terminate, which has been implicated in various addictions, urge-driven behaviors, reward-based learning and motivation; considered part of the brain reward circuitry.

Obsessive–compulsive spectrum—A group of disorders hypothesized to share common clinical and biological characteristics of obsessive–compulsive disorder. These disorders include, but are not limited to, Tourette's syndrome, body dysmorphic disorder, hypochondriasis, depersonalization disorder, pathological skin picking, trichotillomania, and pathological gambling.

Psychopathy—A psychiatric condition characterized by chronic antisocial and immoral behavior.

Topiramate—A sulfamate-substituted monosaccharide derivative used as an anticonvulsant to treat partial seizures.

Ventral tegmental area—A region in the midbrain where the mesocortical and mesolimbic dopaminergic systems originate; dopamine neurons in the ventral tegmental area project to the nucleus accumbens.

Introduction

Pyromania, also referred to as pathological fire setting, is a disorder currently included in the *Diagnostic and Statistical Manual,* 4th edition (DSM-IV), as an impulse control disorder not elsewhere specified. Pyromania is defined by the following criteria according to DSM-IV: (1) deliberate and purposeful fire setting that has occurred on more than one occasion; (2) feelings of tension or arousal preceding a fire-setting act; (3) pleasure, gratification, or relief when setting fires or when watching/participating in the aftermath of the fire; (5) the act of fire setting is not done out of vengeance or for monetary gain; and (6) fire-setting cannot be directly attributed to another mental condition such as conduct or bipolar disorder or impairment due to substance use. Psychosocial problems are common among individuals with pyromania and include impaired functioning and thoughts of suicide. Although pyromania has been documented for almost two centuries, it remains a poorly understood disorder with limited data regarding neurobiology or treatment. This article details what is currently known about the clinical characteristics and treatment of pyromania.

J.E. Grant, N. Thomarios, and B.L. Odlaug, "Pyromania," from the *Encyclopedia of Behavioral Neuroscience: Volume 3*, George F. Koob, Michel Le Moal and Richard F. Thompson, eds., pp. 144–148. Published by Academic Press, 2010. Copyright by Elsevier Science and Technology Books. Permission to reprint granted by the rights holder.

History

Pyromania has been described in medical literature for at least two centuries. The term pyromania derives from the Greek, fire (*pyr*) and madness (*mania*). One of the first descriptions in medical texts was in 1838 by Jean-Etienne Esquirol who referred to the behavior as 'incendiary monomania.' Esquirol included pyromania with kleptomania and erotic monomania of examples of irresistible behaviors. Esquirol differentiated pyromania from simple fire setting by claiming that pyromania was due to an instinctive impulse independent of will. Since that time, although people have debated the validity of the disorder, surprisingly little has been written about pyromania.

Pyromania appeared in the first edition of DSM in 1952 as a supplemental term. Pyromania did not appear in DSM-II. In 1980, DSM-III categorized pyromania as an impulse control disorder not elsewhere classified, the same clinical diagnostic category it currently holds in the DSM-IV-TR.

Epidemiology

Although documented cases have been reported for centuries, very little is known about the prevalence of pyromania. In the only study to examine the rate of pyromania in a community sample, 791 college students were asked about histories of fire setting. The study found eight (1.01%) students who met DSM-IV criteria for lifetime pyromania. An additional 10 (1.26%) students met subsyndromal pyromania criteria, which was defined by the behavior causing significant distress and dysfunction but not meeting full criteria for DSM-IV pyromania. In general, the finding that over 2% of the sample had either clinical or subsyndromal pyromania suggests that pyromania may not be an uncommon disorder.

Several studies of clinical, noncriminal samples also suggest that pyromania may not be uncommon. One study of 107 patients with depression found that three (2.8%) met current DSM-IV criteria for pyromania. A recent study of 204 psychiatric inpatients revealed that 3.4% ($n = 7$) endorsed current symptoms, and 5.9% ($n = 12$) had lifetime symptoms meeting DSM-IV criteria for pyromania. Small studies of individuals with compulsive

buying ($n = 20$) and kleptomania ($n = 20$) have also found frequencies of 10% ($n = 2$) and 15% ($n = 3$), respectively, for lifetime pyromania. Although adolescent fire setting may be a symptom of various psychiatric disorders, a recent study of 102 adolescent psychiatric inpatients found that after excluding those patients who set fires due to conduct disorder, substance use disorders, bipolar disorder, psychotic disorders, or developmental disorders, seven (6.9%) met the criteria for current pyromania. All seven adolescents with pyromania were girls.

Clinical Characteristics of Pyromania

Little data have been published from clinical samples describing the characteristics of individuals with pyromania. Age of onset for pyromania is generally late adolescence or early adulthood, although onset as late as the fourth decade of life is not uncommon. Pyromania appears to occur equally in men and women. Most individuals with pyromania are single, employed, and have at least a high school education. Some may work in jobs that allow them easy access to fires (e.g., firefighter).

Individuals with pyromania frequently report a rush when watching or setting fires. Stress and boredom are common triggers for starting fires. Many people with pyromania set what they consider to be controlled fires in dumpsters, their bathrooms, backyards, or vacant lots. Considerable time is spent on planning the fires, buying utensils to set the fires, and planning what items will burn well and most intensely. In addition, many individuals with pyromania spend considerable time watching fires and traveling to fires when they hear fire engines. The time spent on planning, setting, and watching fires significantly interferes with other responsibilities. Frequency of setting fires increases over the course of the illness, with less time between fires, and the intensity of the fires also increases over time. Many individuals report switching to other types of impulsive behavior after stopping fire setting (e.g., compulsive buying, alcohol or drug addiction, pathological gambling).

Although individuals with pyromania report either pleasure or relief when setting fires, the vast majority also report significant distress following their behavior. Suicidal ideation is common subsequent to setting fires.

Social or occupational impairment due to activities associated with setting fires is common. Although the behavior of pyromania often results in arson, most individuals have not been arrested. Histories of physical or sexual abuse while growing up are fairly common in individuals with pyromania.

Comorbidity

Psychiatric comorbidity appears to be quite common in persons with pyromania. Lifetime rates of mood (62%; most commonly major depressive disorder), impulse control (47%; most commonly kleptomania), anxiety (33%; most commonly posttraumatic stress disorder), and substance use (33%) disorders have been documented in those with pyromania. The majority of individuals with pyromania with mood or substance use disorders indicate that pyromania preceded the other disorders. In addition, pyromania has been associated with attention-deficit/hyperactivity disorder, learning disabilities, dementia, and mental retardation.

Relationship of Pyromania to Other Psychiatric Disorders

Approximately 10 years ago, researchers suggested that one way to understand an impulse control disorder, such as pyromania, was as part of an obsessive–compulsive spectrum. In addition, other models for understanding pyromania have been suggested, and research suggests that behavioral diagnoses such as pyromania may be far more heterogeneous than initially thought.

Pyromania is characterized by repetitive behavioral engagement and impaired inhibition. The difficult-to-resist and difficult-to-control fire-setting characteristics of pyromania suggest a similarity to the frequently excessive, unnecessary, and unwanted rituals of obsessive–compulsive disorder (OCD). There are, however some apparent differences between pyromania and OCD. For example, unlike individuals with OCD, majority of the individuals with pyromania report an urge prior to engaging in the problematic behavior and report their behavior as pleasurable. Individuals with

OCD generally describe their behaviors as ego-dystonic and harm avoidant. Only one study has examined OCD in subjects with pyromania, and it found that a 4.8% co-occurrence of OCD in pyromania. When pyromania has been examined in subjects with OCD, relatively low co-occurrence has also been found (0.3%). Controlled family studies with pyromania are currently lacking, and therefore any putative familial link between pyromania and OCD cannot be precisely determined.

The model of pyromania as a behavioral addiction also has support from recent research. Pyromania shares certain distinct features with substance use disorders: (1) an urge to engage in a behavior with negative consequences; (2) mounting tension unless the behavior is completed; (3) rapid but temporary reduction of the urge after completion of the behavior; (4) return of the urge over hours, days, or weeks; and (5) a pleasurable feeling or rush. In addition, the majority of individuals with pyromania report that the time between episodes of fire setting decreases over time and the intensity of the fires increases over the course of the illness. This element is reminiscent of tolerance in substance use disorders. Finally, pyromania frequently co-occurs with substance use disorders with a lifetime frequency of approximately 33%.

Mood disorders also co-occur frequently with pyromania and have led to the possible inclusion of pyromania within an affective spectrum. Lifetime mood disorders occur in approximately 62% of individuals with pyromania. However, a study of 107 patients with depression found that three (2.8%) met current criteria for pyromania. Individuals with pyromania often report that their symptoms worsen, or are triggered by negative mood states. Fire setting may have an antidepressant effect. In addition, because of the elevated rates of co-occurring bipolar disorder (14%) and because pyromania behavior is risky, pyromania may also be a symptom of subclinical hypomania or mania in some individuals.

Ultimately, an assessment of pyromania's relationship with other psychiatric disorders needs to consider the respective etiologies. Unfortunately, knowledge of this aspect of pyromania is not yet advanced enough to precisely address this topic.

Differences between Pyromania, Fire Setting, and Arson

There is often confusion about the terms used to describe the various types of fire setting. Pyromania is the proper term for fire-setting behavior only when the DSM-IV criteria have been met. In contrast to pyromania, arson is not a diagnosed psychiatric disorder or medical illness and has a distinct definition that differs from that of pyromania. Although state statutes may differ on the explicit language, arson is generally defined as a crime of maliciously, voluntarily, and willfully setting fire to a building or other property of another person or burning one's own property for an improper purpose (e.g., insurance fraud). In general, the motivation of an arsonist is for some type of gain, whether it is revenge for a wrongdoing, insurance fraud, or for sociopolitical or religious reasons. Pyromania, on the other hand, is an impulse- or urge-driven behavior, which affects, among other things, the social and occupational lives of the individuals suffering from the illness. These urges have been described as addictive, and the act of setting a fire produces a sense of calm for the individual.

Unlike true pyromania, arson appears to be a common occurrence that affects many people, both financially and emotionally. In 2004, there were 68,245 reports of arson offenses in the United States, according to statistics from the Federal Bureau of Investigations, with an average dollar loss per incident of $12,017. Recent data provided through the National Epidemiologic Survey on Alcohol and Related Conditions (NESARC) found that 1.13% of a large community sample acknowledged having started a fire, in their lifetimes, for the purpose of destroying someone else's property or just to see it burn. Very few arsonists, however, suffer from pyromania. One study found that only three (3.3%) of 90 arson recidivists had pure pyromania and that an additional nine subjects met DSM criteria for pyromania only when intoxicated at the time of the fire setting. In addition, not everyone who suffers from pyromania is an arsonist. A person meeting DSM-IV criteria for pyromania may also meet the legal definition of arson, but the DSM-IV criteria for pyromania do not require that a person ever set fire to another person's property.

Fire setting may also be associated with a variety of psychiatric disorders even when the diagnostic criteria for pyromania are not fulfilled or when the legal definition of arson is not met. Previous studies have suggested that the lifetime prevalence of fire setting may be approximately 26% in psychiatric patients. In these patients, fire setting has been linked to other self-injurious behaviors. Fire setting may also result from command hallucinations, delirium related to drug use, and manic grandiosity. In these patients, it has also been hypothesized that fire setting may be a manifestation of impulsivity, psychopathy, or affective dysregulation.

Child and Adolescent Fire Setting

A fascination with fire is an occurrence that has been documented for centuries. Usually beginning about the age of 2 or 3 years, attraction for fire may remain constant throughout an individual's life. In fact, behaviors such as playing with matches have been noted to occur in 24.4% of child psychiatric outpatients while fire-setting rates of 19.4% have been found in this sample. Although it is presently unknown how common this behavior is for children in the general population, the consequences of this behavior can be serious. Burn injuries account for 40% of accidental deaths in children under the age of 5, making these injuries the second leading cause of death for this age group.

While child and adolescent fire setting is serious and fairly common, true pyromania is quite rare in this age group. Children generally set fires out of vengeance, peer pressure, or impulse, and not out of an urge to relieve a building tension or as a response to an urge. For example, when 17 young fire setters were asked to identify their respective reasons for starting fires, their responses included revenge, to conceal a crime, for self-harm, due to group peer pressure, denial of the act or accidental, and a fascination with fire. In this sample, the individual endorsing a fascination for fire would be a possible candidate for a diagnosis of pyromania.

As noted above, fire setting itself is quite common in the child and adolescent age groups. Statistics have shown that nearly 50% of arson arrests are juvenile offenders. Common risk factors for this behavior have been identified within the juvenile population. Males have been shown to set fires 10 times more frequently than females. A study of 205 juvenile fire setters revealed that children who had experienced some form of maltreatment (i.e., physical abuse, neglect, or sexual abuse) were more likely to set fires in response to anger and be motivated by a family stressor than those without a history of maltreatment. Although associated with lower socioeconomic income, research has revealed that a variety of socioeconomic backgrounds is prevalent in the juvenile fire-setting population. Research has also shown that many fire-setting individuals in the juvenile population have experienced parental neglect and both emotional and physical abuse. Consistently, juvenile fire setting has been associated with adjustment and conduct disorder.

Etiology of Pyromania

Although abusive childhoods have been associated with fire setting in children and adolescents, little research has investigated possible neurobiological correlates of pyromania. In a study of a single individual with pyromania, neuroimaging using single photon emission computed tomography (SPECT) found left inferior perfusion deficits in the frontal lobe. New-onset fire setting has also been described in an individual with an arachnoid cyst of the cerebellar vermis.

The underlying biological mechanism of urge-based disorders may involve the processing of incoming reward inputs by the ventral tegmental area–nucleus accumbens–orbital frontal cortex circuit. This circuit influences motivations (e.g., urges and cravings) and related behaviors. Dopamine may also play a major role in the regulation of this region's functioning. One hypothesis is that differences in these regions may result in urges seen in pyromania and other impulse control disorders. The efficacy of topiramate (see below) lends further support to this hypothesis. Topiramate is thought to modulate dopaminergic function neurons in this area.

Because serotonergic systems have been implicated in impaired impulse regulation, serotonin dysregulation may also contribute to the pathophysiology of pyromania (as well as other impulse control disorders). Selective serotonin reuptake inhibitors (SSRIs) have shown preliminary promise in the treatment of pyromania. The use of SSRIs is based on the hypothesis that the etiology of impulsive behaviors and disorders may relate to low levels of serotonin in selected brain regions.

Treatment

There are no randomized, controlled, clinical trials examining either pharmacotherapy or psychotherapy for the treatment of pyromania. No medications have been approved by the Food and Drug Administration (FDA) for the treatment of pyromania.

Medications that have been described in case reports and which may show benefit in the treatment of pyromania include topiramate, escitalopram, sertraline, fluoxetine, lithium, and a combination of olanzapine and sodium valproate. An equal number of medications have also shown no benefit in the treatment of pyromania in case reports: fluoxetine, valproic acid, lithium, sertraline, olanzapine, escitalopram, citalopram, and clonazepam.

Another case report, illustrating the treatment of an 18-year-old male with pyromania, described the use of a combination of topiramate with 3 weeks of daily cognitive behavioral therapy (CBT), which included imaginal exposure, relaxation training, response prevention, and cognitive restructuring of fire-setting urges. Other studies describing behavioral treatments of pyromania include methods such as fire safety education, aversive therapy, positive reinforcement, stimulus satiation, and operant structured fantasies and prevention programs designed for pyromania.

There is no standard treatment for pyromania at this time. Given existing data, an approach using both psychotherapy and pharmacological treatment may be most beneficial.

Pyromania often may go undiagnosed. Many reasons exist for why such severely distressing behaviors may not be diagnosed. Shame and secrecy are often associated with pyromania, largely due to the illegal or perceived immoral nature of the behavior. Many people are also embarrassed because of the diminished control they exhibit over the fire-setting behavior. Such embarrassment and shame may explain, in part, why so few patients may volunteer information regarding this behavior unless specifically asked. Often related to the shame and secrecy may be a patient's misunderstanding of what a mental health clinician is required by law to report. Patients suffering from pyromania may believe that the clinician is required to report their illegal behaviors. Clinicians therefore may want to inform patients at the outset of the evaluation concerning what they do and do not have to report.

Conclusions

Pyromania is an impulse control disorder that has received relatively little attention from the psychiatric community. Nonetheless, pyromania may cause significant psychological, social and legal repercussions. Because few individuals volunteer information regarding their fire-setting, it is important that clinicians recognize the disorder and screen patients appropriately. Various treatments have been helpful in case studies but more research examining etiology and treatment is needed.

See also: Compulsive Buying; Impulsive–Compulsive Sexual Behavior; Intermittent Explosive Disorder; Kleptomania; Obesity and Binge Eating Disorder; Pathological Gambling; Problematic Internet Use.

Further Reading

Barnett W and Spitzer M (1994) Pathological fire-setting 1951–1991: A review. *Medicine, Science and the Law* 34: 4–20.

Geller JL (1992) Pathological firesetting in adults. *International Journal of Law and Psychiatry* 15: 283–302.

Geller JL and Bertsch G (1885) Fire-setting behavior in the histories of a state hospital population. *American Journal of Psychiatry* 142: 464–468.

Geller J, McDermett M, and Brown JM (1997) Pyromania? What does it mean? *Journal of Forensic Sciences* 42(6): 1052–1057.

Grant JE (2006) SPECT imaging and treatment of pyromania. *Journal of Clinical Psychiatry* 67: 998.

Grant JE and Kim SW (2007) Clinical characteristics and psychiatric comorbidity of pyromania. *Journal of Clinical Psychiatry* 68: 1717–1722.

Kolko DJ, Day BT, Bridge JA, and Kazdin AE (2001) Two-year prediction of children's firesetting in clinically referred and nonreferred samples. *Journal of Child Psychology and Psychiatry* 42: 371–380.

Lejoyeux M, MoLoughlin M, and Ades J (2005) Pyromania. In: Hollander E and Stein DJ (eds.) *Clinical Manual of Impulse-Control Disorders*, pp. 229–250. Washington, DC: APPI.

Lewis NDC and Yarnell H (1951) *Pathological Firesetting: Nervous and Mental Disease Monograph 82.* New York: Collidge Foundation.

Lindberg N, Holi MM, Tani P, and Virkkunen M (2005) Looking for pyromania: Characteristics of a consecutive sample of Finnish male criminals with histories of recidivist fire-setting between 1973 and 1993. *BMC Psychiatry* 5: 47.

Pilgrim CW (1885) Pyromania (so-called), with report of a case. *American Journal of Insanity* 41: 456–465.

Ritchie EC and Huff TG (1999) Psychiatric aspects of arsonists. *Journal of Forensic Sciences* 44: 733–740.

Robbins E and Robbins L (1967) Arson, with special reference to pyromania. *New York State Journal of Medicine* 67: 795–798.

Wheaton S (2001) Personal accounts: Memoirs of a compulsive firesetter. *Psychiatric Service* 52: 1035–1036.

Relevant Websites

http://www.impulsecontroldisorders.org—University of Minnesota Impulse-Control disorders Clinic.

Trichotillomania (Compulsive Hair Pulling) and Compulsive Skin Picking

By N. Fineberg, J.E. Grant, B.L. Odlaug, V. Boulougouris, and S.R. Chamberlain

Glossary

Habit-reversal therapy—A form of psychotherapy with evidence for efficacy in the treatment of trichotillomania, initially developed by Azrin and Nunn for the treatment of nervous habits. This type of therapy involves training patients to recognize situations where they are likely to undertake hair pulling and to perform competing response strategies, such as clenching fists.

Impulsivity—A multifaceted term in psychiatry referring to behaviors that are premature, risky, inappropriate, and which lead to negative long-term outcomes or harm. In the neurosciences, several dissociable manifestations of impulsivity have been described, including notably impaired response inhibition—difficulty suppressing simple motor responses when instructed to stop by a cue. Impaired response inhibition has been identified in trichotillomania, obsessive–compulsive disorder (OCD), attention-deficit hyperactivity disorder (ADHD), and other conditions.

Noradrenaline—Noradrenaline is a molecule that, within the central nervous system, is involved in neurotransmission. Noradrenaline has been implicated in processes such as arousal, attention, and impulse control.

Obsessive–compulsive (OC) spectrum disorders—Disorders characterized by repetitive habits that are difficult to suppress, purportedly linked to OC disorder (OCD) in terms of etiology and comorbid expression.

Putamen—Part of the basal ganglia that has been implicated in the generation of motor habits, such as tics in Tourette's syndrome or hair pulling in trichotillomania. Patients with trichotillomania show abnormally increased gray matter density in this region compared to healthy volunteer controls.

Trichophagia—Referring to the ingestion of hair, it is often observed in association with trichotillomania and can lead to significant medical complications.

Case Example

Mrs. G, a 24-year-old taxi driver, presented to an academic research unit with a history of repetitive hair pulling since the age of 13. She could not identify any obvious triggering factors during adolescence, and had thus far managed to conceal eyebrow

N. Fineberg, J.E. Grant, B.L. Odlaug, V. Boulougouris, and S.R. Chamberlain, "Trichotillomania (Compulsive Hair Pulling) and Compulsive Skin Picking," from the *Encyclopedia of Behavioral Neuroscience: Volume 3*, George F. Koob, Michel Le Moal and Richard F. Thompson, eds., pp. 429–435. Published by Academic Press, 2010. Copyright by Elsevier Science and Technology Books. Permission to reprint granted by the rights holder.

loss successfully using makeup. More recently, the hair pulling had escalated, now affecting not only her eyebrows but also her scalp, and occupying 3–4 h per day. Consequentially, hair loss had become noticeable to her partner and friends, and was now associated with functional impairment, social avoidance, and comorbid depression.

Introduction

Trichotillomania (compulsive hair pulling) is a common, chronic, poorly recognized, and ill-understood mental disorder. Responsible for considerable shame and distress, its sufferers expend great energy concealing its effects. Trichotillomania is the most researched of several phenomenologically and possibly psychobiologically related grooming behaviors, along with nail biting and skin picking—which in milder forms are common in the background population. Their psychopathology exists in the focus, duration and extent of the behavior, as well as the resulting impairment (e.g., noticeable hair loss or tissue damage, distress, and functional disability). There is increasing awareness of the morbidity associated with these habit disorders, but to date few research trials into neurobiology, pharmacotherapy, or psychotherapeutic strategies have been performed. Patients diagnosed with trichotillomania show similarities to those with compulsive skin picking with respect to demographic characteristics, psychiatric comorbidity, and personality dimensions. In this article, we focus on the psychopathology of trichotillomania, comparing, where possible, data on compulsive skin picking and other grooming disorders. Improved understanding of the underlying neuropsychological mechanisms, including affective and cognitive components, may shed light on the nosological relationships between these conditions and with other impulsive/compulsive mental disorders, paving the pathway for more effective targeted treatments.

Clinical Characteristics and Co-Occurring Disorders

The phenomenon of hair pulling has been recognized for centuries. Accounts are found in the *Old Testament* (*Book of Ezra*), Homer's *The Iliad*, and the plays of William Shakespeare (e.g., *Romeo and Juliet*). The earliest references to hair pulling in the medical literature are attributed to the Greek physician, Hippocrates. In his work, *Epidemics I*, Hippocrates recommended that physicians examine whether a person 'plucks his hair' as part of their general examination to determine if disease is present. In modern medical texts, accounts of trichophagia (hair eating) appeared before hair pulling. In 1889, the French dermatologist Francois Hallopeau coined the term 'trichotillomania' in describing a young man who pulled out his body hair.

Trichotillomania was not formally incorporated into official psychiatric nosology until 1987, revised, third edition of the *Diagnostic and Statistical Manual (DSM-III-R)*. The DSM-III-R diagnostic criteria were essentially the same as those currently in DSM-IV, except that the phrase "recurrent failure to resist impulses to pull" was removed, one of the criteria was expanded to include tension experienced when attempting to resist hair pulling, and distress or impairment due to hair pulling was added as a diagnostic requirement (Figure 1). During the drafting of DSM-IV, trichotillomania was considered for inclusion both in the anxiety disorders (because of presumed similarities to obsessive–compulsive disorder (OCD)) and the disorders first presenting in childhood or adolescence. As in the case of DSM-III-R, the DSM-IV included trichotillomania in the general category of impulse-control disorders not elsewhere classified, together with pathological gambling, pyromania, intermittent explosive disorder, and kleptomania.

Repetitive hair pulling in trichotillomania is usually from the scalp and/or eyebrows, but any body site with hair can be affected. Although rising tension and subsequent pleasure, gratification, or relief are integral to the current diagnostic criteria, in many cases, clinically distressing and noticeable hair pulling exists in people who do not endorse these strict criteria. These individuals should not be overlooked when it comes to providing treatment, and the DSM allows for some clinician discretion in the application of the criteria more generally. Trichotillomania has, in surveys, been linked with reduced work productivity, disruption of family life, and avoidance of sports/social activities. Comorbidity with other mental disorders occurs in the majority (82%) of cases presenting to psychiatrists, of which depression,

A. Recurrent hair pulling
B. Increasing tension immediately before pulling or when resisting the behavior
C. Pleasure, gratification or relief when pulling out the hair
D. Not better accounted for by another mental disorder or dermatological condition
E. Causes clinically significant distress or impairment in social, occupational, or other important areas of functioning

Figure 1 DSM-IV Criteria for trichotillomania (312.39)(APA 1994), abridged by the authors.

OCD, other anxiety disorders and substance abuse are the most common co-occurring Axis I disorders. Medical complications can also arise, including repetitive strain injury, dermatological scarring, and gastrointestinal obstruction following hair consumption (trichophagia). A recent review of 68 trichotillomania patients found that trichophagia was common (16.2%) and most patients with this condition had not received an evaluation for the possibility of medical consequences resulting from the ingestion of hair. Like trichotillomania, compulsive skin picking is also associated with psychosocial distress. For example, researchers found that 12% ($n = 4$) of 34 outpatients with skin picking reported suicidal ideation attributable to their disorder.

In contrast to trichotillomania, there is as yet no specific diagnostic category for other body-focused habit disorders such as skin picking, knuckle cracking, and nail biting. According to the DSM-IV, these may be diagnosed either under the category of stereotypic movement disorder usually first diagnosed in infancy or adolescence (DSM 307.3), or alternatively as impulse-control disorders not otherwise specified (DSM 312.30). Indeed, emerging evidence argues for the inclusion of habit disorders such as trichotillomania and compulsive skin picking in a separate section of OCDs in a revised nosology.

Trichotillomania, Habit Disorders, and the Obsessive–Compulsive Spectrum Disorders

The repetitive motor symptoms of trichotillomania and other body-focused habit disorders appear similar to the repetitive motor tics seen in Tourette's syndrome or even compulsive rituals in OCD. These conditions are thought to share overlapping elements of phenomenology, etiology, and neurobiology and to constitute a putative OC spectrum. Such repetitive, unwanted behaviors may persist due to underlying problems with inhibitory executive neurocognitive control governing habits. Comorbidity between different candidate spectrum disorders is common. For example, whereas compulsive skin picking was found most commonly to present in the context of OCD, it also frequently accompanied body dysmorphic disorder, obsessive–compulsive personality disorder (OCPD), and borderline personality disorder. One other study examined OC-spectrum disorders in OCD subjects and found that trichotillomania clustered with pathological gambling and hypersexual disorder within a proposed reward deficiency group. In contrast, disorders such as self-injurious behavior and body dysmorphic disorder clustered within impulsivity and somatic groups, respectively. The finding that relatives of individuals with OCD showed higher-than-expected rates of grooming disorders (hair pulling, nail biting, and skin picking) lends stronger support to the spectrum theory, although further research is clearly needed.

To further characterize the validity of the OC-spectrum approach, large-scale studies are needed to explore whether rates of habit disorder in OCD-patient relatives (and OCD in habit-disorder-patient relatives) are disproportionately elevated relative to other Axis I conditions. Important differences between trichotillomania and other putative OC-spectrum conditions should not be overlooked. For example, hair pulling in trichotillomania is seldom driven by (or associated with) intrusive thoughts, as distinct from the compulsions seen in OCD. Further research examining impulsive–compulsive neurocircuitry may identify a subtype of trichotillomania more like OCD, and another more like other impulse-control disorders or addictions.

Epidemiology

There have been no population-wide epidemiological studies of trichotillomania, compulsive skin picking, or other body-focused habit disorders. Studies of college students have reported prevalence rates ranging from 0.6% to 3.9% for strictly defined trichotillomania. In addition, hair pulling resulting in noticeable hair-loss (although not meeting diagnostic criteria for trichotillomania) was reported by as many as 1.5% of males and 3.4% of females. Interestingly, one study found that, when the results were analyzed by gender, 4.1% of females and 3.5% of males had trichotillomania. In treatment trials, usually threefold or greater proportions of women than men participated. It remains to be seen whether this reflects genuine female preponderance or selection bias against males in seeking treatment. Archetypal trichotillomania begins in early puberty (age range: 11–13 years) and follows a relapsing-remitting course into adulthood. The majority of sufferers have never received treatment, and patients report disappointing outcomes from the available applied interventions. By contrast, hair pulling in very young children may be regarded as a distinct clinical entity that can resolve before adolescence without the need for medical intervention.

Studies investigating smaller numbers of US and European college students have identified rates of severe skin picking, resulting in significant distress and tissue damage, ranging from 3.8% to 4.6%, of whom the majority (>80%) were female. However, as many as 90% of a cohort of 133 German students reported occasional skin picking. Like trichotillomania, the onset of picking was reported to occur around early puberty. The students primarily squeezed (85%) and scratched (77.4%) the skin, with a primary focus on the face (94.7%) and cuticles (52.6%). About 20% ate the picked tissue afterward. These preliminary findings suggest compulsive skin picking is an under-recognized problem that occurs on a continuum ranging from mild to severe and may be associated with significant medical consequences.

Neuropsychological Models

Affect-Regulation and Reward

Hair pulling is thought to increase during times of both boredom and stress. It has, therefore, been hypothesized that the behavior may, at least in its initial phases, be used to regulate arousal—either by stimulating or soothing. In one study, 39% of individuals with trichotillomania

reported pleasure or a sense of accomplishment from the act of hair pulling which may, therefore, contribute to its repetition. Skin picking and nail biting, likewise, may induce a sense of satisfaction or relief, although for many these symptoms appear to run automatically and to cause distress rather than relief. Mechanisms involved in reinforcement are likely to overlap with those involved in addictive behaviors including substance addiction, and may involve dopaminergic projections within the ventral striatal reward neurocircuitry.

Individuals with trichotillomania and other body-focused repetitive behaviors often exhibit comorbid anxiety and depression. In such cases, individuals may engage in hair pulling to distract themselves from life stressors and unpleasant cognitions. The risk of developing bald spots may be viewed as a relatively minor setback, at least initially. Unfortunately, the development of bald spots can, in turn, exacerbate depression and anxiety, leading to even more pulling as a misguided attempt at symptom management. These findings are consistent with a study that identified negative affective states and poor self-esteem as the primary triggers for trichotillomania. In another more recent study, individuals with trichotillomania were compared to a control group and reported lower life satisfaction, higher levels of distress, and lower self-esteem. Poor self-esteem was related to concerns about appearance, embarrassment, the need to avoid certain activities due to hair loss, and frustration with the inability to control hair pulling.

Nervous habits may begin as a reaction to physical injury or psychological trauma, and there has been speculation over the years as to whether trichotillomania is associated with childhood trauma. Cases of trichotillomania have been described in association with early physical and/or sexual abuse. One study of females with trichotillomania ($n = 60$) found that 18% had histories of childhood sexual abuse. However, it remains to be clearly demonstrated in an appropriate study design whether individuals with trichotillomania experience increased rates of childhood abuse versus people with no history of DSM disorders, or those with other Axis I disorders.

Neurocognitive Impairment

Neurocognitive deficits have been hypothesized as potential contributors to the etiology of habit disorders, either representing vulnerability markers or contributing to the manifestation of symptoms themselves. Such a proposal is based mainly on evidence from research into OCD, where impaired inhibitory control and linked frontostriatal abnormalities have been identified in patients and their unaffected first-degree relatives. Unfortunately, there have been no published studies of cognition in patients with skin picking or nail biting to date. The main studies in trichotillomania are discussed below.

The first neurocognitive investigation in trichotillomania used the Stylus maze test, in which individuals attempt to learn the correct path for navigating across a peg-board, using a stylus. Patients with trichotillomania showed problems on several indices of the test involving a range of abilities including memory, planning, motor execution, and error learning. However, a subsequent study using a similar test (the Austin maze task) found no evidence for deficits in trichotillomania patients who were free from major depression and psychosis.

Impulsivity is a multifaceted term in the neurosciences, and represents a focus of attention in body-focused repetitive behavior research. One form of impulsivity is referred to as 'motor impulsivity'—a diminished ability to suppress motor responses when appropriate to the situation at hand. This ability has classically been measured using tasks that require volunteers to make simple motor responses (e.g., pressing a button) on some computer trials but not on others. Translational research suggests that motor inhibition is dependent on the right inferior frontal gyrus and noradrenergic neurotransmission across species. Using a Go/No-Go task where participants responded to the letter 'X' but not the letter 'O' on-screen (or vice versa) one study reported intact performance in patients with trichotillomania. Another study used a stop-signal task previously validated in ADHD and brain-lesion studies. Using an individually tailored tracking algorithm, the time taken by the brain to suppress an already initiated response—referred to as the stop-signal reaction time (SSRT)—is estimated. In this later study, patients with trichotillomania exhibited impaired inhibitory control compared to healthy controls and patients with OCD. The degree of deficit was similar to that previously reported in studies of adult patients ADHD.

The Wisconsin Card Sorting Test (WCST), which measures rule learning and cognitive flexibility, is a classic test of frontal lobe integrity. Participants attempt to learn a rule governing which of two cards is correct on the basis of trial and error (feedback). The rule is then altered and individuals attempt to show flexibility and acquire the new rule. Two studies have employed this task in patients with trichotillomania, and both reported performance to be intact. A more recent study has used a computerized variant of the WCST called the extradimensional set-shift task (ED-shift task) from the Cambridge Neuropsychological Test Automated Battery (CANTAB). Consistent with these previous WCST studies, patients with trichotillomania exhibited normal performance on all stages of the ED-shift task. OCD patients exhibited cognitive inflexibility on the task, suggesting that there are important differences (as well as some overlap) between the neuropsychological profiles of trichotillomania and OCD. Future work should measure similar functions in skin picking and nail biting in order to clarify the extent of overlap in the cognitive profiles of the body-focused habit disorders.

Neuroanatomical Models

It is important to question whether trichotillomania, skin picking, and nail biting are associated with similar changes in brain structure or function since this would inform neurobiological models, enhance our understanding of the relationships between conditions, and potentially lead to advances in treatment. For example, it is well established that OCD is associated with abnormalities in distributed brain circuitry, including the orbitofrontal cortices and basal ganglia (especially caudate). To the authors' knowledge, there have been no imaging investigations of nail biting or skin picking at this time. The main results from trichotillomania studies are as follows.

Most imaging studies in trichotillomania have used region of interest (ROI) approaches; that is, they have set out to measure whether specific structures of the brain show differences in patients versus controls. This minimizes multiple comparisons but could lead to important regions being overlooked. Based on a possible link between OCD and trichotillomania, one study measured caudate volumes in trichotillomania but detected no abnormalities. Another study reported reduced left inferior frontal gyrus and increased right cuneal cortex volumes in patients compared to controls, while another study found smaller left putamen volumes. Using parcellation techniques, one other study identified reduced cerebellar volumes in trichotillomania patients compared to controls.

A single study has investigated whether trichotillomania is associated with brain changes without restriction to particular ROIs. This study took advantage of recently developed methods of neuroimaging analysis thought to provide greater power to detect group differences than conventional parametric techniques. Patients with trichotillomania showed increased gray matter density in distributed circuitry including the cingulate cortex, amygdala–hippocampal formation, and putamen. These regions have been implicated in action monitoring, affective processing, and motor habit generation, respectively.

In terms of brain function (as opposed to structure), positron emission tomography (PET), single photon emission computed tomography (SPECT), and functional MRI (fMRI) have been used in some trichotillomania studies. In one PET study, normalized resting cerebral glucose metabolic rates were shown to be abnormally increased in the bilateral cerebellum and right parietal cortex in patients with trichotillomania. Another study used SPECT to explore the effects of 12-week pharmacotherapy with the selective serotonin-reuptake inhibitor (SSRI) citalopram on brain circuitry in patients with trichotillomania. Treatment was associated with reduced activity in frontal cortical regions, the left putamen, and the right anterior-temporal lobe. Using a sequence learning task in conjunction with fMRI, another study found no evidence for abnormal brain activation in trichotillomania patients versus controls.

Animal Models

Comprehensive investigation of the neurobiology of any psychiatric condition, or group of conditions, is enhanced by the development of animal models. Etiological models focus on spontaneously arising repetitive or stereotypic behaviors, such as tail chasing, fur chewing and weaving,

and motor behaviors driven by conflict, frustration, or stress—such as grooming, cleaning, and pecking. Laboratory-study behaviors that are induced and not spontaneous (e.g., as resulting from pharmacological or genetic manipulations) may limit the generalizability of results. Barbering (abnormal whisker and fur trimming) is limited to a subgroup of laboratory mice and has been proposed as a mouse model of trichotillomania and possibly other body-focused behaviors. Mouse barbering appears to parallel trichotillomania in terms of phenomenology (hair plucking from the scalp and around the eyes/genitals), demography (female biased, onset during puberty), and etiology (genetic background). The barbering mouse model might provide useful information on genetic and environmental etiological factors in trichotillomania.

Another key animal model, to date, is based upon the observation that mice with mutations of the Hoxb8 gene groom excessively. This model is potentially useful since the excessive grooming of Hoxb8 mutants is similar to the excessive grooming seen in trichotillomania. Critically, the Hoxb8 gene is expressed in the orbital cortex, the anterior cingulate, the striatum, and the limbic system—circuitry which has been recently implicated in the pathophysiology of trichotillomania based on the whole-brain-permutation brain analysis described above.

Treatment

Multiple psychometrically sound instruments for the measurement of trichotillomania have been developed. Assessments of habits in subjects with intellectual disability are well established and rating scales for skin picking now exist. No formal treatment guidelines exist for these disorders since the evidence base is limited by the lack of satisfactory clinical trials. Treatment-development has been further hampered by a failure to take account of overlap with other Axis I conditions.

Psychotherapy

There is some evidence supporting psychotherapy for trichotillomania and compulsive skin picking, albeit the studies have had limitations. In the first formal treatment study for trichotillomania, 34 subjects were randomized to either habit reversal therapy—a form of cognitive behavioral therapy involving attention to triggering situations and practiced resistance to pulling urges—or negative practice where subjects stand in front of a mirror and act out motions of hair pulling without actually pulling. Habit reversal reduced hair pulling by more than 90% after 4 months, compared to 52–68% reduction for negative practice at 3 months. Another study examined 25 subjects randomized to 12 weeks (10 sessions) of either acceptance and commitment therapy/habit reversal or wait list. Subjects assigned to active therapy experienced significant reductions in hair-pulling severity and impairment compared to those assigned to the wait-list, and improvement was maintained at the 3-month follow-up. However, the wait-list lacks credibility as a realistic control treatment.

Recent case studies have also described a positive effect for the use of cognitive behavioral therapies involving habit-reversal elements for the treatment of skin picking. Elsewhere, 372 individuals were consecutively enrolled in an uncontrolled, Internet-based, self-help treatment for self-injurious skin picking. Results revealed significant reductions in frequency of picking episodes and symptom-severity ratings from baseline over a 5-month period, suggesting a role for self-help, computer-based treatments in this field.

Pharmacotherapy

Several controlled pharmacological trials have been performed in trichotillomania. Four of the six published double-blind pharmacological studies examined antidepressants, mainly SRIs. One study compared the serotonergic tricyclic clomipramine to the noradrenergic tricyclic desipramine in a 10-week double-blind, crossover design (5 weeks for each agent). Clomipramine significantly outperformed desipramine, and 12 of the 13 subjects showed significant improvement on clomipramine. A preliminary study reported in poster form, using a randomized, double-blind, nonplacebo, crossover design, compared 10 weeks of fluoxetine with 10 weeks of clomipramine treatment. Both agents demonstrated a similar positive treatment effect.

Fluoxetine has been studied in two small randomized trials with negative results in patients with trichotillomania. In one study, fluoxetine was compared with placebo in a 6-week double-blind crossover study with a 5-week washout period between treatment arms (15 completers). No significant differences were found between fluoxetine and placebo on measures of hair-pulling urges, frequency, or severity. Another crossover study compared 16 subjects on 12 weeks of fluoxetine or placebo, with each agent separated by a 5-week washout period. Fluoxetine again failed to show significant improvement compared to placebo.

The opioid antagonist naltrexone (50 mg per day) was examined in a placebo-controlled, 6-week, randomized, double-blind parallel-arm study in trichotillomania. Of a total of 17 subjects completing the study, significantly greater improvement was noted for the naltrexone group ($n = 7$) than placebo ($n = 10$) on one out of three trichotillomania measures.

A recent double-blind, placebo-controlled study—presented thus far in poster form only—examined olanzapine (mean dose: 10.8 mg per day) for 12 weeks in 25 trichotillomania subjects. Preliminary data reported in conference poster form revealed that 85% of those assigned to olanzapine, compared to 17% of those on placebo, improved during the trial.

Pharmacological agents have also been the most frequently studied treatment approach for compulsive skin picking, with nearly all studies examining the efficacy of SRIs. Twenty-five adult subjects with severe morbid nail biting and no history of OCD participated in a 10-week, double-blind, crossover trial of clomipramine and desipramine. A high dropout rate was observed. In the 14 subjects who completed the study, clomipramine was superior to desipramine hydrochloride in decreasing measures of impairment associated with nail biting. In another study, 21 skin-pickers were randomized to 10 weeks of either placebo or fluoxetine. Eight of the 10 participants in the fluoxetine condition were classified as much improved or very much improved, compared with only three of 11 participants in the placebo condition. In a subsequent study, eight responders, following 6 weeks of open-label treatment with fluoxetine, were then randomized to 6 weeks of double-blind fluoxetine or placebo. The four patients randomized to double-blind fluoxetine maintained clinically significant improvement, whereas the four randomized to placebo returned to their baseline symptom level.

Psychotherapy versus Pharmacotherapy, and Combination Treatment

Two partially controlled studies have compared pharmacological and psychological treatment interventions in trichotillomania. A placebo-controlled, randomized, parallel-treatment design was used to compare cognitive behavioral therapy and clomipramine. Twenty-three subjects entered the 9-week study. The cognitive behavioral therapy was a modified manualized treatment based on habit-reversal therapy. There was no psychological control treatment. Cognitive behavioral therapy was significantly more effective than either clomipramine or pill-placebo. Although clomipramine resulted in greater symptom reduction than placebo, the difference was not statistically significant, possibly owing to lack of power ($n = 6$, in the clomipramine group). In a second comparison study lacking pill-placebo, behavioral therapy was compared to fluoxetine in a 12-week randomized trial using a wait-list control. Forty-three subjects were enrolled and 40 completed the trial (14 in behavior therapy, 11 in the fluoxetine group, and 15 in the wait list). Behavior therapy resulted in statistically significant reductions in trichotillomania symptoms compared to either fluoxetine or wait-list in the completers. One other uncontrolled study investigated the effects of adding habit-reversal therapy for trichotillomania patients who had received 12-week sertraline but had not responded ($n = 24$ completers total). Combination treatment appeared more effective than continuing with sertraline alone.

Treatment: Summary and Future Directions

It is unwise to generate strong recommendations for treating trichotillomania and body-focused habit disorders such as compulsive skin picking on the basis of such limited trial data. Although habit reversal appears promising for trichotillomania, the effectiveness of this treatment requires testing in properly constituted randomized controlled trials. Pharmacotherapy has been studied with more rigor, but trials have been too small and short in duration to be conclusive. For trichotillomania and nail biting, clomipramine demonstrated greater efficacy than did the tricyclic desipramine, but this finding has not been verified against placebo. For trichotillomania, SSRIs have not shown greater benefit than placebo so far, although two small positive studies suggest efficacy for fluoxetine as a treatment for skin picking. Initial promising findings involving olanzapine and naltrexone merit further evaluation. A recent meta-analysis of trichotillomania studies was unable to extend recommendations much further. There exists a need for further double-blind controlled trials to examine potentially beneficial pharmacological treatments in the short and, arguably more importantly, the longer term.

Conclusions

From a phenomenological perspective, trichotillomania and body-focused repetitive behaviors can be considered candidate members of the OC spectrum of disorders. The body-focused disorders may result from the progression of initially mild hair pulling and other grooming behaviors into a repetitive ingrained pathological behavior. Vulnerable individuals may be distinguishable by deficient top–down cortical inhibitory control governing motor habits, or overactive habit-forming circuitry. Brain abnormalities in neural regions involved in cognition and action monitoring (frontal lobes, cingulate cortices, etc.), affect regulation (amygdalo-hippocampal formation), and habit learning (putamen) have been tentatively implicated in trichotillomania and may also be involved in other grooming disorders. Treatment algorithms are lacking, with habit-reversal therapy showing suggestive efficacy but limited availability. SSRIs show promise for treating compulsive skin picking but not for trichotillomania. Clomipramine produced benefit in trichotillomania and comorbid nail biting. Alternative pharmacotherapies merit exploration.

Acknowledgments

This work was adapted in part from Chamberlain SR, Odlaug BL, Boulougouris V, Fineberg NA, Grant JE. Trichotillomania: Neurobiology and treatment. Neuroscience Biobehavioral Reviews 2009 Jun;33(6):831–42. Epub 2009 Feb 20.

See also: Basal Ganglia; Cognition: Attention and Impulsivity; Compulsive Buying; Genes and Behavior: Animal Models; Impulsive–Compulsive Sexual Behavior; Intermittent Explosive Disorder; Kleptomania; Neural Basis of Attention-Deficit/Hyperactivity Disorder; Obesity and Binge Eating Disorder; Pathological Gambling; Problematic Internet Use; Pyromania.

Further Reading

Azrin NH and Nunn RG (1973) Habit-reversal: A method of eliminating nervous habits and tics. *Behaviour Research and Therapy* 11(4): 619–628.

Bloch MH, Landeros-Weisenberger A, Dombrowski P, et al. (2007) Systematic review: Pharmacological and behavioral treatment for trichotillomania. *Biological Psychiatry* 15; 62(8): 839–846.

Chamberlain SR, Fineberg NA, Blackwell AD, Robbins TW, and Sahakian BJ (2006) Motor inhibition and cognitive flexibility in obsessive–compulsive disorder and trichotillomania. *American Journal of Psychiatry* 163(7): 1282–1284.

Chamberlain SR, Menzies LA, Fineberg NA, et al. (2008) Grey matter abnormalities in trichotillomania: A morphometric MRI study. *British Journal of Psychiatry* 193(3): 216–221.

Chamberlain SR, Menzies LA, Sahakian BJ, and Fineberg NA (2007) Lifting the veil on trichotillomania. *American Journal of Psychiatry* 164(4): 568–574.

Christenson GA and Mansueto CS (1999) Trichotillomania: Descriptive statistics and phenomenology. In: Stein DJ, Christenson GA, and Hollander E (eds.) *Trichotillomania,* pp. 1–41. Washington, DC: American Psychiatry Press.

Grant JE and Potenza MN (2006) Compulsive aspects of impulse-control disorders. *Psychiatric Clinics of North America* 29(2): 539–551.

Greer JM and Capecchi MR (2002) Hoxb8 is required for normal grooming behavior in mice. *Neuron* 33(1): 23–34.

Keuthen NJ, O'Sullivan RL, Ricciardi JN, et al. (1995) The Massachusetts General Hospital (MGH) Hairpulling Scale: 1. development and factor analyses. *Psychotherapy and Psychosomatics* 64(3–4): 141–145.

Stein DJ, Chamberlain SR, and Fineberg NA (2006) An A–B–C model of habit disorders: Hair-pulling, skin-picking, and other stereotypic conditions. *CNS Spectrums* 11(11): 824–827.

Obesity and Binge Eating Disorder

By A. Stankovic and M.N. Potenza

Glossary

Body mass index (BMI)—A ratio derived by dividing weight in kilograms by height in meters-squared; useful in the determination of overweight and obesity.

Bulimia nervosa—An eating disorder characterized by bingeing and purging of food.

Cannabinoid—Relating to cannabis. For example, cannabinoid receptors bind cannabis when the drug is introduced in the body. Cannabinoid receptors have been implicated in regulating hunger and this feature may explain patterns of eating behavior (e.g., having the munchies) when smoking cannabis.

Cardiac valvulopathy—A disease involving the valves of the heart,

Diagnostic and statistical manual—A book widely used in psychiatry that categorizes and defines mental health disorders.

FDA—Food and Drug Administration, the US federal agency that regulates drugs and related products, including approving drugs for specific therapeutic indications.

Lipase—An enzyme that breaks down lipids or fats.

Obesity—The condition defined by a BMI ratio above 30; often marked by a co-occurrence of such health complications as hypertension, cardiovascular disease, and type II diabetes.

Overweight—The condition defined by a BMI ratio between 25 and 30; often associated with adverse health measures, albeit to a lesser extent than with obesity.

Type II diabetes—The form of diabetes that typically has its onset in adulthood and is associated with obesity. Type II contrasts with type I diabetes that typically has a childhood onset and is typically not associated with obesity as it has a different pathophysiology.

Introduction

Obesity represents a major public health concern. Although questions remain regarding optimal prevention and treatment approaches, research has illuminated many characteristics of obesity. Binge eating disorder (BED) is characterized by seemingly impulsive or excessive bouts of eating, and BED typically co-occurs with obesity. Both obesity and BED are addressed in the following sections.

Epidemiology of Obesity

Several calculated ratios are used to define overweight states and obesity. The body mass index (BMI)—which is derived by dividing weight in kilograms by height in meters-squared—is the most widely accepted and used measure for the determination and classification of obesity and overweight. Using this system, a BMI value in the 19–25 range generally indicates a healthy, normal weight, while a ratio of 25–30 defines overweight, and a calculation over 30 classifies obesity. Obesity has been subclassified into three types according to BMI: type I (30–34.9); type II (35–39.9), and type III or extreme (≥40). However, BMI might not accurately reflect obesity status in some cases; certain athletes, for example, may have high BMIs related to increased muscle mass. The waist-to-hip ratio serves as another useful tool in the diagnosis of overweight and obese states, with measures over 88 cm in women and greater than 102 cm in men indicating abdominal obesity. According to the World Health Organization (WHO), the global rate of obesity continues to increase at an alarming rate. Over 60% of the US adult population is now classified as overweight. Similar findings are indicated in Europe, Canada, and growing numbers of South American countries. Such startling obesity rates are not localized to Western, industrialized nations. Rather, a growing tendency toward obesity has also been seen in several African nations—despite strained regional demands on limited food supplies—particularly among black African women in areas that have recently experienced socioeconomic growth and increased urbanization. Many Asian countries, also, have demonstrated similar statistics. By WHO estimates, almost 10% of the global population meets the criteria for obesity.

Clinical Characteristics and Co-Occurring Disorders

The increasing prevalence of obesity has been linked with a rise in illness and death from obesity-related health complications. Over a quarter of a million annual obesity-related deaths occur in the United States alone. Being overweight or obese has been linked to multiple health complications including hypertension, cardiovascular disease, stroke, heart attack, congestive heart failure, hypercholesteremia, type II diabetes, osteoarthritis, obstructive sleep apnea, and certain cancers.

In addition to lowering life expectancy, the relationship of obesity to disease may negatively impact quality of life. Overweight or obese individuals experience higher levels of stigmatization and social discrimination than those falling within healthy-weight ranges, perhaps accounting for the markedly increased prevalence of anxiety and affective disorders, especially depression,

in overweight individuals as compared to their healthy-weight counterparts.

Binge Eating Disorder

BED is characterized by episodes of extreme or out-of-control eating. Majority of individuals with BED are either overweight or obese. BED has been proposed as a separate diagnostic category distinct from obesity and bulimia nervosa. Currently, BED is recognized as a provisional diagnosis in need of further study in the *Diagnostic and Statistical Manual of Mental Disorder*, Edition 4, Text Revision (DSM-IV-TR) and is defined in Appendix B by the following criteria:

- recurrent episodes of binge eating in which an individual consumes an abnormally large quantity in a short time; these episodes are typically associated with eating more rapidly than normal, eating until feeling uncomfortably full, eating in the absence of physical hunger, or eating alone due to embarrassment;
- subjective experience of loss of control over eating behaviors during binge-eating;
- distress regarding eating behavior, often marked by feelings of guilt, disgust, or depression after overeating, as well as concern over weight and shape.

Importantly, the occurrence of such behaviors is not seen in conjunction with regular compensatory measures in response to binge episodes, such as purging, laxative abuse, or excessive exercise, thereby distinguishing BED from bulimia nervosa.

Although BED is associated with obesity, findings have indicated differences between overweight/obese individuals with and without BED. Individuals with BED more frequently demonstrate co-occurring Axis I and Axis II psychiatric conditions than do overweight/obese individuals without BED, particularly with respect to major depression and borderline personality disorder. The association between binge eating and depression seems to operate bidirectionally: while the onset of binge eating may follow periods of depression in many individuals, affective disorders often have their onset prior to BED. Other diagnoses frequently seen in people with

BED include other mood disorders, obsessive–compulsive personality disorder, and avoidant personality disorder. Body image disturbances and weight and shape concerns also seem more prominent in obese individuals with BED as compared to those without BED.

Although methodological constraints in the identification of BED (such as the inconsistent and varied use of assessment techniques across different studies) have hindered the precise determination of BED prevalence in the general population, it is estimated that approximately 3% of all adults in the United States, and roughly 8% of all obese adults, suffer from BED. The disorder is seen across ethic and racial groups, with BED having a slightly higher, although not statistically significant, prevalence in women than in men. Such gender-related differences, however, should be considered preliminary as much of the existing BED research has thus far been limited to exclusively female samples.

As few longitudinal studies have been performed, the natural history of BED is poorly understood. Among clinical samples, many individuals with BED report a long history of the disorder, with a fluctuating course defined by intermittent remission and recurrence.

Etiology of Obesity and Binge Eating Disorder

Although many questions exist regarding the etiologies of obesity and BED, genetic, neurobiological, and behavioral features that may influence the course of these disorders have been identified. From a physiological perspective, obesity may be described as a homeostatic energy imbalance in which energy intake significantly exceeds energy expenditure. This imbalance, in turn, is modulated by a complex interaction of factors regulating hunger, satiety, and metabolic rate. Specific genetic factors, when combined with certain environmental factors (such as high-caloric diets, low physical activity, or certain *in utero* factors) may significantly increase the likelihood of developing obesity and BED.

Genetics

Twin and family studies investigating the heritability of obesity and BED suggest significant genetic contributions. Obesity was found to occur twice as frequently among individuals with at least one relative who was overweight or obese. These findings varied with severity of obesity: individuals whose relatives fell within the top 1% of BMI distributions were up to 5 times as likely to be overweight or obese as individuals in the general population.

Similar studies suggest a heritability component of approximately 50% in BED. However, only a limited number of studies have thus far explored the genetic transmission of BED, and methodological concerns—such as the heterogeneity of criteria used for defining BED across investigations—leave precise heritability estimates in question.

Molecular investigations have identified associations between extreme obesity and specific genetic factors. A variant of the gene encoding the melanocortin-4 receptor (Mc4r) has been identified in approximately 3–5% of all morbidly obese individuals. However, not all individuals demonstrating this genetic variation are found to be obese, suggesting that environmental factors and/or multiple genes—such as those contributing toward metabolic regulation, energy conversion, and fat storage—may contribute to determining an individual's propensity to obesity. For example, individuals with overweight or obese spouses or cohabitating partners are frequently overweight or obese themselves; thus, existing data suggest a complex interaction between genetic and environmental factors.

Neuroanatomical and Neurochemical Features

Factors governing hunger, food intake, and body weight play important roles in the etiology of obesity. Multiple appetite-related hormones and signaling factors act on receptors in the hypothalamus to trigger hunger responses and indicate satiety upon sufficient food absorption. These signaling factors include leptin, ghrelin, serotonin, dopamine, norepinephrine (NE), corticotropin-releasing factor, neuropeptide Y, gonadotropin-releasing hormone, and thyroid-stimulating hormone. Dysfunction involving any of these factors or the excitatory or inhibitory pathways they influence may potentially impact upon food-intake regulation and contribute to the development of obesity. Other potential neurochemical elements implicated in the etiology of obesity include dopamine and related systems that influence motivational and emotional states, responses to reward, and reinforcement of behaviors. Prenatal environmental factors may also influence metabolic functioning, with extreme caloric deprivation *in utero,* for example, showing an association with high BMI in childhood.

While no specific neurochemical or structural anomalies have as yet been definitively identified in BED, it has been hypothesized that dysregulation of serotonin pathways regulating mood, appetite, and impulse control may contribute to the disorder. Although few imaging studies have been conducted thus far in BED, early functional imaging data suggest reduced serotonin transporter binding in obese individuals with BED. When exposed to food cues, individuals with BED report a greater subjective desire to eat and demonstrate greater regional cerebral blood flow in the left as compared to the right hemisphere, particularly in frontal brain regions, perhaps suggesting increased reinforcement sensitivity to food-based reward cues in BED. Notably, these findings also seem to indicate that activation patterns in individuals suffering from BED also differ significantly from those seen in subjects diagnosed with bulimia nervosa. Although further imaging work in BED remains to be done, such differential responses to visual food cues between BED and bulimia nervosa subjects seem to highlight the distinctiveness of BED as a condition independent of BN.

Neurocognitive and Behavioral Features

While multiple influences impact disease etiology, environmental factors and lifestyle choices (governed by motivational behavioral decision-making) seem particularly important in the development of obesity. Among these behavioral elements, dietary habits, eating patterns, and physical activity seem particularly relevant.

Obesity co-occurs frequently with mental health disorders, and this relationship seems especially salient for women. In particular, depression and anxiety are reported at higher rates among individuals who are overweight or obese, and the extent to which this relationship reflects genetic influences, environmental contributions such as those related to stigmatization and social discrimination,

or an interaction between genetic and environmental factors remains to be determined.

While an imbalance between energy intake and expenditure may summarize obesity's etiology, caloric intake does not in, and of, itself predict obesity. Rather, the nutritional nature of food eaten seems particularly important, with BMI correlating with dietary fat consumption.

Decreased physical activity is also associated with obesity. Lifestyle changes over the past few decades include substantially decreased levels of average daily physical activity. Frequent usage of motorized transportation, for example, has drastically reduced the reliance on more active methods of travel such as walking or cycling. Daily television viewing hours have significantly increased in many industrialized nations. These factors may contribute to the rapidly increasing rates of childhood obesity.

Factors associated with BED include adverse childhood experiences, including physical or sexual abuse, family problems, bullying, and teasing or negative criticism about weight, shape, or eating. These findings suggest that binge eating may function as a type of maladaptive emotional coping mechanism.

Treatment of Obesity and BED

Today, the three most widely accepted strategies for the treatment of obesity and BED are behavioral therapies such as cognitive behavioral restructuring (often employed in conjunction with training for healthier diet and increased physical activity), pharmacotherapy, and, in extreme cases of obesity, surgery.

Cognitive Behavioral Treatment of Obesity

A goal-oriented treatment strategy focusing on the direct modification of dietary and exercise habits, cognitive behavioral therapy (CBT) is widely used in the treatment of obesity. With a clearly defined objective of behavioral change, this approach centers on building new skill sets and advocates steady, reasonable progress to change, rather than sudden, drastic (and typically short-lived) behavioral modification. Cognitive' behavioral approaches for obesity often include a nutritional education component and strategies for increasing physical activity.

Cognitive restructuring is also typically incorporated within a CBT program to minimize self-defeating thoughts or unrealistic goals which, when not met, may deflate self-confidence and hinder treatment efficacy. The strengthening of skill sets such as communication and self-control in situations which have previously led to overeating is also addressed. Special attention is often given to teaching self-monitoring, or the thoughtful observation of one's behavior, especially with respect to food selection and intake, physical activity, and environmental and emotional cues associated with periods of overeating. By focusing on the development of such skills, CBT in the treatment of obesity aims to help individuals understand circumstances and motivations which may lead to overeating and learn to use a variety of different problem-solving strategies to recognize and avoid such lapses in the future, thereby helping patients gain improved control over eating behaviors.

Behavioral modifications of diet and exercise are presented to help individuals reach a reasonable weight loss goal. Through the course of treatment, individuals learn the importance of well-balanced diets and are encouraged to gradually modify eating patterns to establish healthier, more nutritious eating habits. An integrated exercise component is perhaps one of the most critical aspects of a CBT program for obesity, as sustained increased physical activity seems to be a strong predictor of long-term weight control. Lifestyle changes which may directly lead to increased activity, such as encouraging using the stairs instead of an elevator or walking to a nearby destination instead of riding in the car, are generally advocated over the sudden introduction of more high-intensity exercise approaches. Such small behavioral changes leading to increased energy expenditure have proven more successful in encouraging a long-term commitment to habitual activity.

CBT has shown short-term efficiency in terms of weight loss, with many individuals losing an average of 10% of their initial weight in the short term, although further research remains necessary to examine the long-term success of such treatment strategies. Preliminary findings suggest a typical weight regain of approximately one-third of initial loss in the first year following treatment. Furthermore, almost 50% of patients completing a CBT program for obesity return to baseline weight within 5 years. While studies suggest that follow-up weight-maintenance programs may help individuals continue to utilize weight control skills by emphasizing positive coping with slips and relapses, such courses seem to delay, not prevent, weight regain in the future. To this end, the incorporation of a therapeutic pharmacological component may prove useful in the continued treatment of obesity.

CBT Treatment of BED

Arguably even more so than in obesity, CBT appears helpful for individuals with BED. Because BED shares features with bulimia nervosa, some treatment approaches for BED have been modeled after those for bulimia nervosa.

While focusing primarily on the reduction and control of binge eating episodes, CBT in BED aims to improve an individual's body image and simultaneously address co-occurring psychological disorders. Toward these ends, structured patterns of food intake may be emphasized with the specific goal of reducing instances of binge eating. Concurrently, cognitive restructuring techniques may be employed to help reshape an individual's often negative attitudes toward weight, shape, body image, and food in general. Like with CBT in obesity, other elements may include the teaching of self-monitoring skills, nutritional education, and useful techniques for relapse prevention.

Weight loss, while also important in CBT for BED, is often postponed until an effort has been made toward controlling binge eating behavior. Thus, in addition to nutritional education and an emphasis on regular, structured eating habits, CBT in BED may encourage exercise and increased physical activity. CBT has shown positive results in the treatment of BED, although, as with the treatment of obesity, there may exist limited long-term success in maintaining weight loss and controlling binge eating in obese individuals with BED.

In addition to CBT, other psychotherapy strategies, including interpersonal and dialectical behavior therapy (DBT), have shown promise in the treatment of BED. Modeled after therapeutic treatment programs for depression, interpersonal therapy (IPT) aims to address negative mood and interpersonal conflict arising from repeated episodes of binge eating. DBT, in turn, is structured on the basis of an affect regulation model of binge eating. Under this paradigm, binge episodes are viewed as maladaptive strategies for coping with unpleasant affect. Therefore, DBT aims to help individuals learn to regulate emotion by using healthier coping mechanisms. While both techniques have shown some efficacy in reducing the frequency of binge eating, further investigation is necessary to optimize treatment strategies for BED.

Pharmacological Treatment of Obesity

Pharmacotherapies for obesity might be broadly categorized into two groups: drugs that produce weight loss by interfering with intestinal digestion of fat and those that lead to weight reduction through appetite suppression or other central, brain-based mechanisms.

Of the lipase-inhibiting drugs, orlistat is currently the most widely prescribed. Treatment programs incorporating orlistat have shown modest weight reductions in obese patients and may help reduce the risk of type II diabetes. Due to its mechanism of action, orlistat is not recommended for individuals whose dietary intake is composed of less than 30% fat, as little weight loss is typically seen when these subjects are treated with the drug. Adverse events seen with the use of orlistat may include a decrease in absorption of fat-soluble vitamins presumably related to the drug's inhibition of intestinal triglyceride digestion.

The appetite-suppressing class of drugs, in contrast, reduces weight in obesity by decreasing food intake through several different paths of action. Benzphetamine, phendimetrazine, and diethylpropion stimulate the release of NE and have only been approved by Food and Drug Administration (FDA) for short-term use. Rimonabant, a cannabinoid antagonist which binds CB1a receptors, is indicated for use as an anti-obesity agent. Mazindol acts by blocking NE reuptake, and sibutramine—which has approval for long-term, maintenance treatment of obesity—operates by blocking both NE and serotonin (5-HT) reuptake. Adverse effects related to appetite-suppressing drugs vary and may include dry mouth, constipation, and insomnia. Sibutramine may also produce a small but medically significant increase in pulse and blood pressure, therefore warranting careful observation and contraindicating the drug's use in some individuals with hypertension and heart disease.

In addition to the lipase inhibitors and appetite suppressants currently in use for the treatment of obesity, several other drugs are actively being explored for their potential efficacy. Not currently approved for weight loss, bupropion has been associated with weight loss in the treatment of depression, perhaps related to the drug's noradrenergic properties. Topiramate, a carbonic anhydrase inhibitor used in the treatment of epilepsy and bipolar disorder, has also been associated with weight loss. Antagonists to the melanin-concentrating hormone peptide receptor—which are found primarily in the lateral hypothalamus and regulate food intake—also present a potential future course in the treatment of obesity.

While current and developing pharmacotherapy approaches offer encouraging prospects, drug therapy courses are not without complications and undesirable consequences. For example, fenfluramine, dexfenfluramine, and phentermine have been associated with instances of cardiac valvulopathy and withdrawn from the market. The prescription of other drugs, especially amphetamines and methamphetamines which decrease body weight by stimulating thermogenesis and reducing appetite, should be carefully considered given their addictive potential.

Although pharmacotherapy has shown efficacy in the treatment of obesity, the most effective strategy for the treatment of obesity may involve the combination of medication and behavioral interventions, like CBT, that integrate elements of dietary modification and increased physical activity.

Pharmacological Treatment of BED

While psychotherapeutic approaches such as CBT, IPT, and DBT have shown efficacy in reducing binge frequency, they have demonstrated little success in long-term maintenance of weight loss in BED. To this end, the pursuit of pharmacological approaches to treating BED has been examined.

Although no definitive pharmacological treatment has yet been established for the treatment of BED, at least three different classes are being investigated: serotonergic and noradrenergic drugs used in the treatment of depression, appetite suppressants currently used in the treatment of obesity, and anticonvulsants which have shown efficacy in the treatment of bipolar disorder.

Selective serotonin reuptake inhibitor (SSRI) antidepressant medications, including fluoxetine, fluvoxamine, sertraline, and citalopram, have been found to reduce the frequency of binging episodes and contribute toward a decrease in body weight. Tricyclic antidepressants, such as despiramine and imipramine, which block the reuptake of NE, have also shown some efficacy in the treatment of BED.

In addition to antidepressant medications, centrally acting appetite suppressants that have serotonergic and noradrenergic mechanisms of action, such as sibutramine, have shown some preliminary success in the treatment of BED. Furthermore, anticonvulsants have been associated with modest reductions in both weight and frequency of binge episodes in preliminary investigations. Zonisamide, for example, has shown peripheral weight loss in its use as an antiepileptic and has been found to reduce episodes of binge eating, although further clinical investigations are necessary to explore the efficacy of this drug in the treatment of BED. While these initial findings are encouraging, further research is needed to demonstrate the short- and long-term effectiveness of pharmacotherapies in the treatment of BED and to identify who might respond best to which treatments.

Surgical Approaches to the Treatment of Extreme Obesity

In cases of extreme obesity (BMI greater than 40 or greater than 35 with some comorbid disorders such as type II diabetes, hypertension, heart disease, and significant arthritis in weight-bearing joints) where repeated dietary and exercise modification efforts have been ineffective, surgical techniques may offer a promising treatment alternative. There are three central classes of surgical techniques in practice today for the treatment of extreme obesity: restrictive surgery, malabsorptive procedures, and mixed procedures such as gastric bypass which combine elements of both restrictive and malabsorptive interventions. While all three types of surgeries aim to reduce weight, each has differences with respect to efficacy and adverse effect profiles.

In restrictive procedures—which limit food intake to induce weight loss—surgical techniques are used to reduce stomach size. On average, patients who undergo the procedure lose between 40% and 60% of excess weight within the first 2 years postsurgery. While such surgeries have shown success in treating extreme obesity, they are not encouraged in the treatment of overweight individuals who also suffer from BED, nor in patients whose BMI exceeds 50, in part related to surgical risks. Unfortunately, individuals with extreme obesity who undergo restrictive operations may experience subsequent weight gain and complications, including band slippages or erosions and pouch dilations which may necessitate further corrective surgery.

Malabsorptive procedures, in contrast, reduce nutritional absorption by diminishing the amount of mucosal surface encountered in the process of digestion through a bypass of certain areas of the intestinal tract, thereby resulting in weight loss. Strictly, malabsorptive procedures are now implemented more rarely as they may be associated with malnutrition problems.

Mixed procedures describe an array of surgical techniques which combine elements of both restrictive and malabsorptive surgical strategies. Of these, gastric bypass is the most common operation in use today. In this procedure, a reduced stomach capacity decreases food intake, while an intestinal shortening and bypass incorporates the advantages of malabsorptive procedures. While leading to weight loss, gastric bypass procedures may improve symptoms of diabetes as well. Data suggest that gastric bypass procedures may be superior to restrictive procedures alone in weight loss and in reduction of obesity-related health problems.

Although surgical interventions in the treatment of obesity have been used for several decades, there remains little standardization, and criteria for choosing one intervention over another remain to be established. Toward this end, further research directly comparing the efficacies of various surgical approaches is needed. Such procedures, however, represent a promising development in the treatment of individuals with extreme obesity that fails to respond to other therapeutic strategies.

Obesity in Children and Adolescents

In recent years, the prevalence rates of obesity in children and adolescents have increased at an alarming rate. Today, BMI represents the most effective tool for assessing obesity in children and adolescents, where age- and gender-specific BMI ranges are used to categorize underweight, normal weight, overweight, and obese individuals. One approach uses percentile values along an estimated normal distribution curve of BMI values for each respective age and gender group, with values falling between the projected 85th and 95th percentiles of BMI indicating overweight, and BMI ratings above the 95th percentile describing obesity.

However, current estimates suggest that a much larger percentage of children have BMI ratings falling above the projected 85th percentile mark than would be expected under a pattern of normal distribution. By this classification standard, approximately one-third of all American children are overweight, as are roughly 14–22% of their European counterparts, with about 9–13% of all children falling within the classification ranges for obesity.

Childhood obesity has been associated with multiple negative health measures, including hypertension, glucose intolerance and insulin resistance (both conditions often seen as a precursor to type II diabetes), and respiratory abnormalities. Childhood obesity is linked with both obesity and obesity-related health complications in adulthood. Overweight and obese children may experience stigmatization which may hinder development of social skills in adolescence and negatively impact self-esteem. Emotional and behavioral problems are also often seen in overweight children.

Since being overweight as a child appears to predict adult obesity, early implementation of preventative strategies is important. Behaviorally oriented programs may teach children regarding the importance of proper nutrition and healthy diets while also encouraging physical activity over pastimes such as watching television and playing video games. Therapeutic approaches, such as those based on CBT approaches used in the treatment of adults with obesity, have shown some success when implemented with overweight and obese children. Such programs may be particularly helpful with the involvement of parents (and other family members), who are encouraged to help their children continue at home the techniques learned in treatment sessions.

Binge Eating in Children and Adolescents

While patterns of binge eating may be seen early in life, it remains difficult to assess the prevalence of BED in this population, principally because diagnostic criteria for identifying BED have not been adequately established or validated in children and adolescents. Findings suggest a 7–28% occurrence rate of binge eating episodes in children and adolescents (the broadness of this range is perhaps accounted for by the use of different definitions of binge eating across different investigations). BED as defined in the DSM-IV-TR may be seen in roughly 1–3% of children and adolescents. The relationship between childhood binge eating and adult BED requires further research.

Case Example

The following account of a BED patient's history illustrates one possible course of the illness. Amy, a 29-year-old single female, describes frequent episodes of extreme eating in which she often feels out of control over the quantity of food she consumes, eats more rapidly than normal, and habitually eats when not physically hungry or until she feels uncomfortably full. She does not report ever engaging in any sort of compensatory behaviors (such as purging or excessive exercise) following binge episodes, although she does endorse feelings of guilt, embarrassment, and/or depression after excessive eating. Her medical history reveals that she has experienced at least one major depressive episode in the past 3 years and has previously sought treatment for anxiety. The patient has a BMI of 31 and is being treated for hypertension. Treatment approaches in this case could include cognitive behavioral restructuring coupled with SSRI-based pharmacotherapy to jointly target the reduction of binge episodes. While the primary goal of CBT would be to manage the frequency binge eating, a secondary objective of weight loss through training for healthier diet and increased physical activity would also be pursued once the occurrence of binge episodes has been controlled. The patient's body image and co-occurring psychological disorders would also be addressed.

Conclusion

Although recent research has contributed to an improved understanding of obesity and BED and their symptoms, related features, underlying causes, and potential treatments, many questions still remain. With continued research in this field, however, the development in the near future of new and effective approaches to the prevention and treatment of these conditions seems promising.

See also: Control of Food Intake; Gastrointestinal Peptides and the Control of Food Intake; Stress and Energy Homeostasis.

Further Reading

Brownell KD and Wadden TA (1992) Etiology and treatment of obesity: Understanding a serious, prevalent, and refractory disorder. *Journal of Consulting and Clinical Psychology* 60(4): 505–517.

Fairburn CG and Brownell KD (eds.) (2001) *Eating Disorders and Obesity: A Comprehensive Handbook,* 2nd edn. New York: Guilford.

Flegal KM, Carroll MD, Ogden CL, and Johnson CL (2002) Prevalence and trends in obesity among US adults, 1999–2000. *Journal of the American Medical Association* 288(14): 1723–1727.

Grilo CM (2001) Pharmacological and psychological treatments of obesity and binge eating disorder. In: Sammons MT and Schmidt NB (eds.) *Combined Treatment for Mental Disorders: A Guide to Psychological and Pharmacological Interventions,* pp. 239–269. Washington, DC: American Psychological Association.

Mokdad AH, Ford ES, Bowman BA, Dietz WH, Vinicor F, Bales VS, and Marks JS (2003) Prevalence of obesity, diabetes, and obesity-related health risk factors, 2001. *Journal of the American Medical Association* 289(1): 76–79.

Munsch S and Beglinger C (eds.) (2005) *Obesity and Binge Eating Disorder.* New York: Karger.

Steinbrook R (2004) Surgery for severe obesity. *New England Journal of Medicine* 350(11): 1075–1079.

Striegeil-Moore RH and Franko DL (2003) Epidemiology of binge eating disorder. *International Journal of Eating Disorders* 34: S19–S29.

Diagnostic Criteria for Exercise Dependence in Women

By D.J. Bamber, I.M. Cockerill, S. Rodgers, and D. Carroll

Objective: To formulate diagnostic criteria for exercise dependence.

Method: Fifty six adult female exercisers were interviewed about their exercise behaviour and attitudes. The eating disorders examination, a semistructured clinical interview, was used to diagnose eating disorders. Interviews were taped, transcribed verbatim, and analysed from a social constructionist perspective using QSR NUD*IST. Participants also completed the exercise dependence questionnaire.

Results: Two diagnostic criteria emerged from analysis of the interview data: impaired functioning and withdrawal. Impaired functioning was manifest in four areas: psychological, social and occupational, physical, and behavioural. Impairment in at least two areas was considered necessary for diagnosis. Withdrawal was evident as either an adverse reaction to the interruption of exercise or unsuccessful attempts at exercise control. Either sufficed for diagnosis. The absence or presence of an eating disorder was used to distinguish between primary and secondary exercise dependence. Ten women met these criteria for exercise dependence. All 10 also exhibited eating disorders and, accordingly, should be regarded as showing secondary, rather than primary, exercise dependence. Exercise dependent women had significantly higher scores on the exercise dependence questionnaire than non-dependent women.

Conclusion: These new diagnostic criteria should now be adopted and explored further, particularly among men and individuals with possible primary exercise dependence.

Abbreviations: EDE, eating disorders examination; EXD1, exercise dependence interview; EDO, exercise dependence questionnaire.

Exercise dependence is now the preferred term for a seemingly unhealthy preoccupation with exercising. As eating disorders commonly co-occur with problematic exercise,[1–3] the terms primary and secondary exercise dependence have been coined to differentiate between excessive exercising as an independent pathology and as an associated feature of an underlying eating disorder.[4] Irrespective of its status as a primary or secondary condition, there have now been various attempts to characterise and measure exercise dependence. Some researchers have operationalised exercise dependence in terms of the frequency and/or amount of exercise undertaken.[5 6] For example, Anshel[5] characterised "addicted runners" as "Persons engaging in structured and non-structured activity programs at the (health) club at least 5 days per week for a minimum of 15 hours per week over the past 20 weeks". The main problem with this approach is that it fails to distinguish between committed and problematic exercisers. By focusing only on behavioural criteria, critical attitudinal, emotional, and motivational factors are neglected.

Although not ignoring exercise behaviour, others have emphasised the psychological characteristics of dependence, such as experience of withdrawal symptoms, including anxiety or depression when unable to exercise, as indicative of exercise dependence.[4 7 8] The latter approach has largely informed the numerous questionnaires that have been developed to measure exercise dependence. For example, the exercise dependence questionnaire[9] and the obligatory exercise questionnaire[10] attempt to measure such attributes as withdrawal symptoms, stereotyped behaviour, and interference with social functioning.

However, there are a number of problems with the questionnaire approach at this stage in our understanding of exercise dependence. Firstly, in the absence of agreed and validated criteria for exercise dependence, the choice of items explored on questionnaires must, to an extent, be arbitrary.

Secondly, appropriate cut off points remain to be determined. For example, in a recent study using the exercise dependence questionnaire, the female participants were considered to be exercise dependent if their scores were ≥116.[11] As items are scored on a 1–7 point Likert scale, this cut off represents an average cut off score of at least 4 on each of the 29 items—that is, they did not disagree, on average, with such statements as "The rest of my life has to fit around my exercise" and "If I cannot exercise I feel irritable." However, in the absence of an eating disorder, female exercisers meeting this criterion did not exhibit the sorts of personality profiles, high levels of neuroticism, addictiveness, and impulsivity and the levels of psychological distress that are characteristic of other dependencies.[12–14] Thirdly, existing exercise dependence questionnaires do not differentiate between primary exercise dependence and problematic exercise as an associated characteristic of an eating disorder. In the study by Bamber and colleagues,[11] female exercisers who met the criterion described above, but also showed evidence of an eating disorder on the eating disorders examination questionnaire,[15] displayed the expected morbid personality characteristics and high levels of psychological distress.

As yet, there has only been one attempt to develop proper diagnostic criteria for exercise dependence. Based on clinical experience, Veale[4 8] produced a set of diagnostic criteria for primary and secondary exercise dependence (table 1) analogous to those used for diagnosing other dependence syndromes.[16] However, there has been insufficient evidence to support the existence of primary exercise dependence and, accordingly, to convince the American Psychiatric Association that exercise dependence should be recognised as an independent clinical disorder.

Clearly, there is a need to strengthen the empirical base of exercise dependence. A qualitative approach may be better suited than a quantitative one for exploring potential diagnostic criteria for exercise dependence, as qualitative methods can provide richer accounts of individual experience. As the nature of exercise dependence remains to be determined, a wholly quantitative approach may be premature. Indeed, the general reliance on quantitative methods may well be impeding the further development of diagnostic criteria and, accordingly, our general understanding of exercise dependence. To date, the application of qualitative methods in this context has been limited to a few case studies.[17–20] The present study applied a rigorous and systematic qualitative approach with a view to extracting diagnostic criteria for primary and secondary exercise dependence. Given Veale's preliminary exploration of diagnostic criteria and the expanding literature on exercise dependence, an approach based on a social constructionist mode of grounded theory was adopted.[21] This approach encourages new ideas to emerge while acknowledging and challenging existing ones[22] and was therefore deemed best suited to current research needs.

METHOD

Participants

Interviews were conducted with 56 adult female exercisers recruited from a variety of sources, including: aerobics classes; sports centres; athletics and running clubs; the Eating Disorders Association; a private eating disorder clinic; the readership of *Athletics weekly* and *Runner's world* magazines; the United Kingdom Athletics Organisation. Mean (SD) age was 28.90 (8.36) years, mean (SD) objectively measured body mass index was 22.78 (3.78), and mean (SD) age at menarche was 13.59

TABLE 1 Proposed diagnostic criteria for primary and secondary exercise dependence[4,8]

Primary exercise dependence
1. Preoccupation with exercise which has become stereotyped and routine
2. Significant withdrawal symptoms in the absence of exercise (e.g. mood swings, irritability, insomnia)
3. The preoccupation causes clinically significant distress or impairment in their physical, social, occupational, or other important areas of functioning
4. The preoccupation with exercise is not better accounted for by another mental disorder (e.g. as a means of losing weight or controlling calorie intake as in an eating disorder)
Secondary exercise dependence
1. Narrowing of repertoire leading to stereotyped pattern of exercise with a regular schedule once or more daily
2. Salience with the individual giving increasing priority over other activities to maintaining the pattern of exercise
3. Increased tolerance to the amount of exercise performed over the years
4. Withdrawal symptoms related to disorder of mood after cessation of exercise schedule
5. Relief or avoidance of withdrawal symptoms by further exercise
6. Subjective awareness of a compulsion to exercise
7. Rapid reinstatement of the previous pattern of exercise and withdrawal symptoms after a period of abstinence
Associated features
1. Either the individual continues to exercise despite a serious physical disorder known to be caused, aggravated, or prolonged by exercise and is advised as such by a health professional, or the individual has arguments or difficulties with his/her partner, family, friends, or occupation 2. Self inflicted loss of weight by dieting as a means towards improving performance

(1.69) years. Skinfold thicknesses were taken to derive estimated mean (SD) percentage body fat of 21.65 (7.82).[23] Participants were recruited through mail shots, magazine adverts, or by being given a questionnaire at an exercise class. They were invited to enter a "Lifestyle study", and participation was voluntary. Most of the participants were white (89%); 5% identified themselves as Afro-Caribbean, 2% as Asian, and 4% as mixed ethnicity. Most (80%) were single.

Interview schedule

The two part semistructured interview, comprising the eating disorders examination (EDE)[24] and the exercise dependence interview (EXDI), has been described in detail elsewhere.[11] To improve accuracy and recall, interviews began with a detailed discussion of events over the preceding three months. Participants made notes on a calendar, which was used throughout the interview along with their personal diaries. Detailed probing and use of temporal anchors facilitated accurate recall of more distant past events. A comprehensive debriefing format was used for any participants who expressed disordered eating attitudes and behaviours, and all participants were given the opportunity to ask any questions about the research. Order of administration of the EDE and EXDI was counterbalanced, and all interviews were conducted by the first author who was trained in the administration of the EDE[24] and had completed a one year training course in counselling skills and theory. Interviews were tape recorded and lasted one to three hours. Full written informed consent was obtained before each interview. Finally, before the interview, participants completed the exercise dependence questionnaire (EDQ).[9]

Data preparation and analysis

The procedures used for analysis of the qualitative data have been detailed previously.[11] Briefly, all interviews were transcribed verbatim, participants' responses to the EDE were coded, and eating disorder diagnoses were made.[24] All subjects' names were changed to maintain confidentiality. An inter-rater reliability study was carried out, whereby the third author, a chartered clinical psychologist, assessed 25 interviews for eating disorders and possible exercise dependence. Her assessments agreed 100% with those of the first author. A precis of each interview was made, and any new consistent themes were noted[25] and added to the summary sheet. Interview transcripts, post-interview journal entries, and summary sheets were imported into the QSR NUD*IST 4.0 (non-numerical unstructured data indexing searching and theorising) software package.[26] Interview transcripts were divided into "text units"—lines of text—which were coded and placed into categories in the index system, a framework of nodes for text units that referred to themes—for example, withdrawal. This process continued until no new themes emerged, and theoretical saturation was reached. Again, the third author provided a second opinion at each stage of the analysis. Consensus was reached about the nature and operational definitions of the themes and their position in the index system. An audit trail of theoretical memos was stored within NUD*IST and findings were verified by searching for negative cases.[27]

Diagnoses and quantitative assessment

A second stage of the study involved re-examining the responses of all 56 interviewees using the diagnostic criteria derived from the narratives to characterise participants as primary or secondary exercise dependent. These diagnoses were compared with participants' scores on the EDQ.

RESULTS

Table 2 summarises the findings from the analyses; examples of raw data, higher order themes, and general dimensions are detailed. The four general dimensions pertinent to the diagnosis of exercise dependence that emerged were; impaired functioning, withdrawal presence of an eating disorder, associated features.

Impaired functioning

This dimension referred to significant dysfunction in four areas; (a) psychological; (b) social and occupational; (c) physical; (d) behavioural. Assessment of significance of any functional impairment was based on the evidence provided by participants narratives and was confirmed by the third author's clinical opinion. The following interchange shows impaired psychological functioning manifested as intrusive thoughts about exercise:

> DB: "Over the past four weeks, have you spent much time thinking about exercising?"
>
> Peta: "Oh yes, I plan it every night, I plan it in my head when I get up every morning."
>
> DB: "Has thinking about exercising interfered with your ability to concentrate in the same way that food has?"
>
> Peta: "Yes, yes"
>
> DB: "Have you had to force yourself back to concentrating?"
>
> Peta: "Yes, I am having to do it now, yes."

Millie described how she experienced intrusive thoughts about exercising:

TABLE 2 Emergent themes relating to diagnostic criteria for exercise dependence

Raw data—examples	First order themes	Second order themes	General dimension
"I have to think that people have to sit down in an office day after day … it's like a power of struggle and my brain's never quiet, trying to reason …"	Intrusive thoughts/ruminations Salience of thoughts about exercising Anxiety, depression Anger, frustration, agitation, irritability Guilt, insomnia, lethargy, loss of motivation, impaired concentration, feel confined	Psychological	Impaired functioning
"It's exercise or nothing" "I'd always turn something down if it was going to interfere with my routine" "My exercise is my social life, I don't have a social life outside that"	Salience of exercising above other activities Social isolation/withdrawal Inability to work, late for work, impaired concentration/functioning at work Irritability with colleagues, partners, friends, family Conflict in relationships	Social and occupational	
"I went to the doctor and he said … you have got to slow down, don't do so much exercise, erm, but I didn't"	Medically contraindicated exercising Injury Illness Fatigue	Physical	
"I go (walking) at half past 7 and then I go at half past 10 and then I go at half past 1 and then I go at half past 4, so structured" "I sometimes really push myself … because I am bad, because I have done something that I shouldn't have"	Stereotyped and inflexible behaviour Self harm/punishing	Behavioural	
"I wouldn't think I deserved the food" "I should be feeling very depressed and angry and anxious … I would be ready to be hospitalised"	Change in eating behaviour/cognitions (e.g. bingeing, dietary restriction, fear eating) Fear weight gain Increase alcohol/substance use Severe anxiety, depression, loss motivation	Adverse response to change in/ interruption of exercise habits	Withdrawal
"I'd love to lie on the settee and watch video after video" "It (exercising) speeded up again and now I'm trying to cut down" "The more I do it the more it seems that I need to do it" "It has a tendency to creep up" "If I start doing the exercising … I will start doing more and more of it" "4 and a half to 6 hours per day plus (horse) riding" "There aren't many people in my front room at 5 am"	Fantasies about not exercising Desire to cut down Inability to cut down Feeling exercising is out of own control Increased volume exercise (frequency, intensity, duration) Decreased exercise Fear of addiction Performance/non-performance related High volume Mode, frequency, duration, intensity Solitary exercising	Persistent desire and/or unsuccessful attempts to control/reduce exercise Tolerance Exercise behaviour	Associated: features

Raw data—examples	First order themes	Second order themes	General dimension
"I probably underestimate it" "… a bit economical with the truth … and I don't tell them about the hill profiles and speed" "my main reason for exercising is to be good, but I know that to be good I also need to be thin" "control, control full stop." "because I have to"	Lying about exercising Exercising in secret Denial—self/others Insight/awareness of problem Performance Weight/shape control Mood, sleep Break from work Physical health Social Need to be active Feeling in control Self punishment Regulation emotions Physical self efficacy Sense of compulsion	Deception/ insight Exercise motives	
Responses to each of the 36 EDE items "I always feel guilty after eating" "I feel fat and ugly and I hate myself at the moment" "It (weight) makes me feel awful, it just makes me feel really bad about myself."	EDE interview questions e.g. "Have you felt guilty about eating?" "How have you been feeling about your weight?"	Clinical eating disorder Disordered eating No eating disorder	Presence of an eating disorder (primary or secondary dependence)

EDE, Eating disorders examination.

"It interferes with my concentration for two reasons, one, because I dread it, because I hate those aerobics classes … so I think about it, like, 'Oh no I really don't want to do this', but I feel I must, and then when I don't have the opportunity, that makes me think about it …"

Annie's exercise was the only activity in her life, "It's exercise or nothing." She had given up the occupation for which she was trained to accommodate exercise. Further, when asked if her exercising interfered with her social life she replied, "I don't have a social life anymore … I don't have the energy for a social life." As Annie's exercise regimen involved a 5 am start, evening socialising was out of the question. For others, their exercising threatened intimate relationships. As Jessica described:

"It used to cause so many arguments because, erm, all I wanted to do was exercise, I wasn't interested in anything else at all, I had even got my son, Grant, but everything had to

come second to that, it didn't matter what, as long as I could get my exercise, it was like my fix. I had to get my fix otherwise I was in a foul mood. I felt totally guilty if I missed a lesson, it was mainly, like I say, conflicts between me and my partner, just caused so many arguments."

Unlike non-dependent exercisers, who rarely reported difficulties taking necessary rest when ill or injured, dependent exercisers like Annie would exercise even when medically contraindicated:

"I have knackered my knee joints and I have got arthritis in my knees and ankles from too much exercise, and I have crumbling hip joints from overexercise, so I know I have got permanent knee and shin injuries that I have given myself from overexercise, but I still continue to do it."

Annie even reported having continued to exercise after being thrown off a horse, admitting: "Whenever I am told to rest I always ignore it. If I broke a leg I would find something to do."

Although regular exercising was common to many participants, particularly those involved in competitive sport, dependent exercisers exhibited unusually stereotyped and inflexible behaviour around exercise. For example, Samantha described her exercising as: "Very very structured, it has to be, I like it to be a routine." In contrast, Angie had a much more relaxed attitude towards her exercising:

> "From week to week it's very variable but on average I try to aim for roughly the same kind of things each week, but if I can't make a class and the weather's nice I'll go out for a run instead, I'm not that, my life is not governed to the point where the world stops to get to aerobics for half past five, if I can't go I can't go, I'll do something else, or I'll go home and do nothing occasionally."

Withdrawal

Issues related to withdrawal emerged as two themes. The first was "clinically significant adverse response to a change in or interruption of exercise habits". This was often manifest as anxiety, depression, anger, or guilt. In contrast, non-dependent exercisers did not have a severe reaction to not being able to exercise. For example, when Barbara had to miss her swim she coped: "I felt disappointed but I cheered myself up, I bought myself a new swimming costume. You see, it wasn't earth shattering, it would have been nice, I had planned to go, but it didn't work out." Peta, on the other hand, displayed a marked psychological reaction to missing her swim:

> "I was mad at myself, I felt really angry, I couldn't concentrate on anything and I felt moody and aggressive. I was really sarcastic with my husband and I felt like a big fat blob. Oh it was a dreadful day, I just felt so agitated and so out of control. It was a rotten time, and the other time when I couldn't I felt

angry at that person, I felt angry at everybody because I couldn't go and get my hour in the gym or a swim and just like, less interested, just not interested in anything."

Reported physical symptoms included headaches and insomnia, and common social responses included putting exercising before socialising. Millie's account of a day out was illustrative:

> "I remember one day when I drove my mum over to my sister's and she's there with a new-born baby, obviously struggling, and we were supposed to be there to help, but all I could think about was, "I have got to get out and go for a walk" … we went for this walk and I wanted to leave then and there and go for my walk … they wanted me to go and sit down and have a cup of tea and chat … and all I wanted was to go for a walk, I wasn't thinking about the baby … I brought them back and dumped them … and went off and had my walk anyway."

Laura explained how her need to exercise was a source of conflict in social situations; she gave an example: "Trying to walk to places when other people are trying to go on a bus or something." In contrast, Joan, who was not exercise dependent, said "Exercising doesn't tend to win out [over other activities] these days."

Behavioural responses to not being able to exercise included binge eating or increased rigidity around eating. Meg was one of many who experienced a seeming paradoxical response to not exercising, "If I haven't exercised I tend to eat far more junk stuff and I am at far greater risk of bingeing". Others reacted with extreme dietary restraint, Joan explained "I would stick to very familiar, tried and tested foods … a very narrow range … would be very restrictive. …" Jenny, on the other hand, felt that she would have to continually weigh herself to determine how much she should be eating.

The second theme under the general dimension of withdrawal was "evidence of a persistent desire and/or unsuccessful efforts to control or reduce exercise." Some participants fantasised about not having to exercise.

TABLE 3 New diagnostic criteria for secondary exercise dependence

The following three criteria are necessary for a diagnosis of secondary exercise dependence:
1. Impaired functioning*
The individual shows evidence of impaired functioning in at least two of the following areas:
(a) Psychological—e.g. ruminations or intrusive thoughts about exercise, salience of thoughts about exercise, anxiety, or depression
(b) Social and occupational—e.g. salience of exercising above all social activities, inability to work
(c) Physical—e.g. exercising causes or aggravates health or injury yet continues to exercise when medically contraindicated
(d) Behavioural—e.g. stereotyped and inflexible behaviour
2. Withdrawal
The individual shows evidence of one or more of the following:
(a) Clinically significant adverse response to a change or interruption of exercise habits. Response may be physical, psychological, social, or behavioural,
e.g. severe anxiety or depression, social withdrawal, self harm†
(b) Persistent desire and/or unsuccessful efforts to control or reduce exercise
3. Presence of an eating disorder‡
Associated features
The following features are indicative but not definitive:
(i) Tolerance—i.e. increasing volumes of exercising required
(ii) High volumes of exercising and/or exercising at least once daily
(iii) Solitary exercising
(iv) Deception—e.g. lying about exercise volume, exercising in secret
(v) insight—e.g. denial that exercising is a problem

*Exercise is unreasonably salient and/or stereotyped even when considered in appropriate context—e.g. individual is a competitive athlete:

†If individual had not abstained from exercise, or would refuse to do so, rate withdrawal according to anticipated response.

‡For a diagnosis of primary exercise dependence, ail criteria may be the same as for secondary exercise dependence except for the absence, rather than presence, of an eating disorder.

Peta described the conflict between feeling the need to continue exercising and inner desire for some respite:

"… there's a part of me deep down that would like a rest, you know, I love it, you know when I've got flu, oh it's great to be able to sit down on the settee, because I've got flu, but I'm still agitated at myself, it's a terrible, terrible conflict … I'd love someone to say 'You have to lie down on the settee all day', I'd love to lie down on the settee and watch video after video …"

Annie expressed similar fantasies about not having to exercise: "I think it's a dream that I would love to be able to do at one point in the future but at the moment

I would not be able to, no way." She also reported failed attempts to reduce her exercising to a more reasonable level: "I try to cut down but I know that I won't".

Presence of an eating disorder

The EDE identified 18 participants as having an eating disorder at the time of interview. A further nine participants showed disordered eating—that is, problematic eating behaviour and attitudes that did not currently warrant a clinical diagnosis.

Associated features

Additional themes (table 2) that emerged from the narratives included: tolerance, manifested as a progressive increase in exercise volume; high volumes of exercising and/or daily exercising; solitary exercising; deception, for example, lying about exercising; exercising driven predominantly by the desire to control weight, shape, or body composition.

Diagnostic criteria

Table 3 summarises the diagnostic criteria derived from the analysis of these exercisers' narratives. Associated features were considered indicative but not definitive of exercise dependence. Impaired functioning and withdrawal were regarded by the clinical psychologist on the team (SR) as highly problematic and matters of definite clinical concern. After discussions of the narratives and the emergent themes, there was a consensus between the first author and the clinician that impairments in two or more of the four areas of functioning and withdrawal in either or both of its manifestations strongly intimated pathology and, accordingly, provided appropriate diagnostic criteria for exercise dependence. The presence of an eating disorder qualifies exercise dependence as secondary. The same diagnostic criteria, but in the absence of an eating disorder, are likely to qualify exercise dependence as primary, although evidence from individuals who exhibit possible primary exercise dependence needs to be examined systematically before definitive criteria for primary exercise dependence can be offered.

Diagnoses

When participants' responses were judged against these diagnostic criteria, 10 met the criteria for exercise dependence—that is, they showed impaired functioning in at least two areas and evidence of withdrawal. A further four showed disordered exercising—that is, problematic exercising that failed to meet fully the criteria. The remaining 42 showed symptoms of neither exercise dependence nor disordered exercising. Of the 10 exercise dependent women, all showed evidence of an eating disorder, and, as such, were best regarded as displaying secondary rather than primary exercise dependence. In addition, disordered exercising was only present when accompanied by symptoms of an eating disorder. Of the eight participants diagnosed with an eating disorder but no exercise dependence, one provided evidence of disordered exercising. Similarly, three of the nine participants who showed problematic eating behaviour and attitudes that fell short of a clinical eating disorder, also showed disordered exercising.

Quantitative findings

The mean (SD) score on the EDQ of the 10 participants who met our diagnostic criteria for exercise dependence was 136.3 (19.30). The mean (SD) score on the EDQ for the four people who showed disordered exercising that fell short of exercise dependence was 115.3 (22.87). The mean (SD) EDQ score of the 42 participants who showed no symptoms of exercise dependence or disordered exercising was 100.8 (23.46). A previous study using the EDQ adopted a cut off point for exercise dependence of ≥116,[11] the equivalent of scoring 4 on average on each of the 29 items. Table 4 indicates the accuracy of this criterion in discriminating those identified as exercise dependent, using the present diagnostic criteria. In addition, it indicates the consequences of adopting higher EDQ cut off points. As can be seen, the ≥116 cut off point identified 90% of those diagnosed as exercise dependent, but at some cost in terms of false positives. Thirty per cent of those not regarded as exercise dependent met this cut off point. In contrast, the more severe criterion of ≥145, the equivalent of scoring 5 on average on each of the 29 items, yielded no false positives but a high number of false negatives as it captured only

30% of those judged to be exercise dependent using the diagnostic-criteria derived from the narratives.

TABLE 4 Number of exercise dependent or non-exercise dependent participants as defined by diagnostic criteria and exercise dependence questionnaire (EDQ) score

	Diagnosis	
	Exercise dependent	Non exericise dependent*
EDQ score		
≥116	9	14
<116	1	32
≥130	6	3
<130	4	43
≥145	3	0
≤145	7	46

*Includes four participants who showed symptoms of disordered exercising but did not meet the criteria for exercise dependence.

DISCUSSION

This study represents the first systematic qualitative study of exercise dependence. Using semistructured interviews and an approach based on a social constructionist version of grounded theory, we analysed the narratives of 56 female exercisers with a view to extracting cogent diagnostic criteria for exercise dependence. In general, the themes that emerged are broadly in line with the diagnostic criteria proposed by Veale[4][8] (table 1). The major diagnostic criteria identified in the present study were impaired functioning and withdrawal.

Impaired functioning

There was evidence of impaired functioning in four areas: psychological, social and occupational, physical, and behavioral. Evidence of problems in at least two of these areas was judged necessary for a diagnosis of exercise dependence; only one would risk overinclusion, whereas insisting on three or more was considered to be overly exclusive. The inability to concentrate because of a preoccupation with exercise and exercise induced fatigue were examples of impaired psychological functioning. Medically contraindicated exercising and arguments with partner, family, or friends, rather than being discrete associated features as proposed by Veale,[8] were deemed examples of impaired physical and social functioning respectively. For Meg, her exercise behaviour appeared to serve an almost self harming function, "I sometimes push myself and when I am doing that I know it's because I am bad, because I have done something that I shouldn't have." Many participants described conflict between their exercising and other aspects of their lives. For example, Martine, a middle distance runner explained:

"I always fit my exercise in no matter what, even if it means not doing something else like going out or making myself late for something, because I have got to do my exercise. I am always late for work, terrible, like the other day I was out on my bike and I was just like, 'You have got to be at work in an hour, you have got so much to do', and I am like, 'well, I will finish my bike ride so its tough, they will have to wait' … it's just something that takes priority over other things."

Clearly, Martine's exercising was creating problems for her work.

Attaching a high priority to sport and exercise is not necessarily problematic. The degree of conflict and its context is important. Indeed, it was not unusual for competitive athletes in the present study to indicate some disruption of other activities as a result of their training commitments. Nevertheless, they were generally able to manage successfully sporting and other demands. Exercise only appeared to impair function when it became all consuming. For Annie, for example, exercising was her only priority. It was detrimental to her social life, her career, and her health. She was clearly distressed by her investment in exercise, "I feel it's a great bind, I feel it rules my life and I don't see why I should have to carry this cross when nobody else does."

Withdrawal

This diagnostic criterion was manifested as either a clinically significant adverse response to not exercising or as a persistent desire and/or inability to control or cut back on exercise; the latter sometimes presented as a premature return to exercising after illness or injury. Given that mild withdrawal symptoms are common among athletes, only severe instances of withdrawal should be regarded as symptomatic. As truly dependent exercisers would be unlikely to abstain from exercise for research, diagnostic, or even medical reasons, withdrawal symptoms are difficult to assess. In this study, this problem was addressed by asking participants to respond to the hypothetical situation of not being able to exercise for one week. This tactic yielded important data. For example, Jenny was visibly horrified at the prospect and stated:

> "You wouldn't, you just couldn't do it, well that's what I feel like … you are just depriving me of something that is essential to me … you might as well say, 'stop eating' or 'stop breathing' … I should be really depressed, I should be suicidal … I just wouldn't be able to cope with just sitting in here … without exercising … you would probably have to put me in hospital."

Accordingly, use of such hypothetical questions is recommended in the assessment of exercise dependence. For diagnosis of exercise dependence, it was considered that individuals should display at least one but not necessarily both of the two possible manifestations of withdrawal.

Associated features

A number of additional themes emerged from analysis of the present narratives. However, for reasons explained below, these should, at best, be regarded as indicative rather than definitive of exercise dependence. The present findings support Veale's recommendation that tolerance be abandoned as a criterion for the diagnosis of exercise dependence.[28] The concept of tolerance is a pharmacological one and unlikely to be generally applicable to exercise. Very few of the present participants reported

that increasing exercise loads was a function of compulsion and diminishing subjective benefits, although Joan feared, "If I start doing the exercising … I will start doing more and more of it". In most cases, though, it was difficult to attribute increasing schedules of exercise to tolerance. For some, it was clearly a function of a standard incremental athletic training programme. For others, increased exercise was associated with a desire to lose more weight. Although intentionally increasing exercise levels was a common practice, tolerance cannot be inferred from this behaviour. Accordingly, tolerance was not included as a diagnostic criterion. Nevertheless, occasional declarations of a subjective need for increasing amounts of exercise were considered useful pointers and so tolerance was more properly regarded as an associated feature.

A key finding in the present study was the importance of cognitions, such as ruminations about, or inflexible attitudes towards, exercising, as signifiers of exercise dependence. In contrast, frequency, duration, or overall volume of exercise undertaken did not differentiate unambiguously dependent and non-dependent exercisers. Bamber and colleagues[11] also found no relation between exercise dependence and exercise volume. As such, diagnostic criteria based solely on amounts of exercise would appear to be inadequate. For example, Alison, a triathlete, who was clearly not exercise dependent, reported training seven days a week, often twice daily. On the other hand, analysis of negative cases[27] raised the possibility that exercise dependence could occur at relatively low levels of exercising. For example, Meg insisted on climbing up and down the bottom stair for five minutes every morning and would be in "a bad temper" if she overslept and missed doing it. Similarly, Rebecca felt unable to tolerate not doing her five to ten minutes of daily weight training and sit ups:

> "If I get to the end of the day and I think, 'Oh God I haven't done my exercises' I do feel agitated and I have even got out of bed to do them … its just this overwhelming sensation really that I have to do them, even though I am tired and I just want to go to sleep."

What would seem to be a behavioural discriminator in this context is the stereotyped and rigid character of the exercise. Irrespective of volume, some of the present participants exhibited an inflexible pattern of behaviour that was self imposed. Meg and Rebecca provide striking examples. In contrast with volume, then, rigidity was considered a diagnostic criterion, an example of impaired behavioural functioning.

Veale[8] included a subjective awareness of exercising as a problem in his diagnostic criteria. In the present study, insight was explored by asking participants if they felt their exercising was problematic, excessive, or an addiction. Their subjective definitions of exercise dependence were also explored. Our analysis indicated that some potentially dependent exercisers denied that exercising was a problem. This is illustrated by the following extract from a theoretical memo stored in NUDIST:

> "When coding Roxanne it occurred to me that some individuals have greater or lesser insight into their exercise dependence. For example, Roxanne defined exercise addiction as, 'exercising 7 days a week, 2–3 hours a day, and feeling upset if unable to exercise'. She had described that pattern of behaviour and withdrawal in herself, but when I asked if she felt she was addicted to exercise, she still said, 'No'. It seems she is denying her dependence."
> (DB)

Lack of subjective awareness can be variously manifest as secretive exercising, lying about exercising, and denial of exercising as a problem. In this study, the probe question, "Would other people say that you exercise excessively?" elicited such responses as, "Only the lazy ones in this world". Martine's housemates clearly thought her exercising was excessive, as she recounted their comments, "You are just mad, you go on these futile runs all the time, you know, what's going on? … Martine's going on one of her runs around the world." Martine insisted that she did not have a problem. Interviews with significant others could be valuable to future exercise dependence research. In general, given that many potentially dependent participants were very resistant to any implication that their exercising was problematic or pathological, insight, as a diagnostic criterion, would result in substantial false negatives.

Diagnosis of primary and secondary exercise dependence

Ten of the participants in this study met our new diagnostic criteria for exercise dependence. It is worth noting that their scores on the EDQ were significantly higher than individuals not meeting the criteria. Further, a cut off point on the EDQ of ≥116, in contrast with more stringent EDQ cut off points, captured nine of the 10, although at the cost of a number of false positives. Those who did not meet fully the present diagnostic criteria, and were characterised as disordered exercisers, were not significantly different from non-dependent exercisers on the EDQ. This result could be taken as indicating that diagnosis using the present scheme should be restricted to those who unambiguously meet the criteria for exercise dependence, although it may also reflect the insensitivity of the EDQ. Identifying disordered exercising could be important. Early identification of those at risk—that is, individuals who are not as yet exercise dependent but show many of the characteristics—may help to prevent the development of exercise dependence. Further, it is important to recognise that the EDQ is not a diagnostic instrument; diagnosis should proceed on the basis of interviews of the sort conducted in this study.

Veale[4] has argued that, for exercise dependence to be deemed a primary pathology, it should be independent of any other clinical disorder, particularly an eating disorder. In the present study, impaired functioning and withdrawal were considered likely to characterise both primary and secondary exercise dependence, differentiation being based on the absence or presence of an eating disorder. All 10 exercise dependent women in this study showed evidence of an eating disorder. Thus, all 10 fulfilled the criteria for secondary, rather than primary, exercise dependence. This is in line with the results of a recent study,[11] which concluded that, if primary exercise dependence exists in women, it is a rare phenomenon, and does not have anything like the prevalence rates reported in some previous studies.[29][30] The present results reinforce the importance of systematically screening for eating disorders when studying exercise dependence.

It is worth noting, though, that dieting for performance was not typical of those participants meeting the criteria for secondary exercise dependence. Veale[8] proposed that dieting for performance represented an associated feature of secondary exercise dependence. Although it is difficult to distinguish between dieting as a symptom of an eating disorder and dieting for performance, particularly in weight dependent or aesthetic sports, the present data do not support Veale's proposal. Participants who met the criteria for secondary exercise dependence dieted predominantly to control weight, shape, or body composition rather than to improve athletic performance.

It is important to remember that no women in this study showed evidence of primary exercise dependence. Accordingly, the proposed criteria for primary exercise dependence remain speculative. Indeed, it would seem advisable to extend the proposed criterion for primary exercise dependence, relating to the absence of an eating disorder, to exclude exercise that can be better explained by any other psychiatric disorder. For example, obsessive-compulsive disorder may be manifested as apparent "dependent" exercising. Future attempts to identify primary exercise dependence need to include a full psychiatric assessment to rule out excessive exercising as an associated feature of any other disorder. It remains possible that primary exercise dependence does not exist as a primary clinical disorder.

From these data it is impossible to determine whether the secondary exercise dependence diagnosed is a secondary feature of an eating disorder or a true co-morbidity. However, the concept of secondary exercise dependence implies cause and effect. Given that the cause of exercise dependence and its precise relation to eating disorders remain to be determined, it may be more appropriate to adopt the term "associated exercise dependence", which continues to allow the possibility of genuine co-morbidity. After all, not everyone who exhibited an eating disorder in this study was exercise dependent. Indeed, for some with eating disorders, exercise may have an ameliorative effect. A number of participants reported that exercise encouraged them to eat more healthily and made them less likely to binge. It remains to be established why certain eating disorder sufferers show the symptoms of exercise dependence whereas others do not.

There could be important sex differences in the manifestation of exercise dependence. Primary exercise dependence may be more common among men, because eating disorders are known to occur much more often in women than men. The selection of women for these analyses maximised the opportunity to examine the complex relation between eating disorders and exercise. It is possible that our sampling procedures are responsible for the apparent non-existence of primary exercise dependence: the most "dependent" exercisers may have been unwilling to volunteer their time.

We recommend that these new diagnostic criteria be adopted in favour of earlier criteria for exercise dependence. Clinicians and researchers are invited to test them out in practice and to offer feedback about their replicability among men. Should any evidence for primary exercise dependence emerge, then more definitive diagnostic criteria can be developed.

Take home message

- Diagnostic criteria for exercise dependence in women have been derived from systematic qualitative analysis
- The search for primary exercise dependence continues
- There may be sex differences in the manifestation of exercise dependence

REFERENCES

1 Brewerton TD, Stellefson EJ, Hibbs N, *et al.* Comparison of eating disorder patients with and without compulsive exercising. *Int J Eat Disord* 1995;17:413–16.

2 Davis C, Kennedy SH, Ralevski E, *et al.* Obsessive compulsiveness and physical activity in anorexia nervosa and high level exercising. *J Psychosom Res* 1995;39:967–76.

3 Touyz SW, Beumont PJV, Hook S, Exercise anorexia: a new dimension in anorexia nervosa? In: Beaumont PJV, Burrows GD, Casper RC, eds. *Handbook of eating disorders, part 1.* Amsterdam: Elsevier Science Publishers, 1987:143–57.

4 Veale D. Does primary exercise dependence really exist? In: Annett J, Cripps B, Steinberg H, eds. *Proceedings of Warwick University workshop: exercise addiction: motivation for participation in sport and exercise.* Leicester: The British Psychological Society, 1995:1–5.

5   Anshel MH. A psycho-behavioural analysis of addicted versus non-addicted male and female exercisers. *Journal of Sport Behaviour* 1992;14:145–59.

6   Ogles BM, Masters KS, Richardson SA. Obligatory running and gender: on analysis of participative motives and training habits. *Int J Sport Psychol* 1995;26:233–48.

7   Morgan WP. Negative addiction in runners. *Physician and Sports Medicine* 1979;7:57–70.

8   Veale DMW. Exercise dependence. *Br J Addict* 1987;82:735–40.

9   Ogden J, Veale D, Summers Z. The development and validation of the exercise dependence questionnaire. *Addiction Research* 1997;5:343–56.

10 Blumenthal JA, O'Toole LC, Chang JL. Is running an analogue of anorexia? An empirical study of obligatory running and anorexia nervosa. *JAMA* 1984;252:520–3.

11 Bamber D, Cockerill IM, Carroll D. The pathological status of exercise dependence. *Br J Sports Med* 2000;34:125–32.

12 Blaszczynski AP, Buhrich N, McConaghy N. Pathological gamblers, heroin addicts and control compared on the EPQ "Addiction Scale". *Br J Addict* 1985;80:315–19.

13 Carroll D, Huxley JAA. Cognitive, dispositional, and psychophysiological correlates of dependent slot machine gambling in young people. *J Appl Soc Psychol* 1994;24:1070–83.

14 Gossop MR, Eysenck SBG. A further investigation into the personality of drug addicts in treatment. *Br J Addict* 1980;75:305–11.

15 Fairburn CG, Beglin SJ. Assessment of eating disorders: interview or self-report questionnaire? *Int J Eat Disord* 1994;16:363–70.

16 American Psychiatric Association. *Diagnostic and statistical manual of mental disorders.* 4th ed. Washington DC: American Psychiatric Association, 1994.

17 Cripps B. Exercise addiction and chronic fatigue syndrome: case study of a mountain biker. In: Annett J, Cripps B, Steinberg H, eds. *Proceedings of Warwick University workshop: exercise addiction: motivation for participation in sport and exercise.* Leicester: The British Psychological Society, 1995:22–33.

18 Griffiths M. Exercise addiction: a case study. *Addiction Research* 1997;5:161–8.

19 Sachs ML, Pargman D. Running addiction: a depth interview examination. *Journal of Sport Behaviour* 1979:143–55,

20 Seheult C. Hooked on the "buzz": history of a bodybuilding addict. In: Annett J, Cripps B, Steinberg H, eds. *Proceedings of Warwick University workshop: exercise addiction: motivation for participation in sport and exercise.* Leicester: The British Psychological Society, 1995:40–44.

21 Charmaz K. "Discovering" chronic illness: using grounded theory. *Soc Sci Med* 1990;30:1161–72.

22 Henwood K, Pidgeon N. Grounded theory and psychological research. *The Psychologist* 1995 Mar: 115–18.

23 Jackson AS, Pollock ML. Practical assessment of body composition. *Physician and Sports Medicine* 1985;13:76–90.

24 Fairburn CG, Cooper Z. The eating disorder examination. 12th ed. In: Fairburn CG, Wilson GT, eds. *Binge eating: nature, assessment and treatment.* New York: Guilford Press, 1993:317–60.

25 Miles MB, Huberman AM. *Qualitative data analysis.* London: Sage, 1994.

26 Qualitative Solutions and Research Pty Ltd. *QSR NUD*IST 4 user guide.* 2nd ed. London: Sage, 1997.

27 Strauss A, Corbin J. *Basics of qualitative research: grounded theory procedures and techniques.* London: Sage, 1990.

28 Veale DMW. Psychological aspects of staleness and dependence on exercise. *Int J Sports Med* 1991;12:519–22.

29 Anderson SJ, Basson CJ, Geils C. Personality style and mood states associated with a negative addiction to running. *Sports Med* 1997;4:6–11.

30 Slay HA, Hayaki J, Napolitano MA, *et al.* Motivations for running and eating attitudes in obligatory versus non-obligatory runners. *Int J Eat Disord* 1998;23:267–75.

Empirical Basis and Forensic Application of Affective and Predatory Violence

By J. Reid Meloy

The objective of this paper is to address the empirical basis and forensic application of a bimodal theory of violence. The definitions of affective and predatory violence, the relevant animal and clinical research, and the current empirical evidence in neurochemistry, neuropsychology and psychophysiology are reviewed. Forensic evidence for the relevance of this bimodal theory is investigated. An appropriate methodology for data gathering, and two observational measures along with one self-report measure are explicated. Integration of this bimodal theory into forensic practice is suggested. Affective and predatory modes of violence represent an empirically valid bimodal theory of violence, find application in forensic psychiatry, and scientifically deepen the understanding of discrete violent acts for both retrospective and prospective psychiatric and psychological investigations. This bimodal theory of violence should have a place in forensic psychiatric practice.

Key words: forensic, violence, predatory, affective, instrumental.

Although violence in its myriad forms is a rather stable behaviour in certain members of our species, the exact nature and causes of violence continue to beguile researchers and clinicians throughout the world. Violent behaviour—an intentional act of physical aggression against another human being that is likely to cause physical injury [1]—is, moreover, a fact of professional life in forensic psychiatry and psychology. Its measurement and prediction are dependent upon our keen observation and careful application of the scientific method.

Violent behaviour is no longer conceptualized as a generic, homogeneous phenomenon. It varies in frequency according to the social, psychological and biological determinants that are in play at the time of the violent act. The nature of the violence also varies, and recent advances in the study of violence and aggression have confirmed the usefulness of classifying violent behaviour as either affective or predatory, a tradition that reaches back over 50 years. This study will briefly review the definitions, history and empirical evidence for this bimodal classification of violence, and will then spell out its application to forensic psychiatry and psychology.

Definitions

Affective violence is preceded by high levels of autonomic (sympathetic) arousal, is characterized by the emotions of anger and/or fear, and is a response to a perceived imminent threat [2]. Other researchers refer to affective violence as impulsive [3], reactive [4], hostile [5], emotional [6] or expressive [7]. Its evolutionary basis is self-protection. Predatory violence is not preceded by autonomic arousal, is characterized by the absence of emotion and threat, and is cognitively planned. Other

J. Reid Meloy, "Empirical Basis and Forensic Application of Affective and Predatory Violence," from the *Australian and New Zealand Journal of Psychiatry*, vol. 40, pp. 539–547. Published by Blackwell, 2006. Copyright by John Wiley & Sons. Permission to reprint granted by the rights holder.

researchers refer to predatory violence as instrumental [5], premeditated [8], proactive [9] or cold blooded [10]. Its evolutionary basis is hunting for food. The terms that are preferred in this study—affective and predatory—are chosen for their historical provenance in mammalian research, both animals and humans, and their relatively distinctive psychobiological parameters [11,12]. Although instrumental is more widely used in the research and clinical literature than predatory because of the inference that it is goal-directed behaviour, it suggests that affective violence is not goal-directed, which is mistaken. The goal of affective violence is to successfully defend against a perceived danger through the use of aggression.

The relationship between these two modes of violence, however, continues to be debated. Some have argued that the distinction has outlived its usefulness [5] because it has become a rigid dichotomy and has impeded further research—a claim that is difficult to defend given the dramatic advances in the research concerning this scheme in the past decade [3,4,6,8,10]. Others have more plausibly argued that the two modes of violence may be theoretically important, but should be recognized as prototypes that seldom occur in nature in a pure form [13]. There is also the measurement question as to whether or not such manifestations of violence can be scaled on one dimension or two [7]. It is probably wise at this point to conceive of affective and predatory violence as dimensional rather than categorical, with most violent acts being primarily one or the other, and some violent acts containing elements of both; hence, the suggestion of a bimodal distribution. However, violent acts that appear to be 'mixed' may, in fact, be a sequencing of one mode of violence to another within one event [2]. Heilbrun *et al.* [14] noted that the determination of the mode of violence may be one of the most important criteria in assessing future violence risk and treatment prognosis in criminal offenders.

History

Two excellent recent reviews of affective and predatory violence [11,12] describe in detail the animal, clinical and forensic research which provides the historical database for classifying violence and aggression in this manner. Early investigations focused upon animal models to categorize observable behaviour and suggested both anatomical and neurotransmitter correlates [15,16]. Hess and Brugger coined the terms 'affective defensive behaviour' and 'quiet biting attack' in 1943 when they described the arousal pattern in a cat following stimulation of the hypothalamus [17]. Twenty years later the work of Flynn *et al.* established the anatomical substrates of affective and predatory aggression in felines [18–23]. Reis further clarified these distinctive modes of violence when he noted the differential sympathetic arousal patterns despite some shared limbic structures [24,25], including the ventral and dorsal hippocampus, septal area, amygdala, and portions of the prefrontal cortex, cingulate gyrus and periaqueductal grey matter. Neurotransmitters implicated in the animal research included acetylcholine, gamma-aminobutyric acid (GABA), serotonin, norepinephrine and dopamine, with different effects of some chemicals on the elicitation or suppression of predatory or affective violence [12]. The prototype of affective violence in the cat is the behaviour in the midst of a threat, usually another animal: arched back, piloerection, vocalization, display of teeth and claws, pupil dilation and ears tilted backward. This mode of violence has also been clearly described in mice, rats, dogs and primates [11]. The prototype of predatory violence in the cat is the stalking of a wounded bird: behavioural alerting and focusing upon the target, the absence of any sound and the absence of any sympathetic arousal other than pupil dilation. The cat will move quietly and directly towards the target with ears tilted forward, and there is no display of teeth or claws until the attack is executed [2,12].

Notwithstanding the differences between animal and human subjects, the bridge between the feline research and classification of aggression and violence in humans was constructed by Eichelman in a series of studies which explored their different neuroanatomical and neurochemical basis and potential pharmacological interventions in psychiatric treatment settings [26–29]. Information generated from the animal research has promulgated the widespread use of certain medications, such as beta-blockers, selective serotonin re-uptake inhibitors and anticonvulsants to successfully treat assaultive patients. GABAergic and serotonergic systems appear to inhibit both affective and predatory aggression, while the noradrenergic and dopaminergic systems facilitate affective aggression [12,26–29].

Contemporary Empirical Evidence

Recent research in neurochemistry, neuropsychology and psychophysiology has continued to confirm neurobiological differences between affective and predatory violence [11,12,30].

Neurochemistry

During the past decade Siegel *et al.* [31–33] have provided evidence that opioid, cholecystokinin and substance P receptor activation or blockade differentially affect these two modes of aggression. In particular, the differential effects of peptidergic receptor activation may have important treatment implications in psychiatry settings [11]. Miczek has shown that dopamine facilitates affective aggression and cholinergic stimulation facilitates predatory aggression [34]. Gamma-aminobutyric acid inhibits affective aggression [34]. The serotonergic system has been extensively studied and is primarily associated with the inhibition of affective aggression or violence. Houston *et al.* have reviewed the various research strategies that have demonstrated this relationship [30], including the measurement of serotonin metabolites, platelet binding, prolactin response, pharmacological treatment and regional metabolic activity in response to the serotonin agonist m-CPP. The effect of the dopaminergic system on affective aggression is mixed. Some studies have demonstrated inhibition of affective aggression through the use of dopamine agonists, while most research indicates that dopamine levels and affective aggression positively correlate [12]. Barratt *et al.* [35] and Stanford *et al.* [36] have demonstrated the differential effect of phenytoin in reducing affective aggression while not altering patterns of predatory aggression in incarcerated and hospitalized male adults.

Neuropsychology

While meager in number, neuropsychological studies comparing modes of violence have established a correlation between increased affective aggression and decreased executive functioning, while few cognitive deficits have been found in those who are predatory or premeditated in their violent behaviour [30]. Most recently, Barratt *et al.* showed a negative correlation between affective aggression and verbal skills [37]; and Villemarette-Pittman *et al.* found that verbal deficiencies varied according to executive demands of the task in a sample of affectively aggressive college students [38]. In the first study to compare premeditated or predatory subjects with controls on a variety of neuropsychological tests, Stanford *et al.* found no significant differences except for a single subscale of the Wisconsin Card Sorting Task [39].

Psychophysiology

Studies which have directly compared the psychophysiology of those who engage in affective and predatory violence, although few in number, are promising. Children who are classified as reactive in their aggression accelerated their heart rates during a challenging task, while the proactive aggressive children did not [40]. Gottman *et al.* [6], in a study which is rapidly becoming a classic, found that a subgroup of male domestic batterers, when subjected to a conflict situation in a laboratory with their spouses, showed heart rate deceleration; while the majority of the subjects (84%) showed increased heart rate as conflict became more apparent. The former group had more generalized antisocial histories and were more sadistic (predatory), while the latter group were more emotional, angry and volatile (affective). Although not directly measured, psychopathy in the decelerators was strongly suggested, and would be consistent with the greater frequency of predatory violence among psychopaths [10].

EEG abnormalities are also ubiquitous among those who engage in affective violence, including abnormalities in P1 amplitude, decreased P1-N1-P2 latency, reduced P3 amplitude, and increased P3 latency, inferring sensory, information, and emotional processing dysfunction [30]. Subjects who engage in predatory aggression show fewer differences from non-aggressive controls, including P3 amplitude and latency [37,39].

Although neuroimaging offers a host of measurement possibilities, only one study to date has compared predatorily and affectively violent individuals. Raine *et al.* compared a sample of predatory murderers, affective murderers and controls using PET following a continuous performance task [41]. The affective murderers showed significantly reduced lateral and medial prefrontal activation (although no performance difference) when compared with the controls. The predatory murderers did not significantly differ from the controls in lateral prefrontal activation. Right subcortical measures, however, were significantly greater in both groups of murderers when compared with the controls. Effect sizes were large (1.07–1.27) for differences between affective murderers and controls. The researchers theorized that despite the negative emotionality of the predatory murderers, their executive function facilitated premeditation and planning of their killings (a portion of these individuals were serial murderers); while the negative emotionality of the affective murderers was not effectively managed because of their hypofrontality, resulting in impulsive killing. Another PET study [42] compared impulsive aggressors with controls in response to a serotonin agonist. The controls showed anterior cingulate activation and posterior cingulate deactivation, while the impulsive subjects showed the opposite effect. A third earlier PET study showed that affectively violent psychiatric inpatients had lower relative metabolism in their medial and prefrontal cortices than a normal comparison group [43]. There are no published fMRI studies comparing affective and predatory subjects, although its higher resolution and non-invasive technology when compared with PET strongly invites such work.

Forensic Applications

Are there sufficient data to justify the application of affective and predatory modes of violence to forensic psychiatry and psychology? The answer is yes, and the data are emerging in three applied areas of forensic research.

Domestic violence

As already noted, Gottman *et al.* were the first researchers to measure a physiological difference among spousal batterers [6]; moreover, their research was consistent with the clinical knowledge of three general types of batterers: the over-contolled dependent, the impulsive borderline, and the instrumental antisocial [44]. The first group's violence is much less frequent and they tend to exhibit less obvious psychopathology, but the latter two groups appear to demarcate along the lines of affective

and predatory violence respectively. In a comparison of these two groups, Tweed and Dutton found that the instrumental batterers scored lower on all measures of affect, but reported higher violence scores [3]. Other researchers have suggested that these men are preoccupied with dominating and controlling their partner [44]; and Babcock *et al.* [45] have shown that they are most likely to be violent towards their partner when she attempts to verbally confront his behaviour. The impulsive borderline group of batterers are most likely to be violent when the spouse attempts to withdraw from the argument, suggesting fury at the threat of abandonment [45]. The instrumental (predatory) batterers in Tweed and Dutton's study [3] also did not report a traumatic history, while the impulsive (affective) batterers did—including symptoms of strong negative affect, anger, dysphoria and anxiety. A traumatic history in instrumental batterers would not be consistent with their general autonomic hyporeactivity. Dutton wrote, 'the impulsive group appears to represent a pure sample of … the "abusive personality" whose abusiveness is intimacy-specific and is generated by a cognitive pattern that blames the intimate partner for characterological dysphoria' (6:227). The instrumental (predatory) batterers produced a mean Millon Clinical Multiaxial Inventory III profile prototypic of antisocial personality disorder.

Psychopathy

There is a growing body of research that psychopathic criminals engage in more predatory and affective violence than non-psychopathic criminals [4,46]. Meloy theorized that a predisposition to engage in predatory violence in psychopaths would be due to their low levels of autonomic arousal and reactivity, their disidentification with the victim, their perceived malevolence in others, their emotional detachment and their lack of empathy [2]. He speculated that they may be hard-wired to be the consummate predators. Subsequent research has supported this theorizing, including the quite new findings that psychopaths are more likely to commit instrumental (predatory) rather than impulsive (affective) homicides [10], and individuals who commit sexual homicides are likely to be moderately to severely psychopathic, kill stranger women, and engage in more gratuitous and sadistic violence [47]. Meloy and Meloy found in a large survey of mental health and criminal justice professionals that the majority autonomically responded to being in the presence of a psychopathic individual, and interpreted these data as an evolved visceral reaction which signaled the potential danger of an intraspecies predator [48]. Although it is theorized that all human beings have an evolved capacity for both predatory and affective violence, psychopathy provides the most ideal psychobiological architecture for the behavioural manifestation of predatory violence.

The research on psychopathy and predatory violence is burgeoning, primarily because of the reliable and valid measure of psychopathy using the Psychopathy Checklist-Revised [49], a standardized and normed observational instrument utilizing a comprehensive record review and clinical interview. Psychopathic personality is a more severe and biologically predisposed variant of the Diagnostic and Statistical Manual of Mental Disorders (DSM)-IV-TR antisocial personality disorder diagnosis [50].

Stalking

The research on both male and female stalkers has demonstrated a relatively frequent incidence of physical violence, typically ranging between 25% and 35% [51]. Violence frequencies of stalkers of prior sexual intimates typically exceed 50% [52]. Meloy studied the nature and frequency of violence among stalkers when grouped according to victims: the first group were composed of stalkers of public figures—typically politicians and celebrities—and the second group were composed of stalkers of prior intimates and acquaintances [53]. These 'public' and 'private' stalkers had strikingly contrasting violence patterns. The private stalkers would verbally threaten their victims, and when they assaulted, they would push, choke, punch, fondle, shove, slap, or hair pull, usually in response to a rejection or humiliation. Weapons were typically not used, and medical treatment was usually unnecessary. The violence of the private stalkers across a number of studies exhibited behaviours quite consistent with an affective mode. When stalkers of public figures were violent, they would typically plan their approach and attack for days, weeks, or months; the majority used a weapon, usually a firearm; and in

90% of the cases studied they would not communicate a direct threat to the target or law enforcement before their attack [54]. They often evidenced a downward spiral in their personal lives in the year before the attack, and had a variety of motivations [55]. The violence of the public stalkers exhibited behaviours quite consistent with a predatory mode.

Methods of Data Collection

The determination of the presence of affective or predatory violence in a subject's history is dependent upon several assumptions: (i) there may be both affective and predatory violence in any one individual's history, and the presence of one mode should not exclude the possibility of the other mode of violence at another time; (ii) there may be a sequencing of the two modes of violence in any one discrete event, for example, the psychopathic armed robber who carefully plans his crimes in convenience stores, and then in the course of one robbery is suddenly confronted by the store owner, and angrily kills her for disrupting his course of action; (iii) it is the author's experience that many incarcerated individuals will attempt to redefine their predatory act of violence as an affective act of violence to mitigate responsibility for their behaviour; and (iv) it is also the author's experience that criminal defence attorneys would like every act of violence to be affective, while prosecuting attorneys are convinced that most acts of violence are predatory. The truth must be discerned through the careful sifting of data.

There are numerous methods of information gathering to determine the mode of violence, some better than others. Monahan et al. found that three sources of data gathering, when used concurrently, all contributed to a more reliable and valid assessment of violent behaviour: interview of the subject concerning his violence, review of official records and interview of collateral contacts (individuals who may have witnessed the violence) [56]. It is these combined methods of data gathering that are most effective in retrospectively determining the mode of violence in a subject.

Measurement

There are two observational measures and one self-report measure that hold promise for the determination of affective or predatory violence.

Applied forensic criteria

Meloy developed for forensic practice 10 criteria for distinguishing between affective and predatory violence [2,57,58]. These criteria are listed in Table 1, and were used in an abbreviated form in Raine *et al.* [41] with good interrater reliability (Kappa = 0.86). Although the definitions and details of these criteria are available elsewhere [2,57,58], further elaboration of some of the items is warranted. The presence or absence of intense autonomic arousal (item 1) has emerged as a very important empirical discriminator between affective and predatory violence subsequent to the initial publication of these criteria in 1988 [10,37,39]. There is an acute awareness of anger or fear (item 2) in affective violence, but during events where the intensity of the affect is extreme, it may be dissociated or split off from consciousness. This is often clinically apparent in the subject reporting symptoms of dissociation during the violence and/or partial amnesia. Crime scene evidence, moreover, will confirm the intensity of the emotion at the time of the violence, occasionally manifest as 'overkill' of the victim in a homicide [59]. The reactive violence (item 3) in the affective mode most closely resembles the psychopathol-ogy of 'episodic dyscontrol' identified by Monroe [60] and currently diagnosed as 'intermittent explosive disorder' in the DSM-IV-TR [50]. Unfortunately, the DSM series makes no reference to differentiating between affective and predatory violence, although it does list aggressive behaviour as a clinical indicator in at least 11 Axis I diagnoses [30]. Imminent perceived threats (item 4) may be either internal (e.g. psychotic symptoms, acute anxiety) or external (an actual physical attack), and the presence or absence of an imminent threat is usually an initial, accurate marker for differentiating between the two modes of violence. The public posturing in affective violence (item 8) is often instinctual, and in all mammals is most frequently loud vocalization. Humans will also often fist clench, jaw clench, posture, stare and expand their thorax as a prelude to affective violence: evolution-arily adaptive

behaviours that serve as an 'early warning system' to the threat. The reduction or elimination of the threat is the simple goal of affective violence (item 5), although if the threat is internal, such as symptoms of delusional jealousy, it may not be readily apparent to the forensic examiner. The sequence of events, however, is relatively immutable: perceived threat > sympathetic arousal > consciously felt anger or fear > behavioural posturing to ward off the threat and prepare for violence > affective violence to eliminate the threat. Rapid displacement of aggression (item 6) in affective violence is of great concern, particularly in institutional settings when staff attempt interventions between physically assaultive patients or inmates. In one example from the author's experience, inmates at a maximum security prison at times would consciously feign affectively violent incidents to lure the correctional guard or officer into the fracas and then predatorily attack him. The presence or absence of a major mental disorder or psychosis is independent of the determination of affective violence; although it may determine the perception of an imminent threat, and therefore precipitate the cascading sequence noted above.

In predatory violence autonomic (sympathetic) arousal is minimal or absent, consistent with other mammals (item 1) and indicative of the primarily cognitive, and at times fantasy-based nature of predation. The absence of conscious emotion (item 2) likewise facilitates a successful predatory attack, since both heightened states of autonomic arousal and intense emotion would signal to the target an impending attack and enable its escape. It is speculated that emotion is psychobiologically dampened, muted, or functionally disconnected in predation, an evolved characteristic whose neurochemical basis is unknown at present, but has served our species well as our ancestors successfully hunted to survive another day, reproduce, and raise their young. It is ubiquitous in criminal forensic cases that predatory individuals will report the complete absence of emotion during the commission of their violent act. If any emotion is felt, it is anticipation of the predation, and exhilaration or dysphoria (for those with conscience) in its aftermath [2]. The initial planning of the predatory violence is often reported by subjects to be accompanied by a complete dissipation of anger or fear, and in their place, a resolute calmness.

Table 1. Forensic criteria for determining affective or predatory violence (Meloy [2,57,58])

	Affective violence	Predatory violence
1.	Intense autonomic arousal	Minimal or absent autonomic arousal
2.	Subjective experience of emotion	No conscious emotion
3.	Reactive and immediate violence	Planned or purposeful violence
4.	Internal or external perceived threat	No imminent perceived threat
5.	Goal is threat reduction	Variable goals
6.	Possible displacement of target	No displacement of target
7.	Time-limited behavioural sequence	No time limited sequence
8.	Preceded by public posturing	Preceded by private ritual
9.	Primarily emotional/defensive	Primarily cognitive/attack
10.	Heightened and diffuse awareness	Heightened and focused awareness

Predatory violence is no longer necessary for food gathering for most individuals, but in our species is now commonly used to gratify desires for money, power, dominance, territorial control, sex and revenge. The multiple goals of this mode of violence sharply contrast with the simple goal of affective violence, to reduce a threat. Instead of public posturing, private rituals (item 8) play a dominant role in predatory violence. Such rituals serve to enhance the narcissism of the predator, and may range from certain repetitive grooming behaviours to the selection of certain items of clothing, amulets, other concrete symbols, or weapons [2,61]. Such private rituals may practically increase the likelihood of a successful attack, but

often serve more symbolic psychological goals, such as heightening the sense of omnipotent control over the foreseen victim [2]. In predatorily violent crimes, such as serial rape or murder, such rituals may emerge as signatures at the crime scene that eventually link cases for forensic investigators [62]. The absence of displacement of the target of aggression (item 6) and the selective suppression of other sensory input (item 10), although not yet empirically measured in human subjects, may eventually be understood as psycho-biologically evolved behaviours that have contributed over the generations to the focused awareness and success of any one predatory act.

Research forensic criteria

Woodworth and Porter conceptualized and empirically tested a coding scheme in their study of homicide and its relationship to psychopathy [10]. They devised a 4-point rating scale according to degree of instrumentality (predatory) or reactivity (affective) for each homicide. Purely reactive (rated 1) indicated strong evidence for a high level of spontaneity/impulsivity and a lack of planning surrounding the commission of the offence. There was typically evidence for a rapid and powerful affective reaction and no external goal other than to injure the victim. Reactive/instrumental (rated 2) showed evidence of both reactivity and instrumentality, but the primary factor leading to death was reactivity. Instrumental/reactive (rated 3) showed evidence of both modes, but the primary factor leading to death was instrumental. Purely instrumental (rated 4) indicated a homicide which was goal-orientated, and without evidence of emotional or situational provocation. It was intentional, premeditated, and not preceded by a strong affective reaction.

Instrumental was further classified as either primary or secondary, the former referring to a homicide in which the primary goal was to inflict harm on the victim. The latter referred to a homicide in which the killing was a means to another goal, such as money or drugs. All of the cases were also scored for the dimensions of instrumental gain, impulsivity, and level of antecedent affective arousal.

Interrater reliability for the homicide coding using 21 randomly selected files was K = 0.81, p < 0.001. Nineteen randomly selected cases were used to determine interrater reliability for the three dimensions:

instrumental gain (ICC = 0.90), impulsivity (ICC = 0.95) and affective arousal (ICC = 0.88). All three dimensions contributed in a meaningful way to the coding scheme. Although initially developed for research purposes, the practicality and reliability of the Woodworth and Porter [10] coding scheme shows promise for use in applied forensic work.

Self-report

Although caution is warranted in the applied forensic use of self-report measures to determine the mode of violence due to subject distortion and fabrication, such measures may provide a standardized point of reference against which to evaluate other sources of data in a case. For example, an individual charged with homicide may portray himself as only affectively violent, yet the crime scene characteristics indicate the absence of emotionality and threat, and the presence of careful planning.

Suris *et al.* [63] reviewed over 40 measures of aggression and violence, but found very few which differentiated between mode of violence. The most promising appears to be the Impulsive/Premeditated Aggression Scale (IPAS) developed by Stanford *et al.* [64], a 30-item self-report questionnaire, each item scored on a 5-point Likert Scale. Half of the items describe impulsive aggression and half the items describe premeditated aggression. For example, 'when angry I reacted without thinking', and 'I felt I lost control of my temper during the acts' (scored impulsive [affective]). And further, 'the acts led to power over others or improved social status for me' and 'I planned when and where my anger was expressed' (scored premeditated [predatory]). Initial testing of the instrument [64] indicated that the two factors accounted for 30% of the variance. Those subjects who clustered on the impulsive factor showed a broad range of emotional and cognitive impairments; those who clustered on the premeditated factor showed a greater inclination for aggression and antisocial behaviour. In a recent study of 85 male and female forensic patients [65] admitted to a state hospital with both violent and non-violent felony charges, the IPAS achieved alpha coefficients for the premeditated aggression scale of 0.72 and for the impulsive aggression scale of 0.81, indicating homogeneity of the scale items. The scales correlated 0.40 ($p < 0.01$), suggesting that the modes of violence are not independent of one another when subjects are asked to describe their violence over the previous 6 months. Forty per cent of the sample were predominately premeditated (predatory) in their self-reported aggression. The two aggression factors emerged once again, accounting for 33% of the variance of the instrument. The IPAS has been used in other studies [36,38,39,66] as both an independent and dependent variable to study treatment non-response and non-compliance, as well as other correlates of the two modes of violence.

Integration

The integration of data on mode of violence in forensic psychiatric and psychological evaluations provides a systematic, psychobiologically based description of a specific act of criminal violence, or a historical predisposition to such acts. In risk assessments, such data can be combined with actuarial measures of the likely frequency of future violence risk, such as the Violence Risk Appraisal Guide [67], to individualize each case. Although actuarial measures are empirically impressive, they only give us a probability estimate of large groups of individuals within which a particular subject may fit. They do not specify the probability of risk for a particular subject, nor do they tell us anything about the nature of the violence the subject is likely to commit in the future. For example, a psychopathic individual who has an extensive history of predatory violence and fits into a group which has a 35% probability of future violence over the next 5 years has a very different risk management profile than a non-psychopathic individual with an extensive history of affective violence who also has a 35% probability of future violence over the next 5 years. In the former case, treatment non-response and noncompliance are likely, and an individual who is predatory would be considered much more dangerous than a predominantly affective individual for three reasons: (i) his violence is planned and deliberate; (ii) there are no behavioural signs that foretell his violence; and (iii) predatory violence is often associated with severe character pathology, such as psychopathy.

For the subject who is predominantly affectively violent with the same probability of future violence, risk management is much more feasible because of the greater likelihood of treatment response and compliance, and the ability to foresee affective violence if the subject is placed in emotionally arousing, provocative, or threatening situations. In both cases without a careful delineation of mode of violence, risk management would only be informed by actuarial probabilities, a rather anaemic approach to a complex and demanding task.

Integration of mode of violence into the reconstruction of a violent event for determination of sanity is also quite useful. Review of all evidence in a case, including interviews, witness accounts and crime scene data, will usually lead to a reasonably medically certain opinion that the act was affective or predatory. However, both affective and predatory violence may be motivated by a psychosis, and it is conceivable that a carefully planned and emotionless act of violence may meet jurisdictional criteria for insanity, such as lack of knowledge of wrongfulness [2]. In some cases the presence of delusion brings a resolve to an act of predation that would otherwise be absent [68].

Conclusion

Affective and predatory violence is an empirically established, psychobiologically based, bimodal phenomenon in mammals that has demonstrable relevance to forensic psychiatry and psychology. It is the author's hope that this study has been persuasive, and the analysis and integration of mode of violence will find its way into the lexicon of forensic psychiatric practice.

Acknowledgement

This study was funded by a grant from Forensis, Inc.

References

1. Meloy JR. Stalking and violence. In: Boon J, Sheridan L, eds. *Stalking and psychosexual obsession.* London: Wiley, 2002:105–124.

2. Meloy JR. *The psychopathic mind: origins, dynamics, and treatment.* Northvale, NJ: Jason Aronson, 1988.

3. Tweed RG, Dutton DG. A comparison of impulsive and instrumental subgroups of batterers. *Violence and Victims* 1998; 13:217–230.

4. Cornell DG, Warren J, Hawk G, Stafford E, Oram G, Pine D. Psychopathy in instrumental and reactive violent offenders. *Journal of Consulting and Clinical Psychology* 1996; 64:783–790.

5. Bushman BJ, Anderson CA. Is it time to pull the plug on the hostile versus instrumental aggression dichotomy? *Psychological Review* 2001; 108:273–279.

6. Gottman J, Jacobson NS, Rushe R *et al.* The relationship between heart rate reactivity, emotionally aggressive behavior, and general violence in batterers. *Journal of Family Psychology* 1995; 3:227–248.

7. Campbell A, Muncer S, McManus IC, Woodhouse D. Instrumental and expressive representations of aggression: one scale or two? *Aggressive Behavior* 1999; 25:435–444.

8. Barratt ES, Stanford MS, Dowdy L, Liebman MJ, Kent TA. Impulsive and premeditated aggression: a factor analysis of self-reported acts. *Psychiatry Research* 1999; 86:163–173.

9. Crick NR, Dodge KA. Social information-processing mechanisms in reactive and proactive aggression. *Child Development* 1996; 67:993–1002.

10. Woodworth M, Porter S. In cold blood: characteristics of criminal homicides as a function of psychopathy. *Journal of Abnormal Psychology* 2002; 111:436–445.

11. Weinshenker NJ, Siegel A. Bimodal classification of aggression: affective defense and predatory attack. *Aggression and Violent Behavior* 2002; 7:237–250.

12. McEllistrem J. Affective and predatory violence: a bimodal classification system of human aggression and violence. *Aggression and Violent Behavior* 2004; 10:1–30.

13. Block R, Block CR. Homicide syndromes and vulnerability: violence in Chicago community areas over 25 years. *Studies on Crime and Crime Prevention* 1992; 1:61–87.

14. Heilbrun K, Hart SD, Hare RD, Gustafson D, Nunez C, White AJ. Inpatient and postdischarge aggression in mentally disordered offenders. *Journal of Interpersonal Violence* 1998; 13:514–527.

15. Bard PA. Diencephalic mechanism for the expression of rage with special reference to sympathetic nervous system. *American Journal of Physiology* 1928; 84:490–515.

16. Cannon WB, Britton SW. Studies on the conditions of activity in endocrine glands: XV. Pseudoaffective medulliadrenal secretion. *American Journal of Physiology* 1925; 72:283–294.

17. Hess WR, Brugger M. Das subcorticale zentrum der affektiven abwehrreaktion. *Helvetica Physiologica et Pharmacologica Acta* 1943; 1:33–52.

18. Wasman M, Flynn JP. Directed attack elicited from hypothalamus. *Archives of Neurology* 1962; 27:635–644.

19. Flynn JP. Neural basis of threat and attack. In: Grinnell RG, Gabray S, eds. *Biological, foundations of psychiatry.* New York: Raven, 1976:111–133.

20. Flynn JP. The neural basis of aggression in cats. In: Glass DC, ed. *Neurophysiology and emotion.* New York: Rockefeller University Press and Russell Sage Foundation, 1977:40–60.

21. Flynn JP, Vanegas H, Foote W, Edwards S. *Neural mechanisms involved in cat's attack on a rat: the neural control of behavior.* New York: Academic Press, 1970.

22. Flynn JP, Edwards SB, Bandler RJ. Changes in sensory and motor systems during centrally elicited attack. *Behavioral Sciences* 1971; 16:1–19.

23. Chi CC, Flynn JP. Neuroanatomic projections related to biting attack elicited from hypothalamus in cats. *Brain Research* 1971; 35:49–66.

24. Reis DJ. Brain monoamines in aggression and sleep. *Clinical Neurosurgery* 1971; 18:471–502.

25. Reis DJ. Central neurotransmitters in aggression. *Research Publications of the Association for Research in Nervous and Mental Disease* 1974; 52:119–148.

26. Eichelman B. Aggressive behavior: animal models. *International Journal of Family Psychiatry* 1985; 6:375–387.

27. Eichelman B. Aggressive behavior from laboratory to clinic: quo vadit? *Archives of General Psychiatry* 1992; 49:488–492.

28. Eichelman B, Elliott GR, Barchas JD. *Biochemical, pharmacological, and genetic aspects of aggression biohehavioral aspects of aggression.* New York: Alan Liss, 1981.

29. Eichelman B. Toward a rational pharmacotherapy for aggressive and violent behavior. *Hospital and Community Psychiatry* 1988; 1:31–39.

30. Houston RJ, Stanford MS, Villemarette-Pittman NR, Conklin S, Helfritz L. Neurobiological correlates and clinical implications of aggressive subtypes. *Journal of Forensic Neuropsychology* 2003; 3:67–87.

31. Siegel A, Pott CB. Neural substrate of aggression and flight in the cat. *Progress in Neurobiology* 1988; 31:261–283.

32. Siegel A, Roeling T, Gregg T, Kruk M. Neuropharmacology of brain-stimulation-evoked aggression. *Neuroscience and Biohehavioral Reviews* 1999; 23:359–389.

33. Siegel A, Brutus M. Neural substrates of aggression and rage in the cat. In: Epstein AN, Morrison AR, eds. *Progress in psychobiology and physiological psychology.* San Diego, CA: Academic Press, 1990:135–233.

34. Miczek KA. The psychopharmacology of aggression. In: Iversen LL, Iversen SD, Snyder SH, eds. *Handbook of psychopharmacology: new directions in behavioral pharmacology.* New York: Plenum Press, 1987:183–328.

35. Barrett E, Stanford M, Felthous A, Kent T. The effects of phenytoin on impulsive and premeditated aggression: a controlled study. *Journal of Clinical Psychopharmacology* 1997; 17:341–349.

36. Stanford M, Houston R, Mathias CW, Greve K, Villemarette-Pittman N, Adams D. A double-blind placebo controlled crossover study of phenytoin in individuals with impulsive aggression. *Psychiatry Research* 2001; 103:193–203.

37. Barratt E, Stanford M, Kent T, Felthous A. Neuropsychological and cognitive psychophysiological substrates of impulsive aggression. *Biological Psychiatry* 1997; 41:1045–1047.

38. Villemarette-Pittman N, Stanford M, Greve K. Language and executive function in self reported impulsive aggression. *Personality and Individual Differences* 2003; 34:1533–1544.

39. Stanford M, Houston R, Villemarette-Pittman N, Greve K. Premeditated aggression: clinical assessment and cognitive psychophysiology. *Personality and Individual Differences* 2003; 34:773–781.

40. Pitts TB. Reduced heart rate levels in aggressive children. In: Raine A, Brennan P, Farrington D, Mednick S, eds. *Biosocial bases of violence.* New York: Plenum, 1997:317–320.

41. Raine A, Meloy JR, Bihrle S, Stoddard J, LaCasse L, Buchsbaum M. Reduced prefrontal and increased subcortical brain functioning assessed using positron emission tomography in predatory and affective murderers. *Behavioral Sciences and the Law* 1998; 16:319–332.

42. New A, Hazlett E, Buchsbaum M, *et al.* Blunted prefrontal cortical fluorodeoxyglucose positron emission tomography response to meta-chlorophenylpiperazine in impulsive aggression. *Archives of General Psychiatry* 2002; 59:621–629.

43. Volkow N, Tancredi L, Grant C, *et al.* Brain glucose metabolism in violent psychiatric patients: a preliminary study. *Psychiatry Research: Neuroimaging* 1995; 61:243–253.

44. Meloy JR. Pathologies of attachment, violence, and criminality. In: Goldstein A, ed. *Handbook of psychology,* Vol. 11. *Forensic psychology.* New York: Wiley, 2002:509–526.

45. Babcock J, Jacobson N, Gottman J, Yerington P. Attachment, emotional regulation, and the function of marital violence: differences between secure, preoccupied and dismissing violent and nonviolent husbands. *Journal of Family Violence* 2000; 15:391–399.

46. Serin R. Psychopathy and violence in criminals. *Journal of Interpersonal Violence* 1991; 6:423–431.

47. Porter S, Woodworth M, Earle J, Drugge J, Boer D. Characteristics of sexual homicides committed by psychopathic and nonpsychopathic offenders. *Law and Human Behavior* 2003; 27:459–470.

48. Meloy JR, Meloy MJ. Autonomic arousal in the presence of psychopathy: a survey of mental health and criminal justice professionals. *Journal of Threat Assessment* 2002; 2:21–33.

49. Hare RD. *Hare psychopathy checklist-revised (PCL-R),* 2nd edn. Technical manual. Toronto: Multihealth Systems, 2003.

50. American Psychiatric Association. *Diagnostic and statistical manual of mental disorders,* 4th edn, text revision. Washington, DC: American Psychiatric Press, 2000.

51. Meloy JR, ed. *The psychology of stalking: clinical and forensic perspectives.* San Diego, CA: Academic Press, 1998.

52. Meloy JR. When stalkers become violent: the threat to public figures and private lives. *Psychiatric Annals* 2003; 33:658–665.

53. Meloy JR. Communicated threats and violence toward public and private targets: discerning differences among those who stalk and attack. *Journal of Forensic Sciences* 2001; 46:1211–1213.

54. Fein R, Vossekuil B. Assassination in the United States: an operational study of recent assassins, attackers, and near-lethal approaches. *Journal of Forensic Sciences* 1999; 44:321–333.

55. Meloy JR, James D, Farnham F, *et al.* A research review of public figure threats, approaches, attacks, and assassinations in the United States. *Journal of Forensic Sciences* 2004; 49:1086–1093.

56. Monahan J, Steadman H, Silver E, *et al. Rethinking risk assessment.* New York: Oxford University Press, 2001.

57. Meloy JR. Predatory violence during mass murder. *Journal of Forensic Sciences* 1997; 42:326–329.

58. Meloy JR. *Violence risk and threat assessment.* San Diego, CA: Specialized Training Services, 2000.

59. Meloy JR. *Violent attachments.* Northvale, NJ: Jason Aronson, 1992.

60. Monroe RR. *Brain dysfunction in aggressive criminals.* Lexington, MA: Lexington Books, 1978.

61. Meloy JR. Indirect personality assessment of the violent true believer. *Journal of Personality Assessment* 2004; 82:138–146.

62. Hazelwood R, Warren J. Linkage analysis: modus operandi, ritual, and signature in serial sexual crime. *Aggression and Violent Behavior* 2003; 8:587–598.

63. Suris A, Lind L, Emmett G, Borman P, Kashner M, Barratt E. Measures of aggressive behavior: overview of clinical and research instruments. *Aggression and Violent Behavior* 2004; 9:165–227.

64. Stanford M, Houston R, Mathias C, Villemarette-Pittman N, Helfritz L, Conklin S. Characterizing aggressive behavior. *Assessment* 2003; 10:183–190.

65. Kockler T, Stanford M, Nelson C, Meloy JR, Sanford K. Characterizing aggressive behavior in a forensic population. *American Journal of Orthopsychiatry* 2006 (in press).

66. Houston R, Stanford M. Characterization of aggressive behavior and phenytoin response. *Aggressive Behavior* 2006 (in press).

67. Quinsey V, Rice M, Harris G. *Violent offenders: appraising and managing risk.* Washington, DC: American Psychological Association, 1998.

68. Hempel A, Meloy JR, Richards T. Offender and offense characteristics of a nonrandom sample of mass murderers. *Journal of the American Academy of Psychiatry and the Law* 1999; 27:213–225.

Attention-Deficit/Hyperactivity Disorder in Adults: Recognition and Diagnosis of This Often Overlooked Condition

By David Feifel and Kai MacDonald

Attention-deficit/hyperactivity disorder (ADHD) in adults poses diagnostic challenges. How does it differ from ADHD in children? What are the necessary characteristics to make the diagnosis? What features of a patient's behavior are suggestive of ADHD? Which psychiatric disorders can mask its presence? What is the most important diagnostic procedure? This article provides insight into the behavior patterns of adults with ADHD, presents useful tools for identifying unrecognized cases, and includes several vignettes of actual patients.

It is estimated that 4% to 12% of all children have attention-deficit/hyperactivity disorder (ADHD).[1] About 50% to 60% of children with ADHD continue to experience significant symptoms of the disorder into adulthood. The prevalence of ADHD in the adult population is estimated to be between 4% and 5%, and statistics indicate that the majority of ADHD in adulthood goes unrecognized and undiagnosed.[1,2]

The disability associated with ADHD in adults is enormous and touches on almost all aspects of functioning. Evidence that ADHD is based on brain pathology is overwhelming, and much of this evidence points to dysfunction in the prefrontal cortex and circuits that connect it to subcortical areas.[2] Physicians need to be familiar with the clinical presentation of ADHD in order to recognize potential undiagnosed cases in adults who may present with a host of psychosocial problems and to competently rule out the diagnosis in adults who, having heard about the disorder, suspect they may have it and request treatment.

Diagnosis of ADHD in adults presents several major challenges:

- Unlike children, for whom the classroom represents an almost ideal real world laboratory to detect ADHD behavior in a child that deviates significantly from age-matched classmates, adults represent a more heterogeneous population in terms of occupations, activities of daily living, and compensating techniques that can make impairment much less overt.
- The diagnosis requires a retrospective confirmation of the presence of some impairing ADHD symptoms in childhood.
- The symptoms of many other psychiatric conditions can overlap with, or mimic, symptoms of ADHD and thus produce a clinical picture of "pseudo-ADHD."
- ADHD often coexists with more familiar or recognizable disorders, such as depression, anxiety,

or alcohol or substance abuse, which may mask or confound the recognition of ADHD.

Symptoms

Attention-deficit/hyperactivity disorder is a syndrome of persistent behaviors and symptoms (Table 1). It is composed of 3 potential subsyndromes: inattention or distractibility, impulsivity, and hyperactivity. Children and adults with ADHD do not necessary exhibit significant features of all 3 of these subsyndromes. The *Diagnostic and Statistical Manual of Mental Disorders, Fourth Edition (DSM-IV)*[3] recognizes this heterogeneity in presentation by permitting patients to be classified into one of 3 main subtypes of ADHD based on the burden of symptoms they exhibit: inattentive type, hyperactive-impulsive type, or combined type (Table 2). Most experts also recognize that other symptom clusters are common in adults with ADHD, such as expressions of excessive moodiness.

Inattention or Distractibility

Inattention or distractibility is the most prevalent subsyndrome experienced by adults with ADHD and causes most of the disability in this population. Like their childhood counterparts, adults with ADHD do not seem able to volitionally modulate their attention well. They may be able to focus adequately on an attention-demanding task for a limited time, but sustained focus is extremely difficult.

Typically, people with ADHD have the most difficulty in situations where the task is relatively monotonous and requires mostly sequential information processing where they are required to be relatively passive. Lectures or formal business meetings are classic examples of this type of activity and, not surprisingly, are often extremely difficult for people with ADHD. In such situations, they commonly report "spacing out" unintentionally and getting distracted by irrelevant external or internal stimuli.

The inability to sustain focused attention commonly affects other fundamental activities, such as reading. Adults with ADHD typically report consistently needing to re-read pages because they become aware at the bottom

of a page or end of a section that they have not been concentrating and therefore have not extracted the content of the material. This inattention can be a significant source of social embarrassment with acquaintances and can cause persistent friction with others, who may complain that the person with ADHD often does not appear to be paying attention.

TABLE 1 Frequent Presenting Complaints of Adults with ADHD

Difficulty maintaining a job
Underachievement, performing below intellectual competency in work and/or school
Lack of organization
Poor discipline, procrastination, forgetfulness, memory difficulties
Excessive moodiness or irritability, depression, low self-esteem
Marital or relationship discord
Confusion, trouble thinking

People with ADHD can be highly motivated and ambitious. However, when they do begin a task, seeing it to completion is often a battle because of their proclivity to become distracted and their profound inability to organize tasks that require complex sequential steps. They may start projects with the best intentions and with great enthusiasm; however, they commonly are unable to complete them. The typical pattern of behavior is that soon after starting a task, they get sidetracked onto a different task that comes to mind, and then another and another, until they realize they have engaged in a series of activities that are unrelated to the task they set out to undertake.

Often, adults with ADHD become aversively conditioned and thus avoid activities that require sustained attention and a high degree of organization. They may be consummate procrastinators for certain types of tasks, and this may be perceived by others as laziness or a lack of motivation. For example, a person may avoid paying bills on a monthly basis or filing a tax return, not for lack of funds, but because of the sustained attention

TABLE 2. *DSM-IV* Diagnostic Criteria for Attention-Deficit/Hyperactivity Disorder

A. Must have a minimum of either criteria (1) or criteria (2)
(1) Six (or more) of the following symptoms of inattention have persisted for at least 6 months to a degree that is maladaptive and inconsistent with developmental level:
Inattention
(a) often fails to give close attention to details or makes careless mistakes in schoolwork, work, or other activities
(b) often has difficulty sustaining attention in tasks or play activities
(c) often does not seem to listen when spoken to directly
(d) often does not follow through on instructions and fails to finish schoolwork, chores, or duties in the workplace (not due to oppositional behavior or failure to understand instructions)
(e) often has difficulty organizing tasks and activities
(f) often avoids, dislikes, or is reluctant to engage in tasks that require sustained mental effort (such as schoolwork or homework)
(g) often loses things necessary for tasks or activities (eg, toys, school assignments, pencils, books, tools) (h) is often easily distracted by extraneous stimuli
(i) is often forgetful in daily activities
(2) Six (or more) of the following symptoms of hyperactivity-impulsivity have persisted for at least 6 months to a degree that is maladaptive and inconsistent with developmental level:
Hyperactivity
(a) often fidgets with hands or feet or squirms in seat
(b) often leaves seat in classroom or in other situations in which remaining seated is expected
(c) often runs about or climbs excessively in situations in which it is inappropriate (in adolescents or adults, may be limited to subjective feelings of restlessness)
(d) often has difficulty playing or engaging in leisure activities quietly
(e) is often "on the go" or often acts as if "driven by a motor"
(f) often talks excessively
Impulsivity
(g) often blurts out answers before questions have been completed (h) often has difficulty awaiting turn
(i) often interrupts or intrudes on others (eg, butts into conversations or games)
B. Some hyperactive-impulsive or inattentive symptoms that caused impairment were present before age 7 years.
C. Some Impairment from the symptoms is present in two or more settings (eg, at school [or work] and at home). D. There must be clear evidence of clinically significant impairment in social, academic, or occupational functioning.
E. The symptoms do not occur exclusively during the course of a pervasive developmental disorder, schizophrenia, or other psychotic disorder and are not better accounted for by another mental disorder (eg, mood disorder. anxiety disorder, dissociative disorder, or a personality disorder).
Adapted with permission from the American Psychiatric Association.

to detail and need for organization that the activity may require.

Because memory requires attention, it is not surprising that adults with ADHD often report chronic forgetfulness. They may forget keys, wallets, or appointments far more than the someone without ADHD.

People with ADHD may have difficulty accurately perceiving the passage of time, and they are poor at managing time efficiently.[4] Unable to monitor time while engaged in something, they may get caught up in a conversation or activity and forget an appointment or obligation. This may be expressed in chronic tardiness and missed commitments.

Hyperactivity

Once considered a sine qua non of ADHD, motor hyperactivity is no longer considered a requirement for making the diagnosis. Many children, in particular girls, express the inattentive features of ADHD without the motor hyperactivity.[5] The persistently daydreaming, "spacy" child is a distinct variant of the classic ADHD child, who is a frenetic, disorganized whirlwind of activity.

Even when present in childhood, hyperactivity is the symptom most likely to improve or remit altogether as the ADHD brain matures, so that few adults who otherwise continue to experience the inattentive symptoms display overt hyperactivity. Ironically, the lack of this salient behavior hinders the recognition of ADHD in some children and most adults

Some adults with ADHD do continue to exhibit motor hyperactivity. Clinicians should be vigilant for this excess kinesis because it is easy to overlook during an interview. An interviewer who is suspicious of ADHD in a patient should surreptitiously note the frequency of scratching, gesticulations, position shifts, and limb tapping, which are suggestive of a patient who is struggling with impulses to move. One clue to distinguishing the fidgetiness of a patient who may be experiencing anxiety in a medical context (the "white coat phenomenon") versus the patient with ADHD is that the former phenomenon tends to decrease as the interview proceeds, whereas the latter tends to increase as the stimulating novelty of the meeting diminishes.

ADD or ADHD?

The terms *attention-deficit disorder* (ADD) and *attention-deficit/hyperactivity disorder* (ADHD) refer to the same condition. Attention-deficit disorder is often used to denote a form of the disorder lacking the motor hyperactivity. However, ADHD is the appropriate nomenclature for all patients with this disorder, according to the convention of *DSM-IV*, the recognized authoritative source for the nomenclature and symptoms of the disorder. Patients lacking motor hyperactivity are denoted as ADHD, inattentive type, according to *DSM-IV*.

Impulsivity

Like their childhood counterparts, adults with ADHD typically find activities requiring passive waiting to be a challenge. For example, waiting in line is a provocative situation. Impulsive purchases and impulsive decisions are common. Impulsivity also tends to express itself in conversations. Some adults with ADHD have a self-recognized habit of finishing the sentences of others but cannot inhibit themselves. Worse yet, they may say things that they realize are socially inappropriate.

Case Study: The Accident Victim

Diana, a 45-year-old woman was hospitalized for complications related to a motor vehicle accident. Psychiatric consultation was ordered because the patient was "difficult" and the medical team wanted to rule out bipolar disorder. Psychiatric history taking revealed that the patient had had problems with "poor decisions" and a "short fuse" for her entire life and that her problems in the hospital—verbal outbursts with nursing staff and impulsive medical decisions—were best related to this trait. The patient stated that she was having very brief episodes of "low mood," mostly related to her inability to tolerate the frequent, brief frustrations associated with her treatment. She denied having other symptoms of bipolar disorder. History taking was notable for her tendency to interrupt the interviewer and her reported symptom of a "tendency to do things without thinking that you later regret." Her family history of ADHD (her daughter and 2 brothers) increased the suspicion of ADHD. A diagnosis of ADHD, combined type, was subsequently confirmed.

Comment: The increased risk of motor vehicle accidents in persons with ADHD has been reported extensively in the literature. These persons may present for medical care related to accidents. Their impulsivity can lead to problems with general medical management.

Impulsivity also tends to express itself in driving behavior, often in self-acknowledged dangerous behavior. Heavy traffic can be the bane of adult drivers with ADHD; they may become more frustrated than the average driver and may make reckless or unnecessary attempts to advance their progress. This impulsivity, combined with their deficits in paying close attention and the tendency to be distracted, makes drivers with ADHD a potential large-scale public road hazard. Studies have shown they have statistically higher rates of traffic violations and accidents. Furthermore, the accidents they tend to be involved with are more likely to be highly serious.[6] In a laboratory setting, drivers with ADHD have been shown to perform considerably poorer on driving simulators.[6]

Mood Disturbances

Though not a component of the *DSM-IV* criteria, mood disturbances are a frequent expression of ADHD in adults. Frank clinical depression or anxiety is a common coexisting condition with adult ADHD, but even more common is excessive mood reactivity (situation-dependent), irritability, and low tolerance for frustration, which seem to be congruent. Usually people recognize this as an undesirable component of their personality but are unable to change it.

Distinguishing Features

Difficulty concentrating, moodiness, forgetfulness, lack of patience, and disorganization are not uncommon symptoms and are experienced, if only transiently, by much of the general population. Such symptoms may emerge strongly as part of an active medical condition (eg, thyroid abnormalities, stroke) or psychiatric disorder (eg, mania, depression); during periods of prolonged sleep deprivation; during pregnancy; or after use of certain medications, drugs, or alcohol.

The diagnosis of ADHD should be given only when certain critical criteria are met; these criteria distinguish a deficit in attention due to ADHD from other potential causes. These criteria are as follows:

1. Because ADHD is not an acquired disorder of adulthood, *DSM-IV* requires that clinicians should be satisfied that some impairment from ADHD symptoms were present during childhood to qualify as ADHD. This retrospective determination may be the most difficult aspect of reliably making the diagnosis in adults.

2. ADHD symptoms should display persistence across time and should not display a pattern of spontaneous recurrences and remissions. This is an important distinguishing feature of ADHD from mood disorders such as bipolar affective disorder and major depression, both of which are typically episodic.

    One qualification to this principle must be noted: Whereas the inability to maintain attention and to inhibit impulses remains constant in a person with ADHD, this problem may be more apparent in circumstances that place a heavy demand on these abilities and less apparent in situations that do not. Thus, ADHD symptoms may be less apparent on a leisurely Sunday than 24 hours later on the job.

    For this reason, ADHD not uncommonly comes to the threshold of detection in young adults who have recently started college. The sudden loss of environmental structure and an intense increase in attention-demanding workload (especially reading) associated with the transition from high school to college can make ADHD symptoms worse: symptoms that had been mildly impairing previously may suddenly become debilitating to the point of profound academic problems beyond anything experienced previously. Thus, it is important to be aware that the cognitive deficit of ADHD remains constant, but its saliency and ability to produce impairment may fluctuate, depending on the environmental demand.

3. ADHD-associated symptoms must be present across at least 2 distinct spheres of functioning. The impact of ADHD is generally felt in all spheres of a patient's life—academic, occupational, and social. If someone experiences profound disabilities in one area only, a

non-ADHD cause, perhaps a psychological one, should be suspected. However, more scrutiny may be needed to extract the presence of ADHD features from patients or their significant others in situations where there is less cognitive demand.

Case Study: The Alcohol Abuser

Helen, a 35-year-old woman, presented to a clinic with problems related to alcohol overuse that were affecting her job and marriage. Salient in her history was a lifetime of trouble "staying on task;" she remembered being a "day-dreamer" when she was young, but her innate intelligence allowed her to "get by". She stated that she had trouble prioritizing tasks at work. Even when sober for weeks, she described "spacing out" at work, losing blocks of time, and, according to her husband, having her "head in the clouds." She attributed recent alcohol use as an attempt to mitigate increasing anxiety she felt about losing her job and marriage. The diagnoses of ADHD, inattentive type, anxiety, and alcohol abuse were made. After entering an alcohol rehabilitation program, she was treated with an approved ADHD medication. After a few weeks, she noted improved ability to stay focused and prioritize at work, improved ability to moderate her alcohol use "without even really thinking about it," and reduced anxiety about work and marriage. Six months later, she had been promoted at work because of her markedly improved organizational ability, she had dramatically reduced her drinking to a responsible manner, and relationships with others were improving

Comment: A significant number of ADHD patients have coexisting substance use and mood anxiety disorders, which in many cases may be related to underlying ADHD and may obfuscate diagnosis of ADHD and complicate treatment issues. Such cases can be complex and may warrant a referral.

Coping Strategies and Underachievement

A common misconception is that high levels of achievement and success preclude the diagnosis of ADHD. Thus, the evaluating clinician must not adopt a criterion of debilitation based purely on external elements. To determine debilitation, the clinician must take into account an

individual's potential for success (eg, intelligence, training) as well as the person's ambition and the effort put forth.

The clinician also should take into account an individual's ability to compensate for or mitigate his/her ADHD. An important strategy (conscious or not) is to avoid circumstances in which ADHD deficits are most prominent. Thus, an adult with ADHD might gravitate toward an occupation involving high levels of independence, diverse activity, and mobility. For example, a sales position might be highly favored over a deskbound job such as bookkeeping. However, even the most highly ADHD-friendly occupations invariably involve some administrative requirements, and it is with these elements of the job that the person will struggle. Furthermore, a person doing well in a job that is highly compatible with ADHD often reports disastrous experiences when asked about previous jobs that were less ADHD-friendly.

People with ADHD can compensate for their poor memory and poor innate organizational skills by incorporating external aids and strategies. A heavy reliance on "to-do" lists, elaborate daily planners, or highly organized personal assistants (or spouses) can neutralize much of the practical handicaps emanating from ADHD. Whereas millions of people choose occupations in which they function well and utilize organizing tools, the person with ADHD is more dependent on these, and any change in job responsibilities (ie, added administrative responsibilities) or elimination of coping aids may have a disproportionate negative effect on performance.

Coexisting Conditions

One reason why diagnosis of ADHD in adults is difficult is the extremely high psychiatric comorbidity associated with it. Depression, anxiety, and alcohol and substance abuse are among the conditions that most frequently coexist with ADHD.[7] These illnesses are often more salient to the clinician, who may be much more facile at identifying them than identifying ADHD. In this way, ADHD is often overlooked. The problem with this diagnostic failure is not only the lost opportunity of treating ADHD, but the fact that in many cases the recognized coexisting condition is largely secondary to lifelong ADHD. In such cases, attempts to address the non-ADHD condition alone, with, for example, antidepressant medication or referral to a substance use rehabilitation program, may be unsuccessful or produce only transient benefits. In contrast, successful treatment of ADHD not only may bolster treatment of the coexisting condition, but in many cases can, by itself, produce significant improvement in coexisting conditions and thus obviate the need for additional treatment.

Diagnosis

An informed interview is the most important diagnostic procedure, and rating scales, collateral reports, and neuro-psychological testing can be useful (Table 3). In a primary care setting, other features that should raise suspicion for diagnosis of ADHD are listed in Table 4.

Clinical Interview

Nothing is more central and indispensable to the accurate diagnosis of ADHD than an effective clinical interview. Given the exigencies of busy practice, it is important to develop an efficient approach to screening. High-yield screening questions should be the first goal. Because the majority of adults with ADHD have the inattentive or combined type, screening should focus on the inattentive rather than the hyperactive-impulsive cluster. If a patient endorses a generic symptom, for example, "has difficulty organizing tasks," the clinician should ask the patient to provide specific examples from the past month. The clinician can then assess the extent to which these symptoms are excessive in type and frequency relative to the population.

Case Study: The Underachiever

James, a 45-year-old firefighter, presented to a clinic after reading about ADHD in a popular magazine. He had a sense that he had never accomplished what he felt he was capable of and said that the article about ADHD described him perfectly. He reported a tendency to "always get lost" driving places, missing exit ramps, losing important things (eg, keys, wallets), and difficulty with prioritizing tasks. Reading was extremely difficult because his mind wandered unless the topic was highly interesting to him. Developmental history revealed "boredom"

in school, being labeled as "hyper" when he was a child, early involvement with a negative peer group, and subsequent legal problems. Assessment revealed that the patient had above-average intelligence and what appeared to be a good work ethic, but he had been passed over for promotion many times because he was unable to success-fully complete professional development coursework that was required for promotion. After treatment for several weeks, he first noted that he no longer got lost driving places, and that he finished a novel for the first time in his life. A year later, he felt his ability to read and learn had improved so much that he had decided to take evening college courses and successfully received additional course training for work promotion.

Comment: The poor "mainstream" performance of some patients with ADHD, as well as their involvement in negative peer groups, can influence their "trajectory" in life. Despite superior intelligence, this patient never considered attending college because of the inability to succeed in academic settings and activities (eg, reading). The discrepancy between potential and actual achievement was a clue to diagnosis.

The use of rating scales for screening or diagnosing ADHD is highly recommended. It is best to use one anchored in the *DSM-IV* criteria, such as the Adult Self-Report Scale (ASRS), developed in conjunction with the World Health Organization (http://www.add.org/pdf/who_screening.pdf).

If the current symptoms seem to be sufficiently endorsed, the next step should be to try to establish whether some ADHD symptoms existed during childhood.

An education and occupational history should also be included, and a characteristic pattern of chronic underachievement or excessive effort needed to obtain a level of achievement, marked by ADHD-like symptoms, should be noted. A family history is vital because ADHD is highly heritable.[1,2] Neuromedical risk factors such as head injury and problems incurred during gestation or delivery of the patient should be assessed as part of a thorough medical history since these can also contribute to ADHD.

TABLE 3. Components of an ADHD Assessment

Goals of Clinical Interview
Presence of ADHD symptoms at least during last 6 months?
Presence of ADHD symptoms since childhood?
Presence of functional impairment (ie, underachievement)?
Other psychiatric condition causing symptoms or co-occuring
(eg, mood/anxiety disorders, substance abuse)?
Presence of medical condition that may account for symptoms
(eg, thyroid)?
Observe for hyperkinesis impulsive speech, distractibility
Neuropsychological Tests
Broadscale IQ testing (eg, Wechsler Adult Intelligence Scale-Revised) Additional tests of sustained attention, executive functioning, and sequential processing (eg, Digit Vigilance, Wisconsin Card Sorting Test, Continuous Performance Task)
Medical Evaluation
Neuroendocrine disorders (eg, thyroid)
Neurologic disorders (eg, cerebrovascular accident), fatigue syndrome
(eg, fibromyalgia, chronic fatigue syndrome)
Other Useful Resources
Self-rating assessments for ADHD, depression, and anxiety (eg, Adult
Self-Report Scale Screener)
Collateral information
Current symptoms (obtained from spouse, employer)
Childhood symptoms (obtained from parent, old report cards previous testing)

TABLE 4. Features that Should Raise Suspicion for ADHD Among Adults In a Primary Care Setting

Reputation among office staff as being 'flaky," "scatterbrained," or "absentminded"
Family history of diagnosed ADHD (eg, child)
Alcohol/substance abuse history
Erratic job history
Smoker (especially with failed attempts to quit)
Is chronically late for appointments or misses them altogether
Legal trouble
Accident-prone
Multiple driving accidents or violations
Relationship problems (eg, multiple divorces)
Financial problems
Evidence of poor judgment
Excessively talkative
Childhood academic or behavioral problems

The interview must focus not only on the presence of ADHD symptoms but also on symptoms consistent with other conditions (eg, mood disorders, anxiety disorders, substance abuse, personality disorders), which may mimic or contribute to an attention and/or impulse-control deficit.

Collateral information

The ability to collect clinical information from another source, when available, is very useful for diagnosing ADHD in adults. For example, having spouses or roommates rate the patient using one of the ADHD scales can be extremely helpful. Parents, when available, can likewise be helpful in retrospectively establishing the presence of ADHD symptoms during childhood.

Neuropsychological Evaluation

There is no single neuropsychological test or battery diagnostic for ADHD. Nevertheless, a neuropsychological assessment can be an important and very useful part of a rigorous assessment for ADHD. Although not required, it can be helpful, especially in unclear cases.

Adults with ADHD often exhibit deficits in subtests that rely heavily on attention (eg, Digit-Span Memory Test, Digit Vigilance Test), sequential processing (eg, Digit Symbol Test, Trail Making Test), and executive functioning (Wisconsin Card Sorting Test). Selective impairments in one or more of these areas within an overall picture of intact or even superior intelligence can be highly suggestive of ADHD.

Neuropsychological testing can also detect other potential causes or contributors to a patient's impairment, for example, the presence of a pervasive learning disorder. Furthermore, testing of this sort can characterize a patient's cognitive strengths and weaknesses and establish a baseline before treatment.

Finally, several tests have been developed or adapted in hopes of developing a highly sensitive and specific objective screen for ADHD. The best examples are computerized continuous performance tests (CPTs), in which patients are instructed to respond when certain visual or auditory patterns are presented. These are thought to be a good test of vigilance, and several commercial versions (eg, the Test of Variables of Attention® [TOVA®], the Conners' Rating Scale) are available. The utility of CPTs in diagnosis of ADHD is controversial.[8] The authors' experience is that such a test is a highly useful tool, so long as it is used in the context of other neuropsychological tests and a strong clinical evaluation (ie, interview). Patients with ADHD who have impaired performance on CPT tasks often improve their performance when taking psychostimulants.[8,9]

Empirical Treatment in Ambiguous Cases

Sometimes it is not possible to make a definitive diagnosis of ADHD in an adult. For example, it may be apparent that current criteria for ADHD are met, but the presence of ADHD symptoms during that person's childhood may not be clear. When no alternative cause for ADHD-like symptoms is apparent, it may be reasonable to consider, together with the patient, an empirical trial of treatment as long as there are no medical contraindications.

When to Refer

A decision to refer a patient for clinical assessment should be based on an individual physician's ability to establish or rule out, with confidence, the presence not only of ADHD-consistent symptoms, but also potential comorbid psychiatric conditions, such as mood disorders, anxiety disorders, substance abuse, and personality disorders. Though it may be a relatively time-consuming process, it is essential that this be done by a comprehensive personal interview and never exclusively by patient self-rating scales. If time factors or expertise factors leave a physician feeling incapable of carrying this out, referral to a psychiatrist or clinical psychologist is appropriate. Furthermore, it is advisable, though not necessary, that every patient strongly suspected of having ADHD undergo baseline neuropsychological assessment, preferably with a CPT included, before beginning what may become lifelong treatment.

Case Study: The Parent

Michael, a 45-year-old twice-divorced father of 2 children was referred by his child's pediatrician because of his "difficulty setting a schedule with his kids." He reported that his children, one of whom was recently diagnosed with ADHD, challenge his ability to be a good parent, and he has frequent angry outbursts with them, which he later regrets. He described working "extremely hard" at "keeping this organized" but routinely having to work late into the night to "catch up" from the work he did not accomplish because of his daytime inattention and inefficiency. He described a relatively successful work history but said he feels like he works much harder than his peers to accomplish the same amount and has friction with his boss, who criticizes him for completing projects too slowly. He is a 27-year, one-pack-a-day smoker and despises the habit but has tried to quit 11 times without achieving more than 4 months abstinence. Attention-deficit/hyperactivity

Brand Name	Chemical Name	Frequency	Typical Duration of Action	Typical Adult Dose Range (mg/day)
Dexedrine®	d-amphetamine	2–3 times per day	5 hours	10–60
Adderall®	Mixed amphetamine salts	2 times per day	5 hours	10–60
Dexedrine® spansules	d-amphetamine	Once in AM	6–9 hours	10–40
Adderall XR®*	Mixed amphetamine salts	Once in AM	8–10 hours	10–60
Ritalin®	Methylphenidate	3 times per day	2–4 hours	20–60
Ritalin LA®	Methylphenidate	Once in AM	8–12 hours	20–60
Focalin®	d-methylphenidate	2 times per day	2–5 hours	10–40
Focalin XR®	d-methylphenidate	Once in AM	8–12 hours	10–40
Ritalin SR®	Methylphenidate	1 or 2 times a day	5 hours	20–60
Metadate CD*	Methylphenidate	Once in AM	8 hours	20–60
Concerta®*	Methylphenidate	Once in AM	8–12 hours	36–72
Vyvansce®*	Lisdexamfecamine	Once In AM	6–12 hours	30–70

TABLE 5. Stimulant Medication Commonly Used to Treat Adult ADHD

*Approved for adults with ADHD

disorder, inattentive type, was diagnosed, and treatment was started with the same ADHD medication that was used to treat his daughter. He had a good response, and his improved efficiency and impulse control allowed him to accomplish more at work and to get along better with coworkers and supervisors as well as his children. He reports the medication allows him to be a better parent.

Comment: The significant heritability of ADHD is well recognized. Patients with predominantly inattentive symptoms may not have been recognized in years past, and problems with their ADHD children may be a clue to their diagnosis.

Treatment

Fortunately, ADHD is highly treatable and most patients will experience significant benefit from appropriate treatment with medication. Medication is the most robust scientifically validated means of improving ADHD symptoms. Treating ADHD in adults with medication is fundamentally similar to treating children.

The stimulant family has been the gold standard treatment for ADHD for decades, and almost all of the currently marketed stimulant medications are formulation variants of one of the 2 primary stimulant molecules, methylphenidate (eg, Ritalin®) and amphetamine (eg, Dexedrine®). Standard formulations of these stimulants produce rapid onset but short-lived effects and thus require dosing 2 to 3 times daily. The biggest advance in the past decade among the stimulants has been improved formulations that obviate the need to take multiple doses and the associated "rollercoaster" pharmacokinetics which often exaggerate side effects and compromise symptom control. Three of these once-a-day stimulant formulations are currently approved for adults with ADHD (Table 5).

While some physicians may be apprehensive about prescribing stimulant drugs, they are generally safe, tolerable, and not highly addictive.[10] Potential side effects include decreased appetite, insomnia, dry mouth, increased heart rate (usually mild) and blood pressure (usually mild), anxiety, jitteriness, headache, nausea or other G1 symptoms, tics, and (rarely) transient psychosis or mania.

The dosing approach for stimulant medication used by the authors is quite straightforward. Patients should be instructed to start with the lowest dose and increase step-wise every 5 to 7 days as tolerated to the highest-tolerated dose within the therapeutic dose range, noting at each dose the benefits on ADHD symptoms and any side effects. At a follow-up visit, the effects experienced at each dose step—therapeutic and adverse—should be reviewed with the patient, and the optimal dose should be selected based on a balance between benefits and side effects.

Atomoxetine (Strattera®) is approved for ADHD in children and adults and represents a nonstimulant alternative. The mechanism of action of atomoxetine is an elevation in brain norepinephrine levels and a more limited increase in dopamine through selective inhibition of norepinephrine reuptake mechanisms. Unlike stimulants, whose therapeutic effects are experienced within minutes and correlate with the pharmacokinetic time course, atomoxetine's therapeutic effects accrue insidiously and typically do not reach maximal levels before 2 to 8 weeks after starting the daily target dose, which can be given once daily. Furthermore, it may take several days to 2 weeks to titrate atomoxetine to its target dose depending on patients' individual sensitivity to its side effects, the most common of which are nausea, insomnia, headache, dizziness, dry mouth, sedation, increased heart rate (usually mild) and blood pressure (usually mild), constipation, and urinary retention. Fewer patients experience a significant improvement in ADHD symptoms compared with stimulants.[11,12] Despite lower rates of efficacy and slower onset compared with stimulants, atomoxetine has potential advantages in patients who do respond well to stimulant treatment. Unlike stimulants, atomoxetine's therapeutic effects seem more continuous throughout the 24-hour day, and since the therapeutic effects are not linked strongly to pharmacokinetic profile,[11,12] timing of the medication is not important so it can reasonably be taken in the morning, midday, or bedtime. Furthermore, unlike stimulants, atomoxetine is not a controlled substance and does not seem to have an addictive propensity.[11,12]

The target dose of Strattera® in adults weighing more than 127 lb is 80 to 100 mg/day. It should be started at 25 to 40 mg/day and titrate rapidly as tolerated to the target dose.

Summary

It is estimated that 4% to 5% of the adult population in the United States suffers from ADHD. Knowledge of the cardinal features of ADHD and certain necessary characteristics will allow physicians to identify both unrecognized cases and also rule out incorrectly self-diagnosed cases. Inattention, distractibility, impulsivity, and hyperactivity are the classic core symptoms in children, but adults with ADHD often do not typically express the full syndrome. Motor hyperactivity, in particular, is often not prominent in adults. On the other hand, mood reactivity (eg, irritability, low frustration tolerance) is often present. Because other conditions—particularly depression, anxiety, and alcohol and drug abuse—commonly occur with ADHD in adults, physicians may overlook the presence of comorbid ADHD. This is a highly unfortunate situation because treating the ADHD may be help resolve the patient's other conditions.

Rating scales, collateral reports, and neuropsychological testing can be useful and should be part of any rigorous assessment for the disorder. Finally, in cases where a definitive diagnosis is not possible, a trial of pharmacologic treatment may be appropriate.

References

1. Faraone SV, Biederman J, Spencer T, et al. Attention-deficit/hyperactivity disorder in adults: an overview. *Biol Psychiatry*. 2000;48(1):9–20.

2. Wilens TE, Dodson W. A clinical perspective of attention-deficit/hyperactivity disorder into adulthood. *J Clin Psychiatry*. 2004;5(10):1301–1313.

3. American Psychiatric Association. *Diagnostic and Statistical Manual of Mental Disorders, Fourth Edition*. Washington, DC: American Psychiatric Association; 1994.

4. Barkley RA, Murphy KR, Bush T. Time perception and reproduction in young adults with attention deficit hyperactivity disorder. *Neuropsychology.* 2001;15(3):351–360.

5. Brown TE, McMullen WJ, Jr. Attention deficit disorders and sleep/arousal disturbance. *Ann NY Acad Sci.* 2001;931:271–286.

6. Barkley RA. Driving impairments in teens and adults with attention-deficit/hyperactivity disorder. *Psychiatr Clin North Am.* 2004;27(2):233–260.

7. Biederman J, Faraone SV, Spencer T, et al. Patterns of psychiatric comorbidity, cognition and psychosocial functioning in adults with attention deficit disorder. *Am J Psychiatry.* 1993;150(12):1792–1798.

8. Nichols SL, Waschibusch DA. A review of the validity of laboratory cognitive tasks used to assess symptoms of ADHD. *Child Psychiatry Human Dev.* 2004;34(4):297–315.

9. Swanson JM, Kinsbourne M. The cognitive effects of stimulant drugs on hyperactive children. In: Hale GA, Lewis M, eds. *Attention and Cognitive Development.* New York, NY: Plenum Press, 1980:249–274.

10. Dodson WW. Pharmacotherapy of adult ADHD. *J Clin Psychol.* 2005;61(5):589–606.

11. Simpson D, Plosker GL. Alomoxetine: a review of its use in adults with attention-deficit/hyperactivity disorder. *Drugs.* 2004;64(2):205–222.

12. Barton J. Atomoxetine: a new pharmacotherapeutic approach in the management of attention-deficit/hyperactivity disorder. *Arch Dis Child.* 2005;90(suppl 1):126–129.

Obsessive-Compulsive Disorder and Tic Syndromes

By Neil R. Swerdlow

ADVANCES IN THE PATHOPHYSIOLOGY AND TREATMENT OF PSYCHIATRIC DISORDERS: IMPLICATIONS FOR INTERNAL MEDICINE

OBSESSIVE-COMPULSIVE DISORDER AND TIC SYNDROMES

Interconnected cortico-striato-pallido-thalamic (CSPT) circuitry long has been implicated in the regulation of movement, thought, and affect; abnormalities within this circuitry have been proposed to contribute to the pathophysiology of many neuropsychiatric disorders. The *motor* loops of CSPT circuitry are known to be the locus of pathology in primary movement disorders, such as Huntington's disease, [79] Parkinson's disease, [38] and hemiballism, [57] and the *limbic* CSPT loops have been proposed as the source of pathology in schizophrenia, [103] depression, [103] Tourette Syndrome (TS), [95] obsessive-compulsive disorder (OCD), [7] [89] attention deficit/hyperactivity disorder (ADHD), [13] substance abuse disorders, [60] temporal lobe epilepsy, [111] and many other seemingly disparate forms of psychopathology. Overlapping anatomic models for these disorders have been accompanied by blurred boundaries at a clinical level, with commonalities identified in symptoms and treatment responsivity among many of these disorders. OCD and TS are perhaps the two most closely connected among the disorders associated with CSPT pathology. OCD and TS are linked by overlapping symptoms, frequent comorbidity, and cosegregation in families. Clinically, there are important similarities and differences between these two disorders (Table 1).

OBSESSIVE-COMPULSIVE DISORDER

OCD is an anxiety disorder characterized by recurrent obsessions, compulsions, or both, with a lifetime prevalence of approximately 2.5%. [81] Symptoms may begin in adolescence and typically are manifest fully by the late teens to mid-20s. Throughout adulthood, OCD symptoms follow a chronic course, with exacerbations accompanying periods of life stress. Pronounced functional impairment in OCD has been documented in measures of education, employment, marital status, life satisfaction, and general health. Among OCD patients, more than 90% report low self-esteem; 75% report impaired family relations; approximately 66% report difficulty maintaining friendships, impaired school performance, and lowered career aspirations; 40% are unable to work for periods averaging about 2 years; and 15% commit suicide. [37] In a series of 100 adult OCD patients in the author's facility, the unemployment rate

	OCD	TS
Prevalence (%)	1.5–2.5	0.1–1.0
M:F	1:1	4:1
Age at onset (y)	18	7
Age at first symptoms (y)	13	?
Lag between first symptoms and correct diagnosis (y)	7	7
Course	Chronic, waxing and waning, considerable variability, stress sensitivity, shifting symptoms and clusters, tics decline with age in about 50% TS patients	
Comorbid TS/OCD (%)	7	10
Comorbid tics/OCS (%)	20	50
Monozygotic concordance (%)	65–85	75–90

OCD = obsessive-compulsive disorder; TS = Tourette Syndrome; OCS = obsessive-compulsive symptoms.

TABLE 1 - General Information: Obsessive-Compulsive Disorder and Tourette Syndrome

*Generalized and integrated across multiple sources of information.

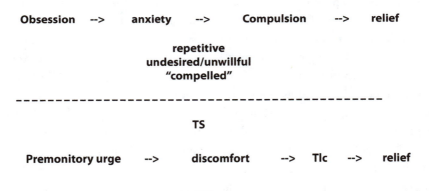

Figure 1. Parallel structure of symptoms in obsessive-compulsive disorder (OCD) and Tourette Syndrome (TS). Relief may only be momentary, and may be accompanied by a complex set of psychologic events, including shame and guilt. Certainly, this is a gross simplification: there are many individuals with OCD who have compulsions but are never consciously aware of an obsession or discrete anxiety. In the same way, there are individuals with TS who have tics, but are never consciously aware of a premonitory urge or discomfort. Nonetheless, this sequence of an anticipatory internal event, followed by an automatic or semiautomatic action, does apply to a large proportion of individuals with either disorder.

Volumetric Measures	
Corpus callosum	Increased volume (children) or length (adults)
Basal ganglia	Approximately 5–10% reduced caudate volume, loss of normal R>L caudate asymmetry
Anterior cingulate	Increased (children, 1 study)
Perfusion/Glucose Uptake/Neuronal Activity	
Resting	Increased glucose uptake orbitofrontal, caudate; bidirectional rCBF inferior frontal, caudate
Regional correlations	Pretreatment but not posttreatment positive correlations in glucose uptake: orbitofrontal to caudate, orbitofrontal to thalamus
Obsession provocation/compulsion suppression	Increased rCBF orbitofrontal, anterior cingulate, caudate; correlation with symptoms and rCBF in right inferior frontal, posterior cingulate, caudate, GP, thalamus, left hippocampus
Cognitive Task	
Implicit learning task	PET imaging revealed failure to activate caudate normally; abnormal activation in medial temporal lobe

rCBF = regional cerebral blood flow; GP = globus pallidus; PET = positron emission tomography; rCBF = regional cerebral blood flow; GP = globus pallidus; PET = positron emission tomography.

TABLE 2—Summary of Neuroimaging Findings in Obsessive-Compulsive Disorder

was 40%, compared with 8.3% among an age-matched group with pure TS. [106]

Obsessions are bothersome and intrusive mental events; compulsions are repetitive, ritualized behaviors typically performed in an attempt to neutralize anxiety caused by obsessions (Fig. 1). Obsessions in OCD include content that ranges from severely aggressive (e.g., violent images) to relatively innocuous (e.g., repetitive musical tunes). Compulsions range in form from excessive washing to checking (e.g., to avoid a perceived harm or threat). Specific clusters of symptoms have been identified that may constitute valid subtypes of OCD, [44] and studies are assessing the degree to which these symptom subtypes can be distinguished in measures ranging from familial transmission to medication responsivity. [1] [59]

Neuroimaging

There are no published reports of neuropathologic findings in OCD. Much of the understanding of the pathophysiology of this disorder comes from neuro-imaging studies, which have identified structural and metabolic abnormalities associated with OCD (Table 2). Striatal volume is reported to be diminished in adult and child OCD patients [55] [82] [84]; in contrast, reductions are not found in volumetric measures of other brain regions, including the amygdala, hippocampus, posterior cingulate, dorsolateral prefrontal cortex, and temporal lobes. [84]

The most critical evidence that OCD symptoms are associated with abnormalities in circuitry connecting orbital cortex, cingulum, and caudate nucleus comes from studies of brain metabolism. Positron emission tomography (PET) studies in OCD reveal elevated metabolic activity in orbital frontal cortex, anterior cingulate cortex, and the head of the caudate nuclei [7]; a direct relationship between OCD symptom intensity and regional hypermetabolism has been reported in symptom provocation studies. [77] At least some regional metabolic abnormalities in OCD diminish after successful pharmacotherapy or behavioral therapy, [7] [89] and relatively lower premedication metabolism in orbitofrontal cortex may be a positive predictor of medication responsivity in OCD. [86] In OCD, symptomatic states are accompanied by orbital cortex and right caudate metabolic activation, and symptom reduction is accompanied by diminished metabolic activity in orbital cortex and caudate.

Metabolic abnormalities in OCD are distributed across several elements of CSPT circuitry. Before treatment, metabolic activity in OCD is highly correlated between caudate nucleus and orbital cortex and between orbital cortex and thalamus, and these correlations are obviated by effective pharmacotherapy or cognitive behavioral therapy. [89] Although it is unclear exactly what neural events correspond to the loss of interregional correlations in metabolism, strong interregion correlations (e.g., right caudate and orbital cortex pretreatment) have been interpreted as a possible synchronization—or *coupling*—of neural activity between these regions. [89] Treatment accompanied by symptom reduction in OCD is paralleled by a *disconnection* of this orbital cortex–caudate metabolic linkage; such *disconnection* also follows anterior cingulotomy, which involves the transection of inputs from the cingulum to the head of the caudate and which is an effective treatment for some individuals with medication-refractory OCD.[31]

In Vivo Neurochemistry

Evidence for serotonin (5-HT) dysfunction in OCD rests primarily on the observations that (1) OCD symptoms are responsive to 5-HT reuptake inhibition (see later), produced by serotonin-selective reuptake inhibitors (SSRIs) or the serotonergic tricyclic antidepressant clomipramine, and (2) OCD symptoms can be exacerbated by the 5-HT1C agonist m-CPP, and this effect is blocked by 5-HT antagonists. [72] Levels of 5-HT metabolites (e.g., 5-HIAA) are not abnormal in OCD, and changes in 5-HIAA levels do not correlate significantly with changes in OCD symptom. [112] In women, symptom exacerbation is noted primarily during the late luteal phase, which is not associated specifically with serotonergic changes, but not during the periovulatory period, which is associated with dropping 5-HT levels. [52] [75] 5-HT activity may play an important role in the pathophysiology of OCD—and certainly in the therapeutic impact of SSRIs—through complex mechanisms that may include regionally specific changes or time dependent changes in receptor (and autoreceptor) sensitivity. It is not yet possible to integrate the neurochemical and metabolic status of CSPT circuitry in OCD into a consistent model.

Pathophysiology

Converging lines of evidence for pathology in CSPT circuitry in OCD comes from neuropsychologic and psychophysiologic studies. Most findings in OCD generally suggest mild deficits: Individuals with OCD perform comparably to normal controls on measures of general alertness and attention, immediate and delayed verbal memory, and general intellectual skills. Many neuropsychologic and psychophysiologic deficits have been reported in studies of OCD. Impaired performance in tasks of central inhibition (e.g., diminished inhibition of reflexive saccades in oculomotor measures), [19] [27] [87] set shifting (e.g., perseverative errors in a number of neuropsychological measures), [18] [35] [36] and visuospatial memory (e.g., deficits in the Rey-Osterrieth Complex Figure Task) [85] are reported most commonly in this disorder and are linked—usually indirectly—with deficits in frontal cortico-striatal function.

Rauch et al [78] provided intriguing evidence for abnormalities in *automatic* or preconscious information processing in OCD and, perhaps just as importantly, for the compensatory recruitment of other brain substrates normally associated with the explicit or volitional engagement of cognitive resources. Regional neuronal activity in OCD and control subjects was measured in a functional imaging paradigm, during the acquisition of an implicit sequence learning task embedded in a serial reaction time paradigm. Learning in controls was accompanied by bilateral inferior striatal activation, consistent with previous reports that this type of learning is regulated critically by the caudate nucleus. In contrast, learning in OCD subjects was not accompanied by bilateral activation but instead was accompanied by activation of medial temporal lobe regions associated with the regulation of explicit memory. Rauch et al [78] hypothesized that certain features of OCD may reflect deficits in automatic or preconscious information processing, normally regulated by the caudate nucleus, which can be compensated—at least in simple tasks—by recruitment of mesial temporal circuitry that normally regulates explicit memory. Such a notion is congruent with the utility of engaging *explicit* information processing in the cognitive therapeutic strategies in OCD and more generally with the notion that deficits associated with failures of automatic mental processes in OCD can be reversed effectively through learning-based therapies. This linkage between striatal pathology and shifts from preconscious/automatic to conscious/explicit information processing and the recruitment of cortical resources for this purpose may reflect a more generalizable response to striatal dysfunction. Automatic motor processes—such as writing one's name—result in striatal activation in normal individuals, whereas in Huntington's disease patients, motor and associational cortices are activated, but striatum is not. Novel or complex motor tasks that require conscious processing of information are accompanied by cortical activation in control and patient groups. These findings in Huntington's disease patients might parallel the observed patterns of deficient striatal activity and aberrant cortical (mesial temporal lobe) activation during implicit learning in OCD patients.

Genetics

Although some individuals with OCD appear to have a *sporadic* form of this disorder, many, perhaps most, forms of OCD are familial. Rates of OCD among first-degree relatives of OCD probands are approximately five times higher than in the general population. [53] [64] Monozygotic concordance rates for OCD are reported to be between 53% and 87%, compared with 22% and 47% among dizygotic twins. [76] Some forms of OCD may be more indicative of a strong genetic cause, including OCD with early onset and with symptoms dominated by symmetry and ordering, [1] [53] As with many common and complex human disorders, ranging from coronary artery disease to breast cancer, an individual's chances of developing OCD reflect an interaction between genetic loading and environmental factors. Substantial efforts have been directed toward identifying the relevant environmental factors in the cause of OCD, focusing on prenatal and perinatal events [46] as well as autoimmune responses to streptococcal infections. [101]

Treatment

For many OCD patients, the most important immediate therapeutic intervention is education and destigmatization. On average, OCD patients wait 7 years after their first symptoms before seeking clinical attention. [37] Initial interviews with such patients are predictable: "I've never told anyone this before, doctor. I'm so ashamed. I get these thoughts, over and over, about [fill in obsession here]." By the time they turn for help, patients often are racked with guilt by the horrific content of these obsessions. A simple therapeutic intervention is to have patients fill out the checklist of the Yale Brown Obsessive Compulsive Scale (YBOCS). As they complete this checklist, patients recognize that others must have had experiences similar to their own. In the ensuing relief, patients can be given the relevant clinical facts about this disorder, emphasizing its *no fault* neurobiology.

Often, with milder forms of OCD, the insight and relief provided by this knowledge is enough to stem the immediate crisis, and patients' energies can be directed toward such important life issues as stress management, coping strategies, nutrition, circadian rhythms, diminishing substance use, and increasing socialization. Self-help OCD therapies often are extremely valuable, such as the specialized four-step cognitive and behavioral therapy program described in *Brain Lock*. [88] Community and national support and advocacy groups are valuable sources of information and support groups for patients and practitioners, including the Obsessive Compulsive Foundation (telephone: 203–315–2190; www.ocfoundation.org).

Educated patients are better able to avail themselves of the benefits of structured behavior therapy and medications. Most forms of behavior therapy for OCD use principles of exposure and response prevention (ERP); some forms of the disorder, including pure obsessional OCD, are not generally amenable to ERP and require more of a cognitive therapeutic component, often in addition to medication treatment. Medication treatments for OCD can be divided roughly into *primary treatments* and *augmentation treatments*. Excellent summaries of medication algorithms for OCD have been published, [39] [74] and specific studies are not reviewed in detail here. In general, *primary* treatments—those known to offer significant symptom relief in controlled studies—include clomipramine; the SSRIs fluoxetine, fluvoxamine, paroxetine, and sertraline; and the mixed uptake inhibitor venlafaxine; citalopram also is being used as a primary OCD treatment. *Augmentation treatments* are added to a primary treatment, to increase effectiveness or to address comorbid conditions. Dopamine antagonists and α_2-adrenergic agonists are useful in the treatment of comorbid OCD and tics, and mood stabilizers are invaluable in the treatment of comorbid OCD and cyclic mood disturbances. Because higher doses of SSRIs generally are necessary in OCD than in the treatment of depression, strategies exist for the use of medications to diminish side effects of these higher SSRI doses. Buproprion and buspirone often are useful for diminishing the sexual side effects of SSRIs, and clonazepam and trazodone often are used to overcome the hyperstimulation and insomnia associated with higher doses of some SSRIs. In more severely ill patients, the combined use of serotonergic agents, such as SSRIs plus trazodone, SSRI combinations, or clomipramine plus an SSRI, may be necessary but should be used with caution because of potential drug-drug interactions. As with affective disorders, the combined use of medication and nonmedication therapies (e.g., cognitive behavior therapy or ERP) offers treatment advantages for OCD.

TOURETTE SYNDROME

TS is a disorder of multiple motor tics and at least one phonic tic that presents in childhood, with a predominance of males over females by almost 4:1. Symptoms wax and wane, and the dynamic patterns have been described in mathematical models. [68] Roughly half of all TS patients experience a significant diminution of symptoms in their early 20s; others experience persistent, lifelong symptoms. [51] Estimates of TS prevalence vary across clinical and field samples because of differences in diagnostic criteria and thresholds, but it is generally accepted that TS is much more common than once believed, with rates now believed to be approximately 0.1% to 1.0%. [40] [58]

The current diagnostic criteria for *Tourette's disorder* (*Diagnostic and Statistical Manual of Mental Disorders, fourth edition*) [DSM-IV] [1A] and *definite Tourette's syndrome* (TS Classification Study Group) [108A] differ only

slightly: Both diagnoses require the frequent occurrence of multiple motor tics and one or more vocal tics, over a continuous interval that involves most of a full year, with the onset of symptoms early in life (before age 18 to 21). The controversial notion that the diagnosis requires that tics cause "marked distress or significant impairment in social, occupational, or other areas of functioning" has been challenged; as presently written in DSM-IV, this criterion excludes individuals who have adjusted well to the presence of tic, because they are not considered to have Tourette's disorder if the syndrome is not a major source of distress.

The DSM-IV lists two specific tic disorders other than Tourette's disorder. Chronic motor or vocal tic disorder is diagnosed when tics are limited to one or the other domain but otherwise meets criteria for Tourette's disorder. Chronic motor tic disorder is the more common of these two conditions, and both often are viewed as part of the *broader phenotype* of TS. To bridge this gradient of *normal* versus *abnormal* tic behaviors in childhood and to span the temporal gap between symptom onset and the 1-year *duration* requirement for the diagnosis of Tourette's disorder, a diagnosis of transient tic disorder can be made if childhood tics, either motor or vocal, are frequent and cause distress and last 1 to 12 months. One in 10 children may meet criteria for this diagnosis, [91] and by extrapolation, fewer than 10% of these children exhibit symptoms for more than 1 year.

Simple tics are short-duration, circumscribed movements or sounds that are fragments or *chunks* of behavior or speech, rather than *self-contained*, meaningful motor sequences or utterances; these might include eye blinking, facial grimacing, mouth movements, head jerks, shoulder shrugs, and arm and leg jerks. *Complex* tics are more elaborate, sustained actions or linguistically meaningful sounds, which often give the appearance of a *willful* event; these might include facial gestures and movements such as brushing hair back, possibly in combination with head jerk, and body shrugs. Audible tics may or may not involve the vocal cords, but true vocal tics can range from grunts and barking sounds to complete, grammatically correct phrases. Only about 10% of individuals with TS express vocal tics with primary obscene content, termed *coprolalia*. [28]

In addition to the outward manifestations of this disorder, many patients report an *internal world* of TS: a variety of sensory and mental states associated with their tics. This awareness—described anecdotally by patients and confirmed in systematic studies by Leckman et al, [47] [48] Cohen et al, [20] [21] and others—that the antecedent to many tics is an *internal experience* and that tics are not just *done* but also are *sensed* is a simple but crucial development in understanding of this disorder. Simple sensory tics, such as simple motor or phonic tics, are rapid, recurrent, and stereotyped and are experienced as a sensation at or near the skin. The sensations typically are bothersome or uncomfortable, and patients may be unusually aware, distracted, and distressed by particular sensory stimuli that most individuals would not notice. One patient explained, "You know the scratchy feeling of a tag on your neck when you put on a new shirt? I have tags on every part of every shirt, all the time." *Premonitory urges* are more complex phenomena, which often include sensory and psychic discomfort that may be relieved momentarily by a tic. The full elaboration of tics can include a four-step sequence: (1) a sensory event or premonitory urge, (2) a complex state of inner conflict over if and when to yield to the urge, (3) the motor or phonic production, and (4) a transient sensation of relief (see Fig. 1).

Although some individuals experience pure tic disorders, functional impairment often is related more directly to the partial or full manifestation of comorbid conditions, such as OCD and ADHD. More than 40% of individuals with TS experience recurrent obsessive-compulsive symptoms. [3] [43] Compared with pure TS, individuals with comorbid TS and OCD experience more lifetime functional impairment in areas such as employment and social relations, and their level of lifetime impairment correlates significantly with the severity of OCD symptoms. [106] Specific obsessive-compulsive symptoms associated with most impairment in individuals with TS include aggressive and sexual obsessions and repeating and counting compulsions. Aggressive and sexual obsessions are associated with more severe motor and phonic tics, even in individuals with TS who do not meet full diagnostic criteria for OCD. [106]

The estimated rates of comorbid ADHD in individuals with TS range from 50% or more in clinical studies [40] to much lower rates in epidemiologic studies. [3] Similar to the functional impact of comorbid OCD,

individuals with comorbid ADHD and TS experience significantly greater impairment than individuals with pure TS. Children with comorbid TS and ADHD are at high risk for several other forms of psychopathology, whereas children who have only TS tend to fare better. [6] [11] [12] [70]

Preliminary Neuropathology Studies

The entire literature of TS neuropathology studies includes seven presumed TS cases; of these, informative clinical and histologic data are available from five cases. Interpretation of the findings from these five cases is clouded by issues of diagnostic uncertainty, comorbidity, and potentially confounding neurologic insults. Preliminary findings have identified four different locations of potential pathology within CSPT circuitry: (1) intrinsic striatal neuron abnormalities (including increased packing density of neurons in the striatum, n = 1 [4]); (2) diminished striato-pallidal *direct* output pathway (reduced dynorphin-like immunoreactivity in the lenticular nuclei, n = 5 [34]); (3) increased dopaminergic innervation of the striatum (increased density of dopamine transporter sites, n = 3 [97]); and (4) reduced glutamatergic output from the subthalamic nucleus (STN) (based on reduced lenticular glutamate content, n = 4 [2]) (Table 3). In a manner more reminiscent of neuropathologic findings in schizophrenia than, for example, Huntington's disease, these preliminary neuropathologic findings in TS do not converge to identify a specific, circumscribed *hole* in CSPT connections, but instead suggest a range of disturbances that affect the *whole* circuit. [102] Many other measures of CSPT biology in TS, including amine levels and receptors, are reported to be normal in these small preliminary studies. Postmortem studies are handicapped by limitations in the nature and number of the brains that have been studied. [105] Efforts by the Tourette Syndrome Association (TSA) to secure adequate material for neuropathologic studies are underway and should allow a new generation of tissue-based research.

TABLE 3—Postmortem Findings in Tourette Syndrome

Finding	n
Increased packing density and reduced neuronal size in caudate	1
Reduced dynorphin (1–7) GPe, VP	5
30% reduced glutamate GPm, GPe, sNR; reduced subcortical 5-HIAA, tryptophan, and 5-HT; normal HVA, TH, NE, DA	4
Increased [^{3}H] mazindol binding caudate (37%) and putamen (50%); normal striatal D1 and D2 receptor binding; DA, DOPAC, HVA levels	3

GP = globus pallidus; e = external; m = medical; VP = ventral pallidum; SNr = substantianigra reticulata.

Neuroimaging

Neuroimaging findings ultimately may provide information crucial to understanding of the pathophysiology of TS. A summary of neuroimaging findings in TS is found in Table 4. Volumetric neuroimaging studies show minimal, if any, consistent abnormalities in TS subjects. Reports of enlarged corpus callosum volume, [5] reduced caudate volume, or diminished R>L caudate asymmetry and L>R asymmetry for putamen and lenticular nucleus [70] [98] have not always been replicated; even if they were replicable, the magnitude of such changes is small, typically on the order of 5%. [15] [62] [70] [98] This small magnitude does not rule out the loss of a crucial cellular element within the basal ganglia, which might account for only a small fraction of its entire volume. The specific cellular or structural processes responsible for the observed modest changes are not known. Concerns regarding sample heterogeneity, comorbidity, misdiagnosis, and effects of chronic medication exposure (described earlier in relation to neuropathologic studies) are equally applicable to neuroimaging studies in TS.

Metabolic neuroimaging studies in TS report *reduced* glucose uptake in orbitofrontal cortex, caudate, parahippocampus, and midbrain regions as well as reduced blood flow in the caudate nucleus, anterior cingulate cortex, and temporal lobes, [8] [62] [80] [93] Regional glucose uptake patterns may reflect distributed CSPT dysfunction, as suggested by the observed covariate relationships between reduced glucose uptake in striatal, pallidal, thalamic, and hippocampal regions. [26] The greatest consistency across metabolic imaging studies in TS—that of distributed *hypometabolism*—contrasts sharply with corticostriatal *hypermetabolism* in patients with OCD (see earlier). The only suggestion of regional activation in TS comes during active tic suppression, which may be associated with increased right caudate neuronal activity, as measured by functional MR imaging; however, tic suppression also is accompanied by bilaterally diminished neuronal activity on functional MR imaging measures in the putamen, globus pallidus, and thalamus. [71]

Neurochemical imaging studies have reported relatively subtle abnormalities in levels of dopamine receptors, [114] dopamine release, [107] 3,4-dihydroxyphenylalanine (DOPA) decarboxylase, [29A] and dopamine transporter [56] in the striatum of some patients with TS. Some of these findings have not been replicated, [33] [59A] [62A] [110] others await replication, [56] and others are evident only in a small subgroup of TS (e.g., 4 of 20 individuals [114]), raising concern about their generalizability to the pathophysiology of TS. A potentially important report of 17% greater caudate D2 receptor binding among more symptomatic TS identical twins [113] was based on five twin pairs and reached statistical significance at the $P<.04$ level through nonparametric analyses. Significant correlations between symptom severity and D2 binding were obtained using aggregate symptom scores from three clinical measures. These latter findings do not address directly the brain mechanisms that distinguish individuals with versus without TS, but rather are more relevant to understanding factors contributing to the heterogeneity of the TS phenotype among affected individuals.

Volumetric Measures

Corpus callosum	Increased volume
Basal ganglia	Approximately 5–10% reduced caudate volume, ? reduced volume GP, loss of normal R>L caudate asymmetry

Perfusion/Glucose Uptake/Neuronal Activity

Resting	Reduced glucose uptake orbitofrontal, caudate, parahippocampus, midbrain, reduced rCBF anterior cingulate, caudate
Regional correlations	Covariate decreases glucose uptake in caudate, GP, thalamus, hippocampus
Tic suppression	fMR imaging activation right caudate, reduction putamen, GP, thalamus

DA Neurochemistry

D2 receptors	Bmax increased in some TS patients, ? correlation with vocal tics, [11 C] raclopride and [123 I] IBZM—not different from controls; increased [123 I]IBZM binding in head of caudate in more symptomatic monozygotic twin; correlated with symptom severity
DA reuptake	Increased striatal DAT sites by [123 I]CIT SPECT and [11 C]WIN 35,428 PET; normal [18 F]DOPA uptake versus elevated uptake left caudate and right midbrain

TABLE 4—Summary of Neuroimaging Findings In Tourette Syndrome

GP = globus pallidus; rCBF = regional cerebral blood flow; DAT = dopamine transporter; fMR = functional magnetic resonance; SPECT = single-photon emission computed tomography; PET = positron emision tomography.

In Vivo Neurochemistry

As reviewed in 1995 by Chokka et al, [17] a variety of techniques have been used to show a wide array of abnormalities in the levels of many major neurotransmitters, precursors, metabolites, biogenic amines, and hormones in blood, cerebrospinal fluid, and urine of TS subjects compared with controls. Attempts to understand the relationship of these abnormalities to the pathophysiology of TS have ranged from a proposed causal role of a single metabolic abnormality (e.g., the reported cerebrospinal fluid elevation of the potential excitotoxin kynurenine [23]) to models for complex imbalances in norepinephrine, dopamine, and 5-HT systems similar to *imbalance* models proposed for other complex forms of psychopathology. [22] [42] One qualitatively different finding, reported by Singer et al, [96] is that of approximately 40% elevations of serum antiputamen antibodies in TS children. This finding may have particular importance, based not only on its magnitude and specific linkage to basal ganglia circuitry, but also based on growing evidence for autoimmune contributions to at least some forms of TS.

Pathophysiology

Converging lines of evidence for pathology in CSPT circuitry in TS comes from neuropsychologic and psychophysiologic studies. These findings generally suggest mild deficits, at most: Response distributions overlap greatly among TS and control subjects, with most TS subjects performing within the normal range. Some forms of TS appear to be accompanied by abnormalities in sensorimotor gating [14] [99] and oculomotor functions [30] consistent with mild cortico-striatal dysfunction. Abnormalities in visuospatial priming [104] and related measures have been reported, but the potential role of comorbidity in these findings has not been excluded.

Genetics

TS is perhaps the most clearly inherited common neuropsychiatric disorder. Across a number of studies, first-degree relatives of TS probands are 20 to 150 times more likely to develop TS compared with unrelated individuals. [65] [67] [73] Concordance rates for TS among monozygotic twins approach 90%, if the phenotypic boundaries include chronic motor or vocal tics, versus 10% to 25% concordance for dizygotic twins, across the same boundaries. [67] [73] The mode of inheritance remains elusive. Some segregation analyses have supported transmission through an incompletely penetrant autosomal dominant major locus, [65] [66] but in other studies, more complex and mixed models could not be ruled out. [90] Perhaps the most conservative assessment is that susceptibility to TS may be determined by a major gene in some families and by multiple genes of small relative effect in others, with a *dose effect* of greater susceptibility for individuals homozygous versus heterozygous for these genes.

The TSA International Genetics Consortium completed the first genome-wide scan in an affected sibling-pairs *(sib-pair)* study. The sib-pair design relies on the comparison of the number of alleles at a given locus that are shared by two affected siblings across all families in the sample. If the number of affected siblings sharing alleles is significantly higher than that expected by chance, it suggests genes of etiologic importance for TS. Using 76 affected sib-pair families with a total of 110 sib-pairs, the multipoint maximum-likelihood scores (MLS) for two regions (4q and 8p) were suggestive of high sharing (MLS > 2.0). Four additional regions also gave multipoint MLS scores between 1.0 and 2.0. [108] Collection of a second replication set of approximately 100 sib-pairs is nearly complete and will be used to map these broad chromosomal regions more narrowly.

Therapeutic Interventions

Much of the distress associated with TS can result from a lack of understanding of the illness. Education about the natural history of TS, emphasizing the involuntary, *no fault* nature of certain brain-behavior relationships, is an essential part of the early treatment of this disorder. As with OCD, community and national support and advocacy groups are crucial sources of information for TS; the TSA provides an invaluable service in this capacity (telephone: 718-224-2999; www.tsa-usa.org). Next, parents and patients should be aware of the waxing and waning nature of the illness. An initial clinical visit may be precipitated by a recent exacerbation of previously subclinical or tolerable symptoms. Given the cyclic pattern of TS, one danger of rapidly initiating a medication treatment in TS is that a *false-positive* response, based on the normal cyclic fluctuation of symptoms, will convince patient, family, or physician that a particular medication is effective. The *bigger picture* of the natural history of TS also is important—that individuals with TS can and should be expected to live full, productive lives, that half of these individuals are largely symptom-free by the time they enter their 20s, and that every individual has strengths that must be nurtured and developed and that ultimately will be more significant determinants of their life quality and character than are tics or other TS symptoms. Within this bigger picture, parents and patients should understand that at present, the benefits of medication treatments of TS are relatively modest, and the potential social, psychologic, and biologic side effects are not trivial.

Because functional impairment in this disorder is linked most closely to comorbid conditions, such as OCD and ADHD, symptoms of these disorders (and their *subclinical* manifestations) often are the first targets of pharmacotherapy in TS. These conditions generally are responsive to pharmacotherapy, and their treatments are relatively free from significant side effects. The prolonged use of stimulants in comorbid TS and ADHD, once avoided because of fears of stimulant potentiation of tics, now has been shown to be safe and effective. [32] Close clinical monitoring is important in all pharmacotherapy, particularly in children. Comorbid major depression and bipolar disorder in TS are generally sensitive to standard pharmacotherapies for these disorders. These pharmacotherapies can be used in combination with anti-tic regimens, but the possibility of iatrogenic depression from dopamine antagonists always should be considered because this might dictate a reduction in neuroleptic dose rather than the addition of an antidepressant.

When tic-suppressing agents are necessary, the cost-to-benefit ratio differs among medications and across clinical conditions. Dopamine antagonists, particularly high-potency, D2-preferential blockers such as haloperidol and pimozide, are the most potent and rapid-acting, tic-suppressing agents that have been studied in controlled trials. [92] These medications may be most useful in individuals with severe, intractable tics, but they have undesirable side effects, causing blunting of cognitive skills, mood, and motivation; when discontinued, these high-potency D2 blockers can precipitate withdrawal dyskinesia and significant worsening of tics. [29] [41] In adults, these drugs are linked to an increased risk for tardive dyskinesia, although in children, this relationship has not been defined as clearly. One newer, *atypical* antipsychotic, risperidone, is a mixed DA/5-HT receptor blocker that is proving to be a useful anti-tic medication, with a side-effect profile preferable to haloperidol or pimozide [10]; however, experience suggests that significant, undesired weight gain with this drug is frequent. The α_2-adrenergic agonists clonidine and guanfacine often are used as first-line anti-tic agents because of their relatively favorable side effect profile and because of some evidence linking these drugs to improved attentional abilities in children with ADHD. [16] [45] These drugs have relatively weaker anti-tic abilities compared with dopamine antagonists, and their benefit generally evolves more gradually than with dopamine antagonists.

Several new therapeutic avenues for TS are being explored in controlled studies. Preliminary studies suggest that one impairing feature of some forms of TS—*rage attacks*—may be sensitive to treatment with SSRIs. [9] Open trials suggest some anti-tic benefit from low doses of dopamine agonists such as pergolide, [54] an effect attributed to *autoreceptor* actions that suppress activity in midbrain dopamine nuclei. Nicotinic manipulations—ranging from nicotine patches to the nicotinic antagonist mecamylamine—may offer significant anti-tic benefit, if controlled studies replicate the impressive series of case reports with these agents. [24] [25] [94] Tetrahydrocannabinol has been reported to diminish tic severity in TS in a large case series [63]; controlled studies with tetrahydrocannabinol are in progress. Certain intractable and localized tics have been treated successfully with repeated injections of botulinum toxin. [109] Generally, tic location and type shifts across the course of an illness so that such a *peripheral* approach may be effective only for short periods of an illness. At another extreme, habit reversal therapy involves the application of cognitive and behavioral therapy principles to TS, [115] analogous to the successful use of these therapies in the treatment of OCD.

SUMMARY

The phenomenology of OCD and TS seem to match perfectly with the existing conceptualization of the functional relationship between frontal cortical and subcortical circuits. Failed editing of thoughts and impulses, perseverative patterns, and inhibitory deficits are the most convenient descriptors of the symptoms, and some operationalized measures can capture evidence for such deficits in TS and OCD patients. Beyond these expectations borne from conceptual models and some broad patterns of distributed metabolic disturbances in neuroimaging studies, a specific causal pathology within CSPT circuitry needs to be identified in these disorders. This is not a criticism of the existing studies of TS and OCD; to the contrary, the scarcity of pathologic material, the limits of resolution of existing technologies, and the heterogeneity of the phenotypes make the accomplishments of these studies more impressive. As clinicians strive to integrate clinical and scientific findings into coherent models for the pathophysiology of OCD and TS, it is useful to identify practical and effective strategies for therapeutic interventions.

ACKNOWLEDGMENTS

The author is grateful for formative discussions with Drs. James Leckman and Jeffrey Schwartz.

References

1. Alsobrook II JP, Leckman JF, Goodman WK, et al: Segregation analysis of obsessive-compulsive disorder using symptom-based factor scores. Am J Med Genet 88:669–675, 1999 **Abstract**

1A. American Psychiatric Association: Diagnostic and Statistical Manual, ed 4. Washington, DC, American Psychiatric Association. 1994.

2. Anderson GM, Pollak ES, Chatterjee D, et al: Postmortem analysis of subcortical monoamines and amino acids in Tourette syndrome. Adv Neurol 58:123–133, 1992 **Citation**

3. Apter A, Pauls DL, Bleich A, et al: An epidemiological study of Gilles de la Tourette's syndrome in Israel. Arch Gen Psychiatry 50:734–738, 1993 **Abstract**

4. Balthasar K: Uber das anatomische Substrat der geralisierten Tic-Krankheit (maladie des tics, Gilles de la Tourette): Entwicklungshemmung des corpus striatum. Arch Psychiatr Nervenkr (Berlin) 195:531–549, 1957

5. Baumgardner TL, Singer HS, Denckla MG, et al: Corpus callosum morphology in children with Tourette syndrome and attention deficit hyperactivity disorder. Neurology 47:477–482, 1996 **Full Text**

6. Bawden HN, Stokes A, Camfield CS, et al: Peer relationship problems in children with Tourette's disorder or diabetes mellitus. J Child Psychol Psychiatry 39:663–668, 1998 **Abstract**

7. Baxter LR, Schwartz JM, Bergman, et al: Caudate glucose metabolic rate changes with both drug and behavior therapy for obsessive-compulsive disorder. Arch Gen Psychiatry 49:681–689, 1992 **Abstract**

8. Braun AR, Stoetter B, Randolph C, et al: The functional neuroanatomy of Tourette's syndrome: An FDG-PET study: I. Regional changes in cerebral glucose metabolism differentiating patients and controls. Neuropsychopharmacology 9:277–291, 1993 **Abstract**

9. Bruun RD, Budman CL: Paroxetine treatment of episodic rages associated with Tourette's disorder. J Clin Psychiatry 59:581–584, 1998 **Abstract**

10. Bruun RD, Budman CL: Risperidone as a treatment for Tourette's syndrome. J Clin Psychiatry 57:29–31, 1996 **Abstract**

11. Carter AS, O'Donnell DA, Schultz RT, et al: Social and emotional adjustment in children affected with Gilles de la Tourette's syndrome: Associations with ADHD and family functioning: Attention Deficit Hyperactivity Disorder. J Child Psychol Psychiatry 41:215–223, 2000 **Abstract**

12. Carter AS, Pauls DL, Leckman JF, et al: A prospective longitudinal study of Gilles de la Tourette's syndrome. J Acad Child Adolesc Psychiatry 33:377–385, 1994

13. Castellanos FX: Toward a pathophysiology of attention-deficit/hyperactivity disorder. Clin Pediatr 36:381–393, 1997 **Abstract**

14. Castellanos FX, Fine EJ, Kaysen D, et al: Sensorimotor gating in boys with Tourette's syndrome and ADHD: Preliminary results. Biol Psychiatry 39:33–41, 1996 **Abstract**

15. Castellanos FX, Giedd JN, Hamburger SD, et al: Brain morphometry in Tourette's syndrome: The influence of comorbid attention-deficit/hyperactivity disorder. Neurology 47:1581–1583, 1996 **Full Text**

16. Chappell PB, Riddle MA, Scahill L, et al: Guanfacine treatment of comorbid attention-deficit hyperactivity disorder and Tourette's syndrome: Preliminary clinical experience. J Am Acad Child Adolesc Psychiatry 34:1140–1146, 1995 **Abstract**

17. Chokka PR, Baker GB, Bornstein RA, et al: The biochemistry of Tourette's syndrome. Metab Brain Dis 10:107–124, 1995 **Citation**

18. Christensen K, Kim S, Dysken M, et al: Neuropsychological performance in OCD. Biol Psychiatry 31:4–18, 1992 **Abstract**

19. Clementz B, Farber R, Lam M, et al: Ocular motor responses to unpredictable and predictable smooth pursuit stimuli among patients with obsessive-compulsive disorder. J Psychiatr Neurosci 21:21–28, 1996

20. Cohen AJ, Leckman JF: Sensory phenomena associated with Gilles de la Tourette's syndrome. J Clin Psychiatry 5:319–323, 1992 **Abstract**

21. Cohen DJ, Leckman JF, Pauls D: Neuropsychiatric disorders of childhood: Tourette's syndrome as a model. Acta Paediatr 422:106–111, 1997

22. De Groot CM, Bornstein RA, Baker GB: Obsessive-compulsive symptom clusters and urinary amine correlates

in Tourette syndrome. J Nerv Ment Dis 183:224–230, 1995 **Abstract**

23. Dursun SM, Farrar G, Handley SL, et al: Elevated plasma kynurenine in Tourette syndrome. Mol Chem Neuropathol 21:55–60, 1994 **Abstract**

24. Dursun SM, Reveley MA, Bird R, et al: Longlasting improvement of Tourette's syndrome with transdermal nicotine. Lancet 344:1577, 1994 **Citation**

25. Dursun SM, Reveley MA: Differential effects of transdermal nicotine on microstructured analyses of tics in Tourette's syndrome: An open study. Psychol Med 27:483–487, 1997 **Abstract**

26. Eidelberg D, Moeller JR, Antonini A, et al: The metabolic anatomy of Tourette's syndrome. Neurology 48:927–934, 1997 **Full Text**

27. Enright SJ, Beech AR: Reduced cognitive inhibition in obsessive-compulsive disorder. Br J Clin Psychol 32:67–74, 1993 **Abstract**

28. Erenberg G, Cruse RP, Rothner AD: Tourette syndrome: An analysis of 200 pediatric and adolescent cases. Cleve Clin Q 53:127–131, 1986 **Citation**

29. Erenberg G, Cruse RP, Rothner AD: The natural history of Tourette syndrome: A follow-up study. Ann Neurol 22:383–385, 1987 **Abstract**

29A. Ernst M, Zametkin AJ, Jons PH, et al: High presynaptic dopaminergic activity in children with Tourette's disorder. J Am Acad Child Adolesc Psychiatry 38:86–94, 1999 **Abstract**

30. Farber RH, Swerdlow NR, Clementz BA: Saccadic performance characteristics and the behavioral neurology of Tourette syndrome. J Neurol Neurosurg Psychiatry 66:305–312, 1999 **Abstract**

31. Fodstad H, Strandman E, Karlsson B, et al: Treatment of chronic obsessive compulsive states with stereotactic anterior capsulotomy or cingulotomy. Acta Neurochir 62:1–23, 1982 **Abstract**

32. Gadow KD, Sverd J, Sprafkin J, et al: Long-term methylphenidate therapy in children with comorbid attention-deficit hyperactivity disorder and chronic multiple tic disorder. Arch Gen Psychiatry 56:330–336, 1999 **Abstract**

33. George MS, Robertson MM, Costa DC, et al: Dopamine receptor availability in Tourette's syndrome. Psychiatry Res 55:193–203, 1994 **Abstract**

34. Haber SN, Kowall NW, Vonsattel JP, et al: Gilles de la Tourette's syndrome: A postmortem neuropathological and immunohistochemical study. J Neurol Sci 75:225–241, 1986 **Abstract**

35. Hartston HJ, Swerdlow NR: Visuospatial priming and Stroop performance in patients with obsessive compulsive disorder. Neuropsychology 13:447–457, 1999 **Abstract**

36. Head D, Bolton D, Hymas N: Deficit in cognitive shifting ability in patients with OCD. Biol Psychiatry 25:929–937, 1989 **Abstract**

37. Hollander E, Kwan J, Stein D, et al: Obsessive compulsive spectrum disorders: Overview and quality of life issues. J Ciin Psychiatry 57 (suppl 8):3–6, 1996 **Abstract**

38. Javoy-Agid F, Ruberg M, Taquet H, et al: Biochemical neuropathology of Parkinson's disease. Adv Neurol 40:189–198, 1984 **Citation**

39. Jefferson JW, Greist JH: The pharmacotherapy of obsessive-compulsive disorder. Psychiatr Ann 26:202–209, 1996

40. Kadesjo B, Gillberg C: Tourette's disorder: Epidemiology and comorbidity in primary school children. J Am Acad Child Adolesc Psychiatry 39:548–555, 2000 **Full Text**

41. Kurlan R: Treatment of tics. Neurol Clin North Am 15:403–409, 1997 **Full Text**

42. Leckman JF, Goodman WK, Anderson GM, et al: Cerebrospinal fluid biogenic amines in obsessive compulsive disorder, Tourette's syndrome, and healthy controls. Neuropsychopharmacology 12:73–86, 1995 **Abstract**

43. Leckman J, Grice D, Barr L, et al: Tic-related vs non-tic-related obsessive compulsive disorder. Anxiety 1:208–215, 1994 **Abstract**

44. Leckman JF, Grice DE, Boardman J, et al: Symptoms of obsessive-compulsive disorder. Am J Psychiatry 154:911–917, 1997 **Abstract**

45. Leckman JF, Hardin MT, Riddle MA, et al: Clonidine treatment of Gilles de la Tourette's syndrome. Arch Gen Psychiatry 48:324–328, 1991 **Abstract**

46. Leckman JF, Price RA, Walkup JT, et al: Nongenetic factors in Gilles de la Tourette's syndrome. Arch Gen Psychiatry 44:100, 1987 **Citation**

47. Leckman JF, Walker DE, Cohen DJ: Premonitory urges in Tourette's syndrome. Am J Psychiatry 150:98–102, 1993 **Abstract**

48. Leckman JF, Walker DE, Goodman WK, et al: "Just right" perceptions associated with compulsive behavior in Tourette's syndrome. Am J Psychiatry 151:675–680, 1994 **Abstract**

49. Leckman JF, Peterson BS, Anderson GM, et al: Pathogenesis of Tourette's syndrome. J Child Psychol Psychiatry 38:119–142, 1997 **Abstract**

50. Leckman JF, Peterson BS, Pauls DL, et al: Tic disorders. Psychiatr Clin North Am 20:839–861, 1997 **Full Text**

51. Leckman JF, Zhang H, Vitale A, et al: Course of tic severity in Tourette syndrome: The first two decades. Pediatrics 102:14–19, 1998 **Abstract**

52. Leibenluft E, Fiero PL, Rubinow DR: Effects of the menstrual cycle on dependent variables in mood disorder research. Arch Gen Psychiatry 51:761–781, 1994 **Abstract**

53. Liang KY, LaBuda M, Walkup J, et al: A family study of obsessive-compulsive disorder. Arch Gen Psychiatry 57:358–363, 2000 **Abstract**

54. Lipinski JF, Sallee FR, Jackson C, et al: Dopamine agonist treatment of Tourette disorder in children: Results of an open-label trial of pergolide. Mov Disord 12:402–407, 1997 **Abstract**

55. Luxenberg JS, Swedo SE, Flament MF: Neuroanatomical abnormalities in obsessive-compulsive disorder detected with quantitative x-ray computed tomography. Am J Psychiatry 145:1089–1096, 1988 **Abstract**

56. Malison RT, McDougle CJ, van Dyck CH, et al: [123I] beta-CIT SPECT imaging of striatal dopamine transporter binding in Tourette's disorder. Am J Psychiatry 152:1359–1361, 1995 **Abstract**

57. Marsden CD: Motor disorders in basal ganglia disease. Hum Neurobiol 2:245–255, 1984 **Abstract**

58. Mason A, Banerjee S, Eapen V, et al: The prevalence of Tourette syndrome in a mainstream school population. Dev Med Child Neurol 40:292–296, 1998 **Abstract**

59. Mataix-Cols D, Rauch SL, Manzo PA, et al: Use of factor-analyzed symptom dimensions to predict outcome with serotonin reuptake inhibitors and placebo in the treatment of obsessive-compulsive disorder. Am J Psychiatry 156:1409–1416, 1999 **Abstract**

59A. Meyer P, Bohnen NI, Minoshima S, et al: Striatal presynaptic monoaminergic vesicles are not increased in Tourette's syndrome. Neurology 53:371–374, 1999 **Full Text**

60. Modell JG, Mountz JM, Beresford TP: Basal ganglia/limbic striatal and thalamocortical involvement in craving and loss of control in alcoholism. J Neuropsychiatr Clin Neurosci 2:123–144, 1990

61. Moriarty J, Costa DC, Schmitz B, et al: Brain perfusion abnormalities in Gilles de la Tourette's Syndrome. Br J Psychiatry 167:249–254, 1995 **Abstract**

62. Moriarty J, Varma AR, Stevens J, et al: A volumetric MRI study of Gilles de la Tourette's syndrome. Neurology 49:410–415, 1997 **Full Text**

62A. Muller-Vahl KR, Berding G, Kolbe H, et al: Dopamine D2 receptor imaging in Gilles de la Tourette syndrome. Acta Neurol Scand 101:165–171, 2000 **Abstract**

63. Muller-Vahl KR, Kolbe H, Schneider U, et al: Cannabis in movement disorders. Forsch Komplementarmed 6(suppl 3):23–27, 1999

64. Pauls D, Alsobrook J, Goodman W, et al: A family study of obsessive compulsive disorder. Am J Psychiatry 152:76–84, 1995 **Abstract**

65. Pauls DL, Leckman JF: The inheritance of Gilles de la Tourette's syndrome and associated behaviors: Evidence for autosomal dominant transmission. N Engl J Med 315:993–997, 1986 **Abstract**

66. Pauls DL, Pakstis AJ, Kurlan R, et al: Segregation and linkage analyses of Tourette's syndrome and related disorders. J Am Acad Child Adolesc Psychiatry 29:195–203, 1990 **Abstract**

67. Pauls DL, Raymond CL, Stevenson JM, et al: A family study of Gilles de la Tourette syndrome. Am J Hum Genet 48:154–163, 1991 **Abstract**

68. Peterson BS, Leckman JF: The temporal dynamics of tics in Gilles de la Tourette syndrome. Biol Psychiatry 44:1337–1348, 1998 **Abstract**

69. Peterson BS, Pine DS, Cohen P, et al: A prospective longitudinal study of tic, obsessive-compulsive and attention deficit-hyperactivity disorders in an epidemiological sample. (submitted)

70. Peterson B, Riddle MA, Cohen DJ, et al: Reduced basal ganglia volumes in Tourette's syndrome using three-dimensional reconstruction techniques from magnetic resonance images. Neurology 43:941–949, 1993 **Abstract**

71. Peterson BS, Skudlarski P, Anderson AW, et al: A functional magnetic resonance imaging study of tic suppression in Tourette syndrome. Arch Gen Psychiatry 55:326–333, 1998 **Abstract**

72. Pigott TA, Hill JL, Grady TA, et al: A comparison of the behavioral effects of oral versus intravenous mCPP administration in OCD patients and the effect of metergoline prior to i.v. mCPP. Biol Psychiatry 33:3–14, 1993 **Abstract**

73. Price RA, Kidd KK, Cohen DJ, et al: A twin study of Tourette syndrome. Arch Gen Psychiatry 42:815–820, 1985 **Abstract**

74. Rasmussen SA, Eisen JL: Treatment strategies for chronic and refractory obsessive-compulsive disorder. J Clin Psychiatry 58(suppl 13):9–13, 1997 **Abstract**

75. Rasmussen SA, Eisen JL: Clinical and epidemiologic findings of significance to neuropharmacologic trials in OCD. Psychopharmacol Bull 24:466–470, 1988 **Citation**

76. Rasmussen SA, Tsuang MT: Clinical characteristics and family history in DSM-III obsessive-compulsive disorder. Am J Psychiatry 143:317–322, 1986 **Abstract**

77. Rauch SL, Jenike MA, Alpert NM, et al: Regional cerebral blood flow measured during symptom provocation in obsessive-compulsive disorder using oxygen 15-labeled carbon dioxide and positron emission tomography. Arch Gen Psychiatry 51:62–70, 1994 **Abstract**

78. Rauch S, Savage C, Alpert N, et al: Probing striatal function in obsessive compulsive disorder: A PET study of implicit sequence learning. J Neuropsychiatr Clin Neurosci 9:568–573, 1997

79. Reiner A, Albin RL, Anderson KD, et al: Differential loss of striatal projection neurons in Huntington disease. Proc Natl Acad Sci U S A 85:5733–5737, 1988 **Abstract**

80. Riddle MA, Rasmusson AM, Woods SW, et al: SPECT imaging of cerebral bloodflow in Tourette syndrome. Adv Neurol 58:207–211, 1992 **Citation**

81. Robins LN, Helzer JE, Weissman MM, et al: Lifetime prevalence of specific psychiatric disorders in three sites. Arch Gen Psychiatry 41:949–958, 1984 **Abstract**

82. Robinson D, Wu H, Munne RA, et al: Reduced caudate nucleus volume in obsessive-compulsive disorder. Arch Gen Psychiatry 52:393–398, 1995 **Abstract**

83. Rosenberg D, Averbach D, O'Hearn K, et al: Oculomotor response inhibition abnormalities in pediatric obsessive compulsive disorder. Arch Gen Psychiatry 54:831–838, 1997 **Abstract**

84. Rosenberg DR, Keshavan MS, O'Hearn KM, et al: Frontostriatal measurement in treatment-naive children with obsessive-compulsive disorder. Arch Gen Psychiatry 54:824–830, 1997 **Abstract**

85. Savage CR, Baer L, Keuthen MJ, et al: Organizational strategies mediate nonverbal memory impairment in obsessive-compulsive disorder. Biol Psychiatry 45:905–916, 1999 **Abstract**

86. Saxena S, Brody AL, Maidment KM, et al: Localized orbitofrontal and subcortical metabolic changes and predictors of response to paroxetine treatment in obsessive-compulsive disorder. Neuropsychopharmacology 21:683–693, 1999 **Abstract**

87. Schall U, Schon A, Zerbin D, et al: Event-related potentials during an auditory discrimination with prepulse inhibition in patients with schizophrenia, obsessive compulsive disorder and healthy subjects. Int J Neurosci 84:15–33, 1996 **Abstract**

88. Schwartz JM: Brain Lock. New York, Regan Books, 1996

89. Schwartz JM, Stoessel PW, Baxter LRJ, et al: Systematic changes in cerebral glucose metabolic rate after successful behavior modification treatment of obsessive-compulsive disorder. Arch Gen Psychiatry 53:109–113, 1996 **Abstract**

90. Seuchter SA, Hebebrand J, Klug B, et al: Complex segregation analysis of families ascertained through Gilles de la Tourette syndrome. Gen Epidemiol 18:33–47, 2000

91. Shapiro AK, Shapiro ES, Braun RD, et al: Gilles de la Tourette Syndrome. New York, Raven Press, 1978

92. Shapiro E, Shapiro AK, Fulop G, et al: Controlled study of haloperidol, pimozide and placebo for the treatment of Gilles de la Tourette's syndrome. Arch Gen Psychiatry 46:722–730, 1989 **Abstract**

93. Sieg KG, Buckingham D, Gaffney GR, et al: Tc-99m HMPAO SPECT brain imaging of Gilles de la Tourette's syndrome. Clin Nucl Med 18:255, 1993 **Citation**

94. Silver AA, Shytle RD, Philipp MK, et al: Case study: Long-term potentiation of neuroleptics with transdermal nicotine in Tourette's syndrome. J Am Acad Child Adolesc Psychiatry 35:1631–1636, 1996 **Abstract**

95. Singer HS: Neurobiology of Tourette syndrome. Neurol Clin North Am 15:357–379, 1997

96. Singer HS, Giulano JD, Hansen BH, et al: Antibodies against human putamen in children with Tourette syndrome. Neurology 50:1618–1624, 1998 **Full Text**

97. Singer HS, Hahn IH, Moran TH: Abnormal dopamine uptake sites in postmortem striatum from patients with Tourette's syndrome. Ann Neurol 30:558–562, 1991 **Abstract**

98. Singer HS, Reiss AL, Brown JE, et al: Volumetric MRI changes in basal ganglia of children with Tourette's syndrome. Neurology 43:950–956, 1993 **Abstract**

99. Smith SJ, Lees AJ: Abnormalities of the blink reflex in Gilles de la Tourette syndrome. J Neurol Neurosurg Psychiatry 52:895–898, 1989 **Abstract**

100. Sutherland RJ, Kolb B, Schoel WM, et al: Neuropsychological assessment of children and adults with Tourette syndrome: A comparison with learning disabilities and schizophrenia. Adv Neurol 35:311–322, 1982 **Citation**

101. Swedo SE, et al: Pediatric autoimmune neuropsychiatric disorders associated with streptococcal infections: Clinical description of the first 50 cases. Am J Psychiatry 155:264–271, 1998 **Abstract**

102. Swerdlow NR: Neuropsychology of schizophrenia: The "hole" thing is wrong. Behav Brain Sci 14:51–53, 1991

103. Swerdlow NR, Koob GF: Dopamine, schizophrenia, mania and depression: Toward a unified hypothesis of cortico-striato-pallido-thalamic function. Behav Brain Sci 10:197–245, 1987

103A. Swerdlow NR, Leckman JF: Tourette's syndrome and related tic disorders. *In* Charney D, Coyle J, Davis K, et al (eds): Fifth Generation of Progress. American College of Neuropsychopharmacology 2000. Baltimore, MD, Lippincott Williams & Wilkins (in press)

104. Swerdlow NR, Magulac M, Filion D, et al: Visuospatial priming and latent inhibition in children and adults with Tourette's disorder. Neuropsychology 10:485–494, 1996

105. Swerdlow NR, Young AB: Neuropathology in Tourette syndrome. CNS Spectrums 4:65–74, 1999

106. Swerdlow NR, Zinner S, Farber RH, et al: Symptoms in obsessive compulsive disorder and Tourette syndrome: A spectrum? CNS Spectrums 4:21–33, 1999

107. Syzmanski S, Galiano J, Yokoi F, et al: Basal ganglia dopamine release in Tourette syndrome. Proceedings of the Society of Nuclear Medicine, San Antonio, TX, 1997

108. Tourette Syndrome Association International Consortium for Genetics: A complete genome screen in sib pairs affected by Gilles de la Tourette syndrome. Am J Hum Genet 65:1428–1436, 1999 **Abstract**

108A. Tourette Syndrome Classification Study Group: Definitions and classification of tic disorders. Arch Neurol 50:1013–1016, 1993 **Abstract**

109. Trimble MR, Whurr R, Brookes G, et al: Vocal tics in Gilles de la Tourette syndrome treated with botulinum toxin injections. Mov Disord 13:617–619, 1998 **Citation**

110. Turjanski N, Sawle GV, Playford ED, et al: PET studies of the presynaptic and postsynaptic dopaminergic systems in Tourette's syndrome. J Neurol Neurosurg Psychiatry 57:688–692, 1994 **Abstract**

111. Van Paesschen W, Revesv T, Duncan JS, et al: Quantitative neuropathology and quantitative magnetic resonance imaging of the hippocampus in temporal lobe epilepsy. Ann Neurol 42:756–766, 1997 **Abstract**

112. Winslow JT, Insel TR: Neurobiology of obsessive compulsive disorder: A possible role for serotonin. J Clin Psychiatry 51(suppl):27–31, 1990 **Abstract**

113. Wolf SS, Jones DW, Knable MB, et al: Tourette syndrome: Prediction of phenotypic variation in monozygotic twins by caudate nucleus D2 receptor binding. Science 273:1225–1227, 1996 **Abstract**

114. Wong DF, Singer HS, Brandt J, et al: D2-like dopamine receptor density in Tourette syndrome measured by PET. J Nucl Med 38:1243–1247, 1997 **Abstract**

115. Woods DW, Miltenberger RG, Lumley VA: Sequential application of major habit-reversal components to treat motor tics in children. J Appl Behav Anal 29:483–493, 1996 **Abstract**

Topics covered in this article have been reviewed in previous reports by the author, [103A] [105]

Self-Regulation: Prospects, Problems, and Promises

By Roy F. Baumeister, Todd F. Heatherton, and Dianne M. Tice

Keep the faculty of effort alive in you by a little gratuitous exercise every day. That is, be systematically heroic in little unnecessary points, do every day or two something for no other reason than its difficulty, so that, when the hour of dire need draws nigh, it may find you not unnerved or untrained to stand the test. Asceticism of this sort is like the insurance which a man pays on his house and goods. The tax does him no good at the time, and possibly may never bring him a return. But if the fire does come, his having paid it will be his salvation from ruin. So with the man who has daily inured himself to habits of concentrated attention, energetic volition, and self-denial in unnecessary things. He will stand like a tower when everything rocks around him, and his softer fellow-mortals are winnowed like chaff in the blast.

—William James, *The Principles of Psychology*

In this book we have taken close looks at a series of spheres of self-regulation failure, one at a time. The final chapter will therefore undertake to summarize some of the common patterns that occurred repeatedly in multiple spheres. This will allow us to reexamine some of the main ideas about self-regulation failure that we proposed at the beginning of the book. In addition, however, we wish to offer some more speculative reflections that these several years of researching self-regulation failure have stimulated. In the spirit of this concluding chapter, therefore, we shall minimize our use of references (quite unlike the rest of the book) and focus on our own general thoughts and impressions.

HOW SELF-CONTROL FAILS

We begin by reviewing the main patterns and issues we have covered with regard to self-regulation failure. In the opening chapters of this book, we noted that self-regulation consists of three components, and so a breakdown or problem with any of them could conceivably be responsible for self-regulation failure. The three components are standards, monitoring, and strength.

Standards

Standards are essential as the targets of self-regulation, and when they are lacking or inconsistent, self-regulation cannot be effective. Problems regarding standards surfaced particularly in two areas, self-management and impulse control.

Regarding self-management, the issue is often a lack of standards. We noted that having both short-term and long-term standards (also known as proximal and distal goals) appears to be necessary for successful self-management. People who lack either one show deficits in self-management.

Another problem arises when people have unrealistic or inappropriate standards. Certain circumstances seem to cause people to set inappropriate goals, with the result that self-regulation is seriously compromised. Thus, people with high self-esteem who are subjected to ego threats seem particularly prone to taking on unrealistic aspirations and doing other things that are destructive for self-management.

Regarding impulse control, the problem is often one of conflicting standards. People have severe approach–avoidance conflicts with many appetitive patterns, such as alcohol and overeating. They are attracted to the activity by the pleasure and satisfaction it offers, but they are held away by their own resolutions, often motivated by recognition of problems that attend overindulgence.

Monitoring

Effective self-regulation depends on monitoring oneself, that is, comparing oneself (and one's circumstances) to the standards. When people are unable to monitor themselves, or when they cease monitoring themselves, self-regulation tends to become ineffective.

Problems with monitoring tend to be associated with underregulation. In some cases people simply do not bother to watch what they are doing. Money problems reflected this pattern; some people simply do not keep track of how much they are spending, with the result that their bills and expenses outstrip their capacity to pay. More generally, an increase in monitoring is often an effective way to improve self-regulation, whether of eating or drinking or studying or exercising or performing a task. Conversely, when people reduce their monitoring of their own behavior, self-regulation is more likely to break down. We noted evidence, for example, that breaking a diet seems to be associated with a serious reduction in monitoring of one's eating behavior.

Some factors seem to interfere directly with the capacity to monitor oneself. When people are under stress, distracted, or preoccupied, it becomes more difficult to continue their ordinary monitoring practices. Alcohol in particular seems to interfere with monitoring. Alcohol may therefore contribute to a broad variety of self-regulation failures, from aggression to task performance—and to escalating abuse of alcohol itself.

Strength Failure

Self-regulation may still fail even if the person has clear goals or standards and monitors himself or herself effectively. This is because it is nonetheless necessary for the person to override whatever action or desire or thought or emotion needs to be changed. We noted that the capacity to bring about these changes in oneself seems to conform to a strength model.

Many of the patterns covered in this book conform to the strength model. Self-regulation failures of many types are most likely to occur late in the day, when people are tired; this is true for dieting failures, aggressive acts, alcohol, and other substance abuse patterns. It is common knowledge that task performance, endurance, and persistence decline with tiredness. Furthermore, there is evidence that coping with stress consumes some of people's strength, and so many forms of self-regulation break down when people are under stress. (Even the aftereffects of stress have been shown to decrease self-regulation in some ways, consistent with the view that once one's strength has been depleted, it takes some time to recoup.) People resume smoking, drink too much, eat too much, stop exercising, lose control of their emotions and moods, and more. Emotional distress was repeatedly implicated in self-regulation failure, and although there are several possible ways that emotional distress could produce those effects, it is very plausible that distress consumes or undermines the person's self-regulatory strength.

The concept of strength, has long-term implications as well. A person's degree of self-regulatory strength should be generally consistent across time, although conceivably someone could build up his or her strength through exercise. There was some evidence consistent with those views, but more research is needed. At present, the most relevant findings show that people who are prone to self-regulation failures in one sphere are more likely to have them in other spheres too, which does seem to imply that they have some form of chronic, undifferentiated weakness at self-regulation.

Misregulation

Two main sources of misregulation emerged in this work. One concerns false or misleading beliefs about the self and the environment. Such faulty knowledge leads people to make unrealistic commitments, to make non-optimal trade-offs between speed and accuracy, to use counterproductive strategies in the attempt to control their emotions, and to persist in doomed endeavors.

The other main source is trying to control things that cannot be directly or properly controlled. Focusing self-regulatory efforts on one of these areas is doomed to fail. Thus, people tend to fail when they try directly to alter their mood states. Choking under pressure is likewise a matter of trying to control the uncontrollable, in the sense that choking occurs when people try to override the automatic quality of their skills and consciously control the process of performance. Trying to suppress thoughts directly falls into this category, because efforts at thought suppression are at best partly successful. Trying to control impulses directly—in the literal sense of preventing oneself from having the desires—is far less likely to succeed than focusing on preventing oneself from acting on those impulses.

A variation on this second form of misregulation is that people focus their regulatory efforts on the wrong thing. One common problem we saw was that people focus on regulating their emotions rather than dealing with objective problems; for example, the procrastinator may put off working on a task because to work on it creates anxiety, but even though this strategy will often minimize anxiety, in the long run it is self-destructive. Likewise, people may overeat, abuse alcohol, smoke cigarettes, or quit jobs or tasks as a way of ducking unpleasant emotional states and demands, but in the long run such coping mechanisms may be worse than nothing. A standard finding in the coping literature is that emotion-focused coping is often less adaptive and helpful than problem-focused coping. One important reason may be that emotion-focused coping allows the objective problem to get worse by neglecting the objective causes while one focuses on one's subjective reaction.

Attention and Transcendence

When people lose control of their attention, self-regulation is in jeopardy. Many forms of self-regulation failure begin with a loss of control over attention. Thus, for example, when people fail to delay gratification, the failure is often preceded by a shift of attention onto the immediately available rewards. Control over thoughts is lost when attention runs wild. Emotional states spin out of control when people are not able to move their attention off of some distressing event or stimulus. Task performance deteriorates when people cannot concentrate on the relevant information. Dieting, abstaining from alcohol, and other forms of regulating appetitive behavior break down when the person's attention fixes on the forbidden activity or stimulus.

Transcendence failure was repeatedly found to be a particularly important form of attentional problem. Many forms of self-regulation failure arise when people lose the capacity to see beyond the immediate situation or salient stimuli. Self-regulation often requires one to adopt a long-range context or higher value or abstract frame of reference. When, instead, attention is narrowly focused in the here and now, the capacity to override impulses or delay gratification or calm unwanted feelings or persist at an unpleasant task is reduced.

The effects of emotion on self-regulation failure may well be mediated by transcendence failure. Emotion tends to keep attention focused on the immediate stimulus (which is why some effective ways of controlling emotion emphasize cultivating an attitude of transcendence). In the grip of powerful emotional state, the person may be unable to look past the availability of a bottle of whiskey or a gun or a cheesecake and may therefore succumb to such temptations.

Lapse-Activated Patterns

Our analyses frequently indicated the need to use two panels of causes in order to explain self-regulation failure; for convenience, we have labeled the second set of causes as *lapse-activated*. The first set of causes prompts the initial lapse or misstep, that is, the initial infraction of a self-regulatory regimen. Other causes then come into play, however, and transform the small misstep into a full-blown binge. The latter factors can be said to promote snowballing, and serious self-regulation failure only occurs when such snowballing produces a large breakdown, but there must already be some lapse before snowballing can happen.

The best example of snowballing resulting from lapse-activated causes was alcohol abuse. Initial drinking can occur for a variety of reasons, including false beliefs about the effects of alcohol or the assumption that one is entitled to a small drink as a celebration or as relief from stress. Initial drinks impair the capacity to monitor oneself, however, so that one soon loses track of one's drinking (and with monitoring goes the capacity to control one's drinking). Drinking also seems to enhance the salience and appeal of alcohol and of cues that promote further drinking. Moreover, various beliefs promote the view that an alcoholic loses all control after a single drink, and so such zero-tolerance views may cause the person to believe that it is too late to stop.

The most common form of lapse-activated snowballing, however, was spiraling distress. After an initial breakdown or lapse occurs, people may feel bad, and their response to feeling bad may lead them to do things that compound the problem. This response resembles the pattern we have seen in which people place undue emphasis on regulating their emotions, at the expense of other self-regulatory efforts. The short-term efforts to overcome distress cause them to neglect other self-regulatory efforts, and this neglect in turn leads to more distress as self-control breaks down more and more.

Thus, for example, eating binges or problems occur because dieters feel bad when they eat too much and they eat too much when they feel bad. Shoppers buy things to cheer themselves up, but the realization of having spent money they could not afford causes them to feel worse, and the resulting distress prompts them to shop again. Gamblers feel bad after losing and become determined to recoup their losses by making a big score, so they make further bets. Likewise, in procrastination, once the person has fallen behind schedule, working on the task may bring up so much anxiety and worry that the person has to stop working on the task in order to calm down. Such a pattern will obviously contribute to further procrastination.

ISSUES, REFLECTIONS, AND

SPECULATIONS

The concepts we have reviewed thus far seem adequate to furnish a basic understanding of self-regulation failure. Although there are certainly enough areas of ambiguity and unanswered questions to keep researchers occupied for years to come, there is presently enough knowledge to support the view that the basic dimensions of self-regulation failure involve standards, monitoring, strength, lapse-activated causes, misregulation fueled by misconceptions, and so forth.

At this point we wish to turn to some of the issues that are not so well resolved. The ideas in this section represent tentative conclusions that we have reached from these past five years of reading about self-regulation. That is, we do not consider the evidence conclusive; rather, these are in the nature of our best guesses based on preliminary evidence. These may therefore be considered issues for further research.

Sequence of Control

One of the classic articles in social psychology in the 1980s was the analysis of control furnished by Rothbaum et al. (1982). They made the fundamental distinction between primary control, which is the attempt to change the environment in order to suit the self, and secondary control, which involves changing the self to fit in to the environment.

Although we have suggested that self-regulation can in many respects be equated with secondary control, our review has suggested that the theoretical issues may be deeper and more complex. After all, people do sometimes manipulate the environment in the service of dealing with their feelings or impulses.

When self-regulation is the issue, the theoretical relationship is perhaps the reverse of the sequence proposed by Rothbaum et al. (1982) for controlling the world. They assumed that people would always begin by trying to alter the environment to suit the self, which is why they labeled that form of intervention *primary* control; only if it failed, they reasoned, would people resort to changing the self (secondary control). Much of the control that people seek is control over their environment or things external to themselves; people want control over their career paths, over their interpersonal options, control over the things that affect their lives. In these cases, seeking control over their environment is likely to be primary, and control by changing the self will remain secondary.

When self-regulation is the issue, however, the sequence is reversed. In self-regulation, one begins by trying to alter the self directly. Most people can succeed at this most of the time, and so nothing else is needed. That is, most people can exert sufficient control over their appetites, impulses, thoughts, and feelings. For those individuals who repeatedly fail at such control, however, the alternate response becomes one of changing the environment. These few people may have to remove all alcohol or fattening foods or cigarettes or dangerous weapons from their homes, because they find they cannot stop themselves from misusing them when available.

Thus, for self-regulation, the primary and most common strategy is to exert control directly on the self. Only when that fails do people resort to the secondary strategy of altering the environment.

Acquiescence

In this book we have repeatedly found that self-regulation failures involve active participation by the individual. This pattern applied mainly to underregulation, rather than misregulation. The question of whether people ever acquiesce in misregulation remains an interesting issue for research on self-defeating behavior patterns, but in general misregulation does not seem to involve acquiescence. In underregulation, however, the person does accept and participate in the self-regulation failure.

Popular conceptions of self-regulation failure depict people becoming overwhelmed by irresistible impulses that they are powerless to control. Some of our own concepts may convey similar notions, such as the concept of strength, which when depleted presumably leaves the person a passive and helpless victim of inner and outer promptings. These are caricatures, however, not reality. A brief consideration of the active role people take in their own self-regulation failures should be enough to discredit them.

A more accurate view may be that people do feel that their strength is depleted and their capacity overwhelmed, and so they decide to give up trying to control themselves. Then they go on and take an active role in indulging their impulses.

Thus, a woman who goes on an eating binge continues to participate actively in that she finds the food, puts it in her mouth, and chews and swallows it. Possibly at the moment she abandoned self-control she felt weak and helpless, but afterward (while eating) she is far from helpless. A man who goes on a drinking binge shows the same pattern: He continues to order or prepare drinks and to raise the glass to his lips. Likewise, smokers must exert themselves substantially and creatively in order to indulge in uncontrolled smoking, because American society now places so many restrictions and obstacles in the way of smoking. A performer suffers from fatigue or boredom and allows the self to quit—and then actively withdraws from the performance and does other things instead.

Along the same lines, we cited evidence that people who suffer from obsessional thoughts experience the obsession as a weakness of their capacity for control rather than as some overwhelming power of the troubling thought. In their experience, it is more a matter of giving in to some constant inner nagging than being overcome by an irresistible thought. Likewise, emotions often cannot be directly controlled, but people can control whether they express their feelings and whether they act on them, and those choices do exert a potent effect on whether the emotion increases or dissipates. This particularly includes aggressive actions performed in the heat of anger. Once self-control is abandoned, the person may take a very active role in performing violent, aggressive actions.

Yet more examples can be found in self-management. In order to fail at delay of gratification, one must often make an active choice to take the immediate rewards, and the process of obtaining and enjoying them often involves active participation. Self-handicapping, meanwhile, is generally recognized as a strategic maneuver that the person performs with some degree of planning and insight (including the careful attention to how other people will perceive one's actions). Failing to set proper goals may sometimes be something the person acquiesces in doing, although it may often be merely passive. With procrastination, it seems likely that the person usually acquiesces to some degree, to the extent that the person knowingly puts off working on the task as the deadline approaches.

There are, certainly, some forms of self-regulation failure that do not (or do not always) entail acquiescence. With the self-regulation of inference processes and with self-deception, the degree of conscious acquiescence is difficult to establish (and is controversial among researchers). Choking under pressure is not usually a matter of acquiescing, nor is a failure to concentrate. There are some aspects to alcohol abuse that do not seem to involve acquiescence, such as the fact that once one has become somewhat inebriated, it becomes difficult to monitor one's behavior and regulate further drinking.

Still, there is plenty of evidence that most cases of underregulation involve the clear and active acquiescence by the individual. Self-regulation failure is not so much something that happens to you as something that you allow to happen. This analysis suggests that the crux of the matter is that a momentary loss of self-control is followed by a refusal to reinstate control. The person starts the eating or drinking binge but probably could stop after a few minutes. Yet the notion of stopping does not arise for a long time. The person postpones the issue of stopping, of reestablishing self-control, while indulging in the impulses.

The popular notion of the "irresistible impulse" must therefore be questioned. In recent years this notion has gained ever wider usage in the society, partly as defense lawyers in criminal trials have used it to argue that their clients should not be punished for performing violent actions (because they could not help what they did), and partly because addicts have used it to explain their destructive, pleasure-seeking behavior. The common thread is of course the excuse from responsibility. If an impulse is truly irresistible, one cannot be blamed for failing to resist it.

Undoubtedly there are some cases of truly irresistible impulses—but not very many. A truly irresistible impulse will be enacted regardless of perceived consequences and other rational calculations. Even if someone is holding a gun and threatening to shoot you, you will act on an irresistible impulse. For example, the urge to urinate or to lie down can eventually become irresistible, and under extreme conditions a person will do either of those things even when someone is threatening to shoot him or her for doing so. But overeating, or smoking a cigarette, or

beating one's spouse would almost certainly not qualify as an irresistible impulse by that criterion. Self-regulation failure thus seems to involve a relinquishing of control because the exertion of controlling oneself is too unpleasant, and not because the impulse is too powerful.

Once the person has begun to indulge the impulse, it may become that much more difficult to control. We have cited ample evidence of inertia. Yet it is possible to reinstate control; eventually, after all, people do stop whatever "uncontrollable" behavior they are doing. The theoretical focus should perhaps be not on the initial impulse but on the failure to reinstate control. An angry person may have an impulse to kill someone who has provoked him. As we said, it may be impossible to prevent oneself from feeling the impulse, but it is possible to refrain from carrying out the action. Even if the anger becomes so intense that the person cannot stop himself from standing up to stomp out of the room, however, there would be ample opportunity to stop before one goes upstairs, fetches and loads the gun, and returns downstairs to shoot the person with whom one is angry. Yet sometimes people do not stop, just as they often fail to stop consumptive behavior after a few bites of ice cream or a single beer. In all of this, there would seem to be an element of passive self-deception. Having once decided to abandon control, the person refrains from reconsidering, even though in fact considerable self-control is necessary in carrying out the acts that accompany self-regulation failure.

The issue of acquiescence is thus an important one for further study. In our view, the direction that the incoming evidence points toward is greater recognition of acquiescence. We are less inclined now than we were when we started this book to regard people who fail at self-regulation as innocent, helpless victims; they look more like accomplices, or at least willing targets of seduction.

Yet it cannot be denied that there is still an important element of self-regulation failure, in the sense that at some level the person still wishes that he or she did not lose control. Seduction may indeed be a useful model, insofar as seduction involves manipulating consent—as opposed to rape, which simply overwhelms resistance. Although lawyers and other advocates of people who fail at self-regulation may sometimes wish to compare their clients' failures to being victims of rape, in the sense of being an innocent victim overpowered by irresistible forces, self-regulation failure is far more similar to being seduced than to being raped.

This is not to say that biological differences, genetic differences, or differences in past history and background are irrelevant to behavior. There is abundant evidence suggesting that some people are biologically prepared to become much more aroused than others in response to even a slight provocation, whereas others are more likely to seek out risky, thrilling events, others are much more genetically susceptible to becoming addicted to alcohol, and others to becoming obese. But these biological, genetic, or background differences that predispose people to anger, thrill seeking, alcoholism, obesity, and so forth do not lead directly to ruin. Rather, they suggest areas in which self-control is especially important. A person with a past history of alcohol abuse may need to exercise more self-control at a cocktail party than the person who has never wanted more than a couple of drinks at a time. A person with obese parents may need to exercise more control over dietary intake than a person who never gains weight no matter how many french fries or chocolate bars are eaten. These biological, genetic, or background differences merely predispose people to certain weaknesses where self-control will be particularly important—they do not necessarily condemn people to lives of alcoholism, violence, obesity, or danger.

The notion of transcendence failure may provide a valuable way to understand the complex problem that the person acquiesces in self-regulation failure while at the same time wishing that he or she could maintain control. The desire to maintain self-control exists at a high level of meaning, in a long-term context. You are unlikely to light up a cigarette as long as you are thinking about lung cancer and your promises to your spouse that you would quit. In that context, the tempting cigarette is merely an enemy of the self. What happens, however, is that the person ceases to transcend the immediate situation. Remote medical outcomes and spousal promises recede from awareness, and attention focuses on the immediate pleasure that a cigarette would offer. And once the person has allowed himself to limit awareness to the immediate situation, it presents little problem or conflict to *actively* go about lighting up and smoking.

Most of the evidence about acquiescence supports such a model, with one further provision: People often seem to arrange to lose control. They seek out settings or support groups that encourage them to give in to their impulses and even to regard them as irresistible. Whether the issue is a drinking binge, a shopping spree, a gambling frenzy, quitting early on a tedious task, or assaulting someone, people can find a place and a group where a consensus reigns that such actions cannot be prevented. Then and there, they can give up the wearisome inner struggle to maintain self-control by resisting those impulses. Once the decision is made to give up the struggle, people seem to find it easy to avoid raising the issue again, and they go about indulging themselves—sometimes to wild extremes. During this phase they often show considerable autonomy and active ingenuity in carrying out the behaviors they were previously trying to stop.

The issue of acquiescence may be of considerable importance to the future of our society. We suggested in Chapter 11 that the true meaning of a subculture of violence may be that it is a group of people who support each other's belief in the impossibility of resisting violent impulses. If that is correct, then America may be drifting toward being an increasingly violent culture, not because of any positive love of violence, but because of a growing consensus that human violent behavior is often caused by irresistible violent impulses. The parallel rise in addictive behaviors may be similarly fueled by the belief that people cannot control their desires for drugs or alcohol. Although there are powerful interest groups that advocate such views, it seems imperative that the contrary view be articulated and that people be exhorted to regard their behavior as controllable whenever possible. If the view prevails that self-regulation failure is something that happens to an individual and excuses his or her subsequent behavior, then gradually the culture itself will become a context that supports—and in a powerful sense encourages—such failures. Against this view, it seems essential to note the abundant evidence that self-regulatory failure is something that people actively acquiesce in, and that therefore should not excuse violent, addictive, delinquent, or other socially undesirable actions.

Self-Esteem

Although we did not place much emphasis on self-esteem in our initial exposition of self-regulation theory (in Chapter 2), the concern with self-esteem emerged repeatedly as a factor relevant to self-regulation failures. In particular, it appears that ego threats promote a broad variety of self-regulation failures.

Multiple performance patterns, involving both misregulation and underregulation, were related to ego threats. Drinking, quitting or persisting irrationally, and venting aggression all seem to involve breakdowns in self-regulation that occur following ego threats. Indeed, it may be that ego threats are involved in the process of acquiescence. For example, a person may decide that some humiliating experience or loss of dignity is too upsetting to make it worth the effort to exert oneself at maintaining self-control.

Self-management patterns were frequently undermined by ego threats or, in particular, by the wish to assert a highly favorable view of self in the face of some ego threat. Thus, self-handicapping reflects a destructive approach to managing one's affairs that is driven by the wish to protect and enhance favorable views of self. Overconfident, unrealistic, and hence destructive goal setting was also a common response (especially among people high in self-esteem) to ego threats. Procrastination was often motivated by the fear that one will not perform up to exalted expectations.

It must be noted that ego threats tend to produce emotional reactions too, and so some of the effects of ego threats may be due to the emotional distress that accompanies them. These include, for example, withdrawing effort and giving up after initial failure and consuming alcohol in response to ego threat.

We were somewhat surprised several years ago when ego threat emerged in preliminary laboratory pilot work as the most potent cause of self-regulation failure in the paradigm we were using (Baumeister et al., 1993). The literature review for this book has yielded plenty of additional evidence, although much of it has been indirect. Hence, we conclude that one priority for future research would be a systematic investigation of how and when ego threats contribute to self-regulation failure.

There do seem to be other ways in which self-esteem is tied in to self-regulation failure. As we have noted, evidence suggests that impulse-control problems are often linked to self-esteem, although not in consistent ways. Thus, gamblers tend to have high self-esteem, whereas alcoholics and binge eaters tend to suffer from low self-esteem. Many people who write about violent behavior claim that low self-esteem is a cause of violence, but our own reading of those studies suggests that high self-esteem—again, particularly high self-esteem combined with an ego threat—is more likely the major cause. The correlational nature of much of the data raises further conceptual problems, of course. Even if a link between low self-esteem and self-regulation failures were well established, it would not be clear whether poor self-regulation leads to lower self-esteem or vice versa.

Thus, although popular conceptions seem all too ready to identify low self-esteem as a uniform and central cause of self-regulation failure, we regard the relationship between self-esteem and self-regulation as very poorly understood. It is apparent that both high and low self-esteem can be linked to self-regulation failure, in different ways and under different circumstances (e.g., Heatherton & Ambady, 1993). Very possibly there are complex, reciprocal, and multifaceted relationships. In our view, most of the research on how self-esteem is related to self-regulation failure is yet to be done.

Generalized Disinhibition

In surveying the various literatures on self-regulation failure, we have repeatedly been led to conclude that failure is the product of intrapsychic changes that thwart or undermine all regulatory efforts. Such a conclusion is of course quite plausible and perhaps not in itself all that surprising. Yet it has a corollary that may have considerable theoretical interest. The factors that promote self-regulation failure in one sphere should tend to promote the roughly simultaneous failure in all spheres.

For example, if alcohol undermines people's ability to monitor their own behavior, then people who have consumed alcohol should show reduced inhibitions in all spheres. They should become more aggressive, more impulsive, more willing to engage in illicit sex or to break their diets, and so forth. Although alcohol is reasonably well recognized in the general culture as an all purpose source of disinhibition, the important question is whether other states that reduce self-regulation in one sphere will simultaneously weaken inhibitions in other spheres.

It may also turn out that the matter is more complex. Possibly some factors promote generalized self-regulation failure while others are specific. Thus, a reduction in monitoring, a failure of transcendence, or a loss of strength may promote generalized failure. In contrast, acquiescence may be specific to certain spheres, as are particular beliefs that may foster misregulation or lapse-activated patterns.

Cultural Change

We began the book by noting that self-regulation failure is central to many problems that plague society. One may reasonably ask whether this is universally true or whether something particular about modern American society predisposes it to self-regulation problems.

A historical analysis of self-control is beyond the scope of this book, but several tentative answers can be suggested. It is obvious that self-regulation depends heavily on cultural factors. Among these are beliefs about self-control. For example, it is generally agreed that Europeans lack zero tolerance beliefs about alcohol, unlike Americans, and that—possibly as a result—they have fewer teetotalers *and* fewer alcoholics than America does (e.g., Peele, 1989). A second factor that varies among cultures is the nature and prevalence of temptations. Eating has been a problem for most societies in the history of the world, but the nature of the problem has been the opposite of what modern America faces. More precisely, most societies have faced famines, shortages, and other sources of inadequate food. Ancient Chinese peasants did not go on diets. Compounding the problem is that the material abundance in modern America is combined with advertising, which routinely seeks to encourage consumption (and often does so by trying to stimulate desire). In the view of many critics, the mass media have in general become a choir of voices shouting against self-regulation.

Given these cultural variations, it seems likely that the epidemic of self-regulation problems in modern America is a recent and unusual problem. To understand why it may have arisen, one will almost inevitably have to consider multiple sources. The ubiquitousness and power of the mass media are only one of these.

Much of twentieth-century American society has seen itself as reacting against what it saw as the destructive and possibly absurd excesses of the Victorian (i.e., late nineteenth century) era. Indeed, the term *Victorian* has become a synonym for sexual prudery, against which the twentieth century has waged a long sexual revolution. Middle-class Victorian society had not killed the sex drive, but it had certainly achieved a measure of control over sexual feelings that is now regarded as undesirable and excessive. As is typical for cultural changes in mass attitudes, however, the culture has moved from one extreme to another. Today, in the face of epidemics of AIDS, other venereal diseases, teen pregnancy, and child sexual abuse, some voices are arguing that America has gone too far toward relaxing the control over sexuality. Several newspaper columnists have even created a stir recently by proposing that sexual morality be reintroduced, at least in the form of stigmatizing unwed parenthood ("illegitimacy"). Our intent here is not to enter into this debate but simply to suggest that the general reaction against Victorian self-control may be a factor behind the rising tide of self-regulation problems.

Psychology itself probably bears some of the responsibility. Undoubtedly the most insightful critic of the Victorian mind was Sigmund Freud, and he argued very persuasively that stifling one's impulses and feelings and desires has psychologically harmful effects. We suspect that Freud would be aghast to find that his ideas have been taken as a justification for abandoning self-control on a large scale, but to some extent that is precisely what has happened. The general public's perception of the lesson of Freud does seem to be that one harms oneself whenever one fails to express or enact an emotion or desire (see Tavris, 1989).

A vicious cycle may have arisen. America is also a remarkably tolerant and compassionate society. Its efforts to offer systematic, enlightened help to the afflicted and downtrodden go far beyond what most societies in the past have done. To benefit from this largesse, one need only be a deserving victim. The wish to be free from responsibility for one's misdeeds has made notions of irresistible impulses very broadly appealing. As the number of alcoholics rises, there are more and more people who wish to believe that alcoholics should not be held responsible for their drinking. And as the culture accepts that view, more and more new individuals find that their own drinking is, sure enough, beyond their control. We have already suggested that America's acceptance of the notion of irresistible violent impulses may be an important factor that encourages people to give in to those impulses. What we are saying here is even more broad and general: As the culture believes in and accepts giving in to all sorts of impulses, self-regulation will be systematically undermined.

Still, the main place where self-regulation is instilled is in the parent–child interactions, and so it is to changes in parental socialization that one should look most carefully in order to find possible reasons for the spread of self-regulation problems. Two fundamental changes in parent–child relations dominate most analyses of the twentieth-century family, and both may have a hand in contributing to the decline of self-control.

The first change is the transformation of the family from an economic or work unit into a nexus of emotional relations. Burgess and Locke (1945) provided a classic analysis of this change. In their view, families in past eras operated largely as small corporations, in which each member had responsibilities to make a productive contribution and, indeed, most members tended to work together on joint tasks (especially in farming). Authority, discipline, and cooperation were necessarily well structured by the demands of joint work.

But the economic function of the family is largely obsolete. Instead, the family has become a locus of the search for emotional satisfaction. Intimacy, rather than economic production, is the goal of family relations. The need for self-regulation is clearly much lower in the modern family. The change may be especially marked if one accepts the view that instilling self-discipline in a child requires some harsh and firm treatment by the parent (e.g., insisting on firm rules, punishing infractions). In the old family, this would have been accepted as necessary, but modern parents may see it as likely to engender resentment by the child. People may seek intimacy with their children by trying to indulge their children's wishes, forgiving their infractions, and being maximally flexible and supportive. High school principals complain these days that parents want to be "pals" to their children and so shrink from disciplining them. Although such generalizations may have been made on the basis of the most salient examples and cannot be applied to all parents, they may also reflect a growing trend.

The second change in the family is the rise in single-parent households. By all measures and counts, the number and proportion of such households have risen sharply since 1960 and show no sign of letting up. Almost by definition, a single parent cannot spend as much time supervising a child as two parents can. Indeed, the difference may be especially dramatic when one considers that single parents are often chronically exhausted by the demands of supporting the family and providing the basic maintenance of food, shelter, and clothing, and so attending to matters of instilling delay of gratification and other rudiments of self-regulation may be too much to ask. In the last several years, research has continued to indicate that children of single parents are more likely than other children to show signs of self-regulation failure in many diverse spheres, ranging from achievement in school math class to juvenile delinquency and crime.

What can be done? There is little reason to think that single parenthood will decline any time soon. It seems ludicrous to expect day-care centers (which live under constant threats of lawsuits, investigations, and simple loss of business if children complain) to contribute much toward instilling self-regulation. Schools can be a partial substitute for parenting in instilling self-regulatory skills, but many factors, including budget cuts, emphases on noncoercive tolerance, and lack of parental support for school discipline, are weakening schools' ability to do this. (And as many educators complain, instilling self-discipline is not the main mission of the schools anyway and should not be their responsibility.)

Some changes could be made, at least at the level of federal policy. As we write this, the newspapers are full of a recent scandal based on a senatorial investigation (Associated Press, 1994). Some years ago the government began classifying drug and alcohol addiction as a disability, and this has allowed alcoholics and drug addicts to collect disability benefits from the Social Security Administration. In effect, the government mails monthly checks to a couple hundred thousand alcoholics and drug addicts. The investigating panel found that much of this money ends up being spent on alcohol and drugs, which is hardly surprising under the circumstances.

Of particular interest was the fact that the applicant's disability is treated as having begun when he or she first applied for benefits, even if the approval is initially denied and it takes a couple years for the appeals and approval process and the bureaucratic paperwork to finally start sending money. At that point, by the present policy, the person receives a lump sum payment for all the money that would have been sent in the intervening months. These payments, often amounting to $15,000 or even $20,000, have been used for major binges by some addicts and alcoholics. The Senate report documented cases of people who actually died from a drug overdose or alcohol-related tragedy that occurred right after the person received the large sum. In essence, the government financed a fatal binge for these individuals.

In general, it seems likely that American society should seek effective ways to get by under the circumstance that a large segment of the population will be prone to self-regulation failures. It therefore seems imperative that society look for ways to adapt to this likely outcome. Some sources of temptation can be removed, such as by restricting guns; those that cannot be removed can perhaps be managed and even perhaps used for the greater good of society, such as the way that gambling is now used as a source of revenue for many states.

DEVELOPING SELF-CONTROL THEORY

We have already concluded that the present state of the evidence is sufficient to furnish a broad understanding of self-regulation failure. A related but more far-reaching theoretical issue is the nature of self-regulation per se. Unfortunately, we do not think that the current state of available research evidence is ready to furnish a significant step forward in this basic understanding of self-regulation. The field seems to be in a transitional state, and the next generation of self-regulation theory may well be some years away (see Karoly, 1993). In this section, therefore, we offer only partial and fragmentary observations from our work that may be relevant to the next generation of self-regulation theory, whenever it arrives.

Self-regulation theory was greatly advanced by the introduction of feedback-loop models, especially as articulated by Carver and Scheier (1981; see also Miller et al., 1960; Powers, 1973). At present there is no reason to replace or even seriously revise that approach. Feedback-loop models are indeed clearly important and central in the process of self-regulation. The next generation of theory will probably not replace the feedback-loop

approach so much as build on it. The task will therefore be to identify and remedy what is left out by feedback-loop analyses of self-regulation.

One issue concerns timing; that is, when does the feedback loop get activated at all? Carver and Scheier's analysis did begin to address this issue, such as in their explanation of the hierarchy of self-control levels and their discussion of how awareness can move from one level to another. Their contention that blockage or failure at one level initiates a shift to a lower level has been supported by research. Still, there are other factors relevant to the activation of a feedback loop. Sometimes people are motivated to turn off the feedback loop, to stop monitoring, to stop trying to improve. As we have already noted, in many cases people seem to acquiesce in self-regulation failure, and a full understanding of such acquiescence would be a powerful complement to feedback-loop models.

The "test" phase of the feedback loop—the monitoring process itself—is not very mysterious. One perceives oneself and current circumstances and compares against relevant standards. There are some issues to be explored there, including biased perception of self and selection of standards for comparison, but by and large this is not a complex problem at present.

On the other hand, the "operate" phase is much less well understood and must be considered a prime target for further work in theory and research. In other words, we suggest that a main focus of self-regulation should be *how* people change themselves, instead of focusing on how people decide whether to change or not. Our treatment of self-regulation as *process override* reflects this emphasis. What enables a person to succeed at overriding some impulse, resisting some motivation, or interrupting some activity that is in progress? When and why will such efforts fail?

In this connection, the distinction between automatic and controlled processes has to be incorporated into self-regulation theory. This distinction was only becoming a central concern of social psychologists when Carver and Scheier (1981) published their book, and so it is hardly surprising that they paid little attention to it. The next generation of self-regulation theory will undoubtedly place considerable emphasis on this distinction. Unfortunately, prevailing views about the nature of automatic and controlled processes and about the distinction between them are now changing, and so self-regulation theory may have to wait until those views have reached more of a consensus.

In any case, there is one aspect that will have to be effectively integrated into the next generation of self-regulation theory, and that is the distinction between two major kinds of automaticity. The old simple distinction gradually broke down because the term *automatic* was understood in two different ways, and so controversy raged. For self-regulation theory, however, both concepts are needed. The one concept was "true" automaticity, referring to processes that were not controlled and not controllable (Bargh, 1982). The other referred to processes that are not controlled but could potentially be controlled.

For self-regulation theory, the distinction is vital. True automatic processes, in the sense of processes that cannot be controlled, are by definition immune from self-regulation. Focusing self-regulatory efforts there will be futile—they fall into our category of trying to control the uncontrollable. We have suggested, for example, that impulses cannot be prevented when a latent motivation encounters an activating cue. If males are indeed biologically programmed to respond to sexual novelty, then seeing a scantily clad woman on a beach or in a magazine may activate sexual desire for her, and that cannot be prevented; women who want their boyfriends or husbands not to notice other women are likely to be disappointed.

On the other hand, automatic processes in the looser sense—call them semiautomatic, for the moment—are perhaps the best place for self-regulation to intervene. These are habits or familiar responses or ways of doing things that are susceptible to control, and so self-regulatory processes can effectively override them. Women can expect their boyfriends or husbands to refrain from making sexual advances toward these other women, even if preventing the interest or desire is unrealistic. That is because the link between desire and action is not automatic in the narrow sense. It is potentially controllable.

This issue complicates a great deal of the discussion of human social behavior and in particular many social problems. Does poverty cause crime? Does being a victim of abuse make one into an abuser? Do anger and jealousy cause violence? Such things create tendencies, but these are tendencies that can be overridden. Most poor people do not become criminals; many abuse victims do not become abusers themselves; many angry people refrain from inflicting violent harm. The causal process does increase the odds, but the potential for self-regulatory override may be the neglected factor in the moral equation (and in the moral judgment of responsibility).

The notion of overlearning raises another complication for the incorporation of automaticity into self-regulation theory. Controlled processes involve self-regulation, in general, and perhaps by definition. But it is also well known that when some controlled process is repeated over and over, it gradually becomes automatic (at least in the looser sense of the term automatic; this is the essence of overlearning). This logic presumably applies to self-regulation too, and so presumably there is some portion of self-regulation that is automatic. In an important sense, this is what many virtues (in the sense of positive character traits) are: ingrained habits of self-control. If you always do the right thing, it becomes easier to do. Physical exercise may be a good example. In order to exercise regularly, it is usually necessary to have a regular habit or routine, rather than having to face the struggle of making a decision about whether to exercise every day.

It is generally accepted that the reason for having automatic processes is that they conserve resources (Bargh, 1982). Controlled processes consume much more in the way of psychological resources than automatic processes do, by definition. These resources make up a great deal of what we have called self-regulatory strength, and indeed probably the biggest challenge facing further development of self-regulation theory is to explicate the nature of these resources.

Clearly, attention is one of these resources. Attention management emerged as a central factor in *all* self-regulation spheres we studied. Self-distraction was often effective as a means of self-regulation. Losing control of attention was associated with self-regulation failure in nearly every sphere—emotion, thought, task performance, impulse control.

Still, the resources involved in self-regulatory strength go beyond mere attention. Some motivational and dispositional factors probably need to be incorporated. Once researchers devise effective measures of strength, they may begin to investigate how it is depleted by fatigue or stress and whether it can be increased over time through exercise.

Transcendence is another issue that will deserve fuller treatment in future self-regulation theory. We have found that self-regulation failure is often marked by becoming immersed in the immediate situation, so that present, salient stimuli exert a powerful effect on behavior. The implication is that effective self-regulation depends on being able to be aware in a way that goes beyond the immediate situation and salient stimuli. The factors that contribute to the success or failure of transcendence deserve further study. Transcendence may involve a link between attention control and time perspectives, including distal goals and long-term interests.

Ultimately, self-regulation theory will need to draw on a clear understanding of how behavior happens ordinarily and how the individual can override these ordinary patterns to change them. As we said at the outset, self-stopping seems the simplest form of self-regulation, and it deserves emphasis by researchers who undertake to investigate how people override their thoughts, feelings, and actions.

IMPLICATIONS FOR CULTIVATING SELF-REGULATION

Given the widespread benefits of good self-regulation, and in view of the many undesirable outcomes that accompany self-regulation failure, one might well ask how good self-regulatory skills are to be instilled. What enables people to develop effective self-discipline? Although a systematic treatment of such questions is beyond the scope of this work, some speculative comments are in order.

Implications for Parenting

In our view, the weight of the evidence currently points to parental influence as the single most important determinant of self-regulatory capacity. Parents can thus accomplish a great deal in terms of instilling good self-control in their children. From our perspective, this may be the single most important and valuable goal of socializing children. We recommend that parents regard the inculcation of self-control as the premier goal in child-rearing (as opposed to cultivating self-esteem, creativity, obedience, sociability, love for parents, or other goals).

The importance of parental influence on self-regulation, however, also raises some cause for concern in the context of current societal trends. As we have already noted, the dramatic rise in single-parent households and dual-career families generally entails that parents have much less opportunity (as well as much less time and energy) to supervise their children than in previous eras. If the result is that children grow up with less supervision, or even with supervision that places less emphasis on instilling self-control, then society will likely see continuing increases in the problems of self-regulation failure, from impulsive crime to sexual misbehavior to problems with alcohol and eating and drugs.

The project of raising a child with high self-control must presumably involve both having a highly structured set of rules to which the child is held to conform and conferring a substantial and growing degree of autonomy on the child. Conventional wisdom among researchers tends to depict the *authoritative* parenting style (i.e., having firm rules with a rationality that is made clear to the child and that the child has some degree of participation in setting) as most effective for this, and there is no reason to dispute that at present. Consistency of rules and consistency of enforcement are probably of paramount importance, and that includes the notion that letting the child off the hook out of some lenient sentiment must be regarded as a potentially harmful neglect of parental duty. Severity of punishment is presumably much less important than consistency and foreseeability.

Given the importance of the capacity to delay gratification, instilling that capacity should probably be one of the key early emphases. It would be necessary to offer the child choices between immediate and delayed (but greater) rewards, as well as to improve the child's capacity to choose the delayed ones.

It is then of course extremely important that the delayed rewards are actually forthcoming. Indeed, the economic difficulties and other turbulence in lower-class households may often make it especially difficult to foster a capacity to delay gratification. Previous generations of researchers were fond of demonstrating that socioeconomic class was correlated with capacity to delay gratification, but this may simply reflect children's rational adaptation to the fact that promises of delayed rewards are often not kept because of unforeseen emergencies or other exigencies. The lesson one learns from such a chaotic environment is that only immediate and available rewards can be counted on, and so it is always best to choose them. Although that may be an optimal adaptation to such a home environment, it will of course be counterproductive in society at large. We suspect that it would not take very many broken promises to teach a child not to trust them, and the capacity to delay gratification may be seriously undermined in rather short order.

Training attentional skills must also be given high priority by parents, because of the pervasive importance of attention for self-regulation. Activities that require vigilance, concentration, or the genesis of multiple possibilities or multiple ideas should probably get high priority. Although it is now common for parents to complain about the influence of television, such as its high rate of sex and violence, we suspect that another (rarely mentioned) important problem with excessive television watching is that it fails to challenge or develop attentional skills. Watching television takes almost no mental effort, and programming is designed to seize and manipulate attention effectively. This can readily be seen by contrasting television with reading, because reading requires some degree of persistent concentration, and so it may be more effective in instilling the capacity to manage one's attention.

As already noted, a particularly important form of attentional control is transcendence. Teaching children to see beyond the immediate stimuli is probably quite helpful for the development of self-control. The ability to transcend the immediate situation helps overcome dangerous emotional reactions, helps hold impulses and appetites in check, increases long-range rationality, and has many other benefits. How one cultivates the ability to transcend the immediate situation is not easy to say. Possibly games such as chess, which require the player to imagine future outcomes beyond the immediate situation, may be helpful at some ages. Transcendence might

also be taught as a method of dealing with emotional distress.

Perhaps the most important fundamental attitude should simply be to make a point of reinforcing behavior that shows good self-control. It is presumably easy to recognize (and punish) significant failures of self-control in one's children, because the failures create problems and attract attention. Positive feats of self-control, however, are less dramatic and might easily go unnoticed. If parents watch for such feats and are careful to reward them, they may be increased. Reinforcement has been shown to be more effective than punishment for producing desired behavior.

One final implication of these speculations is that effective socialization of self-control in children may demand considerable exercise of self-control on the part of parents. After all, the guidelines we have given require vigilant and consistent behavior on the part of parents. That contingency may have ominous implications about the future of our society, however. As children who grew up neglected by parents or raised with other goals (such as esteeming oneself regardless of one's actions) now become parents, their capacity for optimal parenting may be lacking. Moreover, and more unfortunately, lack of self-control makes it that much easier to become a parent, especially an unwed parent, simply by engaging in unprotected sexual behavior. The escalating patterns of parental neglect and abuse may reflect this "snowballing" of poor self-control from one generation to the next. If so, then this cycle may be extremely difficult to reverse, and society should brace itself for a rapid rise in all the problems that stem from self-regulation failure, as more and more children grow up with parents who themselves lack self-control.

Self-Improvement of Self-Control

For people who wish to increase their own capacity for self-regulation, our analysis offers several suggestions. The place to start would presumably be with the three main ingredients of self-regulation, that is, standards, monitoring, and strength.

Regarding standards, there is not much mystery. Setting appropriate goals and avoiding conflicts between one's goals or ideals is a necessary first step. There are of course two main approaches to setting standards. One is to set very high goals and try to come as close as possible. The other is to set relatively low goals and surpass them frequently (and substantially). The latter is likely to be more pleasant and to yield more in the way of satisfactions and other positive affect.

One should also be explicit about setting rewards and punishments in connection with these standards. Judicious use of self-reward is probably a good aid to self-regulation.

Monitoring of the self is vital to effective self-regulation. Probably most people who have difficulty with self-regulation might find it useful to try external forms of monitoring, such as recording one's progress on the calendar. (It may be easy to skip a day's exercise now and then, but if every glance at the calendar reveals how many days this month one has exercised one may be spurred on to do better than last month, or at least to consider whether one is in fact matching one's target.) Social relationships may also furnish a helpful context for external monitoring; many people find, for example, that involving a nonsmoking spouse is a helpful aid to one's own efforts to quit smoking, if only because the spouse is willing to keep an unbiased record of how much one smokes.

The third ingredient is strength. If our analysis is correct, self-regulatory strength should be able to be increased by effective exercise. In that case, setting oneself small but frequent challenges for self-improvement may be useful for building up a good capacity for self-discipline. Managing strength also suggests that one must sometimes be judicious in where to allocate it. When one is subjected to external demands or stresses, for example, it may be prudent to avoid making other demands on oneself, in order to conserve one's strength.

External sources of discipline may also be useful to some people. Religious and military organizations have always offered strong supports for personal self-control, and there may be other organizations that are also helpful.

Cultivating better control over attention in oneself, starting at adulthood, is not easy. Still, this is essentially what meditation involves (i.e., control over attention). Meditation is not easy and, indeed, making the time to meditate once or twice a day may itself be an undertaking that consumes self-regulatory strength, but if one can do it there may gradually be a substantial payoff in the capacity to control oneself. (At first, however, the effect may seem to be the opposite, because when one starts to meditate one typically realizes how little control one has over one's mind and attentional processes.)

Lastly, the careful pursuit of accurate self-knowledge can help prevent or minimize many forms of misregulation and of poor self-management. This is probably harder than it sounds, because most people believe that they do seek to learn about themselves. Evidence suggests, however, that people actually give a fairly low priority to finding out accurate information about themselves. Instead, they prefer first and foremost to hear positive things about themselves, and when that desire is satisfied they seek information that confirms what they already believe about themselves, leaving the quest for accurate self-knowledge a distant third (Sedikides, 1993). Making a fair list of one's virtues or abilities *and* one's faults and weaknesses is thus a rare and difficult undertaking, but to the extent that one can do this, self-management is likely to be facilitated.

FINAL REMARKS

The importance of self-regulation is only beginning to be appreciated, in social psychology as well as in Western society in general. One of the great misconceptions of modern times is that people have a true self hidden inside, needing only to be found. More likely, people have possibilities that need to be cultivated and realized. To do that requires a great deal of systematic effort to bring one's thoughts, feelings, and actions into agreement with one's ideals. Self-regulation is thus central to the essential nature of human selfhood. It is only by means of self-regulation that human beings can reach their potential and fulfill their ideals.

This book has taken us on a tour through many spheres of human failure and misery. We have examined people who give up too easily, quit their jobs, mismanage their task performances, suffer from unwanted thoughts, deceive themselves, are buffeted by uncontrolled emotions, eat too much, drink too much alcohol, smoke or gamble excessively, and in general ruin their lives. Self-regulation failure is indeed a pervasive source of human unhappiness. Indeed, people who fail at self-regulation often bring trouble and sadness not only on themselves but on people close to them and people who care about them.

Yet one should not despair. Self-regulation failure is the exception, not the rule. It is less remarkable that people sometimes fail at self-regulation than that they usually succeed. The capacity to alter and control oneself is one of the most powerfully adaptive and, indeed, miraculous aspects of the human psyche. Anything that science, therapy, public policy, or individual human beings can do to enhance it—and thereby reduce the painful and costly toll of self-regulation failures—holds the fair promise of being a contribution to the greater good of humanity.

Taming Stress

By Robert Sapolsky

Over the centuries, society's approaches to treating the mentally ill have shifted dramatically. At present, drugs that manipulate neurochemistry count as cutting-edge therapeutics. A few decades ago the heights of efficacy and compassion were lobotomies and insulin-induced comas. Before that, restraints and ice baths sufficed. Even earlier, and we've entered the realm of exorcisms.

Society has also shifted its view of the causes of mental illness. Once we got past invoking demonic possession, we put enormous energy into the debate over whether these diseases are more about nature or nurture. Such arguments are quite pointless given the vast intertwining of the two in psychiatric disease. Environment, in the form of trauma, can most certainly break the minds of its victims. Yet there is an undeniable biology that makes some individuals more vulnerable than others. Conversely, genes are most certainly important factors in understanding major disorders. Yet being the identical twin of someone who suffers one of those illnesses means a roughly 50 percent chance of *not* succumbing.

Obviously, biological vulnerabilities and environmental precipitants interact, and in this article I explore one arena of that interaction: the relation between external factors that cause stress and the biology of the mind's response. Scientists have recently come to understand a great deal about the role that stress plays in the two most common classes of psychiatric disorders: anxiety and major depression, each of which affects close to 20 million Americans annually, according to the National Institute of Mental Health. And much investigation focuses on developing the next generation of relevant pharmaceuticals, on finding improved versions of Prozac, Wellbutrin, Valium and Librium that would work faster, longer or with fewer side effects.

At the same time, insights about stress are opening the way for novel drug development. These different tacks are needed for the simple fact that despite laudable progress in treating anxiety and depression, currently available medications do not work for vast numbers of people, or they entail side effects that are too severe.

Research in this area has applications well beyond treating and understanding these two illnesses. The diagnostic boundary that separates someone who is formally ill with an anxiety disorder or major depression from everyone else is somewhat arbitrary. Investigations into stress are also teaching us about the everyday anxiety and depression that all of us experience at times.

Out of Balance

When a body is in homeostatic balance, various measures—such as temperature, glucose level and so on—are as close to "ideal" as possible. A stressor is anything in the environment that knocks the body out of homeostasis, and the stress response is the array of physiological adaptations that ultimately reestablishes balance. The response principally includes the secretion of two types of hormones from the adrenal glands: epinephrine, also known as adrenaline, and glucocorticoids. In humans, the relevant glucocorticoid is called Cortisol, also known as hydrocortisone.

This suite of hormonal changes is what stress is about for the typical mammal. It is often triggered by an acute physical challenge, such as fleeing from a predator. Epinephrine and glucocorticoids mobilize energy for muscles, increase cardiovascular tone so oxygen can travel more quickly, and turn off nonessential activities like growth. (The hormones work at different speeds. In a fight-or-flight scenario, epinephrine is the one handing out guns; glucocorticoids are the ones drawing up blueprints for new aircraft carriers needed for the war effort.)

Primates have it tough, however. More so than in other species, the primate stress response can be set in motion not only by a concrete event but by mere *anticipation*. When this assessment is accurate ("This is a dark, abandoned street, so I should prepare to run"), an anticipatory stress response can be highly adaptive. But when primates, human or otherwise, chronically and erroneously believe that a homeostatic challenge is about to come, they have entered the realm of neurosis, anxiety and paranoia.

In the 1950s and 1960s pioneers such as John Mason, Seymour Levine and Jay Weiss—then at the Walter Reed Army Medical Center, Stanford University and the Rockefeller University, respectively—began to identify key facets of psychological stress. They found that such stress is exacerbated if there is no outlet for frustration, no sense of control, no social support and no impression that something better will follow. Thus, a rat will be less likely to develop an ulcer in response to a series of electric shocks if it can gnaw on a bar of wood throughout, because it has an outlet for frustration. A baboon will secrete fewer stress hormones in response to frequent fighting if the aggression results in a rise, rather than a fall, in the dominance hierarchy; he has a perception that life is improving. A person will become less hypertensive when exposed to painfully loud noise if she believes she can press a button at any time to lower the volume; she has a sense of control.

But suppose such buffers are not available and the stress is chronic. Repeated challenges may demand repeated bursts of vigilance. At some point, this vigilance may become overgeneralized, leading an individual to conclude that he must always be on guard—even in the absence of the stress. And thus the realm of anxiety is entered. Alternatively, the chronic stress may be insurmountable, giving rise to feelings of helplessness. Again this response may become overgeneralized: a person may begin to feel she is always at a loss, even in circumstances that she can actually master. Depression is upon her.

Stress and Anxiety

For its part, anxiety seems to wreak havoc in the limbic system, the brain region concerned with emotion. One structure is primarily affected: the amygdala, which is involved in the perception of and response to fear-evoking stimuli. (Interestingly, the amygdala is also central to aggression, underlining the fact that aggression can be rooted in fear—an observation that can explain much sociopolitical behavior.)

To carry out its role in sensing threat, the amygdala receives input from neurons in the outermost layer of the brain, the cortex, where much high-level processing takes place. Some of this input comes from parts of the cortex that process sensory information, including specialized areas that recognize individual faces, as well as from the frontal cortex, which is involved in abstract associations. In the realm of anxiety, an example of such an association might be grouping a gun, a hijacked plane and an anthrax-tainted envelope in the same category. The sight of a fire or a menacing face can activate the amygdala—as can a purely abstract thought.

The amygdala also takes in sensory information that bypasses the cortex. As a result, a subliminal preconscious menace can activate the amygdala, even before there is conscious awareness of the trigger. Imagine a victim of a traumatic experience who, in a crowd of happy, talking people, suddenly finds herself anxious, her heart racing. It takes her moments to realize that a man conversing behind her has a voice similar to that of the man who once assaulted her.

The amygdala, in turn, contacts an array of brain regions, making heavy use of a neurotransmitter called corticotropin-releasing hormone (CRH). One set of nerve cells projecting from the amygdala reaches evolutionarily ancient parts of the midbrain and brain stem. These structures control the autonomic nervous system, the network of nerve cells projecting to parts of the body over which you normally have no conscious control (your heart, for example). One half of the autonomic nervous system is the sympathetic nervous system, which mediates "fight or flight." Activate your amygdala with a threat, and soon the sympathetic nervous system has directed your adrenal glands to secrete epinephrine. Your heart is racing, your breathing is shallow, your senses are sharpened.

The amygdala also sends information back to the frontal cortex. In addition to processing abstract associations, as noted above, the frontal cortex helps to make judgments about incoming information and initiating behaviors based on those assessments. So it is no surprise that the decisions we make can be so readily influenced by our emotions. Moreover, the amygdala sends projections to the sensory cortices as well, which may explain, in part, why sensations seem so vivid when we are in certain emotional states—or perhaps why sensory memories (flashbacks) occur in victims of trauma.

Whether it orchestrates such powerful reimmersions or not, the amygdala is clearly implicated in certain kinds of memory. There are two general forms of memory. Declarative, or explicit, memory governs the recollection of facts, events or associations. Implicit memory has several roles as well. It includes procedural memory: recalling how to ride a bike or play a passage on the piano. And it is involved in fear. Remember the woman reacting to the similarity between two voices without being aware of it. In that case, the activation of the amygdala and the sympathetic nervous system reflects a form of implicit memory that does not require conscious awareness.

Researchers have begun to understand how these fearful memories are formed and how they can be overgeneralized after repeated stress. The foundation for these insights came from work on declarative memory, which is most likely situated in a part of the brain called the hippocampus. Memory is established when certain sets of nerve cells communicate with one another repeatedly. Such communication entails the release of neurotransmitters—chemical messengers that travel across synapses, the spaces between neurons. Repeated stimulation of sets of neurons causes the communication across synapses to be strengthened, a condition called long-term potentiation (LTP).

Joseph LeDoux of New York University has shown that repeatedly placing rats in a fear-provoking situation can bring about LTP in the amygdala. Work by Sumantra Chattarji of the National Center for Biological Science in Bangalore extends this finding one remarkable step further: the amygdalic neurons of rats in stressful situations sprout new branches, allowing them to make more connections with other neurons. As a result, any part of the fear-inducing situation could end up triggering more firing between neurons in the amygdala. A victim—if he had been robbed several times at night, for instance—might experience anxiety and phobia just by stepping outside his home, even under a blazing sun.

LeDoux has proposed a fascinating model to relate these changes to a feature of some forms of anxiety. As discussed, the hippocampus plays a key role in declarative memory. As will become quite pertinent when we turn to depression, glucocorticoid exposure can impair LTP in the hippocampus and can even cause atrophy of neurons there. This phenomenon constitutes the opposite of the stress response in the amygdala. Severe stress can harm the hippocampus, preventing the consolidation of a conscious, explicit memory of the event; at the same time, new neuronal branches and enhanced LTP facilitate the amygdala's implicit memory machinery. In subsequent situations, the amygdala might respond to preconscious information—but conscious awareness or memory may never follow. According to LeDoux, such a mechanism could underlie forms of free-floating anxiety.

It is interesting that these structural changes come about, in part, because of hormones secreted by the adrenal glands, a source well outside the brain. As mentioned, the amygdala's perception of stress ultimately leads to the secretion of epinephrine and glucocorticoids. The glucocorticoids then activate a brain region called the locus coeruleus. This structure, in turn, sends a powerfully activating projection back to the amygdala, making use of a neurotransmitter called norepinephrine (a close relative of epinephrine). The amygdala then sends out more CRH, which leads to the secretion of more glucocorticoids. A vicious circle of mind-body feedback can result.

Assuaging Anxiety

An understanding of the interactions between stress and anxiety has opened the way for new therapies, some of which hold great promise. These drugs are not presumed better or safer than those available today. Rather, if successful, they will give clinicians more to work with.

The medicines that already exist do target aspects of the stress system. The minor tranquilizers, such as Valium and Librium, are in a class of compounds called benzodiazepines. They work in part by relaxing muscles; they also inhibit the excitatory projection from the locus coeruleus into the amygdala, thereby decreasing the likelihood that the amygdala will mobilize the sympathetic nervous system. The net result is a calm body—and a less anxious body means a less anxious brain. While effective, however, benzodiazepines are also sedating and addictive, and considerable research now focuses on finding less troublesome versions.

In their search for alternatives, researchers have sought to target the stress response upstream of the locus coeruleus and amygdala. Epinephrine activates a nerve called the vagus, which projects into a brain region that subsequently stimulates the amygdala. A new therapy curtails epinephrine's stimulation of the vagus nerve.

Chemical messengers such as epinephrine exert their effects by interacting with specialized receptors on the surface of target cells. A receptor is shaped in such a way that it can receive only a certain messenger—just as a mold will fit only the statue cast in it. But by synthesizing imposter messengers, scientists have been able to block the activity of some of the body's natural couriers.

Drugs called beta blockers fit into some kinds of epinephrine receptors, preventing real epinephrine from transmitting any information. Beta blockers have long been used to reduce high blood pressure driven by an overactive sympathetic nervous system, as well as to reduce stage fright. But Larry Cahill and James McGaugh of the University of California at Irvine have shown that the drugs also blunt the formation of memories of emotionally disturbing events or stories. Based on their findings and others, clinicians such as Roger Pitman of Harvard University have started studies in which beta blockers are given to people who have experienced severe trauma in the hope of heading off the development of post-traumatic stress disorder.

Other therapies are being designed to act in the amygdala itself. As described, the amygdala's shift from merely responding to an arousing event to becoming chronically overaroused probably involves memory formation as well as the growth of new synapses. Work in my laboratory is exploring the molecular biology underlying those changes. Because prolonged stress has opposite effects on synapse formation in the hippocampus and the amygdala, we would like to know how the profiles of genes turned on and off by stress differ in those two structures. Our goal is to then try to block the changes by introducing genes into the amygdala that might give rise to proteins that could inhibit synapse formation during stress. In this work, viruses that have been rendered safe are used to ferry genes to the amygdala [see "Gene Therapy in the Nervous System," by Dora Y. Ho and Robert M. Sapolsky; *Scientific American*, July 1997].

Another strategy—for both anxiety and depression—targets CRH, the neurotransmitter used by the amygdala when it sends information elsewhere. Based on insights into the structure of CRH and its receptors, scientists have developed chemical imposters to bind with the receptors and block it. In research by Michael Davis of Emory University, these compounds have proved effective in rat models of anxiety. They have reduced the extent to which a rat anxiously freezes when placed in a cage where it was previously shocked.

Stress and Depression

In contrast to anxiety, which can feel like desperate hyperactivity, major depression is characterized by helplessness, despair, an exhausted sense of being too overwhelmed to do anything (psychomotor retardation) and a loss of feelings of pleasure. Accordingly, depression has a different biology and requires some different strategies for treatment. But it, too, can be related to stress, and there is ample evidence of this association. First of all, psychological stress entails feeling a loss of control and predictability—an accurate description of depression. Second, major stressful events seem to precede depressive episodes early in the course of the disease. Finally, treating people with glucocorticoid hormones to control conditions such as rheumatoid arthritis can lead to depression.

One way in which stress brings about depression is by acting on the brain's mood and pleasure pathways. To begin, prolonged exposure to glucocorticoid hormones depletes norepinephrine levels in the locus coeruleus neurons. Most plausibly, this means that the animal—or person—becomes less attentive, less vigilant, less active: psychomotor retardation sets in.

Continued stress also decreases levels of serotonin—which may be important in the regulation of mood and sleep cycles, among other things—as well as the number of serotonin receptors in the frontal cortex. Serotonin normally arrives in the frontal cortex by way of the raphe nucleus, a structure that also communicates with the locus coeruleus. You can probably see where this is going. Normally, serotonin stimulates the release of norepinephrine from the locus coeruleus. When serotonin becomes scarce, less norepinephrine is released—exacerbating the shortage caused by earlier unremitting glucocorticoid bombardment.

Stress affects dopamine, the main currency of the pleasure pathway, in a way that seems counterintuitive at first. Moderate and transient amounts of stress—and the ensuing presence of glucocorticoids—increase dopamine release in the pleasure pathway, which runs between a region called the ventral tegmentum/nucleus accumbens and the frontal cortex. More dopamine can lead to a feeling of well-being in situations of moderate or transient stress during which a subject is challenged briefly and not too severely. For a human, or a rat, this situation would entail a task that is not trivial, but one in which there is, nonetheless, a reasonably high likelihood of success—in other words, what we generally call "stimulation." But with chronic glu-cocorticoid exposure, dopamine production is curbed and the feelings of pleasure fade.

Not surprisingly, the amygdala also appears relevant to depression. Wayne Drevets of the National Institute of Mental Health reports that the images of the amygdala of a depressed person light up more in response to sad faces than angry ones. Moreover, the enhanced autonomic arousal seen in anxiety- thought to be driver, by the amygdala—is often observed in depression as well. This fact might seem puzzling at first: anxiety is characterized by a skittish torrent of fight-or-flight signals, whereas depression seems to be about torpor. Yet the helplessness of depression is not a quiet, passive

state. The dread is active, twitching, energy-consuming, distracting, exhausting—but internalized. A classic conceptualization of depression is that it represents aggression turned inward—an enormous emotional battle fought entirely internally—and the disease's physiology supports this analysis.

Memory and New Cells

Stress also acts on the hippocampus, and this activity may bring about some of the hallmarks of depression: difficulty learning and remembering. As I explained before, stress and glucocorticoids can disrupt memory formation in the hippocampus and can cause hippocampal neurons to atrophy and lose some of their many branches. In the 1980s several laboratories, including my own, showed that glucocorticoids can kill hippocampal neurons or impair their ability to survive neurological insults such as a seizure or cardiac arrest.

Stress can even prevent the growth of new nerve cells. Contrary to long-held belief, adult brains do make some new nerve cells. This revolution in our understanding has come in the past decade. And although some findings remain controversial, it is clear that new neurons form in the olfactory bulb and the hippocampus of many adult animals, including humans. Many things, including learning, exercise and environmental enrichment, stimulate neurogenesis in the hippocampus. But stress and glucocorticoids inhibit it.

As would be expected, depression is associated with impaired declarative memory. This impairment extends beyond remembering the details of an acute trauma. Instead depression can interfere with declarative memory formation in general—in people going about their everyday routine or working or learning. Recent and startling medical literature shows that in those who have been seriously depressed for years, the volume of the hippocampus is 10 to 20 percent smaller than in well-matched control subjects. There is little evidence that a small hippocampus predisposes someone toward depression; rather the decreased volume appears to be a loss in response to depression.

At present, it is not clear whether this shrinkage is caused by the atrophy or death of neurons or by the failure of neurogenesis. Disturbingly, both the volume loss and at least some features of the cognitive impairments persist even when the depression resolves. (It is highly controversial whether new neurons are required for learning and memory; thus, it is not clear whether an inhibition of neurogenesis would give rise to cognitive deficits.)

Glucocorticoids may act on the hippocampus by inhibiting levels of a compound called brain-derived neurotrophic factor (BDNF)—which may aid neurogenesis. Several known antidepressants increase amounts of BDNF and stimulate hippocampal neurogenesis in laboratory animals. These findings have led some scientists to speculate that the stress-induced inhibition of neurogenesis and of BDNF are central to the emotional symptoms of depression. I find it to be somewhat of a stretch to connect altered hippocampal function with the many facets of this disease. Nevertheless, these hippocampal changes may play a large part in the substantial memory dysfunction typical of major depression.

New Drugs for Depression

The current generation of antidepressants boost levels of serotonin, dopamine and norepinephrine, and there is tremendous ongoing research to develop more effective versions of these drugs. But some novel therapies target steps more intimately related to the interactions between stress and depression.

Not surprisingly, some of that work focuses on the effects of glucocorticoids. For example, a number of pharmaceuticals that are safe and clinically approved for other reasons can transiently block the synthesis of glucocorticoids in the adrenal glands or block access of glucocorticoids to one of their important receptors in the brain. Fascinatingly, the key compound that blocks glucocorticoid receptors is RU486, famous and controversial for its capacity to also block progesterone receptors in the uterus and for its use as the "abortion drug." Beverly Murphy of McGill University, Owen Wolkowitz of the University of California at San Francisco and Alan Schatzberg of Stanford have shown that such antiglucocorticoids can act as antidepressants for a subset of severely depressed people with highly elevated glucocorticoid levels. These findings are made even more promising by the fact that this group of depressed individuals

tend to be most resistant to the effects of more traditional antidepressants.

Another strategy targets CRH. Because depression, like anxiety, often involves an overly responsive amygdala and sympathetic nervous system, CRH is a key neurotransmitter in the communication from the former to the latter. Moreover, infusion of CRH into the brain of a monkey can cause some depressionlike symptoms. These findings have prompted studies as to whether CRH-receptor blockers can have an antidepressant action. It appears they can, and such drugs are probably not far off.

Using the same receptor-blocking strategy, researchers have curbed the action of a neurotransmitter called Substance P, which binds to the neurokinin-1 (NK-1) receptor. In the early 1990s workers discovered that drugs binding with NK-1 prevent some aspects of the stress response. In one trial and several animal studies, Substance P has worked as an antidepressant.

Other approaches center on the hippocampus. Investigators are injecting BDNF into the brains of rats to counteract the inhibitory effects of glucocorticoids on neurogenesis. My own laboratory is using gene therapy to protect the hippocampus of rats from the effects of stress—much as we are doing in the amygdala to prevent anxiety. These genes are triggered by glucocorticoids; once activated, they express an enzyme that degrades glucocorticoids. The net result blocks the deleterious effects of these hormones. We are now exploring whether this treat-ment can work in animals.

As is now clear, I hope, anxiety and depression are connected. Yet a state of constant vigilance and one of constant helplessness seem quite different. When does stress give rise to one as opposed to the other? The answer seems to lie in how chronic the stress is.

The Stress Continuum

Imagine a rat trained to press a lever to avoid a mild, occasional shock—a task readily mastered. The rat is placed into a cage with the lever, and the anticipatory sense of mastery might well activate the pleasurable dopaminergic projections to the frontal cortex. When the increase in glucocorticoid secretion is moderate and transient—as would likely be the case here—the hormone enhances dopamine release.

Suppose that in this circumstance, however, the lever has been disconnected; pressing it no longer prevents shocks. Initially this alteration produces a wildly hypervigilant state in the rat as it seeks a new coping response to stop the shocks. The animal presses the lever repeatedly, frantically trying to regain control. This is the essence of anxiety and of the multiple, disorganized attempts at coping. Physiologically, this state is characterized by massive activation of the sympathetic nervous system by epinephrine and of the norepinephrine projection from the locus coeruleus, as well as moderately increased glucocorticoid secretion.

And as the shocks continue and the rat finds each attempt at coping useless, a transition occurs. The stress response becomes more dominated by high glucocorticoid levels than by epinephrine and the sympathetic nervous system—which are largely in control of the immediate fight-or-flight reaction. The brain chemistry begins to resemble that of depression as key neurotransmitters become depleted and the animal ceases trying to cope. It has learned to be helpless, passive and involuted. If anxiety is a crackling, menacing brushfire, depression is a suffocating heavy blanket thrown on top of it.

Stress and Genes

I do not want to conclude this article having given the impression that anxiety and depression are "all" or "only" about stress. Obviously, they are not. Both illnesses have substantial genetic components as well. Genes code for the receptors for dopamine, serotonin and glucocorticoids. They also code for the enzymes that synthesize and degrade those chemical messengers, for the pumps that remove them from the synapses, for growth factors like BDNF, and so on.

But those genetic influences are not inevitable. Remember, if an individual has one of the major psychiatric disorders, her identical twin has only about a 50 percent chance of having it. Instead the genetic influences seem to be most about vulnerability: how the brain and body react to certain environments, including how readily the brain and body reequilibrate after stress.

Experience, beginning remarkably early in life, also influences how one responds to stressful envi-ronments. The amount of stress a female rat is exposed to during pregnancy influences the amount of glucocorticoids that cross the placenta and reach the fetus; that exposure can then alter the structure and function of that fetus's hippocampus in adulthood. Separate a newborn rat from its mother for a sustained period and it will have increased levels of CRH as an adult. Seymour Levine, one of the giants of psychobiology, illustrates this point with a quotation from William Faulkner: "The past is not dead. It's not even the past."

An understanding of the role of stress in psychiatric disorders offers much. It teaches us that a genetic legacy of anxiety or depression does not confer a life sentence on sufferers of these tragic diseases. It is paving the way for some new therapies that may help millions. Given that there is a continuum between the biology of these disorders and that of the "normal" aspects of emotion, these findings are not only pertinent to "them and their diseases" but to all of us in our everyday lives. Perhaps most important, such insight carries with it a social imperative: namely, that we find ways to heal a world in which so many people learn that they must always feel watchful and on guard or that they must always feel helpless.

CPSIA information can be obtained
at www.ICGtesting.com
Printed in the USA
FSHW020333290920
74234FS